# Mobile Payments, Consumer Policy, and the Law

Mobile technology offers an innovative and cost-effective channel for delivering a range of financial services, including mobile payments. In some jurisdictions, mobile payments simply provide a convenient option for facilitating payment transactions. In other jurisdictions, mobile payments are viewed as potentially transformative because they present an opportunity to expand access to financial services. However, as with other innovations, mobile payments raise consumer protection concerns and require robust regulatory mechanisms to address such concerns. Against this backdrop, the book adopts a typology of consumer policy tools which can be used to address the identified consumer concerns. This typology guides the enquiry into the existing consumer protection frameworks applying to mobile payments in selected jurisdictions (Canada, Kenya, and the United Kingdom). The main objective of this endeavour is to identify best practices that national authorities seeking to leverage mobile payments and similar innovations can emulate.

This book will be of interest to policymakers, regulators, industry stakeholders, students, and scholars interested in the regulation of innovative financial services, particularly from a consumer protection perspective.

**Nwanneka V Ezechukwu** is a lecturer at the School of Law, University of Sheffield, UK.

## Routledge Research in Finance and Banking Law

**The European Sovereign Debt Crisis**
Breaking the Vicious Circle Between Sovereigns and Banks
*Phoebus L. Athanassiou and Angelos T. Vouldis*

**Global Finance in the 21st Century**
Stability and Sustainability in a Fragmenting World
*Steve Kourabas*

**Banking Regulation in Africa**
The Case of Nigeria and Other Emerging Economies
*Folashade Adeyemo*

**Crypto-Finance, Law and Regulation**
Governing an Emerging Ecosystem
*Joseph Lee*

**Regulation and Governance of Mutual Funds**
United Kingdom and United States of America Perspectives on Investor Protection
*Mohammed Khair Alshaleel*

**Regulation of Debt Collection in Europe**
Understanding Informal Debt Collection Practices
*Cătălin-Gabriel Stănescu*

**The Regulation of Megabanks**
Global Systemically Important Banks and their Legal Frameworks
*Katarzyna M. Parchimowicz*

**Regulating Open Banking**
Comparative Analysis of the EU, the UK and Taiwan
*Chang-Hsien Tsai and Kuan-Jung Peng*

For more information about this series, please visit: www.routledge.com/Routledge-Research-in-Finance-and-Banking-Law/book-series/FINANCIALLAW

# Mobile Payments, Consumer Policy, and the Law

## A Comparative Analysis

**Nwanneka V Ezechukwu**

Routledge
Taylor & Francis Group
LONDON AND NEW YORK

First published 2023
by Routledge
4 Park Square, Milton Park, Abingdon, Oxon OX14 4RN

and by Routledge
605 Third Avenue, New York, NY 10158

*Routledge is an imprint of the Taylor & Francis Group, an informa business*



*British Library Cataloguing-in-Publication Data*
A catalogue record for this book is available from the British Library

ISBN: 978-0-367-34706-2 (hbk)
ISBN: 978-1-032-45445-0 (pbk)
ISBN: 978-0-429-32729-2 (ebk)

DOI: 10.4324/9780429327292

Typeset in Times New Roman
by Deanta Global Publishing Services, Chennai, India

# Contents

*Preface* ix
*Acknowledgements* xi
*List of Abbreviations* xii
*Table of Legislation* xiv
*List of Cases* xvi

**1 Introduction** 1

*1.1 Setting the Context 1*
*1.2 The Scope of the Book 4*
*1.2.1 Why Mobile Payments? 6*
*1.2.2 Why Focus on Consumer Protection? 8*
*1.2.3 Why Canada, Kenya, and the United Kingdom? 11*
*1.3 Road Map: Navigating This Book 12*
*References 13*

**PART I**
**Mobile Payments and Consumer Protection – Contextual Analysis** **17**

**2 Mobile Payments: Understanding the Service** 19

*2.1 Introduction 19*
*2.2 A Brief Note about Payment Services 20*
*2.3 Mobile Payments: Clarifying Key Terms 23*
*2.4 Mobile Payments: Understanding the Technology 27*
*2.5 Mobile Payments: Core Stakeholders and Business Models 30*
*2.6 Mobile Payments as an Additive Payment Service 32*
*2.7 Mobile Payments as a Transformative Payment Service 34*
*2.8 Conclusion 38*
*References 38*

**3 Consumer Protection and Mobile Payments: Why Intervene?** 43

*3.1 Introduction 43*
*3.2 Financial Services in Context 44*
*3.3 Economic Rationales for Regulatory Intervention 50*
*3.3.1 The Perfect Market 50*
*3.3.2 Market Realities 53*
*3.4 Non-Economic Rationales for Regulatory Intervention 57*
*3.4.1 Distributive Justice 57*
*3.4.2 Paternalism 60*
*3.4.3 Community Values 63*
*3.5 Conclusion 65*
*References 66*

**4 Consumer Policy Tools for Regulating Mobile Payments** 70

*4.1 Introduction 70*
*4.2 Provision of Information 73*
*4.2.1 Mandatory Disclosures 74*
*4.2.2 Consumer Education 80*
*4.3 Withdrawal Rights and Cooling-Off Periods 87*
*4.4 The Regulation of Business Conduct 90*
*4.4.1 Regulating Unfair Commercial Practices 91*
*4.4.2 Regulating Contract Terms 94*
*4.4.3 Regulating False and Misleading Information 98*
*4.5 Liability Rules 99*
*4.6 Dispute Resolution 104*
*4.6.1 Internal Dispute Resolution Procedures 106*
*4.6.2 External ADR Mechanisms 108*
*4.6.3 Financial Ombudsman Services 110*
*4.7 Conclusion 111*
*References 112*

**PART II**
**Mobile Payments and Consumer Protection – Country Studies** **119**

**5 Consumer Protection and Mobile Payments: Canada** 121

*5.1 Introduction 121*
*5.2 Provision of Information 122*
*5.2.1 Mandatory Disclosures 122*
*5.2.2 Consumer Education 128*
*5.3 Withdrawal Rights and Cooling-Off Periods 131*
*5.4 The Regulation of Business Conduct 133*
*5.4.1 Regulating Unfair Commercial Practices 133*

*5.4.2 Regulating Contract Terms 140*
*5.4.3 Regulating False and Misleading Information 145*
*5.5 Liability Rules 148*
*5.6 Dispute Resolution 152*
*5.6.1 Internal Dispute Resolution Procedures 152*
*5.6.2 External ADR Mechanisms 154*
*5.7 Conclusion 160*
*References 161*

**6 Consumer Protection and Mobile Payments: Kenya** 165

*6.1 Introduction 165*
*6.2 Provision of Information 167*
*6.2.1 Mandatory Disclosures 167*
*6.2.2 Consumer Education 171*
*6.3 Withdrawal Rights and Cooling-Off Periods 174*
*6.4 The Regulation of Business Conduct 177*
*6.4.1 Regulating Unfair Commercial Practices 177*
*6.4.2 Regulating Contract Terms 181*
*6.4.3 Regulating False and Misleading Information 182*
*6.5 Liability Rules 184*
*6.6 Dispute Resolution 186*
*6.6.1 Internal Dispute Resolution Procedures 186*
*6.6.2 External ADR Mechanisms 189*
*6.7 Conclusion 191*
*References 192*

**7 Consumer Protection and Mobile Payments: The United Kingdom** 194

*7.1 Introduction 194*
*7.2 Provision of Information 195*
*7.2.1 Mandatory Disclosures 195*
*7.2.2 Consumer Education 198*
*7.3 Withdrawal Rights and Cooling-Off Periods 200*
*7.4 The Regulation of Business Conduct 203*
*7.4.1 Regulating Unfair Commercial Practices 203*
*7.4.2 Regulating Contract Terms 211*
*7.4.3 Regulating False and Misleading Information 220*
*7.5 Liability Rules 224*
*7.6 Dispute Resolution 229*
*7.6.1 Internal Dispute Resolution Procedures 229*
*7.6.2 External ADR Mechanisms 232*
*7.7 Conclusion 234*
*References 235*

**PART III**
**Mobile Payments and Consumer Protection – Conclusions and Best Practices** **239**

**8 Conclusions** 241

*8.1 Introduction 241*
*8.2 Provision of Information 241*
*8.2.1 Mandatory Disclosures 241*
*8.2.2 Consumer Education 246*
*8.3 Withdrawal Rights and Cooling-Off Periods 248*
*8.4 The Regulation of Business Conduct 250*
*8.4.1 Regulating Unfair Commercial Practices 250*
*8.4.2 Regulating Contract Terms 254*
*8.4.3 Regulating False and Misleading Information 260*
*8.5 Liability Rules 263*
*8.6 Dispute Resolution 265*
*8.6.1 Internal Dispute Resolution Procedures 265*
*8.6.2 External ADR Mechanisms 267*
*8.7 Conclusion 268*
*References 269*

*Index* 273

# Preface

The average mobile phone weighs significantly less than a kilogram. Yet, a device so small has become one of the remarkable inventions of our time. The mobile phone's capacity to facilitate on-demand communication is not its most ingenious feature. Instead, it is the device's ability to support additional functions: a feature that allows it to reinvent and even replace more established products, services, and delivery channels. In our everyday lives, mobile phones make the separate purchase of ordinary devices like a torch, an alarm clock, an audio recorder, and a calculator unnecessary. The additional functions provided by the mobile phone are not limited to the mundane. The mobile phone also provides a platform that improves accessibility to specialised services. For example, people can access medical advice, fitness, and diet plans by merely downloading software applications on their phones.

The mobile phone goes further – building on inroads provided by telephone banking in the 1980s, it now offers a cost-effective channel for delivering a range of financial services. Mobile-based innovations in the financial services industry promise increased accessibility, efficiency, and convenience to consumers. But, as with all forms of innovation, these raise specific questions from a legal perspective. Do innovations based on mobile technology pose any particular risks for consumers? Are existing regulatory frameworks equipped to deal with any identified risks? Are there best practices or guides that regulators can adopt to address loopholes? It is these queries that underpin the discussion that I have covered in this book.

In this book, I focus on a specific innovation: mobile payments (m-payments). My interest in m-payments stems from my background as a sub-Saharan African. Sub-Saharan Africans are more likely to access a mobile phone than a bank account. Banks are unlikely to site branches in rural areas, where most of the populace resides because they are not profitable. This results in a situation where many cannot access bank accounts and other financial services. To fill this gap, new business models leverage the accessibility of mobile phones. Remittances from friends and relatives in urban areas top the list of services in demand. Unsurprisingly, m-payments which facilitate such transfers have become popular. While this innovation presents an important opportunity for extending financial services to excluded and underserved persons, many sub-Saharan

African countries have underdeveloped consumer protection frameworks. This means that those consumers who are least able to bear adverse outcomes are, in many circumstances, left without legal protections. Hence, the central aim of the analysis carried out in the book is to highlight best practices which can inform legislative and regulatory reform aimed at protecting consumers who choose to adopt mobile payments.

To achieve this aim, I have presented the discussion in the book in three parts. In the first part, I have aimed to set the necessary context for the enquiry covered in the book. In brief, I introduce the specific innovation at the centre of the discourse, i.e., m-payments, highlighting the technology and business models which drive the service. For further context, I also discuss the justification for regulatory intervention to protect m-payment consumers. Finally, the first part of the book ends with identifying a typology of consumer policy tools that can address the consumer issues highlighted.

In the second part of the book, I examine the consumer protection frameworks applying to m-payments in three jurisdictions (i.e., Canada, Kenya, and the United Kingdom). The typology highlighted in the first part of the book is used as the basis for enquiry in each jurisdiction. This ensures consistency in the discussion, making it easier to identify converging and diverging regulatory trends. In the third and final part of the book, I highlight recommendations that reflect some of the best practices observed in the jurisdictions reviewed and supported in the broader academic literature.

At its core, this book reinforces the understanding that financial services innovation provides opportunities to re-examine the continued relevance of existing regulatory frameworks and the potential need to clarify, revise, or introduce new approaches that serve identified regulatory objectives. With this book, I hope to contribute meaningfully to discussions on these themes.

I have attempted to state the law as of June 2022. Any errors or omissions remain my own.

Nwanneka V Ezechukwu
June 2022, Wakefield

# Acknowledgements

In completing this project, I have benefitted immensely from the support of so many to whom I owe enormous thanks. This book is based on my PhD thesis, which I completed at the University of Nottingham in February 2018. Therefore, I owe a great debt of gratitude to my supervisors, Professor Peter Cartwright and Professor Richard Hyde, who provided excellent mentorship throughout my doctoral studies and encouraged me to transform my thesis into a book.

Since starting this project, I have benefitted from stimulating discussions with incredibly supportive colleagues, too numerous to mention. To them, I owe sincere thanks. I wish to thank, in particular, Dr Emilie Ghio, Chipo Mwale, Suresh Birdi, Anil Matoo, and Dr Iju Chen for their encouragement while I wrote this book.

I also owe great appreciation to my family. This book would not have been possible without my superheroes – my loving parents, Ikechukwu and Ebele, who provided the financial and emotional support that enabled me to complete my PhD. I'm also grateful to my brothers, IK and Ifeanyi, who were a source of constant cheer and encouragement throughout the journey that led to this book. Finally, I would like to thank my husband, Ugo, for the daily motivation, 'high fives,' support, and understanding which allowed me to complete this book.

# Abbreviations

| | |
|---|---|
| **ADR** | Alternative Dispute Resolution |
| **ADRBO** | ADR Chambers Banking Ombuds Office |
| **Alberta's CPA** | Alberta's Consumer Protection Act |
| **ATM** | Automated Teller Machine |
| **BIS** | Bank for International Settlements |
| **British Columbia's BPCPA** | British Columbia's Business Practices and Consumer Protection Act |
| **CAK** | Competition Authority of Kenya |
| **CBA** | Canadian Banking Association |
| **CBK** | Central Bank of Kenya |
| **CCA** | Canadian Competition Act |
| **CCRs** | Consumer Contracts (Information, Cancellation, and Additional Charges) Regulations (UK) |
| **CFEB** | Consumer Financial Education Body |
| **CIN** | Consumer Information Network (Kenya) |
| **CJEU** | Court of Justice of the European Union |
| **CMA** | Competition and Markets Authority |
| **COBRs** | Cost of Borrowing (Banks) Regulations |
| **CPUTRs** | Consumer Protection from Unfair Trading Regulations (UK) |
| **CRA** | Consumer Rights Act (UK) |
| **DFID** | Department for International Development |
| **DISP** | Dispute Resolution Complaints Sourcebook |
| **ECB** | European Central Bank |
| **EMI** | E-money Institution |
| **EMRs** | Electronic Money Regulations (UK) |
| **ExCB** | External Complaints Body |
| **FATF** | Financial Action Task Force |
| **FCA** | Financial Conduct Authority |
| **FCAC** | Financial Consumer Agency of Canada |
| **FCPRs** | Financial Consumer Protection Regulations |

| | |
|---|---|
| **FEPP** | Financial Education and Consumer Protection Partnership |
| **FI** | Financial Institution |
| **FOS** | Financial Ombudsman Service |
| **FRFI** | Federally Regulated Financial Institution |
| **FSD** | Financial Sector Deepening Trust (Kenya) |
| **FSMA** | Financial Services and Markets Act (UK) |
| **FSRs** | Financial Services (Distance Marketing) Regulations (UK) |
| **ICT** | Information and Communications Technology |
| **KCA** | Kenyan Competition Act |
| **KCPA** | Kenyan Consumer Protection Act |
| **KICRs** | Kenya Information and Communications (Consumer Protection) Regulations |
| **M-payment** | Mobile Payment |
| **Manitoba's BPA** | Manitoba's Business Practices Act |
| **MaPS** | Money and Pensions Service |
| **MAS** | Money Advice Service |
| **MNO** | Mobile Network Operator |
| **Newfoundland's CPBPA** | Newfoundland's Consumer Protection and Business Practices Act |
| **NFC** | Near Field Communication |
| **NOBRs** | Negative Option Billings Regulations (Canada) |
| **NPSA** | National Payments Systems Act (Kenya) |
| **NPSRs** | National Payment Systems Regulations (Kenya) |
| **OBSI** | Ombudsman Service for Banking Services and Investments |
| **ODR** | Online Dispute Resolution |
| **OECD** | Organisation for Economic Cooperation and Development |
| **Ontario's CPA** | Ontario Consumer Protection Act |
| **PDA** | Personal Digital Assistant |
| **PGCP** | Prudential Guidelines on Consumer Protection (Kenya) |
| **POS** | Point of Sale |
| **PSP** | Payment Service Provider |
| **PSRs** | Payment Services Regulations (UK) |
| **QR Code** | Quick Response Code |
| **SIM** | Subscriber Identity Module |
| **SMS** | Short Message Service |
| **UKSC** | UK Supreme Court |
| **UN** | United Nations |
| **UNFCOG** | Unfair Contract Terms and Consumer Notices Regulatory Guide (UK) |
| **USSD** | Unstructured Supplementary Service Data |
| **WIM** | Wireless Identity Module |

# Table of Legislation

## Canada

Bank Act, SC 1991, c 46
Budget Implementation Act 2018, No.2 SC 2018, c 27
Competition Act, RSC 1985 c C–34.
Cost of Borrowing (Banks) Regulations, SOR/2001–101
Disclosure of Charges (Banks) Regulations, SOR/92–324
Financial Consumer Agency of Canada Act, SC 2001, c 9
Financial Consumer Protection Regulations, SOR/2021–181
Negative Option Billing Regulations, SOR/2012–23.
The Constitution Act 1867, 30 & 31 Vict, c 3
Business Practices Act (Manitoba)1990 CCSM, c B120
Business Practices Act (Prince Edward Island) RSPEI 1988 c B-7
Business Practices and Consumer Protection Act (British Columbia) SBC 2004
Consumer Protection Act (Alberta) RSA 2000, c 26.3
Consumer Protection Act (Manitoba) 1987 CCSM, c 200
Consumer Protection Act (Ontario) SO 2002, c 30,
Consumer Protection and Business Practices Act (Newfoundland and Labrador) SNL 2009 c 31.1
Consumer Protection and Business Practices Act (Saskatchewan) SS 2013 c C-30.2

## Kenya

Banking Act 2012
Competition Act 2010 (as amended)
National Payment System Act 2011
The Constitution of Kenya 2010
The Kenya Information and Communications (Consumer Protection) Regulation 2010
The Kenya Information and Communications (Dispute Resolution) Regulations 2010
The National Payment Systems Regulations 2014

## The United Kingdom

Consumer Credit Act 1974
Consumer Protection (Amendment) Regulations 2014
Consumer Rights Act 2015
Enterprise Act 2002
Financial Guidance and Claims Act 2018
Financial Services Markets Act 2000 (as amended)
The Consumer Protection from Unfair Trading Regulations 2008
The Electronic Money Regulations 2011
The Enterprise Act 2002 (Part 8) (Designation of the Consumers' Association) Order 2005 (SI 2005, No.917)
The Financial Services (Distance Marketing) Regulations 2004
The Financial Services and Markets Act 2000 (Regulated Activities) Order 2001
The Payment Services Regulation 2017
The Unfair Terms in Consumer Contracts Regulation 1999

## Europe

Council Directive 2005/29/EC of 11 May 2005 concerning unfair business-to-consumer commercial practices in the internal market and amending Council Directive 84/450/EEC, Directives 97/7/EC, 98/27/EC and 2002/65/EC of the European Parliament and of the Council and Regulation (EC) No 2006/2004 of the European Parliament and of the Council [2005] OJ L 149/22

Council Directive 2009/110/EC of 16 September 2009 on the taking up, pursuit and prudential supervision of the business of electronic money institutions amending Directives 2005/60/EC and 2006/48/EC and repealing Directive 2000/46/EC [2009] OJ L 267/7

Council Directive 2011/83/EU of 25 October 2011 on consumer rights, amending Council Directive 93/13/EEC and Directive 1999/44/EC of the European Parliament and of the Council and repealing Council Directive 85/577/EEC and Directive 97/7/EC of the European Parliament and of the Council [2011] OJ L 304/64

Council Directive 2015/2366 of 25 November 2015 on payment services in the internal market, amending Directives 2002/65/EC, 2009/110/EC and 2013/36/EU and Regulation (EU) No 1093/2010, and repealing Directive 2007/64/EC [2015] OJ L 337/35

Council Directive 93/13/EC of 5 April 1993 on unfair terms in consumer Contracts [1993] OJ L 95/29

# Cases

## Canada

*32262 B.C. Ltd. v. Balmoral Investments Ltd* [1999] BCCA 184
*Bank of Montreal v. Javed* [2016] ONCA 49
*Bank of Montreal v. Marcotte* [2014] SCC 55
*Bhasin v. Hrynew* [2014] SCC 71
*Tilden Rent-A-Car Co. v. Clendenning* [1978] 83 DLR (3d) 400

## The United Kingdom

*British Airways Plc v. Ryanair Ltd* [2001] E.T.M.R 24
*Clark v. In Focus Asset Management & Tax Solutions* [2014] EWCA Civ 118
*Director General of Fair Trading v. First National Bank Plc.* [2001] UKHL 52
*Erven Warnink Besloten Vennootschap v. J. Townend & Sons (Hull) Ltd* [1979] AC 731
*Financial Ombudsman Service Ltd v. Heather Moor & Edgecomb Ltd* [2008] EWCA Civ 643
*Interfoto Picture Library Ltd. v. Stiletto Visual Programmes Ltd* [1989] QB 433
*Meridian Global Funds Management Asia Ltd v. Securities Commission* [1995] 2 AC 500
*Office of Fair Trading v. Abbey National Plc* [2009] UKSC 6
*Office of Fair Trading v. Purely Creative Ltd* [2011] EWHC 106 (Ch)
*ParkingEye Ltd v. Beavis* [2015] UKSC 67
*Secretary of State for Business Innovation & Skills v. PLT Anti-Marketing Limited* [2015] EWCA Civ 76
*Tesco Supermarkets v. Nattrass* [1972] AC 153
*West v. Ian Finlay and Associates* [2014] EWCA Civ 316
*Yam Seng Pte Ltd v. International Trade Corp* [2013] EWHC 111 (QB)

## Europe

*Aziz v. Caixa d'Estalvis de Catalunya, Tarragona i Manresa (Catalunyacaixa)* (C-415/11) EU:C:2013:164

*Heininger v. Bayerische Hypo-und Vereinsbank AG* (C-481/99) ECR (2001) I-09945
*Mostaza Claro v. Centro Movil Milenium SL* (C-168/05) EU:C:2006:675
*Oceano Grupo Editorial SA v. Quintero* (C-240/98) EU:C:2000:346
*Pannon GSM Zrt. v. Erzsébet Sustikné Győrfi* (C-243/08) [2009] ECR I-4713

# 1 Introduction

## 1.1 Setting the Context

Consumers are important economic actors, and as such, they should have access to the tools which allow them to fully participate in the economy and society. To build wealth in the long term and to ensure that they are remunerated for contributing to economic activities, consumers should be able to manage, save, and invest funds if they choose to. They should also have access to safe and efficient ways to transfer value in exchange for other products and services that they need. In the same vein, where necessary, consumers should also be able to access credit for personal and economic reasons. Should adverse events occur, consumers should also be able to rely on arrangements that insure them against the consequences of such events. In other words, at a minimum, consumers require access to financial services which enable them to save, make payments, and access credit and insurance.

Consumers are said to be financially excluded when they are unable to access these basic financial services (unbanked) or where access is nominal due to reasons such as high costs (underbanked). Available data confirm that while financial exclusion is a problem in many jurisdictions, it is more pronounced in developing countries. For instance, in 2015, the United Nations Conference on Trade and Development (UNCTAD) reported that the share of adults in developed countries with an account with a formal financial institution was more than double that of developing countries.[1] The World Bank's 2017 Global Findex data further reported that at least 1.7 billion adults do not have an account with a financial services provider or mobile money provider.[2] Nearly half of those affected reside in developing countries.[3]

1 United Nations Conference on Trade and Development (UNCTAD), 'Access to Financial Services as a Driver for the Post-2015 Development Agenda' (2015) p.2 <https://unctad.org/system/files/official-document/presspb2015d7_en.pdf> accessed 26 February 2022.

2 Asli Demigruc-Kunt, Leora Klapper Dorothe Singer et al., *The Global Findex Database 2017: Measuring Financial Inclusion and Fintech Revolution* (World Bank 2018) p.4 <https://globalfindex.worldbank.org/sites/globalfindex/files/2018-04/2017 Findex full report_0.pdf> accessed 26 February 2022.

3 Seven countries account for this number including Bangladesh, China, India, Indonesia, Mexico, Nigeria, and Pakistan. Ibid.

DOI: 10.4324/9780429327292-1

Financial exclusion is a pronounced problem in developing countries for many reasons. A top reason is the lack of extensive bank branch networks, which increases the costs of accessing financial services. Banks traditionally provide financial services through branch networks which are often situated in profitable urban areas.[4] However, a significant populace resides in rural areas with high poverty rates. For economic reasons, establishing bank branches and Automated Teller Machines (ATMs) to cover such rural areas is too expensive.[5] Hence, many rural dwellers have zero or limited access to financial services. This has grave implications, as financially excluded persons cannot save or access credit and, thus, cannot insure themselves against unexpected economic shocks such as illness or unemployment.[6] Financial exclusion can also serve as an impediment to income opportunities and the overall welfare of individuals, especially the poor, women, youth, migrants, and rural populations.[7] The result is that such consumers remain vulnerable in circumstances that exacerbate poverty.[8]

Consequently, financial inclusion, which refers to the provision of basic financial services to excluded and underserved persons at affordable costs, continues to draw attention as a development priority.[9] These basic financial services include credit, savings, payments, and insurance provided by formal institutions.[10] Where adults are financially included, they will have 'effective access' to financial services from formal service providers.[11] The Global Partnership for Financial Inclusion explains that in this context, 'effective access' involves the convenient and responsible delivery of financial services at a cost that is affordable to the customer and sustainable for the provider.[12] Financial inclusion, however, is

4 Evan Gibson, Federico Lupo-Pasini, and Ross P Buckley, 'Regulating Digital Financial Services Agents in Developing Countries to Promote Financial Inclusion' (2015) *Singapore Journal of Legal Studies* 26, 26.

5 Claire Alexandre, Ignacio Mas, and Daniel Radcliffe, 'Regulating New Banking Models to Bring Financial Services to All' (2011) 54(3) *Challenge*, 116, 117.

6 Ross P Buckley, Jonathan Greenacre, and Louise Malady, 'The Regulation of Mobile Money in Malawi' (2015) 4 *Washington University Global Studies Law Review* 435, 440.

7 UNCTAD 'Access to Financial Services as a Driver for the Post-2015 Development Agenda' (n 1) p.2.

8 Peter Cartwright, *The Vulnerable Consumer of Financial Services: Law, Policy and Regulation* (Financial Services Research Forum, 2011) p.37 <https://www.nottingham.ac.uk/business/who-we-are/centres-and-institutes/gcbfi/documents/researchreports/paper78.pdf> accessed 18 January 2022.

9 Emily Lee, 'Financial Inclusion: A Challenge to the New Paradigm of Financial Technology, Regulatory Technology and Anti-Money Laundering Law' (2017) 6 *Journal of Business Law* 473, 473.

10 Global Partnership for Financial Inclusion (GBFI), 'Global Standard Setting Bodies and Financial Inclusion: The Evolving Landscape' (2016) p.6 <https://www.gpfi.org/sites/gpfi/files/documents/GPFI_WhitePaper_Mar2016.pdf> accessed 1 March 2022.

11 Global Partnership for Financial Inclusion (GPFI), 'Global Standard-Setting Bodies and Financial Inclusion for the Poor: Toward Proportionate Standards and Guidance' (2011) p.1 <https://www.gpfi.org/sites/gpfi/files/documents/White-Paper-Global-Standard-Setting-Bodies-Oct-2011.pdf> accessed 1 March 2022.

12 Ibid.

not the end goal; rather, it is a means to multiple ends.[13] Financially included individuals are economically resilient: they can save for unforeseen emergencies, plan for recurring expenses,[14] weather financial shocks, and invest in education and health.[15] This can contribute to overall economic growth and the achievement of broader development goals.[16]

There is also growing evidence that financial inclusion can lead to more stable financial systems and economies.[17] In particular, domestic resources can be mobilised through national savings, which helps to boost government revenue.[18] More importantly, financial inclusion has been identified as a key enabler for achieving at least seven of the 17 Sustainable Development Goals.[19] At least 89 countries are members of the Alliance for Financial Inclusion network committed to 'advancing financial inclusion at country, regional and international levels.'[20]

Accordingly, it has become increasingly popular for many financial services regimes to include matters relating to 'financial inclusion, equity or accessibility of regimes' as core policy considerations.[21] This is informed by the belief that in the absence of intervention, the financial services sector is unlikely to extend its services to members of society who are underprivileged due to disability, poverty, and geographic disadvantage.[22] Moreover, in construing a central bank's responsibility to promote and maintain an efficient payment system, financial inclusion is seen as a by-product of a truly efficient system.[23] An efficient system in this

13 United Nations Capital Development Fund, 'Inclusive Digital Economies' <https://www.uncdf.org/inclusive-digital-economies> accessed 28 February 2022.

14 Timothy Adams, 'Why Financial Inclusion Matters' (2018) <https://www.centerforfinancialinclusion.org/why-financial-inclusion-matters> accessed 28 February 2022.

15 The World Bank, 'Financial Inclusion: Overview' <https://www.worldbank.org/en/topic/financialinclusion/overview - 1> accessed 28 February 2022.

16 United Nations Capital Development Fund, 'Financial Inclusion and the SDGs' <https://www.uncdf.org/financial-inclusion-and-the-sdgs> accessed 28 February 2022.

17 Ibid.

18 Ibid.

19 The World Bank, 'Financial Inclusion: Overview' (n 15). These include eliminating extreme poverty (SDG 1), reducing hunger and promoting food security (SDG 2), achieving good health and wellbeing (SDG 3), fostering quality education (SDG 4), promoting gender equality (SDG 5), promoting shared economic growth (SDG 8), promoting innovation and sustainable industrialisation (SDG 9). See Leora Klapper, Mayada El-Zoghbi, and Jake Hess, 'Achieving the Sustainable Development Goals: The Role of Financial Inclusion' (2016) <https://www.cgap.org/sites/default/files/researches/documents/Working-Paper-Achieving-Sustainable-Development-Goals-Apr-2016_0.pdf> accessed 15 January 2022.

20 <https://www.afi-global.org/about/> accessed 15 January 2022.

21 Rhys Bollen, 'A Discussion of Best Practice in the Regulation of Payment Services: Part 2' (2010) 25(9) *Journal of International Banking Law and Regulation* 429, p.432.

22 Ibid.

23 Maria Chiara Malaguti, 'Payment System Regulation for Improving Financial Inclusion.' (2015) p.2 <https://www.cgdev.org/sites/default/files/CGD-Policy-Paper-70-Malaguti-Payment-Systems-Financial-Inclusion-1.pdf> accessed 1 March 2022.

context allows for fair access to the market and supports innovation, all of which are preconditions to financial inclusion.[24]

The financial inclusion agenda has received a boost from technological innovations, which present enormous opportunities for expanding access to financial services. Technology presents traditional financial institutions with a cost-effective channel for serving untapped markets and allows new market players to serve consumers better.[25] The innovations cover a broad range of activities such as offering digital credit, processing online payments, issuing digital currencies, and managing assets, to name a few.[26] One such innovation is mobile payments (m-payments). The ubiquitous nature of mobile devices coupled with a promise of speed and convenience makes m-payments an attractive innovation. However, as with other innovative products, m-payments also raise consumer protection concerns and require robust regulatory mechanisms which respond to such concerns. These themes are given principal attention in this book. This book evaluates the existing consumer protection mechanisms in selected jurisdictions, specifically considering their continued relevance in the face of technological change and highlights regulatory best practices which can inform future reform efforts.

## 1.2 The Scope of the Book

Financial services innovations can introduce regulatory risks. The challenge is to develop regulatory frameworks that are strong enough to withstand those risks yet not so severe that the cost of complying discourages service providers from entering the market.[27] In striking the right balance, it is necessary to analyse existing regulations to establish whether they remain proportionate to identified risks.[28] Thus, innovation presents opportunities to re-examine the continued relevance of existing frameworks and the potential need to clarify, revise, or introduce new approaches that serve identified regulatory objectives.[29] Against this backdrop, this book investigates the existing consumer protection frameworks that apply to m-payments in selected jurisdictions. The inquiry is centred on the premise that for this innovation to remain credible and sustainable, it must function within a clear regulated framework where the parties involved (especially

24 Ibid.

25 Timothy Adams, 'Why Financial Inclusion Matters' (n 14). <https://www.centerforfinancialinclusion.org/why-financial-inclusion-matters>.

26 Rory Van Loo, 'Making Innovation more Competitive: The Case of Fintech' (2018) 65 *UCLA Law Review* 232, 238.

27 Global Partnership for Financial Inclusion, 'The G-20 Principles for Innovative Financial Inclusion' p.5 <https://www.gpfi.org/sites/gpfi/files/documents/G20 Principles for Innovative Financial Inclusion - AFI brochure.pdf> accessed 1 March 2022.

28 Ibid.

29 Matthew W Swinehart, 'Modeling Payments Regulation and Financial Change' (2018) 67 *University of Kansas Law Review* 83, 127.

consumers) are protected.[30] The main objective of this endeavour is to identify best practices that national authorities seeking to leverage m-payments and similar innovations can emulate.

It is important to note at this point that references to the term 'consumer' throughout the book only cover individuals using financial products and services like m-payments in a private capacity. It does not include merchants and other financial and non-financial institutions which qualify as customers in certain business relationships. Also, the book takes a narrower interpretation of the regulatory mechanisms focused on consumer protection. As such, themes falling within the scope of competition law, data protection, and prudential regulation are not considered in the book. While these themes admittedly impact consumer welfare, they address separate objectives, and it would be impossible to do justice to these matters.

There is a range of published works on m-payments. Many of such works focus on the preferred regulatory approach that can enable m-payment services to be scaled and replicated. These works tend to focus on issues such as whether regulation should be ex-ante or ex-post and whether (and how) non-bank players should be regulated. While many works acknowledge the potential consumer issues raised in adopting m-payments, a deeper investigation of existing frameworks and their merits is missing. This book seeks to fill that gap. The argument is simple: m-payments can contribute to achieving policy goals like financial inclusion, but regulatory focus and intervention must not only encourage investment and innovation; it must also serve to protect and inspire consumer confidence.

To achieve this book's objective, the analysis conducted mainly relies on traditional doctrinal legal research. Doctrinal research seeks to understand the law through a detailed examination of authoritative legal texts.[31] This method concerns itself with a search for meaning within legal documents, adopting the language and concepts that are internal to the law.[32] This approach is appropriate, as the discussion in the book relies heavily on primary sources of law (such as legislation and case law) from selected jurisdictions and secondary sources of law in academic literature. Furthermore, good doctrinal research covers both the systemic reconstruction of existing norms and the evaluation of these norms against identified normative standards.[33] Bearing this in mind, the discussion in this book looks to international soft law instruments to determine the objective normative

30 Maria C Stephens, 'Promoting Responsible Financial Inclusion: A Risk-based Approach to Supporting Mobile Financial Services Expansion' (2011) 27 *Banking and Finance Law Review* 229, 330.

31 Douglas W Vick, 'Interdisciplinarity and the Discipline of Law' (2004) 31(2) *Journal of Law & Society* 163, 178.

32 Steven Cammiss and Dawn Watkins, 'Legal Research in the Humanities' in Dawn Watkins and Mandy Burton (eds), *Research Methods in Law* (Routledge 2013) p.72; Stephen A Smith, 'Taking Law Seriously' (2000) 50 *The University of Toronto Law Journal* 241, 255.

33 Vick 'Interdisciplinarity and the Discipline of Law' (n 31).

standards that will guide the evaluation and analysis in the book.[34] Accordingly, the book discusses a typology of consumer policy tools relevant to m-payments in *Chapter 3*.

### *1.2.1 Why Mobile Payments?*

Belonging to a bouquet of mobile-based financial services, m-payments cover payment transactions in which a mobile device and mobile telecommunication network are used to facilitate the exchange of financial value. While numerous payment innovations exist, this book focuses on m-payments owing to the attention that they have generated in the financial inclusion discourse. This attention has been attributed to several reasons. First, the Bank for International Settlements reports that about a fifth of reported innovations target financial inclusion and many focus on m-payments.[35] This can be explained by the growth in the ownership of mobile phones and the relatively extensive mobile network coverage in many developing countries. Mobile phones provide a communications channel which can be conveniently used to initiate and execute transactions.[36] This communication channel helps reduce the cost of financial services as they are well suited for rural and isolated areas, where providing physical points of access to financial services can be expensive relative to the potential revenue streams.[37] With at least 5.2 billion unique mobile subscribers around the world,[38] the ubiquity of the mobile phone provides a compelling business case and continues to be an influential factor in the adoption of m-payment systems.[39] Therefore, it is unsurprising that many innovative financial services focus on m-payments.

34 e.g., The UN Guidelines for Consumer Protection (2016) <https://unctad.org/system/files/official-document/ditccplpmisc2016d1_en.pdf> accessed 26 February 2022; The OECD Consumer Policy Toolkit (2010) <https://www.oecd-ilibrary.org/governance/consumer-policy-toolkit_9789264079663-en> accessed 26 February 2022; The G20 High Level Principles on Financial Consumer Protections (2011) <https://www.oecd.org/daf/fin/financial-markets/48892010.pdf> accessed 26 February 2022.

35 Committee on Payments and Markets Infrastructure, 'Innovations in Retail Payments' (2012) p.16 <https://www.bis.org/cpmi/publ/d102.pdf> accessed 28 February 2022.

36 David Porteous, 'The Enabling Environment for Mobile Banking in Africa' (2006) p.3 <https://www.findevgateway.org/sites/default/files/publications/files/mfg-en-paper-the-enabling-environment-for-mobile-banking-in-africa-may-2006_0.pdf> accessed 2 March 2022.

37 The World Bank, 'Payment Aspects of Financial Inclusion' (2016) para.42 <https://documents1.worldbank.org/curated/en/806481470154477031/pdf/107382-WP-REPLLACEMENT-PUBLIC-PAFI-Report-final-in-A4.pdf> accessed 2 March 2022.

38 The GSM Association (GSMA), 'The Mobile Economy 2020' p.6 <https://www.gsma.com/mobileeconomy/wp-content/uploads/2020/03/GSMA_MobileEconomy2020_Global.pdf> accessed 2 March 2021.

39 Dennis Dennehy and David Sammon, 'Trends in Mobile Payments Research: A Literature Review' (2015) 3(1) *Journal of Innovation Management* 49, 49.

Second, m-payments can serve as an important gateway to other financial services.[40] Payment services form a core part of the overall package of financial services. Hence, access to such services is only one aspect of being financially included.[41] Other financial services such as savings, credit, and insurance are important in maximising the development role of remittances because they facilitate options to invest remitted funds in productive activities, social services, and infrastructure.[42] When a person opens an m-payments account, they effectively open a transaction account that can facilitate access to other financial services.[43] For example, regular use of an m-payment service may help establish a pattern of transactions which could build a previously excluded person's financial profile, allowing them to qualify for credit.[44] In essence, by building a financial profile, an m-payments transaction account may be eligible to be upgraded to an account with more functionalities beyond payment services.

Finally, and on a related note, given the link between financial inclusion and development, governments will continue to push for greater access to and use of financial services.[45] Regulators acknowledge that financial access can reduce poverty and lead to more inclusive and sustainable development, which helps in achieving broader economic and social goals.[46] Increasing innovations involving mobile devices have spurred regulatory interest in leveraging this trend to deliver financial services to underserved or excluded individuals. Sub-Saharan Africa is reported to have the largest number of registered mobile money accounts globally.[47] There are also examples of m-payment success in the region, which informs interest in the subject matter. For example, Kenya's successful m-payment service, M-pesa, is often touted as demonstrating the possibility of leveraging mobile technology to extend financial services to large segments of unbanked poor people.[48] Research also suggests that M-pesa has lifted at least 2 per cent of Kenya's population out of poverty and helped improve the economic lives of disadvantaged groups like women.[49] Therefore, it seems reasonable to focus on the regulatory policies that support consumers adopting this innovation.

40 Morten L Bech and Jenny Hancock, 'Innovations in Payments' (2020) *BIS Quarterly Review*, 21, 30.
41 The World Bank, 'Payment Aspects of Financial Inclusion' (n 37) para.13.
42 UNCTAD, 'Access to Financial Services as a Driver for the Post-2015 Development Agenda' (n 1) p.4
43 The World Bank, 'Payment Aspects of Financial Inclusion' (n 37) para.14.
44 Ibid.
45 Klapper et al., 'Achieving the Sustainable Development Goals' (n 19) p.9.
46 Ibid, pp.2 & 7.
47 Albert G Zeufack, Cesar Calderon, and Gerard Kambou et al., 'An Analysis of Issues Shaping Africa's Economic Future' (2020) 21 *Africa's Pulse* 1, 69.
48 Ignacio Mas and Daniel Radcliffe 'Mobile Payments Go Viral: M-pesa in Kenya' (2011) 32 *Journal of Financial Transformation* 169, 172.
49 UN Capital Development Fund, 'Financial Inclusion and the SDGs' (n 16).

### *1.2.2 Why Focus on Consumer Protection?*

Llewellyn reports that the regulation of financial services has three principal objectives. The first is to sustain systemic stability, the second to maintain the safety and soundness of financial institutions, and the third to protect the consumer.[50] Research and regulatory efforts focusing on financial services (and resulting innovations) generally cover one or more of these themes. While acknowledging the equal importance of these objectives, this book focuses on consumer protection for several reasons.[51]

First, the opportunities presented by m-payment services are exciting, especially in the context of financial inclusion. The biggest beneficiaries of m-payments will be those excluded consumers who, for the first time, will access a relatively cheaper and secure payment service. These beneficiaries will likely be those who are vulnerable and have been excluded for reasons such as poverty, illiteracy, geographic residence, and age. For many such consumers, innovations like m-payments will represent their first engagement with formal financial services. This may be daunting because many first-time users of financial services lack the experience and knowledge required to navigate complexities.

Being unfamiliar with financial services, it is this category of consumers who will be more easily susceptible to abuse by service providers.[52] It is also this group who are least able to bear the consequences of a poorly regulated service as even minor disruptions in their financial life can have significant ripple effects.[53] Therefore, strong consumer protection frameworks must be prioritised to ensure that consumers, especially those who are vulnerable and poor, are subject to adequate safety mechanisms which minimise the risk and impact of unscrupulous business practices. This is especially so as the Global Partnership for Financial Inclusion has pointed out that effective financial consumer protection is an essential element of financial inclusion as it reinforces the benefits of inclusion while also mitigating the risks involved.[54]

Second, the widespread availability of m-payments will depend on whether the service can reach a critical mass. Guru argues that a payment product must satisfy certain conditions for it to be successfully launched and remain viable in

50 David Llewellyn 'The Economic Rationale for Financial Regulation' (1999) p.9 <https://www.fep.up.pt/disciplinas/pgaf924/PGAF/Texto_2_David_Llewellyn.pdf> accessed 26 March 2022.

51 Broadly speaking, it could be argued all objectives/techniques of regulation aid in protecting the consumer.

52 Malaguti, 'Payment System Regulation for Improving Financial Inclusion.' (n 23) p.14.

53 Rajiv Lal and Ishan Sachdev, 'Mobile Money Services – Design and Development for Financial Inclusion' (2015) p.8 <https://www.hbs.edu/ris/Publication Files/15-083_e7db671b-12b2-47e7-9692-31808ee92bf1.pdf> accessed 20 February 2022.

54 GPFI, 'Global Standard-Setting Bodies and Financial Inclusion for the Poor' (n 11) p.5 <https://www.gpfi.org/sites/gpfi/files/documents/White-Paper-Global-Standard-Setting-Bodies-Oct-2011.pdf>.

the long run.[55] First, the service providers must recognise the financial feasibility of the service in the medium to long term; products which will save costs and increase revenue streams are likely to generate interest from these parties. Second, regulators must be convinced that introducing such products will not compromise the security and stability of the financial system. Third, the consumer must be convinced that the product offers convenience, minimal cost, and maximum security.[56]

Against this background, one must note that an important characteristic of the retail payments market is that it is two-sided because there are two distinct users involved, i.e., consumers and merchants.[57] In two-sided markets, success depends on network effects[58] as it is difficult to achieve a critical mass if both sides of the market do not adopt a payment service.[59] The implication is that if more consumers adopt m-payments, then more merchants will and vice versa.[60] An example can be seen with the adoption of credit cards in Europe. Credit cards could take off successfully because consumers were willing to use them in place of the popular Eurocheque and despite the unwillingness of banks and merchants to leave a percentage of their revenue to card companies.[61] This suggests that if an m-payments provider intends to scale, it is in their interest that consumers adopt their product as this can, in turn, encourage merchants to adopt it. Amongst other variables, rapid consumer adoption of m-payments will depend on whether they trust the service.[62] Trust in this context would include trust in the service provider's brand and the security of the technology being deployed. It would also include confidence that transactions would be fulfilled as expected and that remedial actions would be available if anything went wrong.[63]

One aspect of fostering trust in a new product requires that there are clear legal frameworks which proportionately outline the duties and liabilities of all

55 Balachandher K Guru, 'E-banking Developments in Malaysia: Prospects and Problems' (2000) 15(10) *Journal of International Banking Law* 250, 252–253.

56 Ibid.

57 This is often described as the-chicken-and-egg dilemma because each side has to adopt an innovation at the same time, or no side will have the incentive to adopt it. Committee on Payments and Markets Infrastructure, 'Innovations in Retail Payments' (n 35) p.19.

58 Network effects is based on the understanding that a user's perception of the value of a product or service depends on the size of the network, i.e., how many other persons are also using it. Consultative Group to Assist the Poor (CGAP), 'The Challenges of Two-sided Markets in Merchant Payments' (2019) <https://www.cgap.org/research/publication/challenge-two-sided-markets-merchant-payments> accessed 23 February 2022.

59 Committee on Payments and Markets Infrastructure, 'Innovations in Retail Payments' (n 35) p.19.

60 Marc Bourreau and Marianne Verdier, 'Cooperation for Innovation in Payment Systems: The Case of Mobile Payments' (2010) 79(3) *Communications & Strategies* 95, p.103.

61 Nina Kreyer, Key Pousttchi, and Klaus Turowski, 'Mobile Payment Procedures: Scopes and Characteristics' (2003) 2(3) *E-service Journal* 7, 9.

62 Lal & Sachdev 'Mobile Money Services – Design and Development for Financial Inclusion' (n 53) p.7

63 Ibid.

stakeholders as well as the protections available to end-users.[64] Where the consumer protection rules applying to an innovative service are poor, ineffective, or non-existent, negative experiences in using a product will discourage consumers from adopting similar offerings in the market.[65] On the other hand, service providers will enjoy positive externalities if appropriate levels of consumer protection are available to address concerns that consumers may have.[66] Thus, clear and effective consumer protection frameworks will inspire consumer confidence, especially for first-time users of formal financial services, which can positively impact the adoption of innovation.

On a broader note, in recent years, global policymakers have increasingly highlighted the need for clear complementary synergy between policy objectives like financial stability, financial integrity, financial inclusion, and financial consumer protection.[67] There is the understanding that well implemented and effective financial consumer protection regulatory frameworks can positively affect the financial sector as a whole.[68] This is because strong consumer protection frameworks encourage transparency and strengthen consumer confidence, which can spur competition amongst financial institutions.[69] This can lead to financial innovations, which can provide more benefits and greater inclusion for consumers.[70]

In conclusion, an equitable and transparent consumer protection regime is an integral part of a broader financial inclusion framework.[71] As technology changes rapidly, it is often difficult for regulators to catch up, but they can learn from each other. As stated earlier, a key objective of this book is to identify best practices in regulating consumer issues in m-payments. Identifying best practices can help provide regulators with concrete ideas which can be useful in reforming and strengthening consumer protection frameworks. Many developing countries are constrained by the underdevelopment of effective regulatory frameworks that maintain financial integrity and consumer protection. In developed countries with more mature consumer protection frameworks and which historically have had a bank-centric payment sector, the changes introduced by innovation, particularly the introduction of new non-bank players, may question the seamless extension

64 Niels Vandezande, 'Between Bitcoins and Mobile Payments: Will the European Commission's New Proposal Provide More Legal Certainty' (2014) 22(3) *International Journal of Law & Information Technology* 295, 296.

65 Porteous, 'The Enabling Environment for Mobile Banking in Africa' (n 36) para.4.1.2.

66 Ibid.

67 The World Bank 'Good Practices for Financial Consumer Protection' (2017) p.1 <https://openknowledge.worldbank.org/bitstream/handle/10986/28996/122011-PUBLIC-GoodPractices-Web-Final.pdf?sequence=5&isAllowed=y> accessed 27 February 2022.

68 The World Bank, 'Institutional Arrangements for Financial Consumer Protection' (2015) p.4 <https://openknowledge.worldbank.org/bitstream/handle/10986/25196/108122.pdf?sequence=4&isAllowed=y>.

69 Ibid.

70 Ibid.

71 Ibid.

and relevance of existing regulations.[72] These factors may prevent m-payments from reaching their full potential.[73] Consequently, countries hoping to leverage m-payments to meet financial inclusion goals must develop or rethink the appropriate regulatory frameworks which support consumer protection.

### *1.2.3 Why Canada, Kenya, and the United Kingdom?*

The book investigates the consumer protection frameworks in three countries which serve as case studies. The use of case studies helps in meeting the book's objective of examining existing consumer protection frameworks applying to m-payments. This inquiry will also assist in highlighting best practices observed. As stated earlier, the book identifies a typology of consumer policy tools relevant to m-payments. This typology provides an objective reference point which forms the basis for inquiry in each selected jurisdiction. This approach is based on the premise that different jurisdictions deal with similar consumer problems and that the practical effect of the solutions they adopt to solve these problems may be somewhat similar.[74] One critique of this approach may point out that problems faced in different legal systems are steeped within respective cultural and historical contexts and thus cannot be similar.[75] However, this book leans on the increasingly accepted assertion that consumer problems are quite similar around the globe, a point reinforced by the fact that consumer markets are becoming globalised.[76]

Canada, Kenya, and the United Kingdom have been selected for several reasons. First, the three countries showed an early interest in regulatory issues affecting m-payments, including consumer protection. Canada's Financial Consumer Protection Agency was one of the first to conduct a detailed thematic review of consumer issues in m-payments.[77] Kenya's m-payment platform, M-pesa, was launched under a close collaborative process with the Central Bank of Kenya.[78]

72 Swinehart, 'Modeling Payments Regulation and Financial Change' (n 29) p.137.

73 Nir Kshetri and Sharad Acharya, 'Mobile Payments in Emerging Markets' (2012) 14(4) *IEEE IT Professional* 9, 11.

74 Stephen A Smith, 'Comparative Legal Scholarship as Ordinary Legal Scholarship' (2010) 5 *Journal of Comparative Law* 331, 344–345

75 Julie De Coninck 'Comparisons in Private Patrimonial Law: Towards a Bottom-Up Approach Using (Cross-Cultural) Behavioural Economics' in Maurice Adams and Jacco Bomhoff (eds), *Practice and Theory in Comparative Law* (Cambridge University Press 2012) p.261

76 Geraint Howells, Iain Ramsay, and Thomas Wilhelmson, 'Consumer Law in its International Dimension' in Geraint Howells, Iain Ramsay, and Thomas Wilhelmson (eds), *Handbook of Research on International Consumer Law* (Edward Elgar Publishing 2010) p.1.

77 Steve Trites, Charles Gibney, and Bruno Lévesque, 'Mobile Payments and Consumer Protection in Canada' (2013 Research Division, Financial Consumer Agency of Canada) <https://www.canada.ca/content/dam/canada/financial-consumer-agency/migration/eng/resources/researchsurveys/documents/fcac_mobile_payments_consumer_protection_accessible_en.pdf> accessed 27 January 2022.

78 International Finance Corporation, 'M-Money Channel Distribution Case – Kenya (Safaricom M-pesa)' p.1 <https://www.ifc.org/wps/wcm/connect/e0d2a9bd-16b9-4a36-8498-0b2650b9af8b

The United Kingdom's Financial Conduct Authority also conducted two thematic reviews focusing on m-payments.[79]

Second, the three countries also present important characteristics from a consumer protection perspective which justify their choice as case studies. Kenya's M-pesa is a prime example of m-payment success in sub-Saharan Africa. Their early experience with m-payments, amongst other factors, led to important legislation such as the Consumer Protection Act 2012. As a developing country with an established m-payments market, it is useful to consider their experience with m-payments and how their consumer protection frameworks address relevant consumer issues. Canada and the United Kingdom represent jurisdictions with established retail payment markets that support traditional and innovative payment solutions. Notably, both countries also have relatively mature consumer protection frameworks, though set in different contexts. While consumer protection frameworks are centralised in the United Kingdom, Canada's federal system of government allows for a more decentralised approach. For the purposes of this book, it is useful to consider the practice in both countries as their strong consumer protection frameworks may provide helpful pointers on general best practices. It is also beneficial to consider how consumer protection regimes function in centralised and decentralised systems as this can provide valuable insights.

## 1.3 Road Map: Navigating This Book

This book is divided into three parts. Following this introduction, the **first part** of the book commences with discussing the specific innovation that lies at the centre of the discourse, i.e., m-payments. Specifically, *Chapter 2* introduces the concept of m-payments and provides the working definition adopted in the book. The chapter also highlights the parties involved in the transaction process and the technology used to facilitate it. The chapter further highlights that m-payments can take on a transformative significance depending on the jurisdiction.

*Chapter 3* discusses the justification for regulatory intervention to protect consumers. This sets the background for why regulatory intervention is necessary with regards to m-payments. This part of the book concludes with discussions in *Chapter 4* which highlight a typology of consumer policy tools relevant to the consumer issues in m-payments. This typology is adapted from policy principles contained in the UN Guidelines for Consumer Protection,[80] the G20 High-Level Principles of Consumer Financial Protection,[81] and the OECD Consumer Policy Toolkit.[82]

/Tool%2B6.7.%2BCase%2BStudy%2B-%2BM-PESA%2BKenya%2B.pdf?MOD=AJPERES&CVID=jkCVy-n> accessed 27 January 2022.

79 Financial Conduct Authority, 'Mobile Banking and Payments – Supporting an Innovative and Secure Market' (2013) <http://www.fca.org.uk/static/documents/thematic-reviews/tr13-06.pdf> accessed 27 January 2022; Financial Conduct Authority, 'Mobile Banking and Payments' (2014) <https://www.fca.org.uk/publication/thematic-reviews/tr14-15.pdf> accessed 27 January 2022.

80 (n 34).

81 (n 34).

82 (n 34).

The discussions in this chapter provide a theoretical analysis of the selected consumer policy tools to explain their relevance in achieving consumer protection. Thus, the analysis of the tools identified in this chapter sets out the context for the discussion and recommendations in the second and third parts of the book.

The **second part** of this book focuses on examining the consumer protection frameworks applying to m-payments in selected jurisdictions. The typology highlighted in *Chapter 3* is used as the basis for inquiry in each jurisdiction. This ensures consistency in the discussion, making it easier to identify converging and diverging regulatory trends. Accordingly, *Chapters 5*, *6*, and *7* examine the present consumer framework available to m-payment consumers in Canada, Kenya, and the United Kingdom, respectively.

The **third part** of the book concludes the work. *Chapter 8* discusses the conclusions extrapolated from the inquiry and puts forward recommendations that reflect some of the best practices observed in the jurisdictions reviewed and supported in the wider academic literature.

## References

Albert G Zeufack, Cesar Calderon and Gerard Kambou et al, 'An Analysis of Issues Shaping Africa's Economic Future' (2020) 21 *Africa's Pulse* 1.

Asli Demigruc-Kunt, Leora Klapper and Dorothe Singer et al, 'The Global Findex Database 2017: Measuring Financial Inclusion and Fintech Revolution' (World Bank 2018) <https://globalfindex.worldbank.org/sites/globalfindex/files/2018-04/2017 Findex full report_0.pdf> accessed 26 February 2022.

Balachandher K Guru, 'E-banking Developments in Malaysia: Prospects and Problems' (2000) 15(10) *Journal of International Banking Law* 250.

Claire Alexandre, Ignacio Mas and Daniel Radcliffe, 'Regulating New Banking Models to Bring Financial Services to All' (2011) 54(3) *Challenge* 116.

Committee on Payments and Markets Infrastructure, 'Innovations in Retail Payments' (2012) <https://www.bis.org/cpmi/publ/d102.pdf> accessed 28 February 2022.

Consultative Group to Assist the Poor (CGAP), 'The Challenges of Two-sided Markets in Merchant Payments' (2019) <https://www.cgap.org/research/publication/challenge-two-sided-markets-merchant-payments> accessed 23 February 2022.

David Llewellyn 'The Economic Rationale for Financial Regulation' (1999) <https://www.fep.up.pt/disciplinas/pgaf924/PGAF/Texto_2_David_Llewellyn.pdf> accessed 26 March 2022.

David Porteous, 'The Enabling Environment for Mobile Banking in Africa' (2006) <https://www.findevgateway.org/sites/default/files/publications/files/mfg-en-paper-the-enabling-environment-for-mobile-banking-in-africa-may-2006_0.pdf> accessed 2 March 2022.

Dawn Watkins and Mandy Burton (eds), *Research Methods in Law* (Routledge 2013).

Dennis Dennehy and David Sammon, 'Trends in Mobile Payments Research: A Literature Review' (2015) 3(1) *Journal of Innovation Management* 49.

Douglas W Vick, 'Interdisciplinarity and the Discipline of Law' (2004) 31(2) *Journal of Law & Society* 163.

Emily Lee, 'Financial Inclusion: A Challenge to the New Paradigm of Financial Technology, Regulatory Technology and Anti-Money Laundering Law' (2017) 6 *Journal of Business Law* 473.

Evan Gibson, Federico Lupo-Pasini and Ross P Buckley, 'Regulating Digital Financial Services Agents in Developing Countries to Promote Financial Inclusion' (2015) *Singapore Journal of Legal Studies* 26.

Financial Conduct Authority, 'Mobile Banking and Payments – Supporting an Innovative and Secure Market' (2013) <http://www.fca.org.uk/static/documents/thematic-reviews/tr13-06.pdf> accessed 27 January 2022.

Financial Conduct Authority, 'Mobile Banking and Payments' (2014) <https://www.fca.org.uk/publication/thematic-reviews/tr14-15.pdf> accessed 27 January 2022.

Geraint Howells, Iain Ramsay and Thomas Wilhelmson (eds), *Handbook of Research on International Consumer Law* (Edward Elgar Publishing 2010) p.1.

Global Partnership for Financial Inclusion (GPFI), 'Global Standard-Setting Bodies and Financial Inclusion for the Poor: Toward Proportionate Standards and Guidance' (2011) <https://www.gpfi.org/sites/gpfi/files/documents/White-Paper-Global-Standard-Setting-Bodies-Oct-2011.pdf> accessed 1 March 2022.

Global Partnership for Financial Inclusion (GPFI), 'Global Standard Setting Bodies and Financial Inclusion: The Evolving Landscape' (2016) <https://www.gpfi.org/sites/gpfi/files/documents/GPFI_WhitePaper_Mar2016.pdf> accessed 1 March 2022.

Global Partnership for Financial Inclusion (GPFI), 'The G-20 Principles for Innovative Financial Inclusion' <https://www.gpfi.org/sites/gpfi/files/documents/G20 Principles for Innovative Financial Inclusion - AFI brochure.pdf> accessed 1 March 2022.

The GSM Association (GSMA), 'The Mobile Economy 2020' <https://www.gsma.com/mobileeconomy/wp-content/uploads/2020/03/GSMA_MobileEconomy2020_Global.pdf> accessed 2 March 2021.

Ignacio Mas and Daniel Radcliffe 'Mobile Payments Go Viral: M-pesa in Kenya' (2011) 32 *Journal of Financial Transformation* 169.

International Finance Corporation, 'M-Money Chanel Distribution Case – Kenya (Safaricom M-pesa)' <https://www.ifc.org/wps/wcm/connect/e0d2a9bd-16b9-4a36-8498-0b2650b9af8b/Tool%2B6.7.%2BCase%2BStudy%2B-%2BM-PESA%2BKenya%2B.pdf?MOD=AJPERES&CVID=jkCVy-n > accessed 27 January 2022.

Leora Klapper, Mayada El-Zoghbi and Jake Hess, '"Achieving the Sustainable Development Goals" The Role of Financial Inclusion' (2016) <https://www.cgap.org/sites/default/files/researches/documents/Working-Paper-Achieving-Sustainable-Development-Goals-Apr-2016_0.pdf> accessed 15 January 2022.

Marc Bourreau and Marianne Verdier, 'Cooperation for Innovation in Payment Systems: The Case of Mobile Payments' (2010) 79(3) *Communications & Strategies* 95.

Maria C Stephens, 'Promoting Responsible Financial Inclusion: A Risk-based Approach to Supporting Mobile Financial Services Expansion' (2011) 27 *Banking and Finance Law Review* 229.

Maria Chiara Malaguti, 'Payment System Regulation for Improving Financial Inclusion' (2015) <https://www.cgdev.org/sites/default/files/CGD-Policy-Paper-70-Malaguti-Payment-Systems-Financial-Inclusion-1.pdf> accessed 1 March 2022.

Matthew W Swinehart, 'Modeling Payments Regulation and Financial Change' (2018) 67 *University of Kansas Law Review* 83.

Maurice Adams and Jacco Bomhoff (eds), *Practice and Theory in Comparative Law* (Cambridge University Press 2012).

Morten L Bech and Jenny Hancock, 'Innovations in Payments' (2020) *BIS Quarterly Review* 21.

Niels Vandezande, 'Between Bitcoins and Mobile Payments: Will the European Commission's New Proposal Provide More Legal Certainty' (2014) 22(3) *International Journal of Law & Information Technology* 295.

Nina Kreyer, Key Pousttchi and Klaus Turowski, 'Mobile Payment Procedures: Scopes and Characteristics' (2003) 2(3) *E-service Journal* 7.

Nir Kshetri and Sharad Acharya, 'Mobile Payments in Emerging Markets' (2012) 14(4) *IEEE IT Professional* 9.

Peter Cartwright, The Vulnerable Consumer of Financial Services: Law, Policy and Regulation (Financial Services Research Forum, 2011) <https://www.nottingham.ac.uk/business/who-we-are/centres-and-institutes/gcbfi/documents/researchreports/paper78.pdf> accessed 18 January 2022.

Rajiv Lal and Ishan Sachdev, 'Mobile Money Services - Design and Development for Financial Inclusion' (2015) <https://www.hbs.edu/ris/Publication Files/15-083_e7db671b-12b2-47e7-9692-31808ee92bf1.pdf> accessed 20 February 2022.

Rhys Bollen, 'A Discussion of Best Practice in the Regulation of Payment Services: Part 2' (2010) 25(9) *Journal of International Banking Law and Regulation* 429.

Rory Van Loo, 'Making Innovation more Competitive: The Case of Fintech' (2018) 65 *UCLA Law Review* 232.

Ross P Buckley, Jonathan Greenacre and Louise Malady, 'The Regulation of Mobile Money in Malawi' (2015) 4 *Washington University Global Studies Law Review* 435.

Stephen A Smith, 'Taking Law Seriously' (2000) 50 *The University of Toronto Law Journal* 241.

Stephen A Smith, 'Comparative Legal Scholarship as Ordinary Legal Scholarship' (2010) 5 *Journal of Comparative Law* 331.

Steve Trites, Charles Gibney and Bruno Lévesque, 'Mobile Payments and Consumer Protection in Canada' (2013 Research Division, Financial Consumer Agency of Canada) <https://www.canada.ca/content/dam/canada/financial-consumer-agency/migration/eng/resources/researchsurveys/documents/fcac_mobile_payments_consumer_protection_accessible_en.pdf> accessed 27 January 2022.

The G20 High Level Principles on Financial Consumer Protections (2011) <https://www.oecd.org/daf/fin/financial-markets/48892010.pdf> accessed 26 February 2022.

The UN Guidelines for Consumer Protection (2016) <https://unctad.org/system/files/official-document/ditccplpmisc2016d1_en.pdf> accessed 26 February 2022; The OECD Consumer Policy Toolkit (2010) <https://www.oecd-ilibrary.org/governance/consumer-policy-toolkit_9789264079663-en> accessed 26 February 2022.

The World Bank, 'Institutional Arrangements for Financial Consumer Protection' (2015) <https://openknowledge.worldbank.org/bitstream/handle/10986/25196/108122.pdf?sequence=4&isAllowed=y>

The World Bank, 'Payment Aspects of Financial Inclusion' (2016) <https://documents1.worldbank.org/curated/en/806481470154477031/pdf/107382-WP-REPLLACEMENT-PUBLIC-PAFI-Report-final-in-A4.pdf> accessed 2 March 2022.

The World Bank, 'Good Practices for Financial Consumer Protection' (2017) <https://openknowledge.worldbank.org/bitstream/handle/10986/28996/122011-PUBLIC-GoodPractices-WebFinal.pdf?sequence=5&isAllowed=y> accessed 27 February 2022.

The World Bank, 'Financial Inclusion: Overview' <https://www.worldbank.org/en/topic/financialinclusion/overview - 1> accessed 28 February 2022.

Timothy Adams, 'Why Financial Inclusion Matters' (2018) <https://www.centerforfinancialinclusion.org/why-financial-inclusion-matters> accessed 28 February 2022.

United Nations Capital Development Fund, 'Financial Inclusion and the SDGs' <https://www.uncdf.org/financial-inclusion-and-the-sdgs> accessed 28 February 2022.
United Nations Capital Development Fund, 'Inclusive Digital Economies' <https://www.uncdf.org/inclusive-digital-economies> accessed 28 February 2022.
United Nations Conference on Trade and Development (UNCTAD), 'Access to Financial Services as a Driver for the Post-2015 Development Agenda' (2015) <https://unctad.org/system/files/official-document/presspb2015d7_en.pdf> accessed 26 February 2022.

# Part I

# Mobile Payments and Consumer Protection – Contextual Analysis

# 2 Mobile Payments: Understanding the Service

## 2.1 Introduction

Globalisation has increased the flow of finance both domestically and internationally. Consequently, there is a continuous quest to find the most convenient, safe, and cost-effective method to exchange value. This quest has been propelled by several technological developments. In the financial services market, technological innovation has been significant for several reasons. First, it has transformed the channels relied on for delivering financial services to consumers. Owing to the growth of electronically mediated self-service technologies, there has also been a growing shift, over the decades, in how banks serve their customers.[1] For instance, in the 1960s, Automated Teller Machines (ATMs) sprang up and were followed by telephone banking services in the 1980s.[2] By the 1990s, internet banking became a viable medium for serving customers. All these developments, supported by the proliferation of mobile technologies, have arguably prepared the stage for the continuing innovations in the financial services sector.[3]

Second, technological innovation has disrupted the institutions that have historically dominated the financial services market.[4] With new players entering the market, the line separating financial and non-financial institutions has been blurred. Traditional financial institutions like banks initially held the monopoly of providing financial services, but with the liberalisation of such services in many countries, this is so longer the case. In the payments sector, for example, while banks continue to play a principal role in the provision of payment services, many non-traditional financial institutions have entered the arena. Electronic money

1 Hartmut Hoehle, Eusebio Scornavacca, and Sid Huff, 'Three Decades of Research on Consumer adoption and Utilization of Electronic Banking Channels' (2012) 54 *Decision Support Systems* 122, 122.

2 Douglas W Arner, Janos N. Barberis, Ross P Buckey, 'FinTech, RegTech, and the Reconceptualization of Financial Regulation' (2017) 37 *Northwestern Journal of International Law & Business* 371, 378.

3 Hoehle et al. (n 1) p.122.

4 Augustin Carstens, 'Shaping the Future of Payments' (2020) *BIS Quarterly Review* 17, 17.

DOI: 10.4324/9780429327292-3

institutions and mobile network operators (MNOs) now compete with banks in areas such as mobile and internet payments that are yet to be dominated by banks.[5]

Against this background, this chapter considers the innovation that is central to the discussion in this book. It is necessary to clarify what mobile payments (m-payments) mean in the context of our discussion. A better appreciation of the discourse in this book also requires that a brief commentary on the technology and business models supporting the provision of m-payments is included. While m-payments are increasingly gaining acceptance in several countries, this chapter also highlights how this payment service can take on an additive or transformative character depending on the prevailing conditions in a given jurisdiction. Overall, the discussion in this chapter contributes to setting the relevant context for the book's focus on m-payments.

## 2.2 A Brief Note about Payment Services

Payment services represent the arrangements that facilitate the transactions enabling the transfer of value around the economy.[6] These services are broad and national authorities often define the scope of activities that qualify as payment services within their jurisdictions. Generally, examples of payment services could include services that enable the placement and withdrawal of funds from a payment account, services that facilitate the transfer of funds in furtherance of executing a payment transaction, or services that support the domestic and international remittance of money. These services are usually provided by entities known as *payment service providers*. Payment service providers can include deposit-taking institutions like banks, non-financial institutions like MNOs, and other specialised entities like electronic money issuers.[7]

At a minimum, a *payment transaction* often involves four parties: the payer, the payer's payment service provider, the payee, and the payee's payment service provider.[8] A transaction commences when the payer issues the payment order or agrees to the transfer of funds to the payee.[9] The transfer of funds is made when the payer's service provider debits the payer's account and the payee's service

5 Despina Mavromati, *The Law of Payment Services in the EU* (Kluwer Law International 2008) p.150.

6 Rhys Bollen, 'A Discussion of Best Practice in the Regulation of Payment Services: Part 1' (2010) 25(8) *Journal of International Banking Law and Regulation* 370, 370.

7 Committee on Payments and Market Infrastructures, World Bank Group, 'Payment Aspects of Financial Inclusion' (2016) p.65 <https://www.bis.org/cpmi/publ/d144.pdf> accessed 13 September 2021.

8 Committee on Payments and Settlement Systems (Bank for International Settlements), 'Innovations in Retail Payments' (2012) p.10 <https://www.bis.org/cpmi/publ/d102.pdf> accessed 13 September 2021.

9 European Central Bank, 'Glossary of Terms related to Payment, Clearing and Settlement Systems' (2009) p.20 <https://www.ecb.europa.eu/pub/pdf/other/glossaryrelatedtopaymentclearingandsettlementsystemsen.pdf> accessed 13 September 2021.

provider credits the payee's account.[10] A payment transaction usually involves a front end through which the payer initiates the payment and several back-end arrangements that clear and settle the payment.[11] The *front end* comprises the funding source (e.g., a bank account), the service channel used to initiate the payment (e.g., a mobile banking application), and the payment instrument (e.g., a payment card).[12] The *back end* comprises the arrangements for the clearing and settlement of payments.[13]

As stated earlier, a payment transaction usually starts when payment instructions are initiated. To initiate a payment transaction, a payer will typically need an access/service channel and a payment instrument issued by a monetary authority or a payment service provider. *Access channels* connect the payer, payee, and payment service providers involved to ensure that payment instructions can be initiated or received.[14] They may include branch offices, Point of Sale (POS) terminals, ATMs, telecommunication networks, and the internet.[15]

*Payment instruments* are a means of exchange and act as access devices which ensure that the holder can link and use the access channels to facilitate payments.[16] These instruments can be classified in many ways.[17] For the purposes of this discussion, these instruments can be categorised into two broad categories: cash payment instruments and non-cash payment instruments.[18] As the name suggests, *cash payment instruments* include the use of banknotes and coins to facilitate transactions. *Non-cash payment instruments* are numerous, ranging from traditionally recognisable instruments like cheques, payment cards, credit transfers, and direct debits to more innovative instruments like crypto-currencies. Using these payment instruments may require the physical handling of paper (e.g., cheques) or can be facilitated by electronic or mobile telecommunication channels.[19]

The initiation of payment transactions will usually require the validation of the payment instruments, the verification of the parties' identities, and their ability to

10 Committee on Payments and Settlement Systems, 'Innovations in Retail Payments' (2012) p.10 <https://www.bis.org/cpmi/publ/d102.pdf> accessed 13 September 2021.
11 Morten Bech and Jenny Hancock, 'Innovations in Payments' (2020) *BIS Quarterly Review*, 21, 22.
12 Ibid. p.23.
13 Ibid.
14 Committee on Payments and Settlement Systems, 'Innovations in Retail Payments' (n 10) p.11.
15 Ibid.
16 Committee on Payments and Settlement Systems, 'Innovations in Retail Payments' (n 10) p.11; Committee on Payments and Market Infrastructures, 'Payment Aspects of Financial Inclusion' (n 7) para.45.
17 See Valerie-Anne Bleyen, Leo Van Hove, and Monika Hartmann, 'Classifying Payment instruments: A Matryoshka Approach' (2010) 79(3) *Communications & Strategies* 73.
18 Jean Paul, 'Payment, Payment Instruments and Payment Systems' (2017) <https://www.paiementor.com/payments-instruments-and-systems/> accessed 5 September 2021.
19 European Central Bank, 'What are Retail Payments' <https://www.ecb.europa.eu/paym/integration/retail/html/index.en.html> accessed 5 September 2021.

pay.[20] Once this initiation process is completed, the back-end operations involving clearing and settling the transaction and facilitating the receipt of funds kick in. *Clearing* refers to the process of transmitting, reconciling, and in some cases confirming transactions before settlement. On the other hand, *settlement* involves the process of transferring funds to discharge monetary obligations between two or more parties.[21] The transaction process is completed when settlement occurs.[22]

Innovations in payment services often aim to exploit perceived gaps in the supply of retail payment services.[23] The innovations typically focus on one or more of the different stages in a payment transaction. For instance, innovation may concentrate on revolutionising the access channels/payment instruments used to initiate a payment transaction, or they may focus on speeding up clearing and settlement processes.[24] However, despite the wide range of innovations available and although payment services come in different packages, at the very core, payment services are essentially variations on a theme because they all involve fund transfers using book entries maintained by one or more intermediaries.[25]

Cumulatively, the payment services provided, the instruments facilitating payment transfers, the participants, and the applicable procedures and rules governing transactions make up what is commonly described as a *payment system*.[26] Payment systems can be distinguished by the type of payments that they are designed to process. A payment system that is designed to cater to person-to-person payments, person-to-business payments, business-to-person payments, and business-to-business payments is described as a *retail payment system*.[27] In contrast, payment systems dedicated to transactions between financial institutions are described as *wholesale payment systems*. This book is primarily concerned with retail payments, particularly business-to-person consumer payments.

The initial scope of regulation and oversight was mainly dedicated to wholesale payment systems, which were considered more systemically relevant to financial markets.[28] However, over the years, regulatory attention has been extended to retail

20 Committee on Payments and Settlement Systems, 'Innovations in Retail Payments' (n 10) p.11.
21 Bech & Hancock (n 11) p.23.
22 European Central Bank, 'Glossary of Terms related to Payment' (n 9) p.24.
23 Committee on Payments and Settlement Systems, 'Innovations in Retail Payments' (n 10) p.15.
24 The Committee on Payments and Settlement Systems indicates that most of the innovation in payments focus on the initiation stage. Ibid., p.11.
25 Bollen, 'A Discussion of Best Practice in the Regulation of Payment Services: Part 1' (n 6) p.370.
26 Bech & Hancock (n 11) p.22. Note that payment system is sometimes used as a synonym for a funds transfer system. In this context it would mean a 'formal arrangement based on a private contract or legislation, with multiple membership, common rules and standardised arrangements for the transmission, clearing, netting and/or settlement of monetary obligations arising between its members.' European Central Bank, 'Glossary of Terms related to Payment' (n 9) p.12.
27 Bech & Hancock (n 11) p.22.
28 Maria Chiara Malaguti, 'Payment System Regulation for Improving Financial Inclusion' Centre for Global Development Policy Paper 070 2015) p.4 <https://www.cgdev.org/sites/default/files/CGD-Policy-Paper-70-Malaguti-Payment-Systems-Financial-Inclusion-1.pdf> accessed 6 September 2021.

payment systems.[29] This is because, while retail payments systems process low-value transactions compared to wholesale systems, they can have a considerable impact on the financial system because of the large volume of transactions handled within a short time.[30] The growing regulatory focus on retail payment systems has also been extended to non-cash retail payment instruments, i.e., cash alternatives that can be used to facilitate low-value transactions.[31]

Retail payments can be completed with a wide variety of instruments. Several innovations have emerged in this area with a focus on improving the safety, speed, and efficiency of payment processing and extending service delivery to untapped demographics. In many cases, these innovations represent simple incremental developments to existing and more established payment instruments.[32] However, in countries where the payments infrastructure is underdeveloped, these innovations can represent significant leaps. Recent discussions surrounding retail payment instruments cover a broad range of issues, including but not limited to matters concerning their viability as efficient long-term alternatives to cash, the role of technology, and innovative business models in widening the range of instruments available, their potential for increasing financial inclusion, and the regulatory implications of such technological and business innovation. It is within this context that the discussions in this book are placed.

## 2.3 Mobile Payments: Clarifying Key Terms

A perusal of the existing literature and regulatory documents on digital financial services indicates that there is no generally accepted definition of the term 'mobile payments.' Some definitions emphasise the use of a mobile device as a distinguishing characteristic. For instance, Au and Kauffman define m-payments as 'any payment where a mobile device is used to initiate, authorise and confirm an exchange of financial value in return for goods and services.'[33] Somewhat similarly, Crowe et al. define m-payments as 'the use of a mobile phone to make a payment at a physical retail location, whether or not the phone actually accesses the mobile network to make the payment.'[34]

29 Ibid.

30 Ibid.

31 Ibid.

32 Committee on Payments and Settlement Systems, 'Innovations in Retail Payments' (n 10) p.2.

33 Yoris A Au, Robert J Kauffman, 'The Economics of Mobile Payments: Understanding Stakeholder Issues for an emerging Financial Technology application' (2007) 7 *Electronic Commerce Research and Applications* 141, 141.

34 Marianne Crowe, Marc Rysman, and Joanna Stavins, 'Mobile Payments in the United States at Retail Point of Sale: Current Market and Future Prospects' Public Policy Discussion Papers, (2010) Fed. Reserve Bank of Boston, No. 10-2,) p.2 <https://www.bostonfed.org/publications/public-policy-discussion-paper/2010/mobile-payments-in-the-united-states-at-retail-point-of-sale-current-market-and-future-prospects.aspx> accessed 6 September 2021.

Guibert provides a slightly different definition that emphasises the type of mobile device used, i.e., a smartphone. He explains that m-payments can be broadly described as

> those payment services that generally allow consumers to make purchases, pay bills, transfer money and send international remittances or pay for goods and services using smartphones (Internet-enabled telephones) by either accessing a web page through the phone's web browser or by using a downloadable app on the smartphone or even by sending a text message in case of payments between individuals.[35]

Other definitions emphasise the connection to a mobile communications network. For instance, the Bank for International Settlements (BIS) defines m-payments as 'payments initiated and transmitted by access devices that are connected to the mobile communication network ....'[36]

A common point in the definitions available is that a mobile device or a mobile telecommunication network is central to the exchange of financial value. Hence for the purposes of this book, m-payments refer to the exchange of financial value which is initiated, authorised, transmitted, or confirmed using a mobile device and facilitated through a mobile telecommunication network. Departing from Guibert's definition, our definition excludes payments initiated via the internet using mobile phones as these are better categorised as internet/online payments.[37] Our definition covers remittances and domestic payments and includes person-to-person transactions and person-to-business transactions. It also covers contactless payments at physical POS using a mobile device as envisaged by Crowe et al. but goes beyond their definition to include remote transactions facilitated by the use of software applications on mobile devices to support funds transfer.[38]

Although Guibert proffers a narrow definition of m-payments, which only recognises the use of a smartphone, the definitions provided by Au and Kauffman and the BIS are broader and allow for a wider range of mobile devices to be taken into consideration. Accordingly, the mobile devices envisaged in our adopted definition include mobile phones broadly conceived (i.e., whether smartphones or mere cellular phones), personal digital assistants (PDAs), wireless tablets, and any other portable device that can be connected to a mobile telecommunications network to facilitate a payment transaction.[39] In staying true to the payment services

35 Sancho Guibert, 'Mobile Payments in the EU: Overview, Legal Framework and Infrastructure and Challenges' (2016) 9 *International In-House Counsel Journal* 1, 2.

36 Committee on Payments and Settlement Systems, 'Innovations in Retail Payments' (n 10) p.13.

37 Ibid.

38 Ben Regnard-Weinrabe, Mark Taylor, and Rachel Shepherd, 'Mobile Payments and the New E-money Directive' (2011) 17(5) *Computer and Telecommunications Law Review* 117, 117.

39 Au & Kauffman (n 33) p.141.

process, the mobile device may be used to communicate payment instructions and/or as a means of storing and transmitting digital cash.[40]

M-payments fall under a broader category of digital/electronic financial services, often labelled as 'mobile financial services.' Mobile financial services is an umbrella term that covers a range of financial services offered and accessed through a mobile device. These services may facilitate the deposit and withdrawal of funds, the completion of payments and remittances and the provision of credit, etc. These services present us with a reality where consumers can leave their wallets at home and still have the confidence to carry out essential financial transactions.[41] In some contexts, the term 'mobile financial services' is used interchangeably with the term 'mobile money.'[42] However, mobile money more accurately refers to a subset of electronic money recorded and stored on mobile telecommunication networks.

Mobile financial services are often grouped as examples of 'branchless banking.' Branchless banking represents the delivery of financial services outside conventional bank branches.[43] This can involve the use of agent networks and information and communications technologies to transmit transaction data.[44] By relying on agent networks and communication technology, branchless banking reduces the cost of delivering financial services and allows providers to establish their presence in underserved areas.[45]

Finally, there is a tendency to use m-payments synonymously with 'mobile banking.' However, both terms connote different things. Mobile banking involves the use of a mobile device to access a range of banking services. It presupposes the existence of a bank account and merely represents an alternative electronic delivery channel for services that a bank customer would usually receive physically at a bank branch. M-payments can form part of the services offered on a mobile banking platform. However, m-payments generally do not require the existence of a prior banking relationship or access to a mobile banking platform. A consumer

40 Gilberto Martins De Almeida, 'M-Payments in Brazil: Notes on how a Country's background may determine the timing and design of a Regulatory Model' (2013) 8(3) *Washington Journal of Law, Technology & Arts* 347, 351.

41 Meena Aharam Rajan, 'The Future of Wallets: A Look at the Privacy Implications of Mobile Payments' (2012) 20 *Commercial Law Conspectus* 445, 445.

42 See for example Kevin Donovan, 'Mobile Money for Financial Inclusion' (World Bank 2012) <https://web.worldbank.org/archive/website01523/WEB/IMAGES/IC4D_2-4.PDF> accessed 14 September 2021.

43 Consultative Group to Assist the Poor (CGAP), 'Branchless Banking Diagnostic Template' (2010) p.1 <https://www.cgap.org/sites/default/files/researches/documents/CGAP-Branchless-Banking-Diagnostic-Template-Feb-2010.pdf> accessed 14 September 2021.

44 CGAP Branchless Banking Diagnostic Template (n 43) p.1.

45 Timothy R Lyman, Gautam Ivatury, and Stefan Staschen, 'Use of Agents in Branchless Banking for the Poor: Rewards, Risks and Regulation' (CGAP Focus Note No.38, 2006) p.2 <https://www.cgap.org/sites/default/files/CGAP-Focus-Notes-Use-of-Agents-in-Branchless-Banking-for-the-Poor-Rewards-Risks-and-Regulation-Oct-2006.pdf> accessed 14 September 2021.

wishing to employ m-payments only needs to maintain a mobile account with a service provider. The service provider may be a bank or a non-bank.

Arguments abound as to whether m-payments are just a new access channel to existing services or a new payment method, or both.[46] While some may argue that using a mobile device to facilitate payments is in itself novel, others point out that the novelty is more about the access channel (telecommunications network) than the access device (mobile phone).[47] Some commentators further point out that the innovation in m-payments lies not only in the method of giving instructions to execute financial transactions but also in the identity of new intermediaries involved, such as MNOs, which provide telecommunication services. Additionally, one's assessment of novelty may be influenced by the delivery structure of a specific m-payment service. An m-payments provider may deliver the service either by accessing existing payments systems (using an overlay system) or by developing a standalone system.[48] With an overlay system, the service provider merely builds a mobile interface which makes it easier for consumers to facilitate payment transactions.[49] Existing payment infrastructures are also used to process and settle payments. Examples include ApplePay and Google Pay. With standalone systems, providers develop distinct infrastructure and process, clear, and settle transactions independent of other established systems.[50] Examples include M-pesa and Alipay.

A m-payment service using an overlay system is more likely to be interpreted as merely a new access channel, while standalone systems may be viewed as more revolutionary. Whichever side of the divide one aligns with, one can easily concede that m-payments are a step forward in the quest to make payment services more accessible and convenient for consumers. However, it is also important not to lose sight of the fact that underneath the supposed novelty, m-payments still fit within a basic payments framework involving a payer and payee accepting variations to their balance, vis-à-vis a third party, as payment.[51] Thus, as with traditional payment methods, m-payments still involve three basic steps in payment processing – authorisation, settlement, and funding.[52]

46 Tomi Dahlberg, Niina Mallat, Jan Ondrus, and Agnieszka Zmijewska, 'Past, Present and Future of Mobile Payments Research: A Literature Review' (2008) 7(2) *Electronic Commerce Research and Applications* 165, 178.

47 Committee on Payments and Settlement Systems, 'Innovations in Retail Payments' (n 10) p.13.

48 Kathryn Petralia, Thomas Philippon, Tara Rice, and Nicolas Véron, 'Banking Disrupted? Financial Intermediation in an Era of Transformational Technology' (*Geneva Report on the World Economy*, no. 22, 2019) p.34 <https://voxeu.org/content/banking-disrupted-financial-intermediation-era-transformational-technology> accessed 16 September 2021.

49 Ibid.

50 Ibid.

51 Rhys Bollen, 'Recent Developments in Mobile Banking and Payments' (2009) 24(9) *Journal of International Banking Law and Regulation* 454, 454.

52 Chase Bank, 'Merchant Services Basics' <https://www.chase.ca/en/support/managing-your-account/merchant-services-basics> accessed 16th September 2021.

## 2.4 Mobile Payments: Understanding the Technology

Mobile devices are multifunctional and can support a variety of communication methods. These methods range from simple voice and text messaging channels to more sophisticated software applications.[53] It is these communication protocols that support m-payments by facilitating the transmission of financial data and instructions. M-payments may be enabled using *Short Message Service (SMS) & Unstructured Supplementary Service Data* (USSD). Where SMS technology is used, payments may be initiated directly over the mobile network by sending text messages.[54] Typically, the user establishes an account with a service provider, and this account may be prepaid or may be linked to a bank account or payment card.[55] To initiate a payment transaction, the user sends a payment request to an SMS Short Code provided by the service provider. The payment request would often state the amount to be paid and the payee's mobile phone number. The provider will then require that the user confirms and authenticates the request using a personal identification number.[56] Upon confirming and authenticating the request, the transfer is processed, and the payee is notified.[57] The transaction value is charged to the user's phone bill, prepaid account, or linked bank account/payment card. In a person-to-person transfer, the transaction would typically end here.[58] Where a business is the payee, once notified of successful payment, the merchant will subsequently release the goods or service to the consumer.[59]

Payments may also be made via USSD. This is similar to SMS-based payments. The difference lies in the fact that USSD creates a real-time connection which remains open so that there can be a two-way data exchange between parties instead of the SMS system in which data is stored at a Short Message Service Centre before being sent to the recipient. Although the real-time connection provided by the USSD reduces delays, the SMS technology appears to be more popular. Since the SMS technology only requires an SMS-capable phone and a cellular signal, m-payment services facilitated using this technology are convenient for jurisdictions where access to the internet and smartphones is limited. This is anecdotally reflected in the fact that in many developing countries, successful m-payments services often rely on SMS. The downside of this technology is that poor cellular signals can affect the transmission of payment instructions.[60] It is also thought to have security limitations because text messages may not be encrypted.[61]

53 Donovan (n 42) p.62.

54 Crowe et al. (n 34) p.8.

55 Timothy R McTaggart and David W Freese, 'Regulation of Mobile Payments' (2010) 127 *Banking Law Journal* 485, 488.

56 Ibid.

57 Ibid.

58 McTaggart and David W Freese (n 55) p.488.

59 Ibid.

60 Crowe et al. (n 34) p.8.

61 Ibid.

M-payments may also be enabled through *direct mobile billing*. For example, some e-commerce sites offer direct billing from a mobile account as an alternative to paying with a card. Users shopping on such sites will find a mobile billing option on the usual 'check out' page of the website. If this option is selected, payment can be made through a mobile device by entering a mobile number in the relevant box. The mobile owner then receives an SMS message asking them to confirm the payment, and upon confirmation, the transaction is charged to their mobile phone bill.[62]

Increasingly, many m-payments rely on *near field communication* (NFC) technology. NFC is a wireless transmission protocol which supports the encrypted exchange of payment credentials and data at a close range.[63] With the NFC technology, all a consumer needs to do is simply tap or wave their mobile device at an NFC-enabled POS device to complete a transaction.[64] At close range, the POS device reads the payment account credentials stored via a chip on the NFC-enabled mobile device to complete the transaction.[65] The NFC technology is more secure and is expected to make transactions more efficient by reducing errors, such as those that arise from mistyped numbers.[66] The NFC functionality can also be configured to work even without a cellular signal and thus can bypass any problems associated with poor cellular signals.[67] Despite these advantages, the NFC technology is relatively expensive as it requires investment – merchants will need to purchase and install readers while consumers will need to purchase NFC-enabled phones which will be more expensive than cellular phones since they cost more to manufacture.[68]

Finally, m-payments may also be supported using *Quick Response* (QR) *Codes*. A QR code is a two-dimensional (2D) barcode where information or payment credentials can be encrypted.[69] Though initially developed as a mobile advertising tool, the technology has been extended to supporting m-payments.[70] In some instances, a QR code may be used in conjunction with cloud-based technology.[71]

62 Jessica Long and Mark Taylor, 'Mobile Payments: Part 1' (2011) 17(4) *Computer and Telecommunications Law Review* 105, 106.
63 Erin Fonte, '2017 U.S. Regulatory Overview of Mobile Wallets and Mobile Payments' (2017) 17 *Wake Forest Journal of Business & Intellectual Property Law* 549, 559.
64 Jessica Long and Mark Taylor, 'Mobile Payments: Part 2 – Contactless Near Field Communication' (2011) 17(5) *Computer and Telecommunications Law Review* 132, 132.
65 Fonte (n 63) p.559.
66 Donovan (n 42) p.66.
67 Crowe et al. (n 34) p.7.
68 Ibid.
69 Robin Hui Huang, Abby Oi Ling Lam, et al., 'The Development and Regulation of Mobile Payment: Chinese Experiences and Comparative Perspectives' (2021) 20(1) *Washington University Global Studies Law Review* 1, 8.
70 Pietro Caprara, Marta Infantino, Susan Mancini, et al., 'Mobile Proximity Payment – 5 Things Retailers Should Know' (2016) p.3 <https://www.pwc.com/it/it/publications/assets/docs/mobile-proximity.pdf> accessed 16 September 2021.
71 Fonte (n 63) p.560.

Here the payment credentials are stored in the cloud rather than on the mobile phone and controlled by a trusted third party.[72] A QR code can be read through barcode/QR code readers and camera phones and may be used for payment transactions.[73] To pay using this technology, a consumer's device displays a downloaded barcode or one received through a multimedia message which they can scan at a sales terminal to complete a transaction.[74] QR Codes may be static or dynamic. A static code is unchanging and is often stored on a m-payment application installed on a phone and is used for multiple transactions.[75] With dynamic codes, unique codes are generated for each transaction but are tied to a single user's payment account.[76]

M-payments facilitated using NFC technology or QR codes are often better suited where there is a wide internet coverage and a high smartphone penetration.[77] Reflecting the high ownership of smartphones in many developed countries, m-payment solutions in these jurisdictions often leverage these technologies.[78]

The variety of available technology and communication channels means that consumers can use their mobile devices to support remote and proximity payments. Remote payments include payments made from a distance and which do not require a POS terminal because the payer and payee are not present at the same physical location.[79] Examples of such transactions include remittances, payments for the delivery of digital services, and prepaid top-up services.[80] SMS technology remains the more popular technology for facilitating such remote payments. Proximity payments represent payments made where the payer and the payee are in the same physical location.[81] These will include payments made when a mobile device communicates with a physical POS or an ATM using contactless technologies such as NFC.[82] To facilitate such payments, the mobile phones will need to be equipped with a chip that stores the consumer's account information while the merchants require special POS readers.[83]

72 Huang et al. (n 69) p.9.

73 Tanai Khiaonarong, 'Oversight Issues in Mobile Payments' (IMF working paper WP/14/123 2014) pp.7–8 <https://www.imf.org/external/pubs/ft/wp/2014/wp14123.pdf> accessed 11 September 2021.

74 Fumiko Hayashi, 'M-payments: What's in it for Consumers?' (2012) 1 *Economic Review* 35, 36.

75 Fonte (n 63) pp.560–561.

76 Ibid. p.561.

77 Huang et al. (n 69) p.9.

78 Banco Bilbao Vizcaya Argentaria, 'Dissecting digital Payments: How are they Evolving around the World' <https://www.bbva.com/en/dissecting-digital-payments-how-they-are-evolving-around-the-world/> accessed 10 September 2021.

79 European Central Bank, 'Glossary of Terms Related to Payment' (n 9).

80 Marc Bourreau and Marianne Verdier, 'Cooperation for innovation in Payment Systems: The case of Mobile Payments' (2010) 3 *Communications & Strategies* 95, 99.

81 Ibid.

82 Bourreau & Verdier (n 80) p.100.

83 Ibid.

## 2.5 Mobile Payments: Core Stakeholders and Business Models

M-payments straddle the intersection between finance, technology, and telecommunications and this is reflected in the diverse set of stakeholders and parties involved in providing the service.[84] Broadly speaking, the core parties involved include the service providers and customers. The service providers may consist of firms such as banks, MNOs, payment card firms, technology companies, and retail firms which develop the m-payments product.[85] MNOs and banks stand out as more visible competing providers for important reasons. As a traditional financial institution, banks have a competitive edge because they have decades of experience with payment services and are generally well trusted to handle and process sensitive financial data. Though having limited experience in payment services and the accompanying risks, MNOs have a huge customer base because they control the Subscriber Identity Module (SIM) and/or the Wireless Identity Module Card (WIM) of the mobile device and, therefore, stand as the primary contact point with consumers who need a mobile network platform to engage in m-payments.[86] They are also experienced in providing subscriber acquisition and authentication, customer support, and value-added services, all of which are advantages for deploying an m-payments service.[87]

On the demand side, the customers may include merchants and individual consumers. Merchants may use an m-payment platform to facilitate transactions with consumers (person-to-business) or other merchants (business-to-business). Consumers may use m-payment services to facilitate person-to-person transfers and other remittances for economic and non-economic purposes.

For the successful completion of m-payment transactions, Chatain et al., explain that specific functions must be provided.[88] These include the provision of:

i. Mobile communication services by MNOs
ii. A customer interface which allows the customer to connect to the payment system. This could come in the form of a software application that a customer needs to download on their mobile device

84 Donovan (n 42) p.61.

85 These parties are supported by other stakeholders the mobile device manufacturers and software application providers which provide the necessary hardware and software. Judith Rinearson, 'The Next New Thing: Mobile Payments' (2007) 3 *Journal of Payment Systems Law* 82, 85.

86 Ibid., pp.85–86.

87 Darin Contini, Marianne Crowe, Cynthia Merritt, et al., 'Mobile Payments in the United States: Mapping out the Road Ahead' (25 March 2011, Federal Reserve Bank of Boston) p.7 <https://www.dwt.com/files/Uploads/Documents/Publications/MPIW%203.25.11.pdf> accessed 11 September 2021.

88 Pierre-Laurent Chatain, Andrew Zerzan, et al., *Protecting Mobile Money Against Financial Crimes: Global Policy Challenges and Solutions* (World Bank, 2011) pp.2–14 <http://documents1.worldbank.org/curated/en/854951468337169489/pdf/600600PUB0ID181Mobile09780821386699.pdf> accessed 3 September 2021.

iii. Account services which enable the storage of key account information such as account balance information and transaction history
iv. Transaction processing services which enable the receipt and handling of a consumer's instructions
v. Settlement services between the payer and payee accounts

Banks and MNOs have an exclusive monopoly over two of the functions listed above: while MNOs provide the mobile communications services that allow for the transmission of customer instructions, banks act as the final settlement point and custodian of customer funds.[89] Other functions in the product chain may be delivered by a bank or MNO or provided by parties other than a bank or MNO.[90]

Bearing these functions in mind, one must note that m-payments can be provided using various business models. Traditionally, one popular way of distinguishing m-payment business models is by classifying them as either bank-led or MNO-led. However, this classification can connote different things. First, it may refer to the identity of the party that has created or primarily manages the m-payment scheme. Hence, a scheme is bank-led if it is created and managed by a bank, while a scheme is MNO-led if it is created and managed by an MNO.[91]

Alternatively, a more common understanding of the distinction between both models lies in determining which party holds the direct contractual relationship with the customer. In other words, it depends on the identity of the customer's primary account keeper. In a bank-led model, the primary customer account relationship lies with the bank. Apart from managing the customer relationship, the bank also takes the lead in marketing and branding the product.[92] The major advantage of this model is that banks leverage their wealth of expertise in managing payment transactions.[93]

In the MNO-led model, the primary customer account relationship lies with the MNO. In this model, banks serve as a safe keeper of customer funds and supply settlement services while the MNO maintains the customer account and drives the product's branding and marketing.[94] One key advantage of this model is that MNOs can directly tap into their existing customer base as they are already the primary providers of mobile telecommunication services.[95]

89 Rajiv Lal and Ishan Sachdev, 'Mobile Money Services – Design and Development for Financial Inclusion' (Harvard Business School Working Paper 15-083, 2015) p.5 <https://www.hbs.edu/ris/Publication%20Files/15-083_e7db671b-12b2-47e7-9692-31808ee92bf1.pdf> accessed 13 September 2021.
90 Chatain et al. (n 88) p.23.
91 Malaguti (n 28) p.10.
92 Alliance for Financial Inclusion (Mobile Financial Services Working Group), 'Guideline Note Mobile Financial Services: Basic Terminology' (2012) p.4 <https://www.afi-global.org/sites/default/files/publications/MFSWG%20Guideline%20Note%20on%20Terminology.pdf> accessed 13 September 2021.
93 Thomas Lerner, *Mobile Payment* (Springer Science & Business Media 2013) p.25.
94 Alliance for Financial Inclusion (n 92) p.4.
95 Lerner (n 93) p.29.

In reality, the bank-led and MNO-led categorisation provides a limited picture of the supply side and instead creates an image of two extremes where MNOs are not involved in a bank-led model, and vice versa.[96] As we have pointed out earlier, banks and MNOs are necessarily involved in providing m-payments because of the core services they provide in facilitating the service. From this perspective, a pure MNO-led or bank-led service does not exist (except from a customer's point of view).[97] Also, there are various business models currently in use, and many existing schemes take on a hybrid model, which involves cooperating banks and MNOs maintaining independent account relationships with the customers they serve.[98] Hence, a bank customer accessing an m-payments service supported by a bank will primarily interact with the bank, while an MNO's customer accessing the same service will interact primarily with the MNO.[99]

Moreover, many third-party providers which are not banks or MNOs maintain the primary account relationship with customers in the provision of m-payments. Hence, if classifications must be used, it may be more appropriate to adopt broader categorisation of business models. As providers can broadly be categorised as financial institutions or non-financial institutions, it may be better to categorise business models as financial institution-led, or non-financial institution-led. This approach recognises the variety of providers which, though, cannot be neatly classified as either banks or MNOs, but can broadly fall within the understanding of financial institutions and non-financial institutions.

## 2.6 Mobile Payments as an Additive Payment Service

The development and acceptance of m-payments is at differing levels in several parts of the world. This disparity can be explained by various factors, including the extent of existing banking and electronic payment infrastructure in a given jurisdiction.[100] M-payments are purely additive in many developed countries with established payment systems infrastructure. In such countries, they merely represent an additional channel to enable already banked consumers to carry out payment transactions.[101] Hence, in these jurisdictions, m-payments will primarily serve as a complementary and/or alternative payment instrument to cash, cheques, and payment cards.

While m-payments will compete with more established payment methods in such countries, its success and large-scale adoption will depend on if customers are offered

96 Malaguti (n 28) p.11.
97 Ibid.
98 Ibid.
99 Ibid.
100 Au & Kauffman (n 33) p.148.
101 Oxford Policy Management, 'Testing Remote Access Models for Southern African Countries' (2008) p.1 <https://www.gsma.com/mobilefordevelopment/wp-content/uploads/2012/06/brochure_branchlessbanking.pdf> accessed 10 September 2021.

a service proposition that is superior to existing alternatives.[102] M-payments present certain advantages that may inspire a shift in the established paying habits of consumers in these jurisdictions. One competitive edge that the mobile device has over contactless cards is that it can be used to complete payment transactions in a convenient way.[103] For instance, m-payments are well suited for micro-payment transactions, which attract high costs when made with traditional non-cash alternatives such as payment cards.[104] Thus, they provide a suitable alternative that will be useful for everyday low-value transactions, eliminating the inconvenience of carrying coins and loose change.[105] M-payments can be conveniently used to pay for transportation tickets, restaurant bills, and transfer funds to friends and family where costs are split amongst a group.[106] It can also be used to complete transactions at vending and ticketing machines and to effect payments for premium rate services and digital content like ringtones, logos, music, or games.[107]

Consumers generally carry their payment cards and mobile devices wherever they go and will have the increased choice of using whichever instrument they feel is most appropriate for an intended transaction.[108] However, m-payments comparatively present a high degree of flexibility because they can be funded in several ways. To begin with, funding may be directly from a bank account, or a prepaid account held with a non-bank service provider such as an MNO. M-payment transactions may also be funded through debit, credit, or prepaid cards. Another option is to pay for purchases by including them in a user's monthly phone bill (known as 'direct mobile billing'). These funding options are not mutually exclusive and may all be consolidated in a software application (mobile wallet) installed on a customer's smartphone.[109] The possibility of consolidating several funding instruments in a mobile device arguably gives it an edge in terms of portability. Mobile devices can eliminate the inconvenience of carrying multiple plastic cards in a physical wallet.

Furthermore, m-payments may assist consumers in managing their finances in ways traditional bank cards cannot. For example, because consumers have access to multiple payment platforms on their mobile devices, they can conveniently check and compare their account balances before initiating any transaction. This will enable them to choose the payment platform with the most favourable financial impact. Relatedly, m-payments can also help consumers develop financial discipline if they set purchase thresholds on their devices for different categories

102 Mark Pickens, David Porteous, and Sarah Rotman, 'Scenarios for Branchless Banking in 2020' (CGAP Focus Note 57, 2009), p.5 <https://www.cgap.org/sites/default/files/CGAP-Focus-Note-Scenarios-for-Branchless-Banking-in-2020-Oct-2009.pdf> accessed 10 September 2021.

103 Bourreau & Verdier (n 80) p.100.

104 Bollen, 'Recent Developments in Mobile Banking and Payments' (n 51) p.454.

105 Hayashi (n 74) p.43.

106 Guibert (n 35) p.2.

107 Dahlberg et al. (n 46) pp.165–166.

108 Au & Kauffman (n 33) p.157.

109 Hayashi (n 74) p.37.

of spending. With this functionality, consumers are notified when these thresholds are met, regardless of the underlying funding instrument in use.[110]

Consumers are often concerned about whether payment instruments and transactions are secure because of the detriment they will suffer if, owing to security lapses, unauthorised transactions occur. M-payments may assuage this concern because they can potentially provide a more secure way for completing transactions. Password protection of mobile devices, m-payment applications, and mobile wallets can provide greater security. For instance, m-payments have the potential to reduce fraudulent POS transactions by allowing for dynamic authentication at the POS enabled by a chip embedded in a mobile device.[111] However, these security benefits are dependent on mobile devices being protected from theft, malicious payments software, and hacking attacks.[112]

Even with this increased menu of choices, the potential benefits of m-payments to consumers can also be evaluated by drawing a comparison between traditional payment methods and m-payments. While it can be argued that m-payments share attributes such as convenience, cost, security, and acceptance by merchants with bank cards,[113] it can also be argued that the degree and extent of these advantages may be the differentiating factor. This argument is further strengthened by the degree of flexibility that m-payments introduce because they can link various payment instruments to a single mobile wallet.[114]

In summary, all the advantages outlined above suggest that m-payments in this context provide banked consumers with a convenient, secure, and flexible option for transferring value in addition to the numerous alternatives already available.

## 2.7 Mobile Payments as a Transformative Payment Service

In several developing countries, many persons do not have access to traditional bank accounts and other non-cash payment services like credit cards. The financial exclusion problem disproportionately affects those residing in rural areas.[115] In sub-Saharan Africa, for instance, adults in urban areas with a million or more inhabitants report a higher rate of account ownership, more than double that of adults residing in rural areas with a population of less than 10,000.[116] Persons

110 Ibid. p.55.

111 Ibid. p.49.

112 Emil Slazak, 'Adoption of Innovation in Mobile Payments – Financial Viability Prerequisites for Banks' (2014) p.147 <http://citeseerx.ist.psu.edu/viewdoc/download?doi=10.1.1.964.1052&rep=rep1&type=pdf> accessed 5 September 2021.

113 Hayashi (n 74) p.36.

114 Ibid. p.43.

115 Pascaline Dupas, Sarah Green, et al., 'Challenges in Banking the Rural Poor: Evidence from Kenya's Western Province' (2012), p.1 <https://web.stanford.edu/~pdupas/Challenges_DupasEtAl2011.pdf> accessed 17 August 2021.

116 Lora Klapper, 'Two Persistent Divides in Financial Inclusion: Gender and Rural' (2012) <https://www.cgap.org/blog/two-persistent-divides-financial-inclusion-gender-and-rural> accessed 17 August 2021.

living in rural areas often depend on remittances from relatives in urban areas and abroad, and there is a clear need for a cheap, efficient, and secure way to transfer funds. Barriers to accessing financial services are manifold, encompassing lack of money or irregular income, unemployment, low financial literacy, documentation constraints which affect their ability to meet the requirements for opening bank accounts, and high costs, which manifest in several ways such as high interest rates.[117] Significantly, a lack of access could be due to the non-existence or low availability of bank branches in rural areas where a sizeable population resides. As stated in the introduction, banks traditionally provide services through branch networks which are often situated in urban areas that are considered more profitable urban areas.[118]

Interestingly, there has been a steady growth in mobile phone ownership and mobile network coverage in many of these developing countries. This growth has been facilitated partly because there has been a direct implementation of mobile infrastructures rather than a progression from landline technologies to mobile technology.[119] Being widely available, mobile devices are increasingly perceived as presenting a practical and cost-effective channel for extending basic financial services to excluded persons.[120] The adoption of mobile-based financial services has, therefore, been facilitated by the need to address infrastructure gaps that arise when mobile penetration is high but physical banking infrastructure is deficient.[121] In these jurisdictions, m-payments provide many consumers with the first entry point into the formal financial system. In this context, m-payments take on a transformative character because of their potential to drive access and financial inclusion.

It important to note, however, that the distinction between an additive and transformational m-payment product may be a matter of varying degrees on a spectrum.[122] While one end of the spectrum sees a purely additive product that serves to expand functionality for existing fully banked clients, the other end of the spectrum sees a purely transformational product which serves the unserved

117 United Nations Conference on Trade and Development (UNCTAD), 'Access to Financial Services as a driver for the post-2015 development Agenda' (Policy Brief no.35, 2015) p.3 <https://unctad.org/system/files/official-document/presspb2015d7_en.pdf> accessed 23 August 2021.

118 Evan Gibson, Federico Lupo-Pasini, Ross P Buckley, 'Regulating Digital Financial Services Agents in Developing Countries to Promote Financial Inclusion' (2015) *Singapore Journal of Legal Studies* 26, 26.

119 Arnold S Rosenberg, 'Better than Cash? Global Proliferation of Payment Cards and Consumer Protection Policy' (2006) 60 *Consumer Fin.L.Q. Rep* 426, 437 cited in Angela Angelovska-Wilson, Jaimie Feltault, 'M-payments: The Next Payments Frontier – Current Developments and Challenges in the International Implementation of M-Payments' (2007) 22(11) *Journal of International Banking Law & Regulation* 575, 585.

120 Jane K Winn, Louis de Koker, 'Introduction to Mobile Money in Developing Countries: Financial Inclusion and Financial Integrity' (2013) 8(3) *Washington Journal of Law, Technology & Arts* 155, 162.

121 Arner et al. (n 2) p.380.

122 Oxford Policy Management (n 101) pp.1–2 & 17.

clients outside branched areas.[123] Between both ends of the spectrum are products which extend functionality for existing partially served clients, those that extend the reach of those served outside branched areas and redesigned products which serve more clients in branched areas.[124] Within the spectrum, a model could be more additive or more transformational depending on its engagement with expanding access to underserved customers and affordability.[125]

Nonetheless, there is evidence that suggests that branchless banking services, including m-payments, are relatively cheaper than other cash alternatives and this has important implications for the unbanked.[126] A study by McKay and Pickens found that branchless banking services (including mobile money) were 19 per cent cheaper on average than comparable products offered by banks via traditional channels.[127] The study also found that this figure doubled when lower value transactions were involved as they were 38 per cent cheaper.[128] Lower costs suggest that the poor can keep more money when completing transactions.[129] It also indicates that underbanked consumers (who only have nominal access because the quality of service falls short for reasons relating to cost) can now enjoy cheaper alternatives.[130]

Given the service gaps for a significant financially excluded populace, it is unsurprising that the World Bank estimates that sub-Saharan Africa leads the world in mobile money accounts: while just 2 per cent of adults worldwide have a mobile money account, 12 per cent[131] in sub-Saharan Africa have one.[132] Moreover, it has generally been easier for developing countries in comparison to developed ones to embrace m-payments as 'they can jump directly to that technology [m-payments] without having to work around an existing payment infrastructure as in more developed countries.'[133]

Certain success stories support the possibility of leveraging m-payments to drive financial inclusion and lift people out of poverty. In particular, Kenya's success with its m-payment product 'm-pesa' remains a reference point in this regard. Introduced in 2007, M-pesa is a low-cost SMS-based person-to-person money transfer platform which allows users to deposit, send, and withdraw funds

123 Ibid.

124 Oxford Policy Management (n 101) pp.1–2 & 17.

125 Ibid.

126 Claudia McKay and Mark Pickens, 'Branchless Banking 2010: Who's Served? At What Price? What's Next?' (CGAP Focus Note 66, 2010) p.2 <https://www.cgap.org/research/publication/branchless-banking-2010-whos-served-what-price-whats-next> accessed 22 August 2021.

127 Ibid.

128 Ibid. p.5.

129 Donovan (n 42) p.63.

130 Mckay & Pickens (n 126) p.2.

131 The World Bank, 'The Global Findex Database 2017' (2017) <http://www.worldbank.org/en/programs/globalfindex> accessed 15 August 2021.

132 Ibid. p.20.

133 Angelovska-Wilson & Feltault (n 119) p.589.

using their mobile phones.[134] M-pesa provides a safer alternative for moving cash as early research covering its use in low-income areas found that the risk of thefts declined because cash was used less.[135] Since its introduction, M-pesa has assisted in growing the percentage of the population that can access formal payment services. Total account ownership[136] in Kenya rose from 42 per cent in 2011 to 81 per cent in 2018.[137] M-pesa also increased per capita consumption levels and lifted at least 2 per cent of Kenyan households out of poverty.[138]

Importantly, Kenya's experience with M-pesa also lends credence to the argument that m-payments can provide a gateway to other financial services. From focusing on basic services like facilitating person-to-person payments, airtime purchases, and cash withdrawals from agents, M-pesa has expanded its services over the years to include transfers to and from regular bank accounts, international remittances, and microinsurance.[139] Safaricom, the MNO behind M-pesa, has also partnered with the Commercial Bank of Africa to offer M-Shwari, a micro-credit service.[140] Because many financial services regimes now include matters relating to 'financial inclusion, equity, or accessibility of regimes' as core policy considerations,[141] M-pesa's success has inspired regulators concerned with increasing financial inclusion in their jurisdictions.

From a different but related perspective, m-payments can also be considered transformative because of their potential to disrupt the payment services ecosystem. Banks do not dominate the m-payments ecosystem for certain reasons. First, firms that are not traditionally classified as financial institutions, like MNOs, can independently provide the service. This opens up new distribution networks for

134 Mercy W Buku and Micheal W Meredith, 'Safaricom and M-pesa in Kenya: Financial Inclusion and Financial Integrity' (2013) 8 *Washington Journal of Law Technology & Arts* 375, 378.

135 Donovan (n 42) p.63.

136 The World Bank defines account ownership to include accounts held at a financial institution as well as those held with a mobile money provider. The World Bank, 'Global Findex Database' (n 131) p.17.

137 The World Bank, 'The Little Data Book on Financial Inclusion' (2018), p.84 <https://openknowledge.worldbank.org/bitstream/handle/10986/29654/LDB-FinInclusion2018.pdf?sequence=1&isAllowed=y> accessed 14 August 2021.

138 Tavneet Suri and William Jack, 'The Long-run Poverty and Gender Impacts of Mobile Money' (2016) 354(6317) Science 1288 cited in UN Secretary-General's Special Advocate for Inclusive Finance for Development (UNGSA), 'Early Lessons on Regulatory Innovations to Enable Inclusive FinTech: Innovation Offices, Regulatory Sandboxes, and RegTech' (2019) p.11 <https://www.unsgsa.org/sites/default/files/resources-files/2020-09/UNSGSA_Report_2019_Final-compressed.pdf> accessed 14 September 2021.

139 Nick Hughes and Susie Lonie, 'M-pesa: Mobile Money for the 'Unbanked' Turning Cellphones into 24-hour Tellers in Kenya' (2007) 2(1) *Innovations: Technology, Governance, Globalization* 63, 78.

140 Peter Ondiege, 'Regulatory Impact on Mobile Money and Financial inclusion in African countries – Kenya, Nigeria, Tanzania and Uganda' (2015) p.22 <https://www.cgdev.org/sites/default/files/Background-Paper-Financial-Inclusion-Ondiege.pdf> accessed 12 August 2021.

141 Rhys Bollen, 'A Discussion of Best Practice in the Regulation of Payment Services: Part 2' (2010) 25(9) *Journal of International Banking Law & Regulation* 429, 432.

financial transactions beyond the traditional bank branches, POS, and ATM networks.[142] Second, consumers do not necessarily need a bank account to enjoy m-payment services. An account can be provided and maintained by several firms that can qualify as the main service provider. The disruption of the payment services ecosystem can potentially improve competition, which increases the options available to consumers. To compete, banks may be forced to innovate and develop products that can profitably serve the excluded populace.

For m-payments to be genuinely transformational, regulators must provide an enabling environment that encourages investment and innovation and protects the end users from any potential negative externalities. Subsequent discussions in this book will focus on the latter issue.

## 2.8 Conclusion

This chapter has introduced the payment service, which lies at the heart of the discussion covered in this book. The chapter explained the meaning of m-payments and related terminology. It also highlighted the technology and business models that support the provision of m-payments. While m-payments provide increased choice to some consumers and serve as a first entry point for accessing formal financial services for others, it leaves the question of whether these categories of consumers are well protected against any potential detriment that may occur in adopting the service. In tackling this question, other preliminary questions also need to be answered. For instance, why should there be regulatory intervention in favour of consumers? What justification supports targeted arrangements aimed at protecting consumer interests? It is these preliminary questions that *Chapter 3* will address.

## References

Alliance for Financial Inclusion (Mobile Financial Services Working Group), 'Guideline Note Mobile Financial Services: Basic Terminology' (2012) <https://www.afi-global.org/sites/default/files/publications/MFSWG%20Guideline%20Note%20on%20Terminology.pdf> accessed 13 September 2021.

Angela Angelovska-Wilson and Jaimie Feltault, 'M-payments: The Next Payments Frontier - Current Developments and Challenges in the International Implementation of M-Payments' (2007) 22(11) *Journal of International Banking Law & Regulation* 575.

Augustin Carstens 'Shaping the Future of Payments' (2020) *BIS Quarterly Review* 17.

Banco Bilbao Vizcaya Argentaria, 'Dissecting Digital Payments: How Are They Evolving around the World' <https://www.bbva.com/en/dissecting-digital-payments-how-they-are-evolving-around-the-world/> accessed 10 September 2021.

142 David Porteous, 'The Enabling Environment for Mobile Banking in Africa' (2006) para. 2.3. <https://www.findevgateway.org/paper/2006/05/enabling-environment-mobile-banking-africa> accessed 5 September 2021.

Ben Regnard-Weinrabe, Mark Taylor and Rachel Shepherd, 'Mobile Payments and the new E-money Directive' (2011) 17(5) *Computer and Telecommunications Law Review* 117.

Chase Bank, 'Merchant Services Basics' <https://www.chase.ca/en/support/managing-your-account/merchant-services-basics> accessed 16th September 2021.

Claudia McKay and Mark Pickens, 'Branchless Banking 2010: Who's Served? At What Price? What's Next?' (CGAP Focus Note 66, 2010) <https://www.cgap.org/research/publication/branchless-banking-2010-whos-served-what-price-whats-next> accessed 22 August 2021.

Committee on Payments and Market Infrastructures, World bank Group, 'Payment Aspects of Financial Inclusion' (2016) <https://www.bis.org/cpmi/publ/d144.pdf> accessed 13 September 2021.

Committee on Payments and Settlement Systems (Bank for International Settlements), 'Innovations in Retail Payments' (2012) <https://www.bis.org/cpmi/publ/d102.pdf> accessed 13 September 2021.

Consultative Group to Assist the Poor (CGAP), 'Branchless Banking Diagnostic Template' (2010) <https://www.cgap.org/sites/default/files/researches/documents/CGAP-Branchless-Banking-Diagnostic-Template-Feb-2010.pdf> accessed 14 September 2021.

Despina Mavromati, *The Law of Payment Services in the EU* (Kluwer law International 2008).

Darin Contini, Marianne Crowe et al, 'Mobile Payments in the United States: Mapping out the Road Ahead' (Federal Reserve Bank of Boston March 25, 2011) <https://www.dwt.com/files/Uploads/Documents/Publications/MPIW%203.25.11.pdf> accessed 11 September 2021.

David Porteous, 'The Enabling Environment for Mobile Banking in Africa' (2006) <https://www.findevgateway.org/paper/2006/05/enabling-environment-mobile-banking-africa> accessed 5 September 2021.

Douglas W Arner, Janos N Barberis and Ross P Buckley, 'FinTech, Regtech, and the Reconceptualization of Financial Regulation' (2017) 37 *Northwestern Journal of International Law & Business* 371.

Emil Slazak, 'Adoption of Innovation in Mobile Payments – Financial Viability Prerequisites for Banks' (2014) <http://citeseerx.ist.psu.edu/viewdoc/download?doi=10.1.1.964.1052&rep=rep1&type=pdf> accessed 5 September 2021.

European Central Bank, 'Glossary of Terms related to Payment, Clearing and Settlement Systems' (2009) <https://www.ecb.europa.eu/pub/pdf/other/glossaryrelatedtopaymentclearingandsettlementsystemsen.pdf>

European Central Bank, 'What are Retail Payments' <https://www.ecb.europa.eu/paym/integration/retail/html/index.en.html> accessed 5 September 2021.

Evan Gibson, Federico Lupo-Pasini and Ross P Buckley, 'Regulating Digital Financial Services Agents in Developing Countries to Promote Financial Inclusion' (2015) *Singapore Journal of Legal Studies* 26.

Fumiko Hayashi, 'M-payments: What's in it for Consumers?' (2012) 1 *Economic Review* 35.

Gilberto Martins De Almeida, 'M-Payments in Brazil: Notes on How a Country's Background May Determine the Timing and Design of a Regulatory Model' (2013) 8(3) *Washington Journal of Law, Technology & Arts* 347.

Hartmut Hoehle, Eusebio Scornavacca and Sid Huff, 'Three Decades of Research on Consumer adoption and Utilization of Electronic Banking Channels' (2012) 54 *Decision Support Systems* 122.

Jane K Winn and Louis de Koker, 'Introduction to Mobile Money in Developing Countries: Financial Inclusion and Financial Integrity' (2013) 8(3) *Washington Journal of Law, Technology & Arts* 155.

Jean Paul, 'Payment, Payment Instruments and Payment Systems' (2017) <https://www.paiementor.com/payments-instruments-and-systems/> accessed 5 September 2021.

Jessica Long and Mark Taylor, 'Mobile Payments: Part 1' (2011) 17(4) *Computer and Telecommunications Law Review* 105.

Judith Rinearson, 'The Next New Thing: Mobile Payments' (2007) 3 *Journal of Payment Systems Law* 82.

Kathryn Petralia, Thomas Philippon, Tara Rice and Nicolas Véron, 'Banking Disrupted? Financial Intermediation in an Era of Transformational Technology' (*Geneva Report on the World Economy*, no. 22, 2019) <https://voxeu.org/content/banking-disrupted-financial-intermediation-era-transformational-technology> accessed 16 September 2021.

Kevin Donovan, 'Mobile Money for Financial Inclusion' (World Bank 2012) <https://web.worldbank.org/archive/website01523/WEB/IMAGES/IC4D_2-4.PDF> accessed 14 September 2021.

Lora Klapper, 'Two Persistent Divides in Financial Inclusion: Gender and Rural' (2012) <https://www.cgap.org/blog/two-persistent-divides-financial-inclusion-gender-and-rural> accessed 17 August 2021.

Marc Bourreau and Marianne Verdier, 'Cooperation for innovation in Payment Systems: The case of Mobile Payments' (2010) 3 *Communications & Strategies* 95.

Maria Chiara Malaguti, 'Payment System Regulation for Improving Financial Inclusion' (Centre for Global Development Policy Paper 070, 2015) <https://www.cgdev.org/sites/default/files/CGD-Policy-Paper-70-Malaguti-Payment-Systems-Financial-Inclusion-1.pdf> accessed 6 September 2021.

Marianne Crowe, Marc Rysman and Joanna Stavins, 'Mobile Payments in the United States at Retail Point of Sale: Current Market and Future Prospects' Public Policy Discussion Papers' (Fed. Reserve Bank of Boston, 10–2, 2010) <https://www.bostonfed.org/publications/public-policy-discussion-paper/2010/mobile-payments-in-the-united-states-at-retail-point-of-sale-current-market-and-future-prospects.aspx> accessed 6 September 2021.

Mark Pickens, David Porteous and Sarah Rotman, 'Scenarios for Branchless Banking in 2020' (CGAP Focus Note 57, 2009) <https://www.cgap.org/sites/default/files/CGAP-Focus-Note-Scenarios-for-Branchless-Banking-in-2020-Oct-2009.pdf> accessed 10 September 2021.

Meena Aharam Rajan, 'The Future of Wallets: A look at the Privacy Implications of Mobile Payments' (2012) 20 *Commercial Law Conspectus* 445.

Mercy W Buku and Micheal W Meredith, 'Safaricom and M-pesa in Kenya: Financial Inclusion and Financial Integrity' (2013) 8 *Washington Journal of Law Technology & Arts* 375.

Morten Bech and Jenny Hancock, 'Innovations in Payments' (2020) *BIS Quarterly Review* 21.

Nick Hughes and Susie Lonie, 'M-pesa: Mobile Money for the "Unbanked" Turning Cellphones into 24-hour Tellers in Kenya' (2007) 2(1) *Innovations: Technology, Governance, Globalization* 63.

Oxford Policy Management, 'Testing Remote Access Models for Southern African Countries' (2008) <https://www.gsma.com/mobilefordevelopment/wp-content/uploads/2012/06/brochure_branchlessbanking.pdf> accessed 10 September 2021.

Pascaline Dupas, Sarah Green et al, 'Challenges in Banking the Rural Poor: Evidence from Kenya's Western Province' (2012) <https://web.stanford.edu/~pdupas/Challenges_DupasEtAl2011.pdf> accessed 17 August 2021.

Peter Ondiege, 'Regulatory Impact on Mobile Money and Financial inclusion in African Countries - Kenya, Nigeria, Tanzania and Uganda' (2015) <https://www.cgdev.org/sites/default/files/Background-Paper-Financial-Inclusion-Ondiege.pdf> accessed 12 August 2021.

Pierre–Laurent Chatain, Andrew Zerzan et al, *Protecting Mobile Money Against Financial Crimes: Global Policy Challenges and Solutions* (World Bank, 2011) <http://documents1.worldbank.org/curated/en/854951468337169489/pdf/600600PUB0ID181Mobile09780821386699.pdf> accessed 3 September 2021.

Pietro Caprara, Marta Infantino et al, 'Mobile Proximity Payment –5 Things Retailers Should Know' (2016) <https://www.pwc.com/it/it/publications/assets/docs/mobile-proximity.pdf> accessed 16 September 2021.

Rajiv Lal and Ishan Sachdev, 'Mobile Money Services - Design and Development for Financial Inclusion' (Harvard Business School Working Paper 15-083, 2015) <https://www.hbs.edu/ris/Publication%20Files/15-083_e7db671b-12b2-47e7-9692-31808ee92bf1.pdf> accessed 13 September 2021.

Rhys Bollen, 'A Discussion of Best Practice in the Regulation of Payment Services: Part 1' (2010) 25(8) *Journal of International Banking Law and Regulation* 370.

Rhys Bollen, 'A Discussion of Best Practice in the Regulation of Payment Services: Part 2' (2010) 25(9) *Journal of International Banking Law & Regulation* 429.

Rhys Bollen, 'Recent Developments in Mobile Banking and Payments' (2009) 24(9) *Journal of International Banking Law and Regulation* 454.

Robin Hui Huang, Abby Oi Ling Lam et al, 'The Development and Regulation of Mobile Payment: Chinese Experiences and Comparative Perspectives' (2021) 20(1) *Washington University Global Studies Law Review* 1.

Sancho Guibert, 'Mobile Payments in the EU: Overview, Legal Framework and Infrastructure and Challenges' (2016) 9 *International In-House Counsel Journal* 1.

Tanai Khiaonarong, 'Oversight Issues in Mobile Payments' (IMF working paper WP/14/123 2014) <https://www.imf.org/external/pubs/ft/wp/2014/wp14123.pdf> accessed 11 September 2021.

The World Bank, 'The Global Findex Database 2017' (2017) <http://www.worldbank.org/en/programs/globalfindex> accessed 15 August 2021.

The World Bank, 'The Little Data Book on Financial Inclusion' (2018) <https://openknowledge.worldbank.org/bitstream/handle/10986/29654/LDB-FinInclusion2018.pdf?sequence=1&isAllowed=y> accessed 14 August 2021.

Thomas Lerner, *Mobile Payment* (Springer Science & Business Media 2013).

Timothy R Lyman, Gautam Ivatury and Stefan Staschen, 'Use of Agents in Branchless Banking for the Poor: Rewards, Risks and Regulation' (CGAP Focus Note No.38, 2006) <https://www.cgap.org/sites/default/files/CGAP-Focus-Notes-Use-of-Agents-in-Branchless-Banking-for-the-Poor-Rewards-Risks-and-Regulation-Oct-2006.pdf> accessed 14 September 2021.

Timothy R McTaggart and David W Freese, 'Regulation of Mobile Payments' (2010) 127 *Banking Law Journal* 485.

Tomi Dahlberg, Niina Mallat, Jan Ondrus and Agnieszka Zmijewska, 'Past, Present and Future of Mobile Payments Research: A Literature Review' (2008) 7(2) *Electronic Commerce Research and Applications* 165.

UN Secretary-General's Special Advocate for Inclusive Finance for Development (UNGSA), 'Early Lessons on Regulatory Innovations to Enable Inclusive FinTech: Innovation Offices, Regulatory Sandboxes, and RegTech' (2019) <https://www.unsgsa.org/sites/default/files/resources-files/2020-09/UNSGSA_Report_2019_Final-compressed.pdf> accessed 14 September 2021.

United Nations Conference on Trade and Development (UNCTAD), 'Access to Financial Services as a driver for the post-2015 development Agenda' (Policy Brief no.35, 2015) <https://unctad.org/system/files/official-document/presspb2015d7_en.pdf> accessed August 23 2021.

Valerie-Anne Bleyen, Leo Van Hove and Monika Hartmann, 'Classifying Payment instruments: A Matryoshka Approach' (2010) 79(3) *Communications & Strategies* 73.

Yoris A Au and Robert J Kauffman, 'The Economics of Mobile Payments: Understanding Stakeholder Issues for an emerging Financial Technology application' (2007) 7 *Electronic Commerce Research and Applications* 141.

# 3 Consumer Protection and Mobile Payments: Why Intervene?

## 3.1 Introduction

Regulatory intervention in markets is often justified by specific policy objectives prioritised by governments. Examples of such policy objectives include promoting free competition, protecting the integrity of the financial system, and promoting the fair and secure processing of data, to name a few. Once identified, governments put significant effort into ensuring that economic actors adhere to set regulatory standards that further such objectives. In many countries, consumer protection features prominently as a core policy goal. Generally, consumer protection aims to safeguard the economic interests of consumers by ensuring that market outcomes do not fall short of their potential thereby resulting in welfare losses for the consumer.[1] Consumer protection also extends to pursuing other socially driven goals such as encouraging the fair distribution of resources between market participants as well as protecting vulnerable members of the consumer class.[2]

Financial consumer protection is more specific and is concerned with the 'framework of laws, regulations and other approaches generally designed to ensure fair and responsible treatment of financial consumers in their purchase and use of financial products and their dealings with financial services providers.'[3] The discussion in this chapter recognises that financial consumer protection is a subset of the broader conversation on general consumer protection. This is reflected in the inclusion of analysis relevant to the broader context of consumer protection to support more specific discussions relating to financial services.

This chapter starts by placing financial services in context. In particular, it outlines the unique characteristics of financial services, which often justify closer

1 OECD, 'Consumer Policy Toolkit' (2010) pp.11–12 <http://www.oecd-ilibrary.org/governance/consumer-policy-toolkit_9789264079663-en> accessed 6 September 2021.

2 Geraint Howells and Stephen Weatherill, *Consumer Protection Law* (2nd edn, Ashgate 2005) 32; United Nations, 'Guidelines for Consumer Protection' (2016) <https://unctad.org/system/files/official-document/ditccplpmisc2016d1_en.pdf> accessed 5 September 2021.

3 OECD, 'Financial Consumer Protection Policy Approaches in the Digital Age: Protecting Consumers' Assets, Data and Privacy' (2020) p.7 <https://www.oecd.org/daf/fin/financial-education/Financial-Consumer-Protection-Policy-Approaches-in-the-Digital-Age.pdf> accessed 5 September 2021.

DOI: 10.4324/9780429327292-4

regulatory scrutiny and accompanying interventions. Not everyone is convinced that governments should intervene in markets. There are strong arguments asserting that markets are self-correcting, and that external intervention can backfire. However, this book aligns with the position taken by authors like Howells and Weatherill who contend that modern economic realities indicate that the contemporary debate on state intervention in the market has gone beyond whether the state should have a role in the market and now revolves around 'the appropriate intensity of state participation in the economy.'[4] This is more so because modern economic relationships are affected by the statutory intervention and their legal consequences enforced within the framework provided by the state.[5] Ayres and Braithwaite also point out that the reality of policy debates show that focus centres more on how much intervention is needed and not whether intervention is needed at all.[6] Against this background, this chapter takes regulatory intervention as a given – regulators will intervene and do so in varying degrees. Hence, it is essential to understand the basis on which regulators defend their intervention in a given market.

Accordingly, this chapter is concerned with the justification for intervening in markets to protect consumers. Regardless of the specific market under scrutiny, the rationale for consumer protection is usually understood against the background of the consumer's role in the economy, which inevitably attracts differing interpretations.[7] As Howells and Weatherill put it, 'different perspectives contain their own truths.'[8] Some of these perspectives are considered in this chapter.

## 3.2 Financial Services in Context

Financial services are an integral part of our present and future. Reifner and Herwig capture this notion when they explain that:

> The use of financial services has increased across all classes of society. Its capacity to transport money from the past to the future (savings), from the future to the present (credit), from one person to another (payment systems) and from group risk to individual misfortune (insurance) makes it increasingly important in modem society, where partition of labour, globalisation, mobility and the need for capital have grown rapidly.[9]

4 Howells & Weatherill (n 2) p.4.

5 Statutory rules under Contract law for instance, provide a platform that ensures the enforceability of obligations arising from economic transactions. Ibid. p.8.

6 Ian Ayres, John Braithwaite, *Responsive Regulation: Transcending the Deregulation Debate* (Oxford University Press 1992) p.3.

7 Consumers are a heterogeneous group, thus Howells and Weatherill argue that each theory justifying protection is not completely correct or incorrect. Howells & Weatherill (n 2) p.5.

8 Ibid.

9 Udo Reifner and Isabel Herwig, 'Consumer Education and Information Rights in Financial Services' (2003) 12 *Information & Communications Technology Law* 125, 125

With such a unique role, the financial services market possesses certain characteristics which attract much regulatory attention. This section briefly highlights some of these characteristics, as they will provide further context for the discussions that follow in this chapter and the book generally.

First, there are significant information asymmetries in the financial services market. This can partly be attributed to imperfect information about the institutions providing the services. Take the solvency of banking institutions, for instance; McCoy explains that banks inherently have unstable balance sheets because they borrow 'short' by taking in demand deposits and lend 'long' by making loans with longer maturities.[10] The implication is that a significant fraction of a bank's funds are often tied in illiquid loans, with only a smaller fraction being available at any one time to satisfy withdrawals.[11] This would normally not be a cause for concern unless the demand for withdrawals exceeds the cash on hand.[12] But how will a depositor know if a particular bank is financially sound with enough liquid funds to honour demands for withdrawals at any given time?

As expected, Miles explains that depositors cannot usually ascertain which banking institutions are financially sound.[13] This is due to the high costs involved in accessing, analysing, and understanding the information required to draw such conclusions.[14] This information asymmetry can be exploited, as banking providers will have fewer incentives to maintain optimal capital ratios or to limit the riskiness of their assets.[15] In response, regulators may take steps such as imposing capital adequacy requirements on banks to force them to maintain an optimal level of capital. They may also introduce compensation schemes which, although they do not tackle the information asymmetry, reduce the significance of the choice of financial provider.[16] Since depositors will be compensated if a bank goes bust, deciding which banks to transact with becomes less significant.

Information asymmetries may also exist due to the complex products and transactions involved in the financial services market. Goods are sometimes classified based on how easily consumers can acquire and evaluate information about them before purchase. To this end, goods can be classified as search, experience,

10 Patricia A McCoy, 'The Moral Hazard of Deposit Insurance: Theory and Evidence' (2006) p.4 <https://www.imf.org/external/np/seminars/eng/2006/mfl/pam.pdf> accessed 13 September 2021.

11 Ibid.

12 Ibid.

13 See the discussion in David Miles, 'Optimal Regulation of Deposit Taking Financial Intermediaries' (1995) 39 *European Economic Review* 1365. This can be contrasted with views expressed by Kevin Dowd in his paper 'Does Asymmetric Information Justify Bank Capital Adequacy Regulation' (1999) 19 *Cato Journal* 39.

14 Peter Cartwright, *Banks, Consumers and Regulation* (Hart Publishing 2004) p.18.

15 Jean Dermine, 'Bank Mergers in Europe: The Public Policy Issues' (2000) 38 *Journal of Common Market Studies* 409, 411.

16 Peter Cartwright, 'The Vulnerable Consumer of Financial Services: Law, Policy and Regulation' (Financial Services Research Forum 2011) p.50. <https://www.nottingham.ac.uk/business/who-we-are/centres-and-institutes/gcbfi/documents/researchreports/paper78.pdf> accessed 5 September 2021.

or credence goods.[17] Search goods are those whose attributes can be observed and verified before purchase,[18] while experience goods are those whose quality can only be known after use. Credence goods represent those whose quality or attributes cannot be determined or verified even after purchase and use.[19] Credence goods may also be defined in terms of the asymmetric information between an expert supplier and their customer.[20] Hence, credence goods are sometimes described as 'goods and services where an expert knows more about the quality a consumer needs than the consumer himself.'[21] While true in many cases, this is not always the case because, for some credence goods, it is impossible for either party to fully assess the value of the goods. For example, a financial product based on market instruments may yield lower-than-expected returns, an outcome that neither party could have anticipated in advance.[22]

Financial products are considered complex, in part because they are credence goods. With credence goods, the pre-buying and post-buying costs are high.[23] In deciding whether to purchase a financial product, the customer must depend on the quality claims made by the financial institution as well as the information signalling the credibility of the claims.[24] The credibility of such claims generally depends on the financial institution's credentials. After purchase, the value of the service cannot be precisely determined after consumption, and in many cases, the cost of a bad transaction may be delayed since its value is not immediately assessable.[25]

The difficulty in assessing credence goods like financial services has some implications. First, it can create strong incentives for misbehaviour on the part of financial services providers.[26] Kerschbamer and Sutter note that providers may 'overprovide' by inducing consumers to take on financial products they do not

17 Phillip Nelson, 'Information and Consumer Behaviour' (1970) 78(2) *Journal of Political Economy* 331; Michael R Darby and Edi Karni, 'Free Competition and Optimal Amount of Fraud' (1973) 16(1) *Journal of Law & Economics* 67.

18 OECD Consumer Policy Toolkit (n 1) p.34.

19 Ibid. p.35.

20 Loukas Balafoutas and Rudolf Kerschbamer, 'Credence Goods in the Literature: What the Past Fifteen Years Taught us about Fraud, Incentives and the Role of Institutions' (2020) 26 *Journal of Behavioral and Experimental Finance* 1, 14.

21 Uwe Dulleck and Rudolf Kerschbamer, 'On Doctors, Mechanics, and Computer Specialists: The Economics of Credence Goods' (2006) 44(1) *Journal of Economic Literature* 5, 5.

22 Stephen Lumpkin, 'Consumer Protection and Financial Innovation; A Few Basic propositions' (2010) 1 *OECD Journal: Financial Markets Trends* 117, 124.

23 Men-Andri Benz, *Strategies in Markets for Experience and Credence Goods* (Springer 2007) p.2

24 Esben Sloth Anderson, 'The Evolution of Credence Goods: A Transaction approach to Product specification and Quality Control' (MAPP Working Paper No. 21, 1994) <https://pure.au.dk/portal/files/32299368/wp21.pdf> accessed 13 September 2021.

25 Peter Cartwright, *Consumer Protection and the Criminal Law: Law, Theory and Policy in the UK* (Cambridge University Press 2001) p.27.

26 Rudolf Kerschbamer and Matthias Sutter, 'The Economics of Credence Goods – A Survey of Recent Lab and Field Experiments' (2017) 63(1) *CESifo Economic Studies* 1, 2.

need.[27] Here the additional costs of the product are larger than the benefit to the consumer. In other situations, the provider may 'underprovide' by inducing a consumer to take on products that do not meet their needs, or they may 'overcharge' by charging the consumer a high price that is not representative of the value of the product they have received.[28] Second, it can put consumers in a situation where they are vulnerable to conflicts of interest. Financial services providers and their agents may place their own interests above those of the consumer.[29] For example, where commissions are provided as an incentive to drive sales, financial advisers may sell products to consumers that do not match their needs (mis-selling).[30]

These activities can lead to market inefficiencies, including what is commonly described as the 'lemons' problem.[31] This means that where it is impossible to establish the quality of a product in advance, consumers will only be prepared to pay an average price corresponding to the average expected quality. As a result, sellers of high-quality products will be unwilling to sell at that asking price and will withdraw from the market. The result is that the product quality will decline, as will the price consumers are willing to pay.[32] Consequently, to avoid such market failure, regulators intervene to address some of the difficulties associated with credence goods. For instance, they may impose licensing and conduct of business rules to address the credibility of institutions providing financial services.[33] They may also impose disclosure requirements to bridge information gaps and ban/restrict commissions to prevent perverse incentives.

The financial services market is also characterised by high entry and exit barriers. Ideally, free entry and exit ought to be available to firms operating in a given market. This means that it should be possible for any firm wishing to provide services to enter a market to do so at any given time. Should the firm be unsuccessful, it should be able to exit the market using available insolvency procedures. In reality, this is not always the case as governments impose barriers to free entry and exit in sectors considered strategically important. The financial services market is considered to be one of such strategic importance. In many jurisdictions, firms wishing to provide financial services must secure prior approval from regulators and can only do so if they meet certain minimum criteria.[34] Such authorisation requirements are rationalised on the basis that they protect consumers and the

27 Ibid. p.3.

28 Ibid.

29 Lumpkin (n 22) p.124.

30 See a discussion on this in Roman Inderst and Marco Ottaviani, 'Competition through Commissions and Kickbacks' (2012) 102(2) *The American Economic Review* 780.

31 George Akerlof identified this phenomenon (market for lemons) in his article 'The Market for "Lemons": Quality Uncertainty and the Market Mechanism' (1970) 84(3) *Quarterly Journal of Economics* 488.

32 Ibid.

33 Rhys Bollen, 'A Case Study of Bounded Rationality in the Market for Superannuation Products' (2007) 4 *Macquarie Journal of Business Law* 49, 55.

34 Cartwright, *Banks, Consumers and Regulation* (n 14) p.15.

financial system from the risks associated with unauthorised institutions that may be poorly capitalised.[35]

In a similar vein, governments are also reluctant to allow banking institutions to freely exit the financial services market through insolvency because of the serious impact it will have on the stability of the financial system.[36] It is possible that a single bank failure can induce a domino effect which can ultimately lead to a systemic crisis.[37] Regulators, therefore, put in several mechanisms to guarantee the stability of the banking system. For instance, central banking authorities can intervene to assist financially struggling banks in their role as lender of last resort. Public bailouts may also be used as a tool to prevent bank runs. The establishment of safety nets such as deposit insurance can also be understood against this background.[38] Apart from protecting consumers, deposit insurance provides an incentive for depositors to leave their cash in banks, reducing the danger of bank runs.[39]

While important, these safety nets have been recognised as potentially creating moral hazards.[40] This is because financial institutions may be induced to take on more risks and hold lower levels of capital, while consumers may be less careful in selecting institutions.[41] Consumers may also not demand appropriate risk premiums in their deposit interest rate because insurance will subsidise risks.[42] Also, public bailouts and the implicit designation of institutions as 'too big to fail' leads investors to demand riskier options because the public will bear any losses which threaten bankruptcy.[43] Generally, it is assumed that these moral hazards may be minimised by strong regulations that focus on matters such as limiting entry into the financial services sector, ensuring adequate capitalisation, and demanding high standards of ethical behaviour.

Finally, the financial services market is dynamic, characterised by constant changes due to market, technological, and legal developments.[44] Overall, innovation is desirable in financial markets. Innovations in risk management techniques, payments, and transaction processing, all backed by technology, boost productivity, generate economies of scale, and permit better risk diversification.[45]

35 Cartwright, *Consumer Protection and the Criminal Law* (n 25) p.6.

36 Ibid.

37 Dermine (n 15) p.413.

38 Ibid.

39 Cartwright, 'The Vulnerable Consumer of Financial Services' (n 16) p.50.

40 David Llewellyn, 'The Economic Rationale for Financial Regulation' (FSA Occasional Paper Series 1, 1999) p.28 <https://www.fep.up.pt/disciplinas/pgaf924/PGAF/Texto_2_David_Llewellyn.pdf> accessed 5 September 2021.

41 Ibid.

42 Ibid.

43 Xavier Vives, 'The Financial Industry and the Crisis: The Role of Innovation' in Banco Bilbao Vizcaya Argentina (BBVA), *Innovation Perspectives for the 21st Century* (2011) p.327 <https://www.bbvaopenmind.com/wp-content/uploads/2011/01/BBVA-OpenMind-INNOVATION_Perspectives_for_the_21st_Century.pdf> accessed 3 September 2021.

44 OECD, 'Financial Consumer Protection Policy Approaches in the Digital Age' (n 3) p.7.

45 Vives, 'The Financial Industry and the Crisis (n 43) p.322.

Ultimately, this leads to more choices for consumers and greater efficiency in providing those choices. However, innovation can also introduce further complexities. New players with varying levels of engagement and experience with financial services regulation may enter the market. New business models which do not neatly fall within the ambit of existing regulations may also spring up, leaving loopholes that can be exploited. In many situations, regulators have to play catch-up in a constantly evolving landscape. These challenges are even more significant because the consumer class is also experiencing changes that see younger and older persons becoming more significant actors.[46] In addition, exogenous factors such as the lack of financial education and the use of unfamiliar new technologies[47] places consumers in a more vulnerable position.[48]

If innovation is poorly managed, it can negatively impact the stability of the financial system as well as consumer interests. How innovation is used depends on the incentives of the parties involved, who are in turn influenced by existing regulatory frameworks.[49] Bearing this in mind, regulators are faced with the daunting task of ensuring that there are no loopholes in regulating the sector, which create systemic risks. At the same time, regulators must ensure that they intervene proportionately so as not to deter innovation. The balance is not always easily drawn. In part, the 2007–2008 global financial crisis highlighted the dangers of risky innovation exacerbated by inadequate regulation in the financial services sector.[50] The result, amongst other things, was a significant overhauling of financial services and corporate governance regulatory regimes in many jurisdictions.

Importantly, since the financial crisis, there has been growing international support for dedicated regimes that focus on enhancing financial consumer protection. It has been canvassed that financial consumer protection be included as a core part of general consumer protection frameworks.[51] This is because consumer confidence in a well-functioning financial services market is bound to promote stability, efficiency, growth, and innovation in the long term.[52] Several standard-setting bodies and international organisations such as the Organisation for Economic Cooperation and Development (OECD),[53] United Nations (UN),[54] and

46 OECD, 'Consumer Policy Toolkit' (n 1) p.7.

47 Which may be heightened by other factors such as age.

48 Committee on the Internal Market and Consumer Protection, 'Report on a Strategy for Strengthening the rights of Vulnerable Consumers (Explanatory Statement)' (2012) <http://www.europarl.europa.eu/sides/getDoc.do?type=REPORT&reference=A7-2012-0155&language=EN#title2> accessed 5 September 2021; Lisa Waddington, 'Vulnerable and Confused: The Protection of "Vulnerable" Consumers under EU Law' (2013) 38(6) *European Law Review* 757, 767.

49 Vives, 'The Financial Industry and the Crisis' (n 43) p.327.

50 Ibid. p.323.

51 G20, 'High-Level Principles on Consumer Financial Protection' (2011) p.4 <https://www.oecd.org/g20/topics/financial-sector-reform/48892010.pdf> accessed 5 September 2021.

52 Ibid.

53 OECD, 'Consumer Policy Toolkit' (n 1).

54 UN, 'Guidelines for Consumer Protection' (n 2).

the World Bank[55] have released guidelines to support policymakers in developing dedicated financial consumer protection regimes. For instance, a G20/OECD Task Force on financial consumer protection was set up to develop financial consumer protection policy and practice internationally.[56] The task force is responsible for important policy papers, including the influential High-Level Principles on Financial Consumer Protection which set out evidence-based guidance on how policies could be developed to enhance financial consumer protection.[57]

From the discussions above, it is evident that the core objectives of regulatory intervention in financial markets are to sustain systemic stability, maintain the safety and soundness of financial institutions, and protect consumers.[58] But, if these are the ultimate objectives of financial services regulation, what specific reasons justify using regulations to achieve these objectives? It is these rationales that we will consider in the rest of this chapter.

## 3.3 Economic Rationales for Regulatory Intervention

### *3.3.1 The Perfect Market*

There is the theoretical assumption that if markets (including the market for financial services) operate perfectly, there will be no need for regulatory intervention.[59] Neo-classical economic theory explains the perfect market as one where certain conditions exist to maintain equilibrium in the allocation of resources.[60] In such a perfect market, there are numerous buyers and sellers such that the activity of one economic actor will have a negligible effect on the price or output of the market.[61] There is also free entry into and exit from the market. In addition, the commodity sold in the market is homogeneous as they are perfect substitutes for each other.[62] The economic actors have access to perfect information about the nature and value of the traded commodities and their potential substitutes.[63] These economic actors are also rational and act in their self-interest, entering (fully informed) into

55 World Bank Group, 'Good practices for Financial Consumer Protection' (2017 edn, World Bank Washington DC) <https://openknowledge.worldbank.org/handle/10986/28996> accessed 5 September 2021.

56 OECD, 'Financial Consumer Protection Policy Approaches in the Digital Age' (n 3) p.7.

57 Ibid.

58 See Llewellyn, 'The Economic Rationale for Financial Regulation' (n 40).

59 Cartwright, *Banks, Consumers and Regulation* (n 14) p.14.

60 Alessio M Pacces, Roger J. Van Den Bergh, 'An Introduction to the Law and Economics of Regulation' in Roger J Van Den Bergh, Alessio M Pacces (eds), *Regulation and Economics* (Edward Elgar Publishing 2012) 4–5.

61 Peter Cartwright, 'Consumer Protection in Financial Services: Putting the Law in Context' in Peter Cartwright (ed.), *Consumer Protection in Financial Services* (Kluwer Law International 1999) p.8.

62 Ibid.; Jeanne Lorraine Schroeder, *The Triumph of Venus: The Erotics of the Market* (University of California Press, 2004) p.137.

63 Cartwright, 'Consumer Protection in Financial Services: Putting the Law in Context' (n 61) p.8.

transactions that reflect their needs.[64] There are also no externalities as the cost of producing commodities are borne by the producer alone while the benefits of consuming them are borne by only the consumer.[65]

Cartwright explains that it is assumed that if the conditions of a perfect market are met, then the welfare of economic actors, including consumers, is maximised since resources will be allocated efficiently.[66] This proposition, often associated with the Chicago School of economics, relies on certain assumptions on how markets operate. First, it assumes that economic actors are rational maximisers of their own utility.[67] This means that buyers and sellers act in their own self-interest and are perfectly informed about all products in the market and, taking into account the limited resources available, make the best choices that suit their needs.[68] Second, it assumes that decisions made in the marketplace influence market actors.[69] For instance, consumers play an active role in maintaining market discipline as they can use their purchasing decisions to ensure that suppliers act in their best interest.[70] By making decisions that suit their needs, consumers send important signals to traders, which, if ignored, will result in the trader losing patronage, which eventually forces them to exit the market.[71] These assumptions project consumer sovereignty with a high distrust for paternalism.[72]

The perfect market is appealing from an economic and ideological perspective.[73] From an economic perspective, it is desirable because it is efficient.[74] Broadly speaking, an efficient market is one that puts its resources to their most valuable use.[75] Such a market will have economic actors involved in utility-maximising behaviour driven by access to the necessary information needed to make optimal choices. The market will also be highly competitive, taking into account all external costs and benefits.[76] From an ideological perspective, it is desirable

64 Peter J Boettke and Rosolino A Candela, 'Rational Choice as if the users were human' in Morris Altman (eds) *Handbook of Behavioural Economics and Smart Decision Making: Rational Decision Making Within the Bounds of Reason* (Edward Elgar 2017) pp.68–69.

65 Cartwright, *Consumer Protection and the Criminal Law* (n 25) p.6; Colin Scott and Julia Black, *Cranston's Consumers and the Law* (3rd edn, Butterworths 2000) 27.

66 Cartwright, *Banks, Consumers and Regulations* (n 14) p.14.

67 Ibid.

68 OECD, 'Consumer Policy Toolkit' (n 1) p.33.

69 Cartwright, *Banks, Consumers and Regulations* (n 14) p.14.

70 Howells & Weatherill (n 2) p.1.

71 Cartwright, *Consumer Protection and the Criminal Law* (n 25) p.6.

72 Iain Ramsay, *Consumer Law and Policy* (3rd edn, Hart Publishing 2012) p.62.

73 Cartwright, *Consumer Protection and the Criminal Law* (n 25) p.6.

74 Ibid.

75 Using economic theory, efficiency may further be interpreted using the Pareto test (i.e., allocation of resources is efficient when it is impossible to make any one individual better off without at the same time making someone worse off) or the Kaldor-Hicks test (i.e., a policy is efficient where it results in sufficient benefits for those who gain such that potentially they can compensate fully all the losers and still remain better off): Anthony I Ogus, *Regulation: Legal Form and Economic Theory* (Hart Publishing 2004) 23–25.

76 Ibid.

because it upholds consumer sovereignty, prioritising individual choices which reflect personal preferences rather than choices made by the state on behalf of the individual.[77]

Where all the conditions of the perfect market exist, there is no need for regulatory intervention. However, this does not mean that the state has no role in the free market. Using the mechanism of the law, the state's role is to set up the structures in which the market operates and to enforce the agreements made between economic actors.[78] Simply put, the law determines the rules of the game and acts as an umpire to interpret and enforce those rules.[79] Any deviation from the conditions necessary for the perfect market results in market failure, which should be corrected. Any such intervention should be minimal, solely focusing on addressing the identified market failure.[80] From this perspective, market failure can be singled out as the prima facie justification for government intervention.[81]

Since neo-classical economic theory surmises the ideal market arrangement in which consumer welfare is best protected, authorities can evaluate any real-world departures from this ideal in order to determine how and when to intervene.[82] As we see in the next section, reality confirms that market failures are bound to occur; hence market failure analysis is usually an initial step in policymaking. Market failure analysis, thus, remains relevant in policymaking because it assists with diagnosing the source of such failures, which supports regulators in choosing appropriate interventions and evaluating their success.[83] Many interventions aim to recreate, as much as possible, the conditions of a perfect market.[84] Where such interventions focus on correcting only market failures without concerning themselves with achieving broader social goals, they are described as market-based.[85]

Although market-based interventions are perceived to be less intrusive, some commentators have described them as unnecessary and counter-productive since the market itself is capable of correcting its failures.[86] There is also the argument that it is not always the case that a regulatory solution is more successful than the market or private law in correcting market inefficiencies.[87] While these are fair points, the discussions in the next section highlight important issues

77 Cartwright, *Consumer Protection and the Criminal Law* (n 25) p.6.
78 Ibid. p.7
79 Ibid. citing Milton Friedman, *Capitalism and Freedom* (Chicago University Press 1962).
80 Cartwright, *Consumer Protection and the Criminal Law* (n 25) p.1.
81 OECD, 'Consumer Policy Toolkit' (n 1) p.32; Ramsay, *Consumer Law and Policy* (n 72) p.42.
82 OECD, 'Consumer Policy Toolkit' p.33.
83 Ramsay, *Consumer Law and Policy* (n 72) p.42.
84 Cartwright, Consumer Protection in Financial Services: Putting the Law in Context' (6 21) 8.
85 This differentiation can be controversial as there is sometimes no clear distinction between interventions with pure market-based goals and those with social goals. Cartwright, *Consumer Protection and the Criminal law* (n 25) p.158.
86 See, for instance, George Benston, *Regulating Financial Markets*: A Critique and Some Proposals (Hobart Paper 135; Institute of Economic Affairs 1998).
87 Ogus, *Regulation: Legal Form and Economic Theory* (n 75) p.30.

which show that it is not always desirable to leave the market to correct itself. In many instances, consumer detriment and welfare losses can be widespread and substantial in the absence of targeted intervention.

### *3.3.2 Market Realities*

The perfect market is utopian, and in reality, many of the outlined conditions do not exist. For instance, the product homogeneity expected in perfect markets does not hold up in real-life situations. Product differentiation (even if artificial) often exists, and suppliers may leverage this to build a customer base.[88] Also, while the perfect market ideal presupposes that markets are perfectly competitive and that there is free entry into and exit from the market, this is not always the case. As seen earlier, in some sectors like financial services, governments may themselves impose barriers to entry and exit. Such requirements limit competition but are often justified on the need to maintain minimum quality standards and prevent the entry of unscrupulous suppliers into a market.[89]

From a general consumer protection perspective, three significant market failures often justify regulatory intervention. First, there are information failures that occur when parties do not have access to perfect information as envisaged in a perfect market. To make well-informed decisions as envisioned in a perfect market, consumers need up-to-date information on the price, characteristics, and quality of a commodity (and its substitutes) and the terms on which they are purchasing it.[90] Such information must also be understandable, readily available, and verifiable.[91] However, the perfect information characteristic of a perfect market is rarely found and in reality, obtaining perfect information is costly and sometimes impossible for consumers.[92] Where information is imperfect, consumers can be deprived of the knowledge required to make optimal economic decisions.[93] This is significant as consumer choice plays a central role in the economic notion of allocative efficiency.[94]

Information may be imperfect because it is incomplete, inaccurate, or misleading.[95] This may be due to deliberate actions taken by suppliers who wish to manipulate information to enhance their profits.[96] In other situations, information may simply be unavailable or impossible for economic actors to access, as is

88 Cartwright, *Banks, Consumers and Regulation* (n 14) p.16.

89 Ogus, *Regulation: Legal Form and Economic Theory* (n 75) p.123; Cartwright, *Banks, Consumers and Regulation* (n 14) p.16.

90 Scott & Black, (n 65) p.30.

91 Ibid.

92 Ibid. p.31.

93 Ramsay, *Consumer Law and Policy* (n 72) p.43.

94 In economic theory, this suggests that existing resources be put to their most efficient use; Ulrich Schwalbe and Daniel Zimmer, *Law and Economics in European Merger Control* (Oxford University Press 2009) p.3.

95 Colin Bamford and Stephen Walton, *Economics* (Pearson Education Ltd, 2008) p.57.

96 Ogus *Regulation: Legal Form and Economic Theory* (n 75) p.40.

the case with credence goods which we discussed earlier. Imperfect information can also result from suppliers choosing to emphasise certain information that distracts consumers from other key features of a product.[97] Information may also be presented in a way that is deliberately complex and confusing or deceptively simple.[98] These scenarios often result in a situation where suppliers and sellers have an uneven amount of information.[99] This asymmetry consequently contributes to the inequality of bargaining power between consumers and suppliers.[100]

Information failures, therefore, inform government intervention to protect consumers. Information failures may result in a situation where consumers misallocate their resources and fail to or incorrectly exercise their market power to discipline firms.[101] It may also encourage artificial product differentiation and make consumers susceptible to misleading claims.[102] In addition, it may channel competition based on more observable traits like price, leading to a fall in quality which consumers may be unable to observe. This can result in the 'market for lemons' problem explained earlier. Regulatory intervention may thus be introduced to mitigate these problems and to encourage fair competition among suppliers.[103]

A second market failure prominent in consumer markets is the perceived inability of the institutional framework (private law rules and market forces) to secure the efficiency of the market.[104] An efficient market is dependent upon private institutional frameworks that ensure the performance of economic transactions. Private law rules in areas such as contract and tort law play an important facilitative role in this context. The law of contract, for instance, provides the framework which allows individuals to create and enforce agreements that reflect their preferences.[105] Central to the development of contract law and its relationship with the market is the classical theory of freedom of contract.[106] This theory presupposes that individuals of 'full age and competent understanding shall have the utmost liberty of contracting and that their contracts entered into freely and

97 Scott & Black (n 65) p.31; Akerlof (n 31).

98 Scott & Black (n 65) p.32.

99 Edward Rubin, 'The Internet Consumer Protection and Practical Knowledge' in Jane K Winn (ed.) *Consumer Protection in the Age of the Information Economy* (Ashgate Publishing 2013) 37. Information deficits may also occur where neither party has the required information.

100 Ramsay reports that this idea appeared in the Molony Report and the Crowther Report on Consumer Credit which eventually formed the basis of the UK Consumer Credit Act 1974; Ramsay, *Consumer Law and Policy* (n 72) p.41.

101 Iain Ramsay, 'Rationales for intervention in the Consumer Marketplace' (London, Office of Fair Trading 1984) cited in Ramsay, *Consumer Law and Policy* (n 72) p.51.

102 Ibid.

103 Howells & Weatherill (n 2) p.64.

104 Ramsay, *Consumer Law and Policy* (n 72) p.43.

105 Cartwright, *Consumer Protection and the Criminal Law* (n 25) p.8.

106 Ibid.

voluntarily shall be held sacred and shall be enforced by courts of justice.'[107] Ogus explains that underlying this idea is the belief that as rational actors, individuals know what is best for themselves and act to maximise their utility.[108] Hence, they should be free to enter agreements as they wish.[109] Under this theory, courts enforce individual preferences as expressed in their contracts and do not intervene on substantive matters. Although important literature questions whether the law of contract ever championed this level of freedom, the classical theory was influential, and its emphasis on freedom of contract and judicial non-intervention on substantive issues reflects the belief in free markets.[110]

Important aspects of contract law provide some protection for consumers. For instance, the doctrines of duress, misrepresentation, and undue influence serve to protect weaker contracting parties from improper or fraudulent practices perpetrated by the other party. Experience, however, shows that certain aspects of contract law can limit the protections available.[111] For example, the strict application of the doctrine of privity of contract generally prevents third parties from enforcing contracts.[112] Applying this doctrine can lead to situations where consumers are left without a remedy if they cannot establish a direct contractual relationship with a supplier. Contract law also depends on the aggrieved party for its enforcement which ultimately attracts enforcement costs. To deal with a suboptimal contract, an aggrieved party must actively seek redress, but private law dispute resolution procedures are time-consuming and are not cheap.[113] Further discussions on the limitations of private law dispute resolution procedures are dealt with in *Chapter 4*. The important point to note here is that a rational consumer is unlikely to enforce their rights if the expected costs of doing so exceed the expected benefits.[114] Consequently, redress procedures such as individual litigation are inadequate in deterring socially wasteful activity or compensating violations of rights.[115] From this standpoint, it can be argued that regulatory intervention is justified by the need to correct the perceived limitations of private law institutions.[116]

Another notable deviation from the perfect market ideal is the lack of unbounded rationality amongst economic actors. Behavioural economists have shown that in real-life situations, many neo-classical assumptions of consumer

107 Per Sir George Jessel in *Printing and Numerical Registering Co v. Sampson* (1875) LR 19 Eq 462, 465.

108 Ogus, *Regulation: Legal Form and Economic Theory* (n 75) p.21.

109 Ibid.

110 Cartwright, *Consumer Protection and the Criminal Law* (n 25) p.8.

111 Ibid. p.14.

112 Following law reform in the United Kingdom via the Contracts (Rights of Third Parties) Act 1999, a third party may sue if the contract is made for their benefit or if the contract expressly confers them with a right to sue.

113 Cartwright, *Consumer Protection and the Criminal Law* (n 25) p.14.

114 Ogus, *Regulation: Legal Form and Economic Theory* (n 75) p.24.

115 Ramsay, *Consumer Law and Policy* (n 72) p.43.

116 Cartwright, Consumer Protection in financial services 9.

rationality, unbounded willpower, and unbounded self-interest may not hold.[117] They emphasise that 'regulators and policymakers have to take into account the way consumers actually behave rather than the way the economics textbooks say they should behave.'[118]

When faced with decision-making, consumers may rely on mental shortcuts and rules of thumb to assess risk and justify their choices.[119] Accordingly, consumers may make quick purchasing decisions or overlook superior ones due to too many options or the complexity in evaluating them. This reflects the limitations associated with the human capacity to process information.[120] Consumers are also influenced by cognitive biases, which have a direct impact on their decision-making.[121] These biases can manifest in different forms. For instance, it can be fuelled by overconfidence. Consumers may sometimes believe that in carrying out an action, they will enjoy an outcome better than the average expected outcome.[122] This will, for instance, cause a consumer to ignore generic warnings because they assume that the problem will not affect them.[123] Biases may also be fuelled by hyperbolic discounting. This suggests that in making intertemporal choices on whether to consume now or in the future, consumers may not have consistent preferences over time.[124] This debunks the assumption that consumers weigh present and future costs and benefits when making decisions.[125] In fact, consumers may be myopic in the short term but more rational in the long term.[126] This may lead them to make decisions today which they will regret in the future.[127]

Consumers may also evaluate decisions to be made from a particular perspective or reference point.[128] This is known as anchoring. Consumer choice may thus be influenced by an available or convenient piece of information which serves as an arbitrary reference point or anchor.[129] For example, where a choice is presented as a default option, consumers may regard it as the reference point and

117 Ramsay, *Consumer Law and Policy* (n 72) p.56.

118 Meglena Kuneva, 'Consumers and Competition: The Quest for Real Choice Opportunities' (2012) 8(1) *Competition Law International* 10.

119 Ramsay, *Consumer Law and Policy* (n 72) p.59.

120 Nwanneka V Ezechukwu, 'Consumer Generated Reviews: Time for Closer Scrutiny' (2020) 40(4) *Legal Studies* 630, 641.

121 OECD, 'Consumer Policy Toolkit' (n 1) p.116.

122 Ibid.

123 Consumers may also suffer from illusory superiority where they believe they are above average and overestimate their abilities. Ramsay, *Consumer Law and Policy* (n 72) p.58.

124 Ibid. p.57.

125 Ibid.

126 Ibid.

127 People who suffer from hyperbolic discounting may have self-control problems such as procrastination and may be reluctant about changing the status quo if it requires efforts in the present to gain larger benefits gradually in the future; OECD, 'Consumer Policy Toolkit' (n 1) p.45.

128 Ibid. p.46; see also Amos Tversky and Daniel Kahneman, 'Loss Aversion in Riskless Choice: A Reference Dependent Model' (1991) 106(4) *Quarterly Journal of Economics* 1039.

129 Judith Mehta (ed.), *Behavioural Economics in Competition and Consumer Policy* (ESRC Centre for Competition Policy 2013) p.59.

may be induced to choose it. This may be because consumers perceive selecting the default option as a way of avoiding the cost of making a decision or because they may feel that whoever has set the default knows more about making the right decision than they do.[130] Commentators point out that suppliers may exploit these biases to manipulate consumer decision-making. [131]

Consequently, and even with access to information, these biases may prevent consumers from exercising their choices in a rational manner.[132] This is worsened by market practices that take advantage of these biases.[133] This suggests that although markets may be competitive, they may not be optimal for consumer welfare.[134] In essence, these findings demonstrate that consumers may 'have a voice which is much louder in theory than in practice.'[135] These findings are important for regulators who may have based previous policy responses on the assumption that consumers are rational decision-makers.[136]

In this light, some regulatory responses may be justified by the need to deter specific manipulations that may distort consumer decision-making.[137] Regulatory responses which regulate how businesses communicate with consumers can be understood from this perspective. For instance, many regulators require that businesses do not provide (or omit) information in a manner that is misleading, as this can affect the transactional decisions made by consumers. Insights from behavioural science also assist authorities in formulating responses that aim to support consumer decision-making. For instance, some regulators provide withdrawal rights that allow consumers to take advantage of a cooling-off period so that they can carefully reconsider their decisions. These regulatory responses are considered in more detail in *Chapter 4*.

## 3.4 Non-Economic Rationales for Regulatory Intervention

### *3.4.1 Distributive Justice*

Regulatory intervention is not always justified by a need to correct deviations from the perfect market ideal. Instead, it may hinge on other social, ethical, or politically motivated reasons.[138] Certain regulatory interventions may be sustained from a standpoint that emphasises 'social concerns rooted in equality and the

130 OECD, 'Consumer Policy Toolkit' (n 1) p.46.

131 Jon D Hanson, Douglas A Kysar, 'Taking Behaviouralism Seriously: Some Evidence of Market Manipulation' (1999) 112(7) *Harvard law Review* 1420.

132 Toni Williams, 'Empowerment of Whom and for What? Financial Literacy Education and the New Regulation of Consumer Financial Services' (2007) 29(2) *Law & Policy* 226, 245.

133 Dee Pridgen, 'Sea Changes in Consumer Financial Protection: Stronger Agency and Stronger Laws' (2013) 13(2) *Wyoming Law Review* 405, 437.

134 Ramsay, *Consumer Law and Policy* (n 72) p.62.

135 Howells & Weatherill (n 2) p.2.

136 Ramsay *Consumer Law and Policy* (n 72) p.61.

137 Pridgen (n 133) p.437.

138 Howells & Weatherill (n 2) p.7.

protection of human dignity.'[139] These social concerns may not be adequately addressed under an exclusive private law system hence necessitating regulatory intervention.[140]

In a perfect market, resources are limited and only allocated where they can be put to the most valuable use. This means that resources will be allocated based on the contributions that economic actors make to the market. Consequently, those actors that make less significant contributions will have limited access to available resources. A response to this reality is to intervene to ensure that resources are redistributed on a just and fair basis.

While there are different views of what specifically qualifies as 'just and fair' and what characterises distributive justice more generally,[141] there is some agreement that the idea recognises that it is desirable to help those who are in need even if it may not be economically efficient to do so.[142] Ramsay points out that although poor and disadvantaged consumers are seldom identified as the specific beneficiary of consumer protection initiatives, alleviating the problems plaguing this class of consumers remains an undercurrent in consumer protection.[143] In this context, consumer protection legislation is sometimes viewed as a response to 'the limitations of contractual freedom as a basis for delivering a fair and just distribution of resources.'[144] This suggests that in some circumstances, regulation is justified by the belief that resources need to be 'distributed on the basis of what is just rather than what is economically efficient.'[145]

Distributive efforts are also significant when it is understood that some consumers are more vulnerable than others. While consumers may be subject to varying degrees of vulnerability, it is important to note, as Fineman points out, that vulnerability is a constant and universal feature of human existence. Hence all consumers will be vulnerable at one point or another.[146] Although a detailed examination of this is beyond the scope of our discussion, it is important to note

139 Ibid. p.33.

140 Ibid. p.49.

141 See Serena Olsaretti, 'Introduction: The idea of Distributive Justice' in Serena Olsaretti, *The Oxford Handbook of Distributive Justice* (Oxford University Press 2018) p.2.

142 Cartwright *Banks, Consumers and Regulation* (n 14) p.23.

143 Ramsay *Consumer Law and Policy* (n 72) p.70.

144 Howells & Weatherill (n 2) p.32. Note that the terms 'fair and just' are both very subjective and their interpretation will be dependent on the school of thought one favours. Liberal theories will interpret resource distribution as fair where the process by which resources are acquired is just. Socialist theories, on the other hand, will use equality and justice as standards to judge how fair and just resource distributions are: Ogus *Regulation: Legal Form and Economic Theory* (n 75) p.22.

145 Cartwright, 'Consumer Protection in Financial Services' (n 61) p.12.

146 Martha A Fineman, 'The Vulnerable Subject: Anchoring Equality in the Human Condition' (2008) 20 *Yale Journal of Law & Feminism* 1, 8–12.

that several factors contribute to vulnerability.[147] Cartwright provides a helpful taxonomy which incorporates some significant causes of vulnerability.[148]

Following this taxonomy, consumers may be vulnerable because they do not have access to the relevant information needed to make well-informed decisions.[149] Consumers may also be affected where they are put under pressures that deprive them of the ability to make voluntary economic decisions.[150] Consumer vulnerability may also be heightened because certain classes of consumers may feel the impact of poor decision-making more than others for reasons such as low income and/or wealth.[151] Due to the high costs of litigation which is exacerbated by poverty, some consumers face substantial difficulties in obtaining redress where their rights are breached.[152] Furthermore, where consumers are deprived of a wide range of choices, especially for commodities that may be classed as necessities, they may suffer from what is described as supply vulnerability.[153] In reality, the vulnerabilities highlighted above can co-exist and often reinforce each other. Even where market failures are addressed, such vulnerable consumers transact from a disadvantaged position, which increases their likelihood of suffering detriment. Regulatory intervention addressing and mitigating the impact of these vulnerabilities can thus be justified by the need to protect disadvantaged consumers.

In financial markets, governments may and often intervene to set ground rules which have a cumulative distributive effect.[154] An example can be seen in the consumer credit markets where regulations are put in place to protect lower-income and disadvantaged consumers.[155] Ramsay explains that:

> Consumer credit regulation changed the ground rules of consumer credit transactions, attempting to move the market from a seller's to a buyer's market and changing the culture of the market so that consumers could have

147 With regards to the susceptibility to detriment, some commentators draw a distinction between 'vulnerable,' 'disadvantaged,' and 'less privileged' consumers. For instance, the Consumer Affairs Victoria Discussion paper argues that a consumer is better described as 'disadvantaged' where the characteristics of vulnerability persist. See Consumer Affairs Victoria, 'What do we mean by Vulnerable and Disadvantaged Consumers?' (Consumer Affairs Victoria Discussion Paper, 2004) p.3 <https://www.consumer.vic.gov.au/library/publications/resources-and-education/research/what-do-we-mean-by-vulnerable-and-disadvantaged-consumers-discussion-paper-2004.pdf> accessed 3 September 2021.

148 Cartwright, 'The Vulnerable Consumer of Financial Services' (n 16) p.2.

149 i.e., information vulnerability.

150 i.e., pressure vulnerability.

151 i.e., impact vulnerability.

152 i.e., redress vulnerability.

153 Cartwright, 'The Vulnerable Consumer of Financial Services' (n 16) p.37.

154 Iain Ramsey, 'Consumer Credit Law, Distributive Justice and the Welfare State' (1995) 15(2) *Oxford Journal of Legal Studies* 177, 193–195.

155 Ibid. p.181.

> greater trust and confidence in their use of credit. An important goal was therefore that of changing the balance of power in the marketplace.[156]

To achieve these aims in consumer credit markets, regulators have turned to techniques such as requiring disclosures which ensure that consumers have access to the credit terms, imposing cooling-off periods which give consumers additional time to reconsider and back out of a credit agreement without consequence, and directly regulating contract terms to prevent the use of unfair terms.[157]

A further example of a regulatory intervention that is influenced by redistributive efforts can be seen in the context of our discussions on financial inclusion. As we saw in *Chapters 1* and *2*, poorer consumers may be underserved or excluded from accessing basic financial services because it is not profitable for banks to serve them. One may argue that banks act as rational economic actors, exercising their freedom to contract by siting branches and investing in more profitable areas. However, such decisions have a socio-economic impact on persons excluded from accessing financial services. Against this background, governments intervene to prevent market discrimination and to encourage investments and innovation that support financial inclusion. Hence, while it may not be profitable to commit resources to serve poorer customers, it is just and fair to ensure that they are not financially excluded. Such interventions serve to meet the socially desirable goal of reducing inequalities and can be understood in the context of distributive justice.

### *3.4.2 Paternalism*

Consumer choice is central to the economic notion of allocative efficiency.[158] Consumers make decisions which reflect their preferences, and such decisions are dependent on access to adequate information and the ability to process the information correctly.[159] However, as we have seen earlier, information deficits and cognitive limitations mean that consumers may make suboptimal decisions which are not in their best interest. This suggests that while individual decision-making is essential to preserving autonomy, external intervention may be necessary to protect individuals from their own limitations.[160] Against this background, governments may intervene on the basis that preventing or forcing certain choices are necessary for a consumer's own good.[161] Such interference in individual decision-making, whether by a third party or the government, is

156 Ibid. p.181–182.
157 Ibid. p.181.
158 Ogus, *Regulation: Legal Form and Economic Theory* (n 75) p.35.
159 Ibid.
160 Jeremy A Blumenthal, 'Expert Paternalism' (2012) 64 *Florida Law Review* 721, 721.
161 Colin Camerer, Samuel Issacharoff et al., 'Regulation for Conservatives: Behavioral Economics and the Case for Asymmetric Paternalism' (2003) 151(3) *University of Pennsylvania Law Review* 1211, 1211.

generally described as paternalistic.[162] Rationalising the justification for such intrusion, Rachlinski explains that:

> Restricting individual choice in a free society is as perilous as it is essential. Because the aggregation of individual choices directs the production of goods and services, meddling with these choices risks misdirecting the economy. But if collective foolishness governs individual choice, then allowing an unchecked market to direct the economy can also produce an undesirable allocation of resources.[163]

As one would expect, paternalistic interventions are controversial and have been the subject of many debates. On the one hand, proponents argue that experts often know better than individuals and that there are benefits in relying on them in policymaking.[164] Ogus points out that this view conflicts with notions of liberty and could result in authoritarianism.[165] Other commentators contend that paternalistic responses cannot be viable because of individual differences. Individuals differ in their capacity to acquire, process, and act on information.[166] Hence, the one-size-fits-all nature of paternalistic regulations creates the problem of under- and over-inclusion because regulators do not have full information about the distribution of individual abilities or behavioural biases.[167] The consequence is that those persons who are well equipped to make their decisions are deprived of a choice by the state.[168] It has also been argued that individuals ought to be given the liberty to make their own decisions and determine their preferred ends regardless of whether they are unwise.[169] Any mistakes made in decision-making and the consequences which follow should be seen as the price paid for the liberty to make choices.[170]

In reality, these debates are more nuanced because commentators draw distinctions between different types of paternalism based on the degree of government intrusion. One such distinction draws a line between what is known as hard and soft (or libertarian) paternalism.[171] Hard paternalism suggests a more direct

162 Blumenthal (n 160) p.721.

163 Jeffrey J Rachlinski, 'Cognitive Errors, Individual Differences, and Paternalism' (2006) 73 *University of Chicago Law Review* 207, 207.

164 Blumenthal (n 160) p.721.

165 Ogus, *Regulation: Legal Form and Economic Theory* (n 75) p.36.

166 Ibid. p.35.

167 Mario J Rizzo, Douglas Glen Whitman, 'The Knowledge Problem of New Paternalism' (2009) 4 *Brigham Young University Law Review* 905, 960; Contrast with Blumenthal (n 160) pp.738–739.

168 Ogus, *Regulation: Legal Form and Economic Theory* (n 75) p.35.

169 Gregory Mitchell, 'Libertarian Paternalism is an Oxymoron' (2005) 99(3) *Northwestern University Law Review* 1245, 1263.

170 Ibid. p.1263.

171 Jan Schnellenbach, 'Nudges and Norms: On the Political Economy of Soft Paternalism' (2012) 28(2) European Journal of Political Economy 266, 266. Note that other categories are sometimes used to differentiate conceptual issues relating to paternalism, e.g., differences in paternalism may be described as narrow v. broad, pure v. impure; moral v. welfare; see Gerald Dworkin,

and coercive intrusion on consumer decision-making where policymakers force consumers to avoid certain risks.[172] It may include regulators prohibiting consumers from making certain choices, e.g., the use of illicit drugs or mandating them to make certain choices, e.g., requiring the use of seatbelts. Here, the consumer is left with no say as the policymaker has made a choice on their behalf. In contrast, soft paternalism involves the deliberate design of choice frameworks that ensure that cognitively restrained individuals are nudged to make optimal choices.[173] Without coercion, the regulator nudges the consumer away from certain risks.[174] Soft paternalism is championed on the basis that it is less intrusive on individual autonomy. This is because policymakers do not deprive individuals of their liberty to make decisions; instead, they nudge them towards making better ones.[175]

Soft paternalism often relies on insights provided by behavioural economics about consumer behaviour. Understanding consumer behaviour allows regulators to adopt nudges[176] that encourage consumers to make choices that are considered to be in their best interest. For instance, regulators use default rules to nudge individuals into making certain decisions. Default enrolment on pension plans is a popular example. Individuals may be automatically enrolled on a pension plan, although they can exercise the option to opt out if they wish. Reliance on behavioural science is increasingly popular, and governments are investing in this approach. In the UK, for instance, the government set up a Behavioural Insights Team ('the Nudge Unit') in 2010 to 'generate and apply behavioural insights to inform policy….'[177] Other countries such as Australia, Canada, Germany, the Netherlands, and the United States have established similar units.[178]

Despite the arguments in support, some commentators raise questions about the use of mechanisms relying on behavioural science such as nudges. For instance, Cooper and Kovacic point out that the policymakers who have been empowered to decide what is in the best interest of consumers may themselves be subject

'Paternalism' in Edward N Zalta (ed.) *The Stanford Encyclopaedia of Philosophy* (Fall 2020 Edition) <http://plato.stanford.edu/entries/paternalism/> accessed 16 September 2021.

172 Anthony Ogus, 'The Paradoxes of Legal Paternalism and How to Resolve Them' (2010) 30(1) *Legal Studies* 61, 62.

173 Schnellenbach (n 171) p.266.

174 Ogus, 'The Paradoxes of Legal Paternalism and How to Resolve Them' (n 172) p.62.

175 Cass R Sunstein and Richard H Thaler, 'Libertarian Paternalism is not an Oxymoron' (2003) 70 *University of Chicago Law Review* 1182.

176 The term 'nudging' is attributed to the work of Sunstein and Thaler in *Nudge: Improving Decisions About Health, Wealth and Happiness* (Yale University Press 2008) <http://www.telegraph.co.uk/news/politics/9853384/Inside-the-Coalitions-controversial-Nudge-Unit.html> accessed 18 September 2021. See also Cass R Sunstein, 'Nudging: A Very Short Guide' (2014) 37(4) *Journal of Consumer Policy* 583.

177 Although it was formed in partnership with the Cabinet Office, it is independent of the UK government. <https://www.gov.uk/government/organisations/behavioural-insights-team> <https://www.bi.team/about-us/> accessed 5 September 2021.

178 Zeina Afif, '"Nudge Units" – Where They Come From and What They Do' (2017) <https://blogs.worldbank.org/developmenttalk/nudge-units-where-they-came-and-what-they-can-do> accessed 5 September 2021.

to cognitive biases.[179] As a result, these policymakers may adopt policies based on flawed heuristics or policies which are closer to the preferences of political overseers rather than consumers.[180]

While agreeing that soft paternalism is less intrusive than hard paternalism, other commentators contend that soft paternalism could inevitably lead to hard paternalism.[181] Wright and Ginsburg, for instance, argue that the use of behavioural economics as a justification for protecting consumers could effectively mean that consumer choices are controlled more by the government and less by consumers themselves.[182] It also supports a supposed false assumption that governments can determine and promote the true preferences of consumers, which Glaeser points out is a problem because policymakers are human and may themselves become victims of behavioural biases, thereby undermining the rationality of regulatory choice.[183] Mitchell further contends that a better alternative to soft paternalism would be to assist consumers in overcoming the biases that affect decision-making.[184] This, he believes, will enhance their freedom and improve the quality of their choices.[185]

### *3.4.3 Community Values*

It is commonly accepted that there are certain shared values held by society that ought to be promoted and protected by legislation. These values may include matters such as fair dealing, trust, honesty, and loss sharing.[186] In this context, regulatory intervention is not justified on the basis of counting economic costs and benefits but is instead seen as part of a continuing process of deciding the type of society that is desirable.[187] For instance, it is assumed that most members of society will want vulnerable members to be protected from exploitative business practices. Hence, business conduct legislation that seeks to prevent unfair businesses practices can be justified as reflecting and entrenching such values. In the same vein, product safety regulations can be understood as reflecting the fact that 'citizens want to live healthily and safely … and have confidence in the products

179 James C Cooper and William E Kovacic, 'Behavioural Economics: Implications for Regulatory Behaviour' (2012) 41(1) *Journal of Regulatory Economics* 41, 42.

180 Ibid.

181 Blumenthal (n 160) p.745.

182 Joshua D Wright, Douglas H Ginsburg, 'Behavioural Law and Economics: Its Origins, Fatal Flaws, and Implications for Liberty' (2012) 106 *Northwestern University Law Review* 1033, 1075–1079.

183 Edward L Glaeser, 'Paternalism and Psychology' (2006) 73(1) *University of Chicago Law Review* 133, 133.

184 Mitchell (n 169) p.1245.

185 Ibid. pp.1245, 1258.

186 Ramsay *Consumer Law and Policy* (n 72) p.80.

187 Richard B Stewart and Cass R Sunstein, 'Public Programs and Private Rights' (1982) 95 *Harvard Law Review* 1193, 1238.

and services they consume.'[188] In financial markets specifically, Ramsay notes that values like trust and confidence are necessary for its functioning and that regulations preserving such values are important.[189] Thus, regulatory intervention may be justified by the need to champion values that can help financial markets flourish and at the same time protect consumers.[190]

The idea of sustainable consumption, which includes meeting the needs of present and future generations, is also classified as a community value.[191] Moreover, with its recognition as an objective in the UN Guidelines for Consumer Protection, it is now considered a matter that should be incorporated into consumer protection policy.[192] Against this background, governments often seek to use regulations to encourage the design, development, and use of environmentally sound products and services that are considered to positively impact consumption patterns.[193] Consequently, green claims[194] are increasingly popular as businesses seek to signal to consumers that their products are less damaging to the environment than those offered by competitors.[195]

Reliance on community values as the basis for consumer protection is not without controversy. For example, Hyde points out that although this is a popularly quoted rationale for regulation, it is an 'amorphous concept' which is difficult to define.[196] Though speaking on the issue of judicial activism justified by communal values, Heydon also raises the following key questions relevant in our context.

> How are contemporary 'community values' to be discovered? How are 'community values' in former times to be discovered? Do applicable 'community values' exist when the community is pluralist and divided on many questions? How can searchers for community values distinguish between their personal values and the values of the community which are distinct from their own?[197]

188 Commission of The European Communities, 'Proposal for a decision of the European Parliament and of the Council establishing a Programme of Community action in the field of Health and Consumer protection 2007–2013' COM (2005, 115 final) Para. 1.1 <https://eur-lex.europa.eu/legal-content/EN/TXT/PDF/?uri=COM:2005:115:FIN&from=EN> accessed 18 September 2021.

189 Ramsay, *Consumer Law and Policy* (n 72) p.80.

190 Cartwright, *Consumer Protection and the Criminal Law* (n 25) p.8.

191 Ramsay *Consumer Law and Policy* (n 72) p.82.

192 See objective (h) of the UN Guidelines for Consumer Protection (n 2).

193 Ibid.

194 Or environmental claims.

195 Bert Keirsbilck, Evelyne Terryn, et al., 'Sustainable Consumption and Consumer Protection Legislation: How can Sustainable Consumption and Longer Lifetime Products be Promoted through Consumer Protection Legislation' (2020) p.11 <https://www.europarl.europa.eu/RegData/etudes/IDAN/2020/648769/IPOL_IDA(2020)648769_EN.pdf> accessed 18 September 2021.

196 Richard Hyde, 'Why Separate the Regulatory Regimes Applicable to Food Safety and Product Safety' (2013) 33 *Legal Studies* 509, 520.

197 Dyson Heydon, 'Judicial Activism and the Death of the Rule of Law' (2004) 10 *Otago Law Review* 493, 513.

When regulators justify intervening based on shared values, are the values actually those held by the community or do the values represent those that the regulators believe the community should aspire to hold? These are difficult questions that are not easy to answer. Nonetheless, many regulators allude to entrenching commonly held values when justifying regulatory intervention.

On a final note, it is important to point out that the distinction between economic and non-economic rationales may not always be clear cut. As Cartwright points out, this may be because interventions that appear to be justified from a non-economic perspective may improve the market, while market-based responses addressing market failure can lead to desirable social benefits.[198] Moreover, in some situations, a matter of concern and the accompanying regulatory response to tackle it can be understood from an economic and non-economic perspective. An example may illustrate this: where an individual's action negatively affects third parties or society, such effects are an externality. In a perfect market, there are no externalities, so if an individual's decision impacts an unrelated third party, it indicates market failure. An intervention by the state to minimise or prevent such an externality can thus be rationalised from an economic perspective. Yet, the same intervention may also be interpreted as paternalistic where to prevent the externality, individuals are prevented from carrying out certain actions.[199] For instance, an individual's decision to drive under the influence can create burdens on other third parties. The drunk driver may cause bodily harm to themselves and others and may also destroy property in the process.[200] These negative outcomes are externalities that generate costs for the third party and society. Regulators often respond with rules penalising drunk driving or decreasing the availability of alcohol. One can rationalise such rules from an economic perspective (to prevent the private and social costs – all externalities associated with drunk driving) and from a paternalistic perspective (since the state interferes with a driver's decision to drive in a sober state or not).[201]

## 3.5 Conclusion

To appreciate regulatory interventions aimed at protecting consumers, it is important to understand the rationales justifying regulations. As seen in this chapter, consumer protection regulation can be justified on economic grounds or non-economic grounds. The line between these justifications can be blurry because many interventions can be explained using multiple perspectives.

198 Cartwright, *Consumer Protection and the Criminal Law* (n 25) pp.27–28.

199 See Ogus, 'The Paradoxes of Legal Paternalism and How to Resolve them' (n 172) pp.64–65.

200 See Thomas K Greenfield, Yu Ye, William Kerr et al., 'Externalities form Alcohol Consumption in the 2005 US National Alcohol Survey: Implications for Policy' (2009) 6(12) *International Journal of Environmental Research and Public Health* 3205.

201 Harry Clarke, 'The Economist's Way of Thinking about Alcohol Policy' (2008) 15(2) *Agenda – A Journal of Policy Analysis and Reform* 27, 30.

The financial services industry has unique characteristics, which explains why it is a heavily regulated industry. Importantly, these characteristics highlight the paramount importance of protecting financial services consumers. Identifying consumer protection as a policy objective and rationalising the necessity of regulatory intervention is only one part of a government's responsibility. It must go a step further in identifying the most appropriate regulatory tools or mechanisms for achieving its objectives. In the next chapter, we consider the regulatory tools that regulators can rely on to protect consumers who choose to adopt mobile payments.

## References

Amos Tversky and Daniel Kahneman, 'Loss Aversion in Riskless Choice: A Reference Dependent Model' (1991) 106(4) *Quarterly Journal of Economics* 1039.

Anthony I Ogus, *Regulation: Legal Form and Economic Theory* (Hart Publishing 2004).

Anthony I Ogus, 'The Paradoxes of Legal Paternalism and How to Resolve Them' (2010) 30(1) *Legal Studies* 61.

Bert Keirsbilck, Evelyne Terryn, et al, 'Sustainable Consumption and Consumer Protection Legislation: How can Sustainable Consumption and Longer Lifetime Products be Promoted through Consumer Protection Legislation' (2020) <https://www.europarl.europa.eu/RegData/etudes/IDAN/2020/648769/IPOL_IDA(2020)648769_EN.pdf> accessed 18 September 2021.

Cass R Sunstein, 'Nudging: A Very Short Guide' (2014) 37(4) *Journal of Consumer Policy* 583.

Cass R Sunstein and Richard H Thaler, 'Libertarian Paternalism is not an Oxymoron' (2003) 70 *University of Chicago Law Review* 1182.

Cass R Sunstein and Richard H Thaler, *Nudge: Improving Decisions About Health, Wealth and Happiness* (Yale University Press 2008).

Colin Bamford and Stephen Walton, *Economics* (Pearson Education Ltd, 2008).

Colin Camerer, Samuel Issacharoff et al, 'Regulation for Conservatives: Behavioral Economics and the Case for Asymmetric Paternalism' (2003) 151(3) *University of Pennsylvania Law Review* 1211.

Colin Scott and Julia Black, *Cranston's Consumers and the Law* (3rd ed., Butterworths 2000).

Commission of The European Communities, 'Proposal for a decision of the European Parliament and of the Council establishing a Programme of Community action in the field of Health and Consumer protection 2007–2013' *COM* (2005, 115 final) <https://eur-lex.europa.eu/legal-content/EN/TXT/PDF/?uri=COM:2005:115:FIN&from=EN> accessed 18 September 2021

Committee on the Internal Market and Consumer Protection, 'Report on a Strategy for Strengthening the rights of Vulnerable Consumers (Explanatory Statement)' (2012) <http://www.europarl.europa.eu/sides/getDoc.do?type=REPORT&reference=A7-2012-0155&language=EN#title2> accessed 5 September 2021.

Consumer Affairs Victoria, 'What do we mean by Vulnerable and Disadvantaged Consumers?' (Consumer Affairs Victoria Discussion Paper, 2004) <https://www.consumer.vic.gov.au/library/publications/resources-and-education/research/what-do-we-mean-by-vulnerable-and-disadvantaged-consumers-discussion-paper-2004.pdf> accessed 3 September 2021.

David Llewellyn, 'The Economic Rationale for Financial Regulation' (FSA Occasional Paper Series 1, 1999) <https://www.fep.up.pt/disciplinas/pgaf924/PGAF/Texto_2_David_Llewellyn.pdf> accessed 5 September 2021.

David Miles, 'Optimal Regulation of Deposit Taking Financial Intermediaries' (1995) 39 *European Economic Review* 1365.

Dee Pridgen, 'Sea Changes in Consumer Financial Protection: Stronger Agency and Stronger Laws' (2013) 13(2) *Wyoming Law Review* 405.

Dyson Heydon, 'Judicial Activism and the Death of the Rule of Law' (2004) 10 *Otago Law Review* 493.

Edward L Glaeser, 'Paternalism and Psychology' (2006) 73(1) *University of Chicago Law Review* 133.

Edward N Zalta (ed) *The Stanford Encyclopaedia of Philosophy* (Fall 2020 Edition). <http://plato.stanford.edu/entries/paternalism/> accessed 16 September 2021.

Esben Sloth Anderson, 'The Evolution of Credence Goods: A Transaction approach to Product specification and Quality Control' (MAPP Working Paper No. 21, 1994) <https://pure.au.dk/portal/files/32299368/wp21.pdf> accessed 13 September 2021.

G20, 'High-Level Principles on Consumer Financial Protection' (2011) <https://www.oecd.org/g20/topics/financial-sector-reform/48892010.pdf> accessed 5 September 2021.

George Akerlof, 'The Market for 'Lemons': Quality Uncertainty and the Market Mechanism' (1970) 84(3) *Quarterly Journal of Economics* 488.

George Benston, *Regulating Financial Markets: A Critique and Some Proposals* (Hobart Paper 135; Institute of Economic Affairs 1998).

Geraint Howells and Stephen Weatherill, *Consumer Protection Law* (2nd ed., Ashgate 2005).

Gregory Mitchell, 'Libertarian Paternalism is an Oxymoron' (2005) 99(3) *Northwestern University Law Review* 1245.

Harry Clarke, 'The Economist's Way of Thinking about Alcohol Policy' (2008) 15(2) *Agenda: A Journal of Policy Analysis and Reform* 27.

Iain Ramsay, *Consumer Law and Policy* (3rd ed., Hart Publishing 2012).

Iain Ramsey, 'Consumer Credit Law, Distributive Justice and the Welfare State' (1995) 15(2) *Oxford Journal of Legal Studies* 177.

Ian Ayres and John Braithwaite, *Responsive Regulation: Transcending the Deregulation Debate* (Oxford University Press 1992).

James C Cooper and William E Kovacic, 'Behavioural Economics: Implications for Regulatory Behaviour' (2012) 41(1) *Journal of Regulatory Economics* 41.

Jan Schnellenbach, 'Nudges and Norms: On the Political Economy of Soft Paternalism' (2012) 28(2) *European Journal of Political Economy* 266.

Jane K Winn (ed), *Consumer Protection in the Age of the Information Economy* (Ashgate Publishing 2013).

Jean Dermine, 'Bank Mergers in Europe: The Public Policy Issues' (2000) 38 *Journal Common Market Studies* 409.

Jeanne Lorraine Schroeder, *The Triumph of Venus: The Erotics of the Market* (University of California Press, 2004).

Jeffrey J Rachlinski, 'Cognitive Errors, Individual Differences, and Paternalism' (2006) 73 *University of Chicago Law Review* 207.

Jeremy A Blumenthal, 'Expert Paternalism' (2012) 64 *Florida Law Review* 721.

Jon D Hanson, Douglas A Kysar, 'Taking Behaviouralism Seriously: Some Evidence of Market Manipulation' (1999) 112(7) *Harvard law Review* 1420.

Joshua D Wright, Douglas H Ginsburg, 'Behavioural Law and Economics: Its Origins, Fatal Flaws, and Implications for Liberty' (2012) 106 *Northwestern University Law Review* 1033.

Judith Mehta (eds), *Behavioural Economics in Competition and Consumer Policy* (ESRC Centre for Competition Policy 2013).

Kevin Dowd 'Does Asymmetric Information Justify Bank Capital Adequacy Regulation' (1999) 19 *Cato Journal* 39.

Lisa Waddington, 'Vulnerable and Confused: The Protection of 'Vulnerable' Consumers under EU Law' (2013) 38(6) *European Law Review* 757.

Loukas Balafoutas and Rudolf Kerschbamer, 'Credence Goods in the Literature: What the Past Fifteen Years Taught us about Fraud, Incentives and the Role of Institutions' (2020) 26 *Journal of Behavioral and Experimental Finance* 1.

Mario J Rizzo, Douglas Glen Whitman, 'The Knowledge Problem of New Paternalism' (2009) 4 *Brigham Young University Law Review* 905.

Martha A Fineman, 'The Vulnerable Subject: Anchoring Equality in the Human Condition' (2008) 20 *Yale Journal of Law & Feminism* 1.

Meglena Kuneva, 'Consumers and Competition: The Quest for Real Choice Opportunities' (2012) 8(1) *Competition Law International* 10.

Men-Andri Benz, *Strategies in Markets for Experience and Credence Goods* (Springer 2007).

Michael R Darby and Edi Karni, 'Free Competition and Optimal Amount of Fraud' (1973) 16(1) *Journal of Law & Economics* 67.

Morris Altman (eds) *Handbook of Behavioural Economics and Smart Decision Making: Rational Decision Making Within the Bounds of Reason* (Edward Elgar 2017).

Nwanneka V Ezechukwu, 'Consumer Generated Reviews: Time for Closer Scrutiny' (2020) 40(4) *Legal Studies* 630.

OECD, 'Consumer Policy Toolkit' (2010) <http://www.oecd-ilibrary.org/governance/consumer-policy-toolkit_9789264079663-en> accessed 6 September 2021.

OECD, 'Financial Consumer Protection Policy Approaches in the Digital Age: Protecting Consumers' Assets, Data and Privacy' (2020) <https://www.oecd.org/daf/fin/financial-education/Financial-Consumer-Protection-Policy-Approaches-in-the-Digital-Age.pdf> accessed 5 September 2021.

Patricia A McCoy, 'The Moral Hazard of Deposit Insurance: Theory and Evidence' (2006) <https://www.imf.org/external/np/seminars/eng/2006/mfl/pam.pdf> accessed 13 September 2021.

Peter Cartwright (ed), *Consumer Protection in Financial Services* (Kluwer Law Int'l 1999)

Peter Cartwright, *Consumer Protection and the Criminal Law: Law, Theory and Policy in the UK* (Cambridge University Press 2001).

Peter Cartwright, *Banks, Consumers and Regulation* (Hart Publishing 2004).

Peter Cartwright, 'The Vulnerable Consumer of Financial Services: Law, Policy and Regulation' (Financial Services Research Forum 2011) <https://www.nottingham.ac.uk/business/who-we-are/centres-and-institutes/gcbfi/documents/researchreports/paper78.pdf> Accessed 5 September 2021.

Phillip Nelson, 'Information and Consumer Behaviour' (1970) 78(2) *Journal of Political Economy* 331.

*Printing and Numerical Registering Co v Sampson* (1875) LR 19 Eq 462.

Rhys Bollen, 'A Case Study of Bounded Rationality in the Market for Superannuation Products' (2007) 4 *Macquarie Journal of Business Law* 49.

Richard B Stewart and Cass R Sunstein, 'Public Programs and Private Rights' (1982) 95 *Harvard Law Review* 1193.

Richard Hyde, 'Why Separate the Regulatory Regimes Applicable to Food Safety and Product Safety' (2013) 33 *Legal Studies* 509.

Roger J Van Den Bergh, Alessio M Pacces (eds), *Regulation and Economics* (Edward Elgar Publishing 2012).

Roman Inderst and Marco Ottaviani, 'Competition through Commissions and Kickbacks' (2012) 102(2) *The American Economic Review* 780.

Rudolf Kerschbamer and Matthias Sutter, 'The Economics of Credence Goods: A Survey of Recent Lab and Field Experiments' (2017) 63(1) *CESifo Economic Studies* 1.

Serena Olsaretti, *The Oxford Handbook of Distributive Justice* (Oxford University Press 2018).

Stephen Lumpkin, 'Consumer Protection and Financial Innovation: A Few Basic Propositions' (2010) 1 *OECD Journal: Financial Markets Trends* 117.

Thomas K Greenfield, Yu Ye, William Kerr et al, 'Externalities form Alcohol Consumption in the 2005 US National Alcohol Survey: Implications for Policy' (2009) 6(12) *International Journal of Environmental Research and Public Health* 3205.

Toni Williams, 'Empowerment of Whom and for What? Financial Literacy Education and the New Regulation of Consumer Financial Services' (2007) 29(2) *Law & Policy* 226.

Udo Reifner and Isabel Herwig, 'Consumer Education and Information Rights in Financial Services' (2003) 12 *Information & Communications Technology Law* 125.

Ulrich Schwalbe and Daniel Zimmer, *Law and Economics in European Merger Control* (Oxford University Press 2009).

United Nations, 'Guidelines for Consumer Protection' (2016) <https://unctad.org/system/files/official-document/ditccplpmisc2016d1_en.pdf> accessed 5 September 2021.

Uwe Dulleck and Rudolf Kerschbamer, 'On Doctors, Mechanics, and Computer Specialists: The Economics of Credence Goods' (2006) 44(1) *Journal of Economic Literature* 5.

World Bank Group, 'Good Practices for Financial Consumer Protection' (World Bank Washington DC 2017 ed.) <https://openknowledge.worldbank.org/handle/10986/28996> accessed 5 September 2021.

Xavier Vives, 'The Financial Industry and the Crisis: The Role of Innovation' in Banco Bilbao Vizcaya Argentina (BBVA) (ed), *Innovation Perspectives for the 21st Century* (2011) <https://www.bbvaopenmind.com/wp-content/uploads/2011/01/BBVA-OpenMind-INNOVATION_Perspectives_for_the_21st_Century.pdf> accessed 3 September 2021.

Zeina Afif, '"Nudge Units" – Where They Come From and What They Do' (2017) <https://blogs.worldbank.org/developmenttalk/nudge-units-where-they-came-and-what-they-can-do> accessed 5 September 2021

# 4 Consumer Policy Tools for Regulating Mobile Payments

## 4.1 Introduction

In *Chapter 3*, we established that consumer protection is a regulatory priority in financial services markets. With innovations like mobile payments (m-payments), this objective is even more paramount where authorities seek to leverage m-payments in driving financial inclusion goals. This is because the absence of appropriate protective measures exposes previously excluded and inexperienced consumers to abusive commercial practices, perpetuating their vulnerability.[1]

With m-payments, the benefit to consumers is increased choice, while the downside is the paucity and uncertainty of regulations to protect them.[2] The latter is due to the lack of industry standards and the rapid pace of technological development.[3] As the Organisation for Economic Cooperation and Development (OECD) points out, many countries do not have specific legislation governing m-payments.[4] The extent to which existing general consumer protection rules cover m-payments also remains largely untested.

To better appreciate the concerns associated with m-payments, it is important to highlight some of the key consumer issues that may arise in the use of m-payments, which require close attention from stakeholders.[5] First, as with many financial products, there are concerns linked to the information asymmetry and power imbalance between m-payment service providers and consumers. Consumers may not have

1 Global Partnership for Financial Inclusion (GPFI), 'Global Standard-Setting Bodies and Financial Inclusion for the Poor' (2011) p.33 <https://www.gpfi.org/sites/gpfi/files/documents/White-Paper-Global-Standard-Setting-Bodies-Oct-2011.pdf> accessed 19 July 2021.

2 Eleanor Lumsden, 'Securing Mobile Technology and Financial Transactions in the U.S.' (2012) 9 *Berkeley Business Law Journal* 139, 153.

3 Elizabeth Eraker, Colin Hector, and Chris J Hoofnagle, 'Mobile Payments: The Challenge of Protecting Consumers and Innovation' (2011) 10 *Privacy & Security Law Report* 212, 213.

4 OECD, 'Report on Consumer Protection in Online and Mobile Payments' (OECD Digital Economy Papers No. 204, 2012), p.16 <http://Dx.Doi.Org/10.1787/5k9490gwp7f3-En> accessed 10 September 2021.

5 The book chooses a narrower approach to identifying consumer protection themes and does not discuss issues related to data and security protection, competition, and interoperability. While these areas admittedly have an impact on consumer protection, they address different regulatory priorities.

DOI: 10.4324/9780429327292-5

adequate information on m-payments, and even where they have access to information, they may not be able to process it. This becomes a problem, as effective competition in price and quality requires meaningful and comparable product disclosure that prevents poor purchasing decisions.[6] Second, consumers may also become victims of deceptive and fraudulent commercial practices. This may be due to consumer inexperience or illiteracy. It may also be due to the entrance of new providers who have not been previously subject to the conduct of business regulations prevalent in the financial services industry. Deceptive and fraudulent business practices distort consumer decision-making, thereby affecting fair competition.

Third, consumers may be subject to inconsistent liability regimes owing to the different funding sources supporting m-payments. As we have seen in *Chapter 2*, m-payment transactions may be funded in different ways, and this has far-reaching consequences on how liability may be allocated. Lastly, there can be a lack of clarity with respect to dispute resolution frameworks applicable to m-payments. Owing to the numerous parties involved in providing the service, it is sometimes not clear who bears the primary responsibility for resolving consumer disputes. It is also unclear if ombudsman services ordinarily available to consumers dealing with traditional financial institutions will remain accessible where new non-traditional providers are involved.

Some of these issues are not novel because they are also present when traditional retail payment services are used. For example, information asymmetry is a problem with most financial products due to reasons discussed in *Chapter 3*. Also, consumers can be subjected to unfair terms when purchasing any financial product, and liability may be imposed unfairly if there are disputed payments. However, the consumer issues in innovative services like m-payments appear amplified due to two points. First, m-payments are still a burgeoning service in many jurisdictions, with authorities having to respond on the go to regulatory issues that arise. Authorities have had more time to understand and fashion dedicated regulatory responses to address consumer issues when established payment instruments and traditional financial institutions are involved. For instance, many countries impose disclosure requirements on financial institutions issuing traditional payment services to reduce information asymmetry. Regulations also exist in many jurisdictions to deter abusive contracting. For example, statutes like the United Kingdom's Consumer Credit Act 1974 contain provisions favouring consumers wishing to recover disputed payments if certain conditions are met.

Second, the novelty surrounding m-payments – new technology, new parties, and new business models heighten consumer concerns. The OECD explains a consequence of this novelty is that:

> Consumers may … have difficulty determining what their rights are, and how these may vary depending on factors, such as: i) the payment mechanism

6 Katalin Judit Cseres, *Competition Law and Consumer Protection* (Kluwer Law International 2005) p.213.

> used (e.g. payment charged on mobile phone bills vs. credit, debit or prepaid payment card); and ii) the device being used… . Determining which parties are responsible for addressing any problems that arise, the procedures for seeking redress, and the types of remedies that may be obtained, can also be problematic for consumers.[7]

These concerns question whether existing consumer protection arrangements remain robust and fit for purpose. Financial consumer protection frameworks are usually designed with traditional financial institutions and services in mind. This can mean that the direct application of these frameworks to innovative services like m-payments may not be straightforward.[8] This issue is even more significant when considering the complexities arising from the different business models driving m-payment services. For example, an m-payment service may be integral to another financial service such as a current account or designed as a separate and distinctive service.[9] In some cases, if non-bank service providers like mobile network operators (MNOs) allow consumers to reload their accounts as desired and keep funds in the account for indefinite periods, the m-payment services may be considered a hybrid of deposit and payment services, thereby combining concerns relevant to both distinctive services.[10] In this light, it is, thus, not surprising that there is an increased focus on the consumer issues associated with the use of m-payments. International bodies such as the OECD, the Financial Action Task Force (FATF), and the European Central Bank (ECB) have released policy guidelines on m-payments.[11] In countries like the United Kingdom and Canada, there have also been specific thematic reviews by regulatory authorities focusing on the consumer issues that arise in m-payments.[12]

7 OECD, 'Consumer Policy Guidance on Mobile and Online Payments' (2014) (OECD Digital Economy Papers, No. 236) <http://dx.doi.org/10.1787/5jz432cl1ns7-en> accessed 12 September 2021.

8 The World Bank Group, 'Good Practices for Financial Consumer Protection' (2017 edn, World Bank) p.177 <https://openknowledge.worldbank.org/handle/10986/28996> accessed 12 September 2021.

9 Ibid. p.173.

10 Ibid. p.175.

11 OECD, 'Policy Guidance for addressing Consumer Protection and Empowerment Issues in Mobile Commerce' (2008) OECD Digital Economy Papers, No. 149 <http://dx.doi.org/10.1787/230363687074> accessed 10 August 2021; The Financial Action Task Force (FATF), 'Guidance for a Risk-Based Approach: Prepaid Cards, Mobile Payments and Internet-Based Payment Services' (2013) <http://www.fatf-gafi.org/media/fatf/documents/recommendations/Guidance-RBA-NPPS.pdf> accessed 2 August 2021; European Central Bank, 'Recommendations for the Security of Mobile Payments: Draft Document for Public Consultation' (2013) <http://www.ecb.europa.eu/paym/cons/pdf/131120/recommendationsforthesecurityofmobilepaymentsdraftpc201311en.pdf> accessed 7 August 2021.

12 Financial Conduct Authority, 'Mobile Banking and Payments' (2014) <https://www.fca.org.uk/publication/thematic-reviews/tr14-15.pdf> accessed 5 September 2021; Steve Trites, Charles Gibney and Bruno Lévesque (2013 Research Division, Financial Consumer Agency of Canada)

The question, therefore, is what regulatory mechanisms can authorities use to deal with the highlighted consumer issues? This chapter seeks to address this question. As stated in the book's introduction, the typology of the relevant regulatory tools draw inspiration from the principles contained in the UN Guidelines for Consumer Protection[13] and the G-20 High-Level Principles of Consumer Financial Protection.[14] These tools are of general significance in the broader consumer policy discourse and of particular relevance to the financial services sector. This reflects the reality that in many countries, general consumer protection rules exist to tackle consumer issues irrespective of industry. Such general frameworks are often complemented by sector-specific regulations.

## 4.2 Provision of Information

In *Chapter 3*, we mentioned that there are significant information deficits in the financial services market. The most apparent solution to this problem is the provision of more information.[15] Most information interventions operate on the premise that consumers are better placed to make efficient decisions if they have adequate information on price, quality, and other terms relating to a product and its substitutes and/or complements.[16] However, obtaining and understanding information introduces transaction and processing costs.[17] A rational consumer is expected to make a cost-benefit analysis of the amount of search that he should engage in, and any decisions made will be based on the results of the information that is obtained.[18]

It is often stated that information has some of the characteristics of a public good. A public good is a commodity that individuals benefit from without contributing to the cost of its provision.[19] Gartner explains that 'their benefits generally cannot be made excludable and their consumption generally cannot be made

---

<https://www.canada.ca/content/dam/canada/financial-consumer-agency/migration/eng/resources/researchsurveys/documents/fcac_mobile_payments_consumer_protection_accessible_en.pdf>.

13 United Nations, 'Guidelines for Consumer Protection' (2016) <https://unctad.org/system/files/official-document/ditccplpmisc2016d1_en.pdf> accessed 5 September 2021.

14 G20, 'High-Level Principles on Consumer Financial Protection' (2011) <https://www.oecd.org/g20/topics/financial-sector-reform/48892010.pdf> accessed 5 September 2021.

15 Colin Scott and Julia Black, *Cranston's Consumers and the Law* (3rd edn, Butterworths 2000) p.35.

16 Iain Ramsay, 'Rationales for intervention in the Consumer Marketplace' (London, Office of Fair Trading 1984) cited in Iain Ramsay, *Consumer Law and Policy* (3rd edn, Hart Publishing 2012) p.50.

17 Anthony I. Ogus, *Regulation: Legal Form and Economic Theory* (Hart Publishing 2004) p.39.

18 Ramsay, 'Rationales for intervention in the Consumer Marketplace' (n 16) p.50.

19 Jeffery Atik, 'Complex Enterprises and Quasi-Public Goods' (1995) 16 University of Pennsylvania Journal of International Law 1, 5–6. It is important to note however that some organisations and businesses now monetise the supply of consumer information. e.g., The UK consumer group known as Which? provides information about some consumer products, which can only be accessed if consumers hold a paid subscription.

exclusive.'[20] This explains one of the reasons why there may be under-provision of product information in consumer markets. Thus, many remedial policies focus on providing market information or aiding the consumer in processing complex information.[21] Consumers may receive information from several sources and in different forms. They may receive information directly from regulators or firms mandated to do so either by law or in line with self-regulatory arrangements. They may also receive information from trade associations, independent consumer bodies and other intermediaries, including other consumers.[22] This book is interested in information that consumers can access as a result of information regulation initiatives. These include information provided by firms due to a regulatory obligation and those obtained through consumer education.

### *4.2.1 Mandatory Disclosures*

Mandatory disclosures are regulatory responses requiring financial services providers to supply certain standardised information.[23] This technique 'requires "the discloser" to give "the disclosee" information which the disclosee may use to make better decisions and to keep the discloser from abusing its superior position.'[24] Mandatory disclosures are usually classified as positive informational responses because they require that suppliers provide specific information.[25] Since consumers are faced with decision-making on complex financial transactions and services, it is reasonable to assume that more information will bolster consumer autonomy since they can make better decisions.[26]

Most disclosure regimes applying to financial services contain similar core requirements. They often explicitly identify:

i. Who should disclose (the regulated firm)
ii. To whom disclosures should be made (consumers transacting with the regulated firm)

20 David Gartner, 'Global Public Goods and Global Health' (2012) 22 *Duke Journal of Comparative & International Law* 303, 304.

21 Iain Ramsay, *Consumer Law and Policy* (3rd edn, Hart Publishing 2012) p.49.

22 See The Office of Communications (Ofcom), 'A Review of Consumer Information Remedies' (2013) p.9 <https://www.ofcom.org.uk/__data/assets/pdf_file/0033/91698/information-remedies.pdf> accessed 25 September 2021.

23 Paul Latimer and Phillip Maume, *Promoting Information in the Marketplace for Financial Services: Financial Market Regulation and International Standards* (Springer 2014) p.28.

24 Omri Ben-Shahar and Carl E. Schneider, 'The Failure of Mandated Disclosure' (2011) 159 *University of Pennsylvania Law Review* 647, 649.

25 Peter Cartwright, 'The Vulnerable Consumer of Financial Services: Law, Policy and Regulation' (Financial Services Research Forum 2011) p.29 <https://www.nottingham.ac.uk/business/who-we-are/centres-and-institutes/gcbfi/documents/researchreports/paper78.pdf> accessed 5 September 2021.

26 Ben-Shahar & Schneider, 'The Failure of Mandated Disclosure' (n 24) p.650.

iii. What should be disclosed (key information deemed necessary for making decisions)
iv. How the disclosure should be made (the medium, language, and format of disclosures)
v. When the disclosures should be made (e.g., shopping, pre-, and post-contractual stages)
vi. The consequences of failing to disclose

The end goal of mandatory disclosure regimes is to provide consumers with the accurate information necessary to make informed and independent decisions.[27] Therefore, it is assumed that disclosures will be beneficial if the information provided is clear, concise, accurate, and easily accessible.[28] Such information should also be comparable because this helps to ensure that consumers and competitors focus on both visible elements like fees and other less visible elements that significantly impact consumers.[29] This has a positive externality because standardised information makes consumer decision-making relatively cheaper and easier.[30] Standardised disclosures can also foster competition since consumers can access standardised information from competitors, enabling them to make optimal choices based on critical comparisons.[31] Comparison tools are sometimes adopted to further support consumers when comparing the attributes of alternatives. These tools may be provided by the government[32] or other third parties.[33]

The breadth of disclosures often depends on the nature of the transaction involved. Where payment services are provided continuously, the information disclosed is often more comprehensive than those disclosed for one-off payment transactions.[34] Apart from the content and breadth of disclosures, the timing is also

27 United Nations, 'Guidelines for Consumer Protection' (n 13) p.13.
28 G20, 'High-Level Principles on Consumer Financial Protection' (n 14) p.6.
29 Office of Fair-Trading, 'Personal Current Accounts in the UK' (2008 Market Study) cited in Anu Arora, 'Unfair Contract Terms and Unauthorised Bank Charges: A Banking Lawyer's Perspective' (2012) 1 *Journal of Business Law* 44, 54.
30 David Llewellyn, 'The Economic Rationale for Financial Regulation' (FSA Occasional Paper Series 1, 1999) p.33 <https://www.fep.up.pt/disciplinas/pgaf924/PGAF/Texto_2_David_Llewellyn.pdf> accessed 5 September 2021.
31 Colin Camerer, Samuel Issacharoff, George Loewenstein, et al., 'Regulation for Conservatives: Behavioural Economics and the Case for "Asymmetric Paternalism"' (2003) 151(3) *University of Pennsylvania Law Review* 1211, 1232; Ben-Shahar & Schneider, 'The Failure of Mandated Disclosure' (n 24) p.649.
32 For instance, the OECD notes that the Italian Ministry of Economic Development runs a website that provides comparative information on different products. OECD, 'Consumer Policy Toolkit' (2010) p.83 <http://www.oecd-ilibrary.org/governance/consumer-policy-toolkit_9789264079663-en> accessed 6 September 2021.
33 Such as suppliers (e.g., UK retailer Tesco, for instance, runs a price check website where its prices may be compared with that of its competitors), or independent businesses (such as Skyscanner and Uswitch) or consumer organisations (e.g., Australian consumer advocacy group 'CHOICE' conducts surveys that compare price). OECD, 'Consumer Policy Toolkit' (n 32) p.83.
34 World Bank Group, 'Good Practices for Financial Consumer Protection' (n 8) p.187.

significant. The OECD advocates that disclosures be made to consumers early in the transaction process.[35] This is expected to arm the consumer with enough information to determine if a transaction would be beneficial. Continuous ongoing disclosures are also essential[36] because they ensure that consumers know about changes that may affect their interests so that they can make necessary adjustments.[37]

In the context of m-payments, mandatory disclosures will serve some important functions. First, as already explained, they will help ensure that consumers focus not only on the price of the service but also on other important product features. Comprehensive disclosures cover important issues such as applicable charges, penalties, risks, liability rules, complaints/redress and termination procedures, privacy policies etc., attached to an m-payment service. Thus, such disclosures will provide a holistic picture of the service. Moreover, where competition focuses on more observable traits like price, there is the risk that in the long run, this may lead to a fall in quality which consumers may be unable to observe.[38] As we saw in *Chapter 3*, if consumers cannot establish the quality of financial products in advance, they might only be willing to pay an average price corresponding to the average expected quality. Providers of high-quality products will be unwilling to sell at that asking price and will withdraw from the market. The result of this is that the quality of products will decline as will the price consumers are willing to pay.[39]

Second, disclosures ensure that consumers have a realistic appreciation of what to expect from an m-payments service. Since an m-payment service will likely conform to the expectations built around disclosed information, it can empower consumers in ways that reduce the likelihood of suffering detriment.[40] For instance, disclosures will serve to increase consumer awareness of the risks involved in using m-payments. This point is critical in light of the security concerns that may arise where a mobile device is stolen or where a consumer downloads malicious software onto their mobile device. Consumers, due to lack of awareness, may fail to adopt available safeguards such as PINs, passwords, device lock features, or anti-virus software. Crowe et al. reason that these 'risky behaviours' will need to be changed if a consumer intends to add a wallet containing payment credentials to their mobile phone.[41] With access to information on risks, consumers can adjust

35 OECD, 'Report on Consumer Protection in Online and Mobile Payments' (n 7) p.7.

36 This covers information on recent charges, current balance, records of recent transactions, and changes in the terms of the contract.

37 Rhys Bollen, 'A Discussion of Best Practice in the Regulation of Payment Services: Part 2' (2010) 25(9) *Journal of International Banking Law and Regulation* 429, 434.

38 George Akerlof, 'The Market For "Lemons": Quality Uncertainty and the Market Mechanism' (1970) 84(3) *Quarterly Journal of Economics* 488.

39 i.e., the lemons problem; ibid.

40 Geraint Howells, 'The Potential and Limits of Consumer Empowerment by Information' (2005) 32(3) *Journal of Law & Society* 349, 355.

41 Marianne Crowe, Susan Pandy, et al., 'US Mobile Payments Landscape: 2 Years Later' (May 2013) p.14 <https://abnk.assembly.ca.gov/sites/abnk.assembly.ca.gov/files/mobile-payments-landscape-two-years-later.pdf> accessed 8 September 2021.

by adopting reasonable risk-mitigating practices when using the service. Such practices, for instance, could include putting passwords on mobile devices and payment applications to reduce the risk of unauthorised use.

Furthermore, if disclosures are streamlined and consistent throughout the m-payments industry, it can generate direct welfare gains for consumers since it will make it easier for consumers to compare and choose the platform that suits their needs.[42] Easing comparison between competing services will lead to a decrease in search and switching costs which should, in turn, encourage effective competition in price and quality.[43]

Providing these comprehensive disclosures may prove challenging owing to the technological constraints of mobile devices. These inherent technical limitations[44] include its relatively small screen, limited storage/memory capacity, battery life, and limited processing power.[45] In recognition of these limitations, Trites et al. suggest a need for specific provisions that support optimised disclosure statements on mobile devices.[46] While optimising disclosure statements on mobile devices can make information more accessible, there are other questions raised about the general effectiveness of mandatory disclosures that we shall consider in the next section.

#### *4.2.1.1 Limits of Mandatory Disclosures*

Significant criticisms lie against techniques like mandatory disclosures because they are thought to rest on 'false assumptions about how people live, think, and make decisions.'[47] Because mandatory disclosures are market-based, they seek to return the market as closely as possible to the perfect market ideal. This suggests that this technique relies on the neo-classical assumption that consumers are rational and are the best judges of their interests, who maximise their utility with the limited resources available.[48] As we saw in *Chapter 3*, this assumption has been questioned by behavioural research which shows that even with access to

42 Fariba Dehghan and Amirhossein Haghighi, 'E-money Regulation for Consumer Protection' (2015) 57(6) *International Journal of Law and Management* 610, 617.

43 Cseres (n 6) p.213; Stephen Lumpkin, 'Consumer Protection and Financial Innovation: A Few Basic Propositions' (2010) 1 *OECD Journal: Financial Market Trends* 117, 138.

44 Some of these limitations have been reduced by technological progress. For example, smartphones tend to have larger memory capacity, and other mobile devices such as tablets have larger screens than smaller mobile phones. Some of these devices also have improved battery life in comparison to earlier models.

45 OECD, 'Policy Guidance for addressing Consumer Protection and Empowerment Issues in Mobile Commerce (n 11); Financial Conduct Authority, 'Mobile Banking and Payments – Supporting an Innovative and Secure Market' (2013) <http://www.fca.org.uk/static/documents/thematic-reviews/tr13-06.pdf> accessed 13 September 2021.

46 Trites et al. (n 12) p.56.

47 Ben-Shahar & Schneider (n 24) p.651.

48 Iain Ramsay, 'Rationales for intervention in the Consumer Marketplace' (London, Office of Fair Trading 1984) cited in Ramsay, *Consumer Law and Policy* (n 21) p.47.

information, consumers tend to process such information incorrectly for several reasons, including the susceptibility to behavioural biases. Financial markets are complex, with enormous marketing material available and additional information obtained through disclosures may result in information overload which can create undesirable results. Owing to the preponderance of behavioural biases, rational decision-making cannot, therefore, be guaranteed with the provision of more information.

Moreover, various consumers react differently to information. What consumers choose to know and what they do with the knowledge acquired is heavily dependent on their intrinsic psychological attributes which result in varying outcomes.[49] Wealthier and better-educated consumers may arguably react to disclosures differently from poorer and uneducated consumers.[50] Cayne and Trebilcock submit that this is because disclosure regimes only benefit consumers who are psychologically and intellectually equipped to apply the information provided.[51] This leads Howells to conclude that those likely to take advantage of and benefit from information initiatives tend to be the more affluent, well-educated, middle-class consumers.[52] Thus, there remains an argument that vulnerable less-educated consumers may benefit the least from disclosure regimes.[53] This is an issue to be considered, in particular, by regulators in developing countries where m-payments are rapidly growing but a significant percentage of consumers remains uneducated and poor.[54]

One may argue in favour of this position because where a consumer is vulnerable owing to deficient literacy skills, mandated disclosures will have no significant effect in improving their decision-making.[55] This is especially so in the case of financial services like m-payments which will be used by a considerable percentage of uneducated users in developing countries. In light of this, commentators like Loewenstein et al. warn that disclosure regimes should not be used as an alternative to more targeted regulatory responses needed to improve consumer welfare.[56]

The complexity of financial transactions can also affect the efficacy of disclosures. For instance, the UK Consumers' Association[57] points out that many

49 David De Meza, Bernd Irlenbusch, and Diane Reyniers, 'Financial Capability: A Behavioural Economics Perspective' (Consumer Research Report N0.69, UK Financial Services Authority, 2008) p.2 <https://www.fca.org.uk/publication/research/fsa-crpr69.pdf> accessed 12 September 2021.

50 Howells (n 40) p.357.

51 David Cayne and Michael J Trebilcock, 'Market Considerations in the Formulation of Consumer Protection Policy' (1973) 23(4) *University of Toronto Law Journal* 396, 406.

52 Howells (n 40) p.357; Scott & Black (n 15) p.372.

53 Ben-Shahar & Schneider, (n 24) p.660.

54 In this context, 'uneducated' covers those lacking both basic education and financial education.

55 This will also be the case where a consumer lacks proficiency in the language that disclosures are made in.

56 George Loewenstein, Cass R Sunstein, Russell Golman, 'Disclosure: Psychology Changes Everything' (2014) 6 *Annual Review of Economics* 391, 412.

57 Also known as Which?

transactions that are perceived as a single package by consumers are in reality multi-faceted from a legal perspective.[58] This is especially so with the convergence of technology and industries.[59] Despite disclosure, consumers may erroneously believe these transactions are a single package when, in fact, they may be comprised of different contracts.[60] This is particularly significant in m-payments. Our discussions in *Chapter 2* show that m-payments may be structured in a way that involves multiple contracts and parties. Thus, consumers may be subject to several separate charges and risk allocation regimes of which they are unaware.[61]

Furthermore, consumers tend to use transaction value as a proxy for risk and are less likely to read the terms of a contract for small value purchases.[62] This may be significant in m-payments as one of its advantages is its potential for supporting micro-payments. It is possible that owing to the small amounts involved, consumers may not feel pressed to read disclosures on key contract terms. These issues corroborate the argument that authorities must look beyond disclosure regimes alone in dealing with consumer problems that may arise in m-payments.

Another argument against the over-reliance on disclosure regimes is the fact that such regimes are designed in a way that demands the active participation of the consumer. This is because they place a responsibility on consumers to respond to disclosures made.[63] This suggests that the success of disclosure regimes depends on consumers actively reacting to information disclosed. However, Scott and Black point out that one of the biggest problems with disclosures is ensuring that consumers are aware of and appreciate the significance of information disclosed and that they respond to it.[64] Thus, disclosure regimes may fail to record any remarkable change where a significant number of consumers do not respond as expected. The inability to predict consumer response to disclosure somewhat points to the fact that it is not sensible to rely solely on it.

Despite these shortcomings, disclosures are still important and may have more impact when combined with rising consumer education levels.[65] It might also be a helpful aid to authorities who can easily identify discrepancies between the substance of business claims and their actual performance when this is a matter for investigation.[66]

58 Which, 'Unfair Terms in Consumer Contracts: A New Approach' (Which? Consultation Response 2012) p.6 <https://www.dropbox.com/s/pwwhdr2sczykdqd/which-response-unfair-terms-in-consumer-contracts-a-new-approach-301590.pdf?dl=0> accessed 9 September 2021.

59 Ibid.

60 Ibid.

61 Which, 'Unfair Terms in Consumer Contracts: A New Approach' (n 58) p.6.

62 Ibid p.7.

63 Cartwright, 'The Vulnerable Consumer of Financial Services: Law, Policy and Regulation' (n 25) p.22.

64 Scott & Black (n 15) p.372.

65 Ibid. p.375.

66 Ibid.

### *4.2.2 Consumer Education*

Consumer education lies at the heart of consumer policy because it provides the avenue for empowering consumers with vital information on core aspects of a consumer protection regime including relevant legislation, redress procedures and agencies/organisations involved in enforcement.[67] Importantly, education initiatives provide information on the suitability of the products in the market which can assist consumers in making more appropriate decisions. The OECD defines financial education, more specifically to mean:

> the process by which financial consumers/investors improve their understanding of financial products, concepts and risks and, through information, instruction and/or objective advice, develop the skills and confidence to become more aware of financial risks and opportunities, to make informed choices, to know where to go for help, and to take other effective actions to improve their financial well-being.[68]

Financial education thus focuses on educating consumers on financial concepts 'with the explicit purpose of increasing knowledge and the skills, confidence, and motivation to use it.'[69] Since the 2007/2008 financial crisis, many national authorities have recognised that financial literacy is an essential life skill because of the rapid developments in financial markets due to deregulation and technological advancement, as well as demographic, economic, and policy changes.[70] In response, policymakers have committed to developing national financial education strategies.[71] A core aim of these strategies is to enhance financial literacy through nationally coordinated and tailored efforts.[72] Increased financial literacy is expected to enable consumers to have an 'appropriate perspective on the financial system.'[73] These initiatives also aim to ensure that consumers learn about the products on offer and how these meet their needs and expectations.[74] They also inform consumers about where to get further information and advice about financial products.[75] In addition, they alert consumers to the importance of shopping around for the best offerings.

67 United Nations 'Guidelines for Consumer Protection' (n 13) p.17.

68 OECD, 'Recommendation on Principles and Good Practices for Financial Education and Awareness' (2005) para.1.1 <https://www.oecd.org/finance/financial-education/35108560.pdf> accessed 13 September 2021.

69 Lauren E. Willis, 'Against Financial-Literacy Education' (2008) 94 *Iowa Law Review* 197, 202.

70 OECD & Russia's G20 Presidency, 'Advancing National Strategies for Financial Education' (2013) p.16 <https://www.oecd.org/finance/financial-education/G20_OECD_NSFinancialEducation.pdf> accessed 13 September 2021.

71 Ibid. pp.11, 17.

72 Ibid. p.11.

73 Peter Cartwright, *Banks, Consumers and Regulation* (Hart Publishing 2004) p.59.

74 Ibid.

75 Ibid p.60.

Overall, education initiatives aim to increase critical consumer awareness and action competence.[76] Unsurprisingly, it has been argued that mandated disclosures will be more effective as a regulatory tool if they are supported by more general attempts to educate consumers about the area in which they must make decisions.[77] Consequently, financial education remains an essential part of the disclosure and informed consent paradigm.[78] Armed with information obtained through awareness campaigns, consumers are expected to be actively involved in policing businesses and ensuring that markets remain effective.[79]

Being of a specialised nature, financial literacy initiatives rely on existing basic literacy[80] and numeracy skills provided under a broader consumer education framework.[81] The absence of these skills presents a fundamental obstacle to achieving financial consumer education objectives.[82] This deficiency may also lead to vulnerability as discussed in *Chapter 3*. However, basic literacy and numeracy skills will be insufficient in situations requiring some form of specialised knowledge. Studies confirm that financial literacy may not be substituted by general education or cognitive training (numeracy).[83] This is because financial literacy covers concepts which are different from those covered by basic education or pure mathematical abilities.[84]

General financial consumer education provides the bedrock for more targeted awareness campaigns covering specific financial products. Targeted efforts are an important way of raising consumer awareness about specific financial products on offer. In the context of m-payments, targeted financial literacy initiatives will serve two broad purposes. First, like disclosure, financial literacy will help reduce information gaps since it will serve as an additional gateway for providing information to consumers. This should, in turn, assist them in making better decisions. For instance, education initiatives can provide consumers with information on the

76 Jette Benn, 'Consumer Education between "Consumership" and Citizenship: Experiences from Studies of Young People' <http://www.mv.helsinki.fi/home/palojoki/english/nordplus/IJC_364%20Benn.pdf> accessed 10 September 2021.

77 Ben-Shahar & Schneider (n 24) p.732.

78 Ibid. p.667.

79 Ramsay, *Consumer Law and Policy* (n 21) p.95; Willis (n 69) p.201.

80 The OECD defines literacy as 'the capacity to understand, use and reflect critically on written information, the capacity to reason mathematically and use mathematical concepts, procedures and tools to explain and predict situations, and the capacity to think scientifically and to draw evidence-based conclusions' – Erik A Hanushek and Ludger Woessmann, 'The Case for Promoting Universal Basic Skills' in OECD, *Universal Basic Skills: What Countries Stand to Gain* (OECD Publishing Paris 2015) p.21 <https://www.oecd.org/education/universal-basic-skills-9789264234833-en.htm> accessed 12 September 2021.

81 Cartwright, *Banks, Consumers and Regulation* (n 73) pp.59–60.

82 Ibid. p.60.

83 Christian D Dick and Lena M Jaroszek, 'Knowing what not to do: Financial Literacy and Consumer Credit Choices' (2013) p.21 <https://www.fdic.gov/news/conferences/consumersymposium/2013/Papers/Jaroszek.pdf> accessed 13 September 2021.

84 Ibid. pp.15, 18.

comparable benefits of using m-payments which will allow them to decide if the service meets their needs and expectations.

Second, targeted m-payment literacy initiatives can increase consumer awareness of the service making them confident when choosing to adopt it.[85] It can further contribute towards shaping consumer expectations about the service. It may also empower them to adopt measures to mitigate any risks attached to the service. For instance, educating consumers on the privacy and security risks as well as the best practices for reducing these risks may enable them to make reasonable adjustments to reflect what they have learned.

Third, targeted literacy efforts may also address some of the shortcomings associated with mandatory disclosures. Mandatory disclosures operate on the premise that consumers will have the intellectual skills required to understand and to act on the information provided. However, as highlighted earlier, this is not always the case. Where consumers do not have the intellectual capacity to understand the significance of information, mandatory disclosures will be of limited help to them. A consumer protection diagnostic study conducted in Kenya sheds some light on the close link between disclosures and consumer education in m-payments.[86] According to the report, Safaricom, the MNO behind a popular m-payment service in Kenya called 'M-pesa,' was said to have adopted transparent pricing schedules with price tariffs being published and made available to users. To ensure that the service was affordable, this pricing schedule adopted a tiered fee model where users were charged according to the monetary value of a transaction.[87] Despite efforts made in disclosing the pricing schedule, Flaming et al. report that owing to literacy and numeracy concerns, some consumers did not fully understand the tariffs and entirely avoided transactions on the complex tariff tiers they could not understand.[88]

Consequently, most consumers made transactions in the lower tariff tiers and did not transact in other tariff tiers they considered more complex. Thus, although tariffs were disclosed transparently, there was still some confusion which indirectly limited the choices open to uneducated consumers who could only transact on less complex tariffs. While this raises questions about the effect of complex disclosures, it also reinforces the argument that only intellectually equipped consumers will benefit from disclosure regimes.[89]

85 OECD & Russia's G20 Presidency (n 70) p.18.

86 Mark Flaming, Alexander Owino, Katharine McKee, et al., 'Consumer Protection Diagnostic Study: Kenya' (2011) pp.12–13 <http://s3-eu-central-1.amazonaws.com/fsd-circle/wp-content/uploads/2015/08/30095758/11-02-22_Consumer_diagnostic_study.pdf> accessed 13 December 2018.

87 International Finance Corporation, 'M-Money Chanel Distribution Case – Kenya (Safaricom M-pesa)' (2010) p.5 <https://www.ifc.org/wps/wcm/connect/e0d2a9bd-16b9-4a36-8498-0b2650b9af8b/Tool%2B6.7.%2BCase%2BStudy%2B-%2BM-PESA%2BKenya%2B.pdf?MOD=AJPERES&CVID=jkCVy-n> accessed 10 September 2021.

88 Flaming et al. (n 86) pp.12–13.

89 Cayne & Trebilcock (n 51) p.406.

Financial education can empower consumers with the knowledge, skill and confidence needed to process and act meaningfully on the information provided.[90] Educating consumers on relevant themes in m-payments can help them put information disclosed in context. Where consumers can appreciate the content and context of disclosures, it is more likely that they will act on such disclosures. For instance, a consumer who is aware that third parties can access their m-payment applications through malicious software may pay more attention to disclosures on how to keep their device safe and how liability for unauthorised transactions will be apportioned.

Finally, having identified the importance of financial education, the next question that follows is who should be responsible for providing such education. National literacy strategies are in many cases initiated by public institutions with a mandate in such areas.[91] This may be a supervisory authority like the central bank or a government department like the finance ministry.[92] Cartwright points out that the implementation and coordination of such strategies may be a bit trickier as several stakeholders will be best placed to tackle different elements of financial illiteracy.[93] Financial illiteracy exists on a spectrum with one end covering consumers who lack basic literacy and numeracy skills.[94] Further along the spectrum are consumers who have the relevant literacy and numeracy skills but lack a satisfactory understanding of the financial system.[95] National authorities with a general education mandate will likely take on a more prominent role with assisting those consumers lacking the basic literacy and numeracy skills. For those consumers who have the required knowledge but lack a proper understanding of the financial system, financial regulators may play a more prominent role in supporting targeted financial education initiatives. This reflects the reality that in many countries the mandate to promote basic literacy skills and financial literacy may not always fall on the same regulatory authority. It appears that in many instances, improving basic numeracy skills will form part of a national education policy which may be outside the direct supervision of financial regulatory authorities.[96] However, this does not mean that efforts should not be coordinated between relevant agencies.

90 Toni Williams, 'Empowerment of Whom and for What? Financial Literacy Education and the New Regulation of Consumer Financial Services' (2007) 29(2) *Law & Policy* 226, 227.

91 OECD & Russia's G20 Presidency (n 70) p.25.

92 Ibid.

93 Cartwright, *Banks, Consumers and Regulation* (n 73) p.59.

94 Ibid.

95 Ibid. p.60.

96 For instance, the UK Financial Services Authority (whose powers have now been inherited by the Financial Conduct Authority) stated that its financial capability strategy did not extend towards teaching more general numeracy skills. It believed that it would be better led by the government; Financial Services Authority, 'Towards a National Strategy for Financial Capability' (2003) p.12 <https://financialliteracygroup.com/wp-content/uploads/2015/10/SM1-UK-National-Strategy.pdf> accessed 13 September 2021.

#### *4.2.2.1 Consumer Education and Matters Arising*

Benn asserts that the aim of consumer education is to increase critical consumer awareness and action competence.[97] Armed with information obtained through awareness campaigns, consumers are expected to be actively involved in policing businesses.[98] Consumers are thus seen as important actors who contribute to ensuring effective markets.[99] While this is the ideal, behavioural studies suggest that increased education and information disclosure may not necessarily result in increased rational choices.[100] It is thus unsafe to place undue weight on the outcomes that may be achieved through these policies.[101] However, there is an argument that financial consumer education may raise awareness about behavioural biases thereby putting consumers in a position to recognise and address impediments that limit rational decision-making. This view finds support with commentators like Posner who argues that it should not be impossible to educate people out of their irrationalities.[102] However, this position is countered by other commentators who insist that it is difficult and often unsuccessful to educate some behavioural biases away.[103]

Moreover, learning is also a complex developmental process 'conditioned by the distinctive values, assumptions, and interpretive repertoires by which individuals make sense of their worlds.'[104] Hence, what consumers choose to do with the knowledge acquired is heavily dependent on their intrinsic psychological attributes which result in varying outcomes. Thus, while Consumers A and B may have access to the same educative resources on m-payments, their use of the knowledge acquired will vary owing to different factors such as their past experiences, socialisation, decision context, personality, cognitive abilities, and values.[105] The consequence is that it is unsafe to place undue weight on the outcomes that may be achieved by educating m-payment consumers.

Commentators argue that education goals within contemporary consumer policy tend to view consumers as regulatory subjects rather than beneficiaries.[106] In this context, financial consumer education is seen as an attempt to reconstruct the consumer as a regulatory subject, a process often referred to as

97 Benn (n 76) p.1.
98 Ramsay, *Consumer Law and Policy* (n 21) p.95.
99 Ibid.
100 Nicola Howell, 'Developing a Consumer Policy for the 21st Century' (2008) 33(2) *Alternative Law Journal* 80, 82.
101 Ibid.
102 Richard A Posner, 'Rational Choice, Behavioural Economics, and the Law' (1997) 50 *Stanford Law Review* 1551, 1575.
103 Jeremy A Blumenthal, 'Emotional Paternalism' (2007) 35(1) *Florida State University Law Review* 1, 57–58; Willis (n 69) p.228.
104 Williams (n 90) p.247.
105 Willis (n 69) p.252.
106 Ramsay, *Consumer Law and Policy* (n 21) p.95; Williams (n 90) p.232.

'responsibilisation.'[107] This projects the financial consumer as a responsible self-regulating subject who does not look to the state for more help than it is willing to provide.[108] Pearson explains that the expectation that financial literacy will increase consumer competence involves both the responsibilisation and empowerment of the consumer.[109] In emphasising the responsibilisation of consumers, it is assumed that literate, well-informed consumers will exhaustively search the market, monitor firms attentively, switch providers effortlessly, and exercise their consumer power to drive out businesses that are incompetent, dishonest, and indifferent to their needs.[110] Williams points out that a serious implication of this approach is that in adopting financial literacy objectives, regulators run the risk of reversing the idea of market failure posing a risk to consumer welfare by focusing instead on the risk of consumer failure threatening the proper functioning of financial markets.[111]

Since financial education aims to enhance a consumer's ability to regulate themselves and other market actors, there is the concern that responsibilisation may justify the decision by regulators to commit fewer resources to patrol markets and to develop substantive regulatory responses to match products.[112] This approach may increase the risks that consumers of novel products are required to bear. For instance, practicality demands that consumers assume some responsibility in keeping their mobile device and personal security details safe when using m-payments. However, in allocating risk for security breaches, consumers may have more liability thrust on them on the basis that they have been well educated against such risks even if mitigating such risks may be outside their control. If regulators are convinced that disclosures and educative materials are available and sufficient, consumer detriment may be interpreted to be a result of poor decision-making by the consumer deflecting a need for a closer investigation into the practices of the industry or the fairness of the existing risk allocation rules.

Pearson also adds that the responsibilisation approach relies on voluntary compliance, persuasion, and imbibing values.[113] This may prove ineffective because it depends on the assumptions of rational choice which has been demystified by behavioural economists.[114] Regulators must thus acknowledge abundant research showing that consumer rationality has its limits. They must also realise that businesses are often involved in exploiting new ways in which consumer behaviour

107 Iain Ramsay, 'Consumer Law, Regulatory Capitalism and the "New Learning" in Regulation' (2006) 28(1) *Sydney Law Review* 9, 13.

108 Williams (n 90) p.233.

109 Gail Pearson, 'Reconceiving Regulation: Financial Literacy' (2008) 8 *Macquarie Law Journal* 45, 53.

110 Williams (n 90) p.236.

111 Ibid. p.243.

112 Willis (n 69) p.264.

113 Pearson (109) p.53.

114 Ibid. p.56.

departs from economic rationality.[115] From the foregoing, it is clear that relying solely on the outcomes of financial literacy initiatives may be insufficient in protecting m-payment consumers.

Given that m-payments operate with different business models, (banks lead some models while non-banks such as MNOs drive others) there remains a question as to which stakeholder should take on the responsibility of educating consumers. Failure to clarify this may generate some confusion since the industry may not always be motivated to provide information through financial education. This is because, as we previously pointed out, information has some of the characteristics of a public good. Because a person may enjoy the benefits of such goods without contributing to their production, there is often the danger that a free-rider problem may occur. As McVea explains, this means that

> those who are inclined to provide such goods may decide on balance not to do so, since others will free-ride on their efforts and there will be no readily effective way of charging these users for the costs associated with providing the good.[116]

What this suggests is that there may be some under-provision of information as some m-payment providers may shirk the responsibility of educating consumers in the hope that their competitors will take the lead.

Perhaps, educating consumers may be best achieved through a collaborative effort between regulators and m-payment service providers (whether a bank or MNO). While regulators are better placed to provide general financial education (which provides the foundation for targeted initiatives), they may not be in the best position to provide in-depth information on new products. This is because regulators suffer an information lag due to the rapid changes that occur in a market which places them in a constant race to keep up with these changes.[117] This information lag can affect the regulator's ability to understand the product well enough to provide timely education to consumers.[118] Consequently, it is argued that service providers will be better positioned to provide specific education on the innovative products they offer because they will likely have more expertise with the product having been involved in developing it. Moreover, in fulfilling their mandated disclosure responsibilities, many providers indirectly already produce educative materials. On this basis, it will be appropriate to place a positive obligation on institutions introducing m-payments to make reasonable efforts towards educating intended consumers.

115 Williams (n 90) p.244.

116 Harry McVea, 'Financial Services Regulation under the Financial Services Authority: A Reassertion of the Market Failure Thesis' (2005) 64(2) *Cambridge Law Journal* 413, 418–419.

117 Henry TC Hu, 'The Modern Process of Financial Innovation and the Vulnerability of a Regulatory Paradigm' (1989) 138(2) *University of Pennsylvania Law Review* 333, 340 cited in Willis (n 69) p.216.

118 Ibid.

## 4.3 Withdrawal Rights and Cooling-Off Periods

What happens where a consumer signs up for a financial product and subsequently, upon further reflection, changes their mind about the suitability of the service? Regulatory intervention in such situations can come in the form of cooling-off periods and withdrawal rights. Cooling-off periods represent legally prescribed time frames within which consumers may reconsider their transactional decisions. Camerer et al. explain that cooling-off periods can take two forms.[119] One form could compel consumers to delay action until after a timeframe elapses.[120] Another form could permit immediate decisions but render them reversible during a specific timeframe.[121] This book focuses on the latter, i.e., where cooling-off periods represent a timeframe within which a consumer may exercise a right to withdraw from a contract without incurring any penalty.

One must note that cooling-off periods and the attendant withdrawal rights are seen as a deviation from the contract law principle of *pacta sunt servanda*[122] which suggests that a contract is binding on the parties once it is concluded.[123] Under traditional contract law, contracts can only be set aside under exceptional circumstances.[124] These often include circumstances where the true consent of a party is lacking owing to wrong assumptions of fact or the use of improper pressure by the other party.[125] Contracts may also be set aside where there has been defective performance or non-performance by a party.[126] However, where a consumer exercises withdrawal rights during a set cooling-off period, they need not provide any reason or prove exceptional circumstances to justify cancelling the contract.[127]

Since cooling-off periods and withdrawal rights are a significant deviation from traditional contractual principles, it is often argued that such rights should be placed within carefully circumscribed policy justifications.[128] Smit reports that two explanations support cooling-off periods: they provide protection against a lack of 'psychological strength' and a lack of 'informational strength.'[129] Consumers lack psychological strength when they cannot exercise their autonomy because they

119 Camerer et al. (n 31) p.1240.

120 e.g., where a person signs a contract to purchase a good but must wait out a specific period before they can take possession of it. Ibid. p.1240.

121 Ibid.

122 Latin for 'promises must be kept.'

123 Caroline Cohen, 'The Contract Law Principle of Pacta Sunt Servanda and Behavioural Economics Literature in Relation to Justifications for the European Consumer's Right of Withdrawal under Directive 2011/83/EC' (2016) 2 *Exeter Student Law Review* 13, 14.

124 Jan M Smits, 'Rethinking the Usefulness of Mandatory Rights of Withdrawal in Consumer Contract Law: The Right to Change Your Mind' (2011) 29 *Pennsylvania State International Law Review* 671, 673.

125 Ibid.

126 Ibid.

127 Ibid.

128 Ramsay, *Consumer Law and Policy* (n 21) pp.102, 209.

129 Smits (n 124) p.676.

are subject to aggressive and high-pressure sales such as doorstep sales where a consumer is taken by surprise and their privacy invaded.[130] Cooling-off periods allow consumers in such circumstances to re-evaluate the appropriateness of their transactional decisions when the immediate pressure from the seller is no longer at play.

In other circumstances, consumers lack informational strength due to information asymmetries. As we saw in *Chapter 3*, it may be because it is impossible to evaluate the product before purchase or because the nature of the transaction (e.g., distance sales) is such that consumers can only rely on limited information and the assumed credibility of the seller before making a purchase. In such circumstances, cooling-off periods arguably provide consumers with the opportunity to seek out additional information during the prescribed time allowed.[131] With access to better information about a product (and its alternatives) during this period, consumers may withdraw from contracts already entered into if they are not optimal.[132] In this context, cooling-off periods and withdrawal rights are critical tools that support disclosure regimes in financial markets. These tools will be of obvious benefit to consumers who decide to subscribe to m-payment services.

Cooling-off periods and withdrawal rights are frequently supported by those who believe that market-based solutions are the appropriate responses to consumer detriment. This is because they avoid high-handed interference with consumer choice, place relatively little burden on business and require low resource commitment to enforcement.[133] Cooling-off periods and withdrawal rights can also reduce switching costs and therefore reinforce consumer choice and competition.[134] Also, knowing that consumers can cancel transactions without penalty incentivises traders to provide goods of reasonable quality.[135] These tools can also be interpreted as a distributive effort because they can aid vulnerable consumers who are at risk of making poor decisions due to inaccurate information or high-pressure sales. In this context, it appears appropriate for the party in a stronger position, i.e., the trader to bear the loss if the consumer withdraws from the contract.[136]

These tools, however, have some drawbacks. First, they may impose costs upon traders and consumers. For traders, there are costs which derive from the uncertainty and delay attached to a transaction as a trader can only be sure that a

130 Ibid.

131 Ramsay, *Consumer Law and Policy* (n 21) p.102.

132 Ibid. pp.102, 209.

133 Geraint Howells and Stephen Weatherill, *Consumer Protection Law* (2nd edn, Ashgate 2005) pp.64–65.

134 Shmuel I Becher, 'Unintended Consequences and the Design of Consumer Protection Legislation' (2018) 93 *Tulane Law Review* 105, 126.

135 Ibid.

136 Cartwright, *Banks, Consumers and Regulation* (n 73) p.26.

sale is firmly completed at the end of the cooling-off period.[137] Naturally, traders pass on these costs to all consumers (including those with no preference for withdrawal rights) in the form of higher prices.[138] Also consumers must themselves incur other costs to take advantage of cooling-off periods and the accompanying withdrawal rights. For instance, to make the best use of cooling-off periods, consumers will also incur search costs in looking up information on alternatives and substitutes.[139] They may also underestimate other costs in terms of anxiety and out-of-pocket expenses.[140] Like other regulatory costs, these additional costs will mainly affect those who least can afford it.[141]

Second, cooling-off periods may only benefit consumers who are relatively well-informed and willing to take advantage of them.[142] Wilhelmsson points out that cooling-off periods fit within consumer regimes that emphasise helping consumers protect themselves and their role in disciplining the market through their actions.[143] He explains that this approach can be dangerous because measures requiring protection based on consumer action may, in fact, reinforce injustice as the vulnerable consumer will be the least likely to take action.[144] Thus, while cooling-off periods can be useful, some vulnerable consumers who need the remedy may not benefit from its protection. This is reminiscent of earlier criticism levelled against consumer policy approaches that rely on the reponsibilisation of consumers.

Even where consumers are not vulnerable, they may generally overestimate their ability and willingness to exercise their rights to withdraw. Cognitive limitations can affect consumers' use of withdrawal rights within the cooling-off period. Status quo bias and inertia are major culprits in this context. Becher and Zarsky point out that

> rescinding a contract requires action. But people tend to maintain the status quo and remain passive, even if by doing so, they fail to maximise utility.

137 Anthony Duggan & Iain Ramsay, 'Front-End Strategies for Improving Consumer Access to Justice' in Michael J. Trebilcock, Lorne Sossin & Anthony Duggan (eds), *Middle Income Access to Justice* (University of Toronto Press 2012) p.112.

138 Kirsten Thommes, Michael Faure, and Klaus Heine, 'The Internal Market and the Consumer: What Consumers Actually Choose' (2014) 21 *Columbia Journal of European Law* 47, 70

139 Cartwright, 'The Vulnerable Consumer of Financial Services: Law, Policy and Regulation' (n 25) p.23.

140 Shmuel I Becher and Tal Z Zarsky, 'Open Doors, Trap Doors, and the Law' (2011) 74 *Law & Contemporary Problems* 63, 80.

141 Ibid.

142 Citizens Advice, 'Can You Cancel It' (CAB Evidence Briefing) cited in Cartwright, 'The Vulnerable Consumer of Financial Services: Law, Policy and Regulation' (n 25) p.36.

143 Thomas Wilhelmsson, *Twelve Essays on Consumer Law and Policy* (University of Helsinki 1996) p.203 cited in Cartwright, 'The Vulnerable Consumer of Financial Services: Law, Policy and Regulation' (n 25) p.36.

144 Ibid.

> Even when choosing an action, they often procrastinate and postpone what has to be done.[145]

Procrastination can, in turn, reinforce the endowment effect. The endowment effect causes consumers to attach additional value to things they own or possess.[146] This is often fuelled by an aversion to loss, i.e., consumers feel more strongly about losing or giving up something than gaining something.[147] Hence, the longer they procrastinate, the more likely it is that the endowment will set in. Ultimately, this leads to a situation where the consumer puts off action and inadvertently misses out on exercising their withdrawal rights during the cooling-off period.[148]

Finally, there is the argument that cooling-off periods might only be effective where the a key problem is that the consumer lacks sufficient time to assess all the information provided.[149] Where the problem relates to other issues such as a lack of transparency in the information provided, cooling-off periods may make no difference because the consumer may still be confused or misled by it, even if they have more time to evaluate it.[150]

## 4.4 The Regulation of Business Conduct

When consumers contract for financial services like m-payments, it is expected that they will be treated fairly at all stages of their relationship with the service provider.[151] In reality, consumers are vulnerable to several forms of unconscionable conduct at different stages of the contractual process. For example, there is the possibility that consumers may be exploited through advertising which misleads them on the suitability of the service or service provider. They may also unduly influence vulnerable consumers or adopt other unconscionable practices to secure a contract. For instance, some consumers may be victims of high-pressure sales where agents of service providers or even bank representatives offer them m-payment contracts unexpectedly and at short notice in situations where they feel compelled to sign up for the service. Providers may also adopt the use of unfair contract terms, which place consumers at a disadvantage. All these circumstances confirm that an important strategy in protecting financial services consumers involves regulating the conduct of the institutions that they deal with.

145 Becher & Zarsky (n 140) p.81.

146 Keith M Marzilli Ericson and Andreas Fuster, 'The Endowment Effect' (National Bureau of Economic Research Working Paper Series 2013) p.2 <https://www.nber.org/system/files/working_papers/w19384/w19384.pdf> accessed 13 September 2021.

147 Ibid.

148 Becher & Zarsky (n 140) p.81.

149 Competition and Markets Authority (CMA), 'Guidance on the Unfair Terms Provisions in the Consumer Rights Act 2015' (July 2015) para.5.20.6. <https://www.gov.uk/government/uploads/system/uploads/attachment_data/file/450440/Unfair_Terms_Main_Guidance.pdf> accessed 23 August 2021.

150 Ibid.

151 The World Bank Group, 'Good Practices for Financial Consumer' (n 8) p.193.

Regulation of these practices is imperative and premised on preserving fair competition and protecting market participants, especially consumers.[152]

Financial services consumers often benefit from broader regulatory efforts to control unfair business practices irrespective of the sector involved. They also benefit from more specific conduct rules applying to the financial services sector. Often contained in legislation and regulatory guidance, these rules target the conduct of providers and how they impact consumers.[153]

In this section, we examine three areas involving the regulation of business conduct relevant to financial services. First, we look broadly at the regulation of commercial practices that can be deemed unfair and unconscionable. Second, we consider the regulation of contract terms. Finally, we consider the regulation of false and misleading information. It is necessary to make a few points about the inclusion of the last category (false and misleading information) in this section. The regulation of false/misleading information can be seen as an information regulation initiative closely related to mandatory disclosures discussed earlier in this chapter. However, one must note that thematically, regulatory tools sometimes overlap, making it difficult to perfectly separate discussions on such tools. The regulation of false/misleading information manifests such difficulty. While it can be classified as an information regulatory initiative, it can also be interpreted as forming an important part of the regulation of unfair business practices aimed at exploiting consumer decision-making. Regulatory responses preventing the use of false/misleading information are often couched as negative informational responses which do not easily fit with the positive nature of mandatory disclosures. Hence the discussion on regulating false and misleading information has been included in this section.

### *4.4.1 Regulating Unfair Commercial Practices*

There is a thin line between smart and sharp commercial practices.[154] Where commercial practices unfairly affect consumer decision-making, regulatory intervention often becomes necessary. These unfair practices can occur at the formation, performance, or enforcement of consumer transactions.[155] They include and are not restricted to deceptive advertising, providing false and misleading

152 Antonina B Engelbrekt, 'An end to fragmentation? The Unfair Commercial Practices Directive from the Perspective of New Member States from Central and Eastern Europe' in Stephen Weatherill and Ulf Bernitz, *The Regulation of Unfair Commercial Practices under EC Directive 2005/29: New Rules and New Techniques* (Bloomsbury Publishing 2007) 54.

153 Norton Rose Fulbright, 'Beyond Law: Understanding the Scope of Conduct Regulation' (2014) <https://www.nortonrosefulbright.com/-/media/files/nrf/nrfweb/imported/beyond-law-understanding-the-scope-of-conduct-regulation.pdf> accessed 13 September 2021.

154 Geraint Howells, Hans-Wolfgang Micklitz, Thomas Wilhelmsson, 'Towards a Better Understanding of Unfair Commercial Practices' (2009) 51(2) *International Journal of Law and Management* 69, 69.

155 Ramsay, *Consumer Law and Policy* (n 21) p.152.

information, omitting material information, high-pressure sales, and the unfair use/enforcement of contractual terms.[156] Apart from preventing the exploitation of all consumers, the regulation of unfair commercial practices is often justified by the need to protect vulnerable consumers specifically.[157] Persons who are vulnerable for reasons such as age, mental disability, and poverty may be more susceptible to certain unfair commercial practices. In addition, the regulation of unfair commercial practices is also linked to regulating unfair competition. This is based on the premise that firms that do not get involved in perpetuating unfair commercial practices should not be put at a disadvantage.[158] Thus, upholding honesty and integrity in the marketplace often justifies regulatory oversight.[159]

With retail payment services, many unfair commercial practices can be traced to the provider's need to make their products 'sticky.'[160] This means that providers put in mechanisms that ensure that consumers continue using their products.[161] While efforts to retain consumers are not necessarily against the consumer's interest, they can easily become disadvantageous when they are supported by mechanisms which make it difficult for consumers to switch to other providers.[162] The need to retain consumers may lead to practices such as conditional sales where the provision of a product is subject to certain conditions, tying – where two or more products are sold together[163] and pure bundling where certain products can only be purchased with other products, all of which can be unfair.[164]

M-payment services may also be susceptible to other unfair commercial practices. For instance, where m-payments are provided by financial institutions, unfair practices may take the form of cross-selling where consumers are forced by their financial services provider to buy additional services from another provider with which it has an exclusive agreement.[165] Thus, a financial service provider in exclusive partnership with a particular mobile network may indirectly force consumers to use the MNO's services. Consumers may also be offered an insurance package with certain firms to cover losses such as the theft of mobile devices. M-payment consumers may also be subject to a practice called 'cramming' where unexpected charges are made to their phone bills by third parties for purchases they did not authorise, products they did not receive, or products with a higher

156 Ibid.
157 Ibid, p.152.
158 Ibid. p.77.
159 Ibid. p.71.
160 The World Bank Group, 'Good Practices for Financial Consumer Protection' (n 8) p.195.
161 Ibid.
162 Ibid.
163 This occurs where two or more products are sold together. Loreta Poro, 'Unfair Commercial Practices in Financial Services: Is the EU Legal Framework Sufficient to Protect Consumers?' (2014) 29(7) *Journal of International Banking Law and Regulation* 422, 425.
164 Ibid. These practices also raise competition law concerns, a discussion of which is outside the scope of this book.
165 Poro (n 163) p.425.

cost than the consumer was led to believe.[166] The possibility of m-payment service providers adopting such practices makes regulatory intervention necessary to ensure that m-payment consumers are equipped for rational market behaviour and that businesses are induced to behave responsibly.[167]

Unfair commercial practices may be deterred by private law mechanisms such as litigation. However, litigation is not cost-effective where losses are small individually but significant in aggregate.[168] This may be worsened in situations such as where 'fly-by-night' traders are involved. In such cases, market discipline tools like reputation and repeat sales will be ineffective in providing adequate redress and litigation will also be challenging to pursue. All these problems will be magnified where the sharp practices are cross-border.[169] Additional problems consumers face may be traced to other inadequacies of private law remedial mechanisms. For instance, in the absence of a direct contract, advertising claims may only be successful where a collateral contract[170] exists or where Common Law remedies for the tort of deceit or negligent misstatements are available.[171] Owing to these factors, it may become desirable to have some form of public regulation in this area.

Public regulation may involve passing targeted legislation to discourage the use of unfair commercial practices. Such legislation may prohibit certain practices outright (e.g., the door-to-door selling of financial services) and may have others regulated (e.g., distance selling of financial services). A selected government agency may also be conferred with powers to monitor and sanction firm behaviour and to make specific regulations targeted at certain markets.[172] The scope of the agency's mandate may also be defined by broad standards set out in relevant legislation. Such broad standards usually give the enforcing agency the flexibility needed to respond to the ever-changing commercial landscape where certain practices that were not previously envisaged become a problem.[173]

Enforcement of regulatory standards against unfair practices varies in approach. While one approach favours public enforcement where specific public agencies deal with complaints lodged by individuals or organisations, another emphasises private enforcement where aggrieved parties may launch civil claims for damages and/or injunctions.[174] In reality, many jurisdictions combine both approaches.

166 OECD, 'Consumer Policy Guidance on Mobile and Online Payments' (n 7) p.19.

167 Howells et al., 'Towards a Better Understanding of Unfair Commercial Practices' (n 154) p.71.

168 Ramsay, *Consumer Law and Policy* (n 21) p.153.

169 Ibid.

170 See *Warlow v. Harrison* [1859] 1 E & E 309; *Barry v. Davies* [2001] EWCA Civ 235. Where a contract exists, remedies for negligent misrepresentation may apply.

171 Ramsay, *Consumer Law and Policy* (n 21) p.139.

172 Ibid. p.155.

173 Ibid.

174 British Institute of Commercial and Comparative Law, 'Unfair Commercial Practices: An analysis of the existing national laws on unfair commercial practices between business and consumers in the new Member States' (2005) pp.12–13. <http://www.biicl.org/files/882_general_report

### *4.4.2 Regulating Contract Terms*

#### *4.4.2.1 Classical Theory and Freedom of Contract*

The classical theory of contract law supports the enforcement of contracts that are freely entered into.[175] This is based on the assumption that parties negotiate contracts on equal terms.[176] Freedom of contract allows parties to choose how they wish to allocate the obligations and risks arising from their agreements – terms that are freely adopted cannot be described as 'unfair' because they represent the voluntary wishes of the parties.[177] It thus follows that where a contract is freely negotiated, it must be enforced even if it is substantively unfair.[178] However, this theory is unsustainable in reality.[179] The term 'unfair' suggests that there may be some value judgement about the content of a bargain which is divorced from the perceptions of the parties at the time of contracting.[180] This implies that negotiation over terms is not simply a matter of contractual freedom, as suggested by the classical theory.[181] In reality, many factors obscure the purity of the individual bargain and contribute to the inability of parties to make informed choices.[182] Contractual parties do not often have equal bargaining power or complete knowledge of the issues at stake. The result is that some contractual terms may be unfair due to this power asymmetry.[183] Thus, the justification for controlling unfair terms may lie in the perceived imbalance between supplier and consumer.[184] In essence, legislating against unfair terms recognises that a balance must be drawn between

_unfair_commercial_practices_new_member_states%5Bwith_dir_table_and_new_logo%5D .pdf> accessed 13 September 2021.

175 See Patrick S Atiyah, *The Rise and Fall of Freedom of Contract* (Clarendon Press 1979) pp.1–7.

176 Alexandra Sims, 'Unfair Contract Terms: A New Dawn in Australia and New Zealand?' (2013) 39(3) *Monash University Law Review* 739, 742.

177 Howells & Weatherill, *Consumer Protection Law* (n 133) p.261.

178 Cartwright, *Banks, Consumers and Regulation* (n 73) p.153. *See Printing & Numerical Registering Co v. Sampson (*1875) LR 19 Eq. 462 where in restating this cardinal principle of contract law, Sir George Jessel MR famously stated that '*[I]f there is one thing which more than another public policy requires it is that men of full age and competent understanding shall have the utmost liberty of contracting and that their contracts entered into freely and voluntarily shall be held sacred and shall be enforced by Courts of Justice*' [p.465].

179 Under the classical theory, contracts can only be challenged on procedural grounds. However, there is an argument that procedural unfairness is a proxy for substantive unfairness. Courts are known to address substantive issues under the guise of procedural unfairness because they do not want to be seen as interfering with freedom of contract. Cartwright, *Banks, Consumers and Regulation* (n 73) p.153.

180 Howells & Weatherill, *Consumer Protection Law* (n 133) p.261.

181 Atiyah (n 175) provides important historical insight into the foundations of the doctrine of freedom of contract. He also contends that certain propositions canvassed in supporting the doctrine may have been based on certain misconceptions about the age of *laissez-faire* popularised by AV Dicey's *Law and Public Opinion*. See pages 231–237.

182 Howells & Weatherill, *Consumer Protection Law* (n 133) p.261.

183 Sims (n 176) p.742.

184 Howells & Weatherill, *Consumer Protection Law* (n 133) p.261.

freedom of contract and protection of contracting parties.[185] Policy responses to unfair contract terms are thus targeted at ensuring that consumers are protected from unfair provisions hidden in contractual small print, especially when those terms are contained in standard form contracts.

### *4.4.2.2 Standard Term Contracts*

Standard term contracts are contracts that have been drawn up in advance by the supplier and presented on a take-it-or-leave-it basis.[186] These contracts are common because they reduce the cost of negotiating individual contracts.[187] They also allow for reasonable expectations between parties if particular terms are used consistently in a given industry.[188] Accordingly, it is not surprising that these contracts are also popular within the m-payments market.

Standard form contracts used in retail payment services often identify the party proposing to contract on standard terms (usually the payment service provider) and includes the main features of the service being provided.[189] These features include (i) the applicable costs, fees and charges that may arise and how they are calculated, (ii) the key rights and responsibilities of the contractual parties (i.e., payment service provider and consumer), (iii) the penalties and remedies available to the parties, (iv) dispute resolution procedures, (v) liability rules and procedures for resolving unauthorised, fraudulent, and mistaken transactions, and (vi) applicable transaction restrictions and balance limits[190] – altogether, these pieces of information form the terms of the contract proposed.

Since standard form contracts are contracts of adhesion,[191] they often put consumers in a position where they have risks and liabilities imposed on them that sellers do not wish to bear.[192] It could be argued that when confronted with unfair terms contained in standard form contracts, consumers have the choice of rejecting them and opting for alternatives with fairer terms.[193] Zumbo however, contends that in reality, the consumer might have 'no choice' at all because other

185 Arora (n 29) p.45.

186 Aonghus McClafferty, 'Effective Protection for the E-Consumer in light of the Consumer Rights Directive?' (2012) 11 *Hibernian Law Journal* 85, 89.

187 Chris Willett, *Fairness in Consumer Contracts: The Case of Unfair Terms* (Ashgate Publishing Ltd 2007) p.16.

188 Howells & Weatherill, *Consumer Protection Law* (n 133) p.90.

189 The World Bank Group, 'Good Practices for Financial Consumer Protection' (n 8) p.187.

190 Ibid.

191 i.e., they are contracts written by one contracting party and presented to the other party on a take it or leave it basis: Roger Miller, Gaylord A Jentz, *Business Law Today: The Essentials* (Cengage Learning 2007) p.246.

192 Friedrich Kessler, 'Contracts of Adhesion: Some thoughts about Freedom of Contract' (1943) 43 *Columbia Law Review* 629.

193 Sims (n 176) p.742; McClafferty (n 186) p.90.

providers may have similar terms in the standard term contracts they offer.[194] Even where some providers offer favourable terms, they may be forced to reduce the quality of services/goods offered in order to compete with competitors and meet their commercial targets.[195]

Recognising the power imbalance where standard term contracts are used, regulatory intervention often seeks to ensure that (i) the terms offered in such contracts are fair, (ii) the terms are disclosed to consumers early in the contractual process, and (iii) the terms are presented in a manner that consumers can understand.

#### 4.4.2.3 Fairness

Where standard term contracts are used, regulators often require that the terms be disclosed to consumers so that they can make informed decisions. For example, in financial services markets, providers are often mandated to furnish consumers at the pre-contractual stage with a key facts statement summarising the main terms and conditions to aid comprehension and comparability.[196] However, the mere disclosure of the contract terms does not resolve the issue of the provider having a stronger bargaining power than the consumer. Hence, authorities often go a step further by putting in place rules which specifically aim to deter the use of unfair contract terms. Fairness in this context applies to both the form and substance of contract terms.[197]

In addressing the use of unfair terms, authorities may adopt several approaches. One approach is to pass legislation that outrightly invalidates specific contract terms that are considered unfair.[198] A variant of this approach would be to put certain terms on a grey list, placing the onus on suppliers to rebut the presumption of unfairness. The main advantage of invalidating specific terms is that it creates certainty.[199] This approach has, however, been criticised for being relatively inflexible in dealing with unanticipated terms.[200] Also, it can leave room for the continued use of unfair terms since suppliers can exploit the use of disingenuous drafting to avoid falling within the scope of specific terms blacklisted.

194 Frank Zumbo, 'Dealing with Unfair Terms in Consumer Contracts: Is Australia Falling Behind?' (2005) 13 *Trade Practices Law Journal* 70, 71 cited in Sims (n 176) p.742. It may be argued that choosing not to buy at all is also a choice. In fact, Posner argues that a purchaser who is offered a printed contract on a take-it-or-leave-it basis has a choice because he can refuse to sign it knowing that if better terms are possible, another seller would offer it to him; Richard A Posner, *Economic Analysis of the Law* (Little Brown and Company 1973) p.85.

195 Michael Schillig, 'Inequality of Bargaining Power Versus a Market for Lemons: Legal Paradigm Change and the Court of Justice's Jurisprudence on Directive 93/13 on Unfair Contract Terms' (2008) 33(3) *European Law Review* 336, 341.

196 The World Bank Group, 'Good Practices for Financial Consumer Protection' (n 8) p.190.

197 Competition and Markets Authority (n 149) p.23.

198 Scott & Black (n 15) p.96.

199 Ibid.; an example is found in Part 1, Schedule 2 of the UK Consumer Rights Act 2015.

200 Scott & Black (n 15) p.97.

A second approach requires that the terms in standard form contracts satisfy a test of good faith.[201] This approach is justified on the premise that the broad standards adopted can cope with unforeseen situations.[202] Authorities are also given more flexibility, unlike where legislation only focuses on an exhaustive list of blacklisted terms.[203] To have a successful impact, Scott and Black argue that a broad standard must focus on the situation at the inception of a transaction and its subsequent performance. In other words, the focus ought to be on both procedural and substantive fairness.[204] Authorities may also decide to combine the aforementioned approaches. This appears to be a favoured method as it allows authorities to enjoy the advantages of both approaches – certainty and flexibility.

A third approach may see authorities requiring that standard form contracts are approved before they are adopted for use by providers[205] It is submitted that this approach may create some form of uncertainty and inconsistency where there are no clear guidelines on what terms will be deemed problematic. It might also put a strain on regulatory authorities which will be expected to look at multiple contracts from different sectors to approve them before use. This process may also slow down business endeavours while increasing costs.[206]

Regulatory responses targeting unfair terms will be more meaningful if supported by effective monitoring and enforcement mechanisms.[207] To this end, legislation may entrust a selected public agency with the authority to monitor consumer contracts and to take legal actions to challenge offending terms being used.[208] Private individuals and consumer organisations may also be empowered to report such terms to the enforcing agency and/or to maintain independent actions challenging them.

### *4.4.2.4 Transparency*

Recognising that contract terms may be couched in lengthy technical terms, which may be difficult for consumers to understand, the idea behind transparency is for contract terms to be put in simple, comprehensible language which consumers may easily understand. Transparency also requires that terms with far-reaching implications be brought to the notice of the consumer.

201 Ibid.
202 Scott & Black (n 15) p.98.
203 Ibid.
204 Scott & Black (n 15) p.99.
205 For example, under Israel's Standard Contract Law (1982), businesses could apply to a Standards Contracts Tribunal to have restrictive terms in standard form contracts approved; S Deutch, 'Controlling Standard Contracts – The Israeli Version' (1985) 30 McGill LJ 458 cited in Scott & Black (n 15) pp.101–102.
206 OECD, *China in the World Economy: An OECD Economic and Statistical Survey, Volume 1* (Kogan Page Publishers, 2003) p.285.
207 OECD, Consumer Policy Toolkit (n 32) p.99.
208 Scott & Black (n 15) p.99.

In principle, enhanced transparency can incentivise providers to adopt fairer terms since consumers have an increased awareness of the applicable contractual terms.[209] However, Willett points out that transparency alone does not always translate to better protection from unfair terms. Thus, he argues that a term should not be enforceable simply because it is transparent; it must also be procedurally and substantively fair.[210] This view is supported by authors such as Sims, who reason that the inability of transparency to legitimise an unfair term is justified on the basis that most consumers do not read contracts.[211] Even where they read, she contends that it is not always pragmatic for them to read all the contract terms.[212] She further points out that with standard form contracts offered on a 'take-it-or-leave-it' basis, consumers do not have the opportunity to negotiate to change the terms.[213] As we shall see subsequently, jurisdictions like the United Kingdom favour this line of thought (i.e., that transparency is incapable of legitimising an unfair term).

### *4.4.3 Regulating False and Misleading Information*

An important point which should be noted is that poor consumer decision-making may not always be the effect of behavioural biases. It may result from the content of and manner in which information is provided. As stated earlier, mandatory disclosures are positive informational responses because they place an obligation on providers to disclose specific pieces of information. While being subject to mandatory disclosure regimes, financial services providers may leave out vital information not explicitly required to be disclosed, even if such information may significantly impact consumer decision-making. In other scenarios, information may be disclosed in a way that deceives or misrepresents the true characteristics of a financial service. Businesses are also known to use advertising/marketing campaigns to relay vital information on the price and characteristics of the services they offer and to build reputational capital designed to communicate the quality and value of services they offer.[214] However, a firm may use these tools to project biased or misleading information, which is in the firm's interest.[215] These scenarios confirm that poor consumer decision-making can be caused by information that is false, incomplete, or misleading. This highlights the importance of adopting a regulatory approach which goes beyond merely requiring that firms provide specific information.

209 Howells & Weatherill, *Consumer Protection Law* (n 133) p.25.
210 Chris Willet, 'The Functions of Transparency in Regulating Contract Terms: UK and Australian Approaches' (2011) 60(2) *International & Comparative Law Quarterly* 355, 384.
211 Sims (n 176) p.770.
212 Ibid.
213 Ibid.
214 Paul Rubin, 'Regulation of Information and Advertising' in Barry Keeting (ed.), *A Companion to the Economics of Regulation* (Blackwell Publishing, 2004) cited in OECD, 'Consumer Policy Toolkit' (n 32) p.35.
215 OECD, 'Consumer Policy Toolkit' (n 32) p.35.

In light of this, it is imperative that providers are obligated not to withhold material information that can impact decision-making. They should also be prohibited from disseminating false or misleading information. In contrast to mandatory disclosures, prohibiting the use of false or misleading information is classified as a negative informational response. Cartwright argues that this is significant because it addresses the other end of the information spectrum – rather than specifying in detail what sort of information must be disclosed, the obligation is not to omit information which an average consumer would rely on to make an informed decision.[216] A combination of positive and negative informational responses will arguably provide a more holistic approach to providing consumers with information as it covers both ends of the information spectrum.

One must note that not all deceptive information involves fraud or outright lies. Thus, the OECD argues that disclosures should also be regarded as deceptive if they leave out vital information or imply something untrue.[217] In such situations, authorities will have the responsibility of determining the message actually received by consumers and what importance they attach to it.[218] This is a complex task as consumers are bound to construe information differently. Authorities may thus adopt objective standards or consumer categories against which such disclosures may be interpreted.[219]

Finally, the OECD warns that regulatory responses tackling deceptive representations should not be excessively prescriptive and restrictive. This is because it may undermine competition and/or cause firms to be overly cautious in providing information that could assist consumers.[220] This warning may be based on the possibility that firms can become excessively cautious because they are uncertain of how consumers will judge the information disclosed.

## 4.5 Liability Rules

There are several risks involved in every financial transaction, and m-payment transactions are no exception in this regard. As with most payment services, there is the risk of data and privacy breaches which may lead to fraudulent and unauthorised transactions. There is also the risk of transactional failure, which may occur for several reasons.[221] Where such risks materialise, one or both parties will bear the losses that follow. Often, the party with the stronger bargaining power

216 Cartwright, 'The Vulnerable Consumer of Financial Services: Law, Policy and Regulation' (n 25) p.29.

217 OECD, 'Consumer Policy Toolkit' (n 32) p.37.

218 Ibid.

219 In the European Union, for instance, the concept of the 'average consumer' is adopted under the Unfair Commercial Practices Directive (Directive 2005/29/EC) to deal with this problem.

220 OECD, 'Consumer Policy Toolkit' (n 32) p.35.

221 This may occur where payments are not effected as intended owing to the wrong amount, payee, or timing or technological problems: Rhys Bollen, 'Recent Developments in Mobile Banking and Payments' (2009) 24(9) *Journal of International Banking Law and Regulation* 454, 465–466.

will attempt to shift such losses to the weaker party, and this can result in unfair outcomes. Hence, in many circumstances, spurred by redistributive concerns, regulators intervene by imposing rules allocating liability between contracting parties to ensure predictable and fairer outcomes.

Liability rules can also be justified from an economic standpoint. Van den Bergh and Visscher explain that the economic goal of liability rules is to incentivise parties who influence the size of the expected loss to ensure they take care.[222] It follows, therefore, that liability will often be placed on the party that is best able to bear it.[223] This may be the party with the least risk-bearing costs or the lowest insurance premium.[224] A more detailed explanation provided by Cooter and Rubin support these points.[225] They explain that the cost of negotiating favourable loss allocation provisions in a contract typically exceeds the potential benefit.[226] Although consumers can instead choose to shop around for alternative contracts with more favourable allocation rules, this also introduces search costs. Information asymmetry also limits the effectiveness of shopping – consumers may be unaware of risk allocation rules and, even if aware, may not understand the legal language in which they are couched.[227] These issues point to a market failure which provides clear justification for regulatory intervention in the form of efficient risk allocation rules.

Cooter and Rubin further suggest that three major principles of economic efficiency influence the design of such rules – i.e., the loss-spreading principle, the loss-reduction principle, and the loss-imposition principle.[228] Their thesis suggests that efficient rules should assign liability to the party that can achieve risk neutrality at the lowest cost (loss-spreading principle).[229] Efficient rules also incentivise the party that is best able to reduce a loss to do so by assigning liability to the party that can reduce losses at the lowest cost (loss-reduction principle).[230] The cheapest approach to loss imposition is to allow losses to fall where they may. However, this is not always efficient or desirable. Therefore, rules may be

222 Roger Van den Bergh and Louis Visscher, 'Consumer Sales Law from an Economic Perspective' in Martin Ebers, Andre Janssen, and Olaf Meyer, (eds), *European Perspectives on Producer's Liability: Direct Producers' Liability for Non-conformity and the Sellers' Right of Redress* (Walter de Gruyter 2009) p.142.

223 Franziska Weber, *The Law and Economics of Enforcing European Law: A Comparative Analysis of Package Travel and Misleading Advertising* (Ashgate Publishing 2014) p.34.

224 Ibid.

225 Robert D Cooter and Edward L Rubin, 'Theory of Loss Allocation for Consumer Payments' (1987) 66 *Texas Law Review* 63.

226 Ibid. p.68.

227 Ibid.

228 Cooter and Rubin (n 225) p.70.

229 Most people are risk-averse (i.e., when faced with the likelihood of a loss, they are willing to pay more than the loss's average value to eliminate the risk of it). In contrast, a risk-neutral person places a value on risk equal to the loss's average value. Financial institutions can be risk-neutral if the loss in question is small in proportion to their wealth and sufficiently predictable for them to spread it amongst their customers. Ibid. pp.70–71.

230 Cooter and Rubin (n 225) p.73.

imposed to increase efficiency by shifting losses to the party that should suffer the final loss (loss-imposition principle). Mechanisms such as strict liability can be understood in the context of the loss-imposition principle and mainly serve to reduce the cost of enforcing the allocation of liability.[231]

To achieve the economic goal that Van den Bergh and Visscher refer to, clarity on applicable liability rules is vital. Such clarity enables parties to adopt appropriate measures such as taking out insurance cover for risks they have elected to bear or those imposed by law.[232] From this perspective, clear rules governing the allocation of risks help increase the efficiency of a market.

Liability may be allocated in different ways. The most obvious way would be based on the agreement entered into between parties. In this context, contract terms such as exclusion and limitation clauses play a significant role.[233] However, the usefulness of such clauses is subject to their being utilised in a manner adjudged fair.[234] For instance, the availability of insurance at a reasonable cost for the party bearing the risk may be a factor considered in evaluating the fairness of a term.[235] Where contractual liability rules fail to meet the requirements of fairness, they can be struck down by courts.

Allocation of liability may also be set under a statute. Statutory documents like the European Union's Product Liability Directive[236] and the United Kingdom's Consumer Credit Act 1974 contain pro-consumer risk allocation rules.[237] A good example can be found in Section 75 of the UK Consumer Credit Act which protects consumers who have made purchases between £100 and £30,000 with a credit card where there has been a breach of contract or misrepresentation. The section holds the trader and credit supplier jointly and severally liable and is justified on the basis that a 'consumer is less well placed to seek redress against a recalcitrant supplier than the creditor; and the creditor should not benefit if the consumer has been let down by the supplier.'[238]

231 Ibid. p.78.

232 See Steven Shavell, 'On Liability and Insurance' (1982) 13(1) *The Bell Journal of Economics* 120, for a detailed discussion.

233 Such clauses also affect the price of a product/service. Where the supplier is sure of where the risk falls, the price can be fixed accordingly. A consumer may be offered a lower price where they are prepared to assume the risk under a contract. Parties may also rely on indemnities and warranties incorporated into their contract. Howells & Weatherill, *Consumer Protection Law* (n 133) p.262.

234 In the United Kingdom, for instance, exclusion clauses in consumer contracts are subject to the Consumer Rights Act, 2015. Some clauses are invalidated outright while others are subject to a test of fairness. See s.62(5)(b) Consumer Rights Act 2015.

235 Competition and Markets Authority (n 149) para.5.31.1

236 Directive 85/374 (as amended).

237 Stephen Weatherill, *EU Consumer Law & Policy* (Edward Elgar Publishing 2005) p.137.

238 Department of Trade and Industry, 'Connected Lender Liability in the United Kingdom Consumer Credit Law: Consultation Document' (1995), *Chapter 5*, paragraph 2 cited in Andrew Campbell, 'Credit Cards and Section 75: Time for a Change in the Law' (1996) 11(12) *Journal of International Banking Law*, 527, 527.

Rules on the allocation of liability may also form part of industry's efforts in building consumer confidence. Hence, individual industry players may develop some risk allocation rules that favour consumers. This is exemplified in the case of debit cards. Debit cards generally do not enjoy as much statutory protection as credit cards in many jurisdictions. Nevertheless, many debit card companies offer customers a chargeback where goods purchased with debit cards do not arrive, do not fit their description, or are faulty.[239] These chargeback provisions are mostly based on private scheme rules and not statutory provisions.[240]

Notwithstanding their source, liability rules often seek to strike a balance between identified consumer interests (e.g., compensation) on the one hand and the business interests (e.g., innovation) on the other hand.[241] In striking this balance, it is important that the formula adopted in allocating liability represents an objectively fair bargain where the consumer's liabilities are reasonably limited.[242] For instance, subject to requirements of fairness, it is reasonable to expect that consumers will bear some liability where they have wilfully breached their contractual obligations or where they have contracted to bear the cost of certain events such as the cost of returning unwanted/unsatisfactory goods to suppliers.

Fair dealing also dictates that parties be expressly informed of what liability rules apply to their transactions. In light of this, the rules on the allocation of liability for payment services are often incorporated into disclosure frameworks.[243] There is also an expectation that important contractual terms defining the parties' liability ought to be reasonably brought to the consumer's attention at the pre-contractual stage. This is even more so when such terms contain unusual provisions that can significantly impact a consumer's rights.[244] The insistence on such disclosures aims to ensure that the consumer can make well-informed decisions on whether to proceed with the contract.

Allocation of liability in m-payments is significant for two principal reasons. First, as shown in *Chapter 2*, numerous parties are involved in the transaction

239 See, for instance, Visa Europe, 'Protected When you Pay' <https://www.visa.co.uk/visa-everywhere/blog/bdp/2019/10/07/protected-when-you-1570458734759.html> accessed 14 September 2021.

240 Which?, 'How do I use Chargebacks' <http://www.which.co.uk/consumer-rights/problem/how-do-i-use-chargeback> accessed 14 September 2021.

241 This is evident in the EU product liability regime, for instance. Article 7(e) of the Product Liability Directive 1985 includes an optional 'development risk' defence for business so as not to stifle innovation. See cases that discuss this defence – *Abouzaid v. Mothercare (UK) Ltd* [2000] EWCA Civ. 348; *Richardson v. LRC Products Ltd* [2000] 59 BMLR 185; *A and Others v. National Blood Authority and Another* [2001] 3 All ER 289. The need for a balancing act may sometimes influence the decision to support a strict liability regime or a fault-based liability regime; Howells & Weatherill, *Consumer Protection Law* (n 133) p.43.

242 Bollen, 'A Discussion of Best Practice in the Regulation of Payment Services' (n 37) p.432.

243 Gail Hillebrand, 'Before the Grand Rethinking: Five Things to do Today with Payments Law and Ten Principles to guide New Payments Products and New Payments Law' (2008) 83(2) *Chicago-Kent Law Review* 769, 808.

244 *Spurling v. Bradshaw* [1956] 1 W.L.R 461.

chain, and clarity will be needed to decide who bears liability for what in the transaction process. The second reason is connected to the fact that transactions are reliant on diverse funding sources, which attract different protections for consumers under the law. For example, as we saw earlier, only credit card users are covered by Section 75 of the UK Consumer Credit Act 1974. This means that while m-payments create flexibility by allowing consumers to adopt the most convenient funding source at a given time, they may create greater uncertainty about which liability regime applies to their transaction.[245]

In many countries, the applicable liability regime for m-payments depends on factors such as the underlying funding and payment instrument used, the nature of the problem, the product or services purchased, and the payment providers involved.[246] Hence, for instance, if a payment card funds an m-payments transaction, the liability regime is determined by the type of card used. Similarly, suppose a consumer opts for direct mobile billing or a prepaid fund with an MNO, in that case, the applicable liability regime may be significantly different from that applying to m-payment services offered by a traditional financial institution.[247] In other words, consumer 'A' who makes an m-payment transaction funded by a credit card under a bank-led m-payment platform may enjoy different levels of protection when compared to consumer 'B' who performs an m-payment transaction funded by a pre-paid account under an exclusive MNO-led service. This state of affairs has been criticised by Hillebrand, who argues that basic consumer protections in payment systems should not be dependent on the payment method or the means of processing.[248]

This inconsistency in liability regimes will prove complex for consumers who do not understand the implications of using different funding sources.[249] The merger of different parties in the m-payment process makes it even more difficult to pinpoint where liability lies.[250] This state of affairs is captured by De Almeida when he raises the following query –

> If a telecommunications-centred model of m-payments is adopted, should banks be considered liable for ultimately providing funds to a MNO that has commercialised electronic money? Conversely, should interruption of airtime availability by a MNO that has partnered with a bank in a joint venture for

245 Fumiko Hayashi, 'M-payments: What's in it for Consumers?' (2012) 1 *Economic Review* 35, 51.

246 Trites et al. (n 12) p.54.

247 OECD, 'Report on Consumer Protection in Online and Mobile Payments' (n 4) p.21.

248 Hillebrand (n 243) pp.788–800.

249 Federal Trade Commission, 'Paper, Plastic or Mobile? An FTC Workshop on Mobile Payments' (2013) p.6 <https://www.ftc.gov/reports/paper-plastic-or-mobile-ftc-workshop-mobile-payments> assessed 14 September 2021.

250 Gilberto Martins De Almeida, 'M-Payments in Brazil: Notes on How a Country's Background May Determine the Timing and Design of a Regulatory Model' (2013) 8(3) *Washington Journal of Law Technology & Arts* 347, 369.

selling m-payment services be subject to the bank's liability in the event airtime is deemed to integrate the financial package of m-payments service?[251]

## 4.6 Dispute Resolution

An important aspect of effective financial consumer protection frameworks is the presence of 'an accessible and efficient recourse mechanism that allows consumers both to know and to assert their rights to have their complaints addressed and resolved in a transparent and just way within a reasonable timeframe.'[252] Consumers can only exert the market discipline anticipated in neo-classical theory if they can make voluntary informed decisions and also take action where goods and services supplied are unsatisfactory.[253] Consumer action in this context may involve switching suppliers and holding them accountable by seeking redress where they have breached their legal obligations.[254]

Effective redress systems contribute to making traders more accountable because it incentivises them to supply quality products and to engage in ethical conduct.[255] Apart from having a deterrent effect on business, an effective redress framework may also increase consumer trust, satisfaction, and confidence in authorities.[256] This is because consumers are assured that their claims are safeguarded.[257] Dispute resolution mechanisms are particularly important for financially excluded and low-income consumers because their vulnerability may be heightened if they cannot pursue redress or where redress mechanisms exclude them because they lack the knowledge, confidence, and resources to act.[258] Since these consumers are likely to suffer the impact of poor redress mechanisms, special consideration should be given to their needs so that they (and their representatives) can easily access legal advice and assistance to pursue redress.[259]

251 Ibid.

252 World Bank Group, 'Complaints Handling within Financial Service Providers Principles, Practices, and Regulatory Approaches' (2019) p.1 <https://openknowledge.worldbank.org/handle/10986/32360?locale-attribute=en> accessed 14 September 2021.

253 Cartwright, 'The Vulnerable Consumer of Financial Services: Law, Policy and Regulation' (n 25) p.43.

254 Ibid.

255 Effective dispute resolution mechanisms may also provide the incentive for consumers to enter contracts with the supplier as they are assured that if disputes arise, they will be resolved efficiently. Cartwright, 'The Vulnerable Consumer of Financial Services: Law, Policy and Regulation' (n 25) p.43.

256 Stefan Wrbka, 'European Consumer Protection Law, Quo Vadis? – Thoughts on the Compensatory Collective Redress Debate' in Stefan Wrbka, Steven Van Uytsel, et al. (eds), *Collective Actions: Enhancing Access to Justice and reconciling Multi-Layer Interests* (Cambridge University Press 2012) p.32.

257 Ibid. p.37.

258 Cartwright terms this 'Redress Vulnerability' and states that this form of vulnerability may exist in connection with other aspects of vulnerability, (n 97) pp.42–43.

259 OECD, 'Recommendation on Consumer Dispute Resolution and Redress' (2007) p.10. <https://www.oecd.org/sti/consumer/38960101.pdf> accessed 14 September 2021.

As with other payment services, it is anticipated that disputes will arise in the use of m-payments for several reasons. First, m-payment transactions are usually completed quickly, and consumers may not be in the position to think thoroughly about the applicable terms and conditions before making a purchase.[260] Second, consumers may not be able to validate the integrity and identity of vendors, nor do they always have the opportunity to inspect goods before completing transactions using m-payment platforms.[261] Additionally, there will likely be cases involving erroneous or unintended transactions which will need to be resolved.[262] Moreover, there is the possibility of transactional failure. This will cover situations where payments are not affected as intended and where limitations in telecommunication infrastructure and mobile network coverage stall a transaction.[263] All these scenarios highlight the importance of effective dispute resolution in m-payments.

Redress mechanisms are generally comprised of multiple routes. These routes may be structured around formal or informal procedures which ought to be accessible, fair, expeditious, affordable, and subject to independent review.[264] They may include individual litigation procedures, collective redress systems, out-of-court alternative dispute resolution (ADR) procedures, and enforcement actions on behalf of consumers by regulatory authorities. This variety of options gives consumers the choice to access the most appropriate route for resolving disputes that may arise.[265] The availability of options might also ensure, to an extent, that the position of vulnerable consumers is not made worse owing to difficulties they face in obtaining redress.[266]

Traditionally, litigation (both individualised and collective procedures) serves as the primary platform for venting consumer grievances. However, the economic, organisational, and procedural obstacles associated with litigation often discourage consumers from taking this route. This reality has led to more emphasis on out-of-court dispute resolution procedures. In the financial services market, consumer complaints usually comprise two types: those handled by financial services providers, and where not satisfactorily resolved, those referred to external dispute resolution providers.[267] Accordingly, this book's discussion on dispute resolution procedures focuses on out-of-court dispute resolution procedures available to financial services users. In our context, these procedures are broadly taken to refer to internal dispute resolution mechanisms provided by financial services provid-

260 OECD, 'Report on Consumer Protection in Online and Mobile Payments' (n 4) p.36.

261 Ibid.

262 Edwin Saidi, 'Mobile Opportunities, Mobile Problems: Assessing Mobile Commerce Implementation Issues in Malawi' (2009) 14(1) *Journal of Internet Banking and Commerce* 8.

263 Ibid.

264 United Nations 'Guidelines for Consumer Protection' (n 13) paras11(f), 37.

265 Appropriate in terms of costs (time, money, and expertise considerations).

266 Cartwright, 'The Vulnerable Consumer of Financial Services: Law, Policy and Regulation' (n 25) pp.42–43.

267 World Bank Group, 'Complaints Handling within Financial Service Providers Principles, Practices, and Regulatory Approaches' (n 252) p.1.

ers and institutional ADR processes (e.g., ombudsmen), which deal with complaints that a service provider has not satisfactorily resolved. These out-of-court procedures are also more relevant to m-payments involving small value transactions where the cost of resolving small claims in civil courts will be prohibitive.

### *4.6.1 Internal Dispute Resolution Procedures*

To resolve disputes, the OECD recommends that financial services providers cooperate with governments in establishing fair, transparent, and effective self-regulatory mechanisms and procedures to address consumer complaints.[268] To also ensure a level playing field, minimum internal dispute resolution obligations are often imposed on all financial services providers in a given jurisdiction.[269]

As a starting point, taking into account the size, nature, and complexity of financial service providers, regulations often mandate that providers design internal dispute resolution procedures that are available to consumers in the first instance.[270] Regulations also determine the timeframe and organisational structure of such mechanisms.[271] Under such arrangements, providers are required to publicise information about the dispute resolution procedures available to consumers and the process and channels for initiating complaints.[272] The information disseminated to consumers also covers the expected costs and duration of the procedures, the possible outcomes, avenues for appeal and the binding status (or otherwise) of the outcome.[273]

Recognising that it might be practically impossible for consumers to have all these pieces of information at once, there should be mechanisms which ensure consumers are aware of their key rights and that they know where to get further advice. Accordingly, information on dispute resolution procedures is often built into mandatory disclosure frameworks and made freely available through a range of channels such as websites, branches, and service points.[274]

The World Bank proposes that to meet these obligations and where the size and nature of the financial service provider permits, providers should establish dedicated complaints handling departments that are operationally independent of other business units. This can be supported by written complaints management

268 OECD 'Policy Guidance for Addressing Consumer Protection and Empowerment Issues in Mobile Commerce' (n 11) p.8.

269 World Bank Group, 'Complaints Handling within Financial Service Providers Principles, Practices, and Regulatory Approaches' (n 252) p.3.

270 Ibid. p.7

271 Ibid. p.3.

272 United Nations 'Guidelines for Consumer Protection' (n 13) para.39.

273 OECD, 'Recommendation on Consumer Dispute Resolution and Redress' (n 259) p.9.

274 World Bank Group, 'Complaints Handling within Financial Service Providers Principles, Practices, and Regulatory Approaches' (n 252) p.7

policies which set out the procedures for the effective, timely, and impartial handling of consumer disputes.[275]

Ideally, consumers can also access a range of channels and communication tools to submit their complaints. For effectiveness, it might also be necessary that providers adapt these channels to cater to illiterate consumers or those who speak languages not spoken by the majority. This is of particular importance in jurisdictions wishing to drive financial inclusion. To ensure accessibility, many regulators also prohibit financial service providers from charging consumers for using the complaints resolution process.[276]

Apart from the obvious benefits of internal dispute resolution mechanisms to consumers, the World Bank points out that they can also be beneficial to financial services providers. They help providers maintain a healthy relationship with consumers based on trust, and they mitigate the reputational risks and costs associated with lengthy legal actions. Importantly, the internal dispute resolution mechanisms generate data that can serve as an invaluable source of consumer feedback which can be used to strategically improve service delivery.[277]

A particular issue arising with m-payments is that it may be unclear whom the consumer should contact in the first instance when a dispute arises. This is due to the complexity of m-payment transactions and the multiple parties involved. Where regulations do not clarify which party will be responsible for resolving consumer complaints, there is the risk that parties involved on the supply side may be unwilling to take up the responsibility.[278] This situation will be challenging for consumers accustomed to dispute resolution mechanisms affiliated with other established payment methods and who may erroneously believe that these apply to m-payments.[279] This confusing situation may make it difficult for consumers to have reasonable expectations about their redress rights or which entity in the transaction chain is responsible for dispute resolution.[280]

This situation is often worsened by the fact that the different parties involved in the m-payment process are often subject to different regulators. Consumers may thus be confused about which regulator[281] to approach if a problem persists.[282] Cumulatively, this can result in a situation where consumers face delays and unnecessary costs in ensuring that their complaints are resolved satisfactorily.[283] One consequence is that consumers, especially those new to using financial ser-

275 Ibid. pp.5, 7.

276 Ibid.

277 Ibid. p.2

278 Trites et al. (n 12) p.33.

279 Ibid. p.22.

280 OECD, 'Report on Consumer Protection in Online and Mobile Payments' (n 4) p.35; Trites et al. (n 12) p.33.

281 These regulatory bodies may themselves be confused about their competence in respect of m-payments.

282 OECD, 'Report on Consumer Protection in Online and Mobile Payments' (n 4) p.35.

283 OECD, 'Consumer Policy Guidance on Mobile and Online Payments' (n 7) p.22.

vices, may lose trust in financial service providers and the sector in general.[284] These consumers may also be put off from using m-payments which will negatively affect its widescale adoption. Regulators can respond to this issue by requiring that service providers expressly clarify which party will be responsible for resolving consumer disputes. This should reasonably be the party that maintains the direct account relationship with the consumer.

Dispute resolution frameworks must also clarify what happens where a consumer is dissatisfied with the outcome of the internal dispute resolution process or where they are not resolved within established timeframes.[285] The prevalent approach in many jurisdictions is that in such situations, regulations or self-regulatory arrangements often guarantee consumers a right of appeal and access to an external and independent out-of-court ADR mechanism.[286] Where such external out-of-court mechanisms are available, there is often a requirement that consumers must be made aware of the relevant procedures for accessing them.

### *4.6.2 External ADR Mechanisms*

External ADR mechanisms come in different forms. They may include semi-formal mediation and negotiation services or more formalised processes or institutions like a government-sanctioned ombudsman. ADR can also take the form of private or quasi-private mechanisms established by industry associations or consumer organisations.[287] In addition, ADR may be available on a collective basis.

In jurisdictions like the European Union, there is a concerted effort towards encouraging the settlement of mass claims through ADR.[288] In encouraging collective ADR, Member States are urged to 'ensure that judicial collective redress mechanisms are accompanied by appropriate means of collective alternative dispute resolution available to the parties before and throughout the litigation.'[289] Collective ADR procedures may be significant in m-payments as consumers may not be willing to go through the hassle of individualised processes (whether litigation or ADR) to recover losses suffered. In other words, where detriment is small, consumers may be unwilling to act individually. However, if this detriment is widespread in the industry, it can be significant since many consumers will effectively be left without redress. Collective ADR procedures, therefore, provide a

284 World Bank Group, 'Complaints Handling within Financial Service Providers Principles, Practices, and Regulatory Approaches' (n 252) p.1.

285 Ibid. p.3.

286 World Bank Group, 'Complaints Handling within Financial Service Providers Principles, Practices, and Regulatory Approaches' (n 252) p.51.

287 Ibid. pp.51–52.

288 See European Commission Recommendation of 11 June 2013 on Common Principles for Injunctive and Compensatory Collective Redress Mechanisms in The Member States Concerning Violations of Rights Granted Under Union Law (2013/396/EU) <https://eur-lex.europa.eu/legal-content/EN/TXT/PDF/?uri=CELEX:32013H0396&from=EN> accessed 14 September 2021.

289 Ibid. Recommendation 26.

sensible solution to this issue by allowing mass individual claims to be 'combined in a procedure that delivers "judicial economy" and thereby increases access to justice.'[290]

In response to changing commercial norms, authorities may also encourage the adoption of Online Dispute Resolution (ODR) mechanisms.[291] ODR represents a synergy between ADR and Information and Communications Technology (ICT) in dealing with the increase of online disputes for which the traditional means of dispute resolution is inadequate.[292] Thus, they have been portrayed as 'a reaction to the constraints of the offline world.'[293] These online platforms are becoming popular because they allow for efficiency and convenience by adopting internet-based processes, information management, and communication tools to resolve complaints.[294] In particular, they bypass linguistic barriers and the need for the physical presence of disputing parties. In the European Union, this has been embraced to improve the internal retail market and enhance redress for consumers.[295] Since m-payments may be used for cross-border transactions, ODR mechanisms can provide a platform for conveniently resolving disputes that arise.

Whichever form of ADR process is selected, it is expected that the mechanism does not impose unreasonable costs, delays, or burdens on consumers.[296] From a regulatory perspective, the World Bank recommends that at a minimum, an effective ADR mechanism is one that:

i. Has powers to issue decisions on each case that are binding on the financial service provider (but not binding on the consumer);
ii. Is independent of both parties and discharges its functions impartially;
iii. Is staffed by professionals trained in the subject(s) they deal with;
iv. Has an adequate oversight structure that ensures efficient operations;

290 Christopher Hodges, 'Current Discussions on Consumer Redress: Collective Redress and ADR' (2012) 13 *ERA Forum* 11, 17.

291 The European Uunion has adopted Regulation No 524/2013 on Online Dispute Resolution for Consumer Disputes, amending Regulation (EC) No 2006/2004 and Directive 2009/22/EC.

292 Ethan Katsh and Janet Rifkin, *Online Dispute Resolution: Resolving Conflicts in Cyberspace* (San Francisco: Jossey-Bass, 2001), p.9 cited in Pablo Cortes, 'Online Dispute Resolution Services: A Selected Number of Case Studies' (2014) 20(6) *Computer and Telecommunications Law Review* 172, 172.

293 Gabrielle Kauffman-Kohler, Thomas Schultz, 'The State of Play in Online Dispute Resolution' in Gabrielle Kauffman-Kohler and Thomas Schultz, *Online Dispute Resolution: Challenges for Contemporary Justice* (Kluwer Law International 2004) p.7.

294 The OECD lists SquareTrade as an example of this. SquareTrade allows parties to use online SquareTrade mediators to resolve their disputes. OECD, 'Consumer Policy Toolkit' (n 32) p.101.

295 Apart from the ODR Regulation, legislative measures in the European Union have tended to favour the utilisation of ODR mechanisms. Examples include the Directive on Electronic Commerce (Directive 2000/31/EC) – Art.17 and the Directive on certain aspects of Mediation in Civil and Commercial Matters (Directive 2008/52/EC) – Recitals 8 and 9; Julio Cesar Betancourt and Elina Zlatanska, 'Online Dispute Resolution (ODR): What is it, and is it the way forward?' (2013) 79(3) *International Journal of Arbitration, Mediation and Dispute Management* 256.

296 G20, 'High-Level Principles on Consumer Financial Protection' (n 14) p.7.

v. Is financed adequately and on a sustainable basis;
vi. Is free of charge to the consumer; and
vii. Is accessible to consumers.[297]

### *4.6.3 Financial Ombudsman Services*

Special mention must be given to ombudsman services which have become prevalent in the financial services sector. These services seek to provide quicker, cheaper, independent, less-formal, and impartial out-of-court platforms for resolving disputes.[298] To ensure that cost is not a barrier, these services often charge minimal fees or are completely free to consumers.[299] Ombudsman services may be established by statute or industry associations. These services are usually be funded by the government out of taxation (if government-backed), or more usually by contributions from the financial services industry that they serve.[300]

Ombudsmen may be established to deal with a single sector in the financial services market (e.g., banking or insurance) or to deal broadly with all sectors.[301] Either way, their mandate must be clear to ensure that their role within the dispute resolution infrastructure is clearly understood. In many jurisdictions with a tiered approach to dispute resolution, access to an ombudsman is often available where the consumer has exhausted the internal dispute resolution processes provided by the financial services provider.

In carrying out their responsibilities of investigating and adjudicating claims, ombudsmen are more interested in producing conciliated outcomes than declaring winners or losers.[302] Furthermore, ombudsmen are often required to publish annual reports about their work. These reports serve important functions. First, they provide statistics about the disputes received and their handling, enabling financial services providers to avoid future problems when serving consumers.[303] Second, they provide information on prevalent consumer issues, applicable rights, and liabilities, which can be used by consumer advisers and the media to help improve the financial capability of consumers.[304] Finally, the reports also generate data that can point to systemic issues, which the ombudsman can feed back

297 World Bank Group, 'Complaints Handling within Financial Service Providers Principles, Practices, and Regulatory Approaches' (n 252) p.51.

298 David Thomas and Francis Frizon, 'Resolving Disputes Between Consumers and Financial Businesses: Fundamentals for a Financial Ombudsman – A Practical Guide Based on Experience in Western Europe' (2012) p.11 <https://documents1.worldbank.org/curated/en/169791468233091885/pdf/699160v10ESW0P0en0Vol10Fundamentals.pdf> accessed 14 September 2021.

299 Ibid.

300 Ibid. p.37.

301 Thomas & Frizon (n 298) p.6.

302 World Bank Group, 'Complaints Handling within Financial Service Providers Principles, Practices, and Regulatory Approaches' (n 252) p.51.

303 Thomas & Frizon (n 298) p.13

304 Ibid.

to authorities.[305] Such feedback can be used by authorities to improve existing consumer protection frameworks.

Some commentators call for caution where financial ombudsmen are established by industry associations. For instance, Thomas and Frizon suggest that consumers may have less confidence in such ombudsmen and recommend that they should only be appointed by legislators, government, or the financial regulator.[306] Others like Hirschman warn that there is a tendency over time for such industry-based mechanisms to be transformed into 'a method of institutionalising and domesticating dissent.'[307] Authorities may address this concern by ensuring that consumers can access independent redress procedures if industry-based mechanisms prove unsatisfactory.[308] In response to this, some countries like the United Kingdom permit consumers to approach civil courts if dissatisfied with an ombudsman's decision.[309]

One issue that may arise in the use of ombudsman services in m-payments is the breadth of their jurisdiction. Where existing ombudsman services in the financial sector are restricted to traditional financial institutions, it will negatively impact consumers. This is because disputes with non-financial institutions providing m-payments will be excluded from their jurisdiction. Where this is the case, m-payment consumers who sign up for services offered by these non-traditional financial institutions will be disadvantaged due to the limited external redress options available to them.

## 4.7 Conclusion

Consumer policy is concerned with responding to market failures that jeopardise consumer welfare and pursuing socially motivated objectives that encourage fairness. These goals are achieved by using regulatory techniques and setting out rules that modify the behaviour of market participants and by providing redress where detriment has occurred.[310]

This chapter has shown that the tools for responding to consumer issues in financial markets vary. Regulatory tools such as consumer education, information disclosures, cooling-off periods, and contract terms regulations may be

305 Thomas & Frizon (n 298) p.8.

306 Ibid. p.35.

307 AO Hirschman, *Exit Voice and Loyalty* (Harvard Uni. Press 1970) cited in Ramsay, *Consumer Law and Policy* (n 21) p.38; see also Shauhin A Talesh, 'How Dispute Resolution System Design Matters: An Organizational Analysis of Dispute Resolution Structures and Consumer Lemon Laws' (2012) 46(3) Law & Society Review 463.

308 G20, 'High-Level Principles on Consumer Financial Protection' (n 14) p.7; Howells & Weatherill, *Consumer Protection Law* (n 133) p.74.

309 The United Kingdom's financial services ombudsman is discussed in more detail in *Chapter 7*.

310 Magdalena Tulibacka, *Product Liability Law in Transition: A Central European Perspective* (Ashgate Publishing Ltd, 2013) p.95.

relied on to strengthen consumers' position.[311] Authorities may also adopt other mechanisms to ensure that the supply side behaves in the interest of consumers.[312] Furthermore, intermediate tools such as dispute resolution and redress mechanisms may be adopted as they could be potent on both sides of the value chain.[313] These tools address issues that consumers may deal with at different stages of their business relationship with the financial service provider. Information requirements and regulations controlling unfair practices usually address the pre-purchase stage; contract terms regulation and cooling-off periods address the purchase stage, while liability rules and dispute resolution mechanisms cover the post-purchase stage.[314]

The next part of this book discusses how selected jurisdictions address the consumer issues in m-payments using the consumer policy tools identified in this chapter. The discussions we have covered so far in this first part of the book provide the background and basis for inquiry in the next part.

## References

Alexandra Sims, 'Unfair Contract Terms: A New Dawn in Australia and New Zealand?' (2013) 39(3) *Monash University Law Review* 739.

Andrew Campbell, 'Credit Cards and Section 75: Time for a Change in the Law' (1996) 11(12) *Journal of International Banking Law*, 527.

Anthony I. Ogus, *Regulation: Legal Form and Economic Theory* (Hart Publishing 2004).

Anu Arora, 'Unfair Contract Terms and Unauthorised Bank Charges: A Banking Lawyer's Perspective' (2012) 1 *Journal of Business Law* 44.

Aonghus McClafferty, 'Effective Protection for the E-Consumer in light of the Consumer Rights Directive?' (2012) 11 *Hibernian Law Journal* 85.

British Institute of Commercial and Comparative Law, 'Unfair Commercial Practices: An analysis of the existing National Laws on Unfair Commercial Practices between Business and Consumers in the new Member States' (2005) <http://www.biicl.org/files/882_general_report_unfair_commercial_practices_new_member_states%5Bwith_dir_table_and_new_logo%5D.pdf> accessed 13 September 2021.

Caroline Cohen, 'The Contract Law Principle of Pacta Sunt Servanda and Behavioural Economics Literature in Relation to Justifications for the European Consumer's Right of Withdrawal under Directive 2011/83/EC' (2016) 2 *Exeter Student Law Review* 13.

Chris Willett, *Fairness in Consumer Contracts: The Case of Unfair Terms* (Ashgate Publishing Ltd 2007).

311 Referred to as 'demand side tools' by the OECD – OECD, 'Consumer Policy Toolkit' (n 32) p.119.

312 These are described as 'supply side tools' and include licensing, accreditations, standards, moral suasion, and codes of conduct: Ibid.

313 OECD, 'Consumer Policy Toolkit' (n 32) p.119.

314 Ioannis Lianos, Despoina Mantzari, et al., 'The Global Governance of Online Consumer Protection and E-commerce Building Trust' (World Economic Forum White Paper 2019) pp.8–10 <http://www3.weforum.org/docs/WEF_consumer_protection.pdf > accessed 14 September 2021.

Chris Willet, 'The Functions of Transparency in Regulating Contract Terms: UK and Australian Approaches' (2011) 60(2) *International & Comparative Law Quarterly* 355.

Christian D. Dick and Lena M. Jaroszek, 'Knowing what not to do: Financial Literacy and Consumer Credit Choices' (2013) <https://www.fdic.gov/news/conferences/consumersymposium/2013/Papers/Jaroszek.pdf> accessed 13 September 2021.

Christopher Hodges, 'Current Discussions on Consumer Redress: Collective Redress and ADR' (2012) 13 *ERA Forum* 11.

Colin Camerer, Samuel Issacharoff, George Loewenstein, et al, 'Regulation for Conservatives: Behavioural Economics and the Case for 'Asymmetric Paternalism'' (2003) 151(3) *University of Pennsylvania Law Review* 1211.

Colin Scott and Julia Black, *Cranston's Consumers and the Law* (3rd ed., Butterworths 2000).

Competition and Markets Authority (CMA), 'Guidance on the Unfair Terms Provisions in the Consumer Rights Act 2015' (July 2015) <https://www.gov.uk/government/uploads/system/uploads/attachment_data/file/450440/Unfair_Terms_Main_Guidance.pdf> accessed 23 August 2021.

David Cayne and Michael J. Trebilcock, 'Market Considerations in the Formulation of Consumer Protection Policy' (1973) 23(4) *University of Toronto Law Journal* 396.

David De Meza, Bernd Irlenbusch and Diane Reyniers, 'Financial Capability: A Behavioural Economics Perspective' (Consumer Research Report N0.69, UK Financial Services Authority, 2008) <https://www.fca.org.uk/publication/research/fsa-crpr69.pdf> accessed 12 September 2021.

David Gartner, 'Global Public Goods and Global Health' (2012) 22 *Duke Journal of Comparative & International Law* 303.

David Llewellyn, 'The Economic Rationale for Financial Regulation' (FSA Occasional Paper Series 1, 1999) <https://www.fep.up.pt/disciplinas/pgaf924/PGAF/Texto_2_David_Llewellyn.pdf> accessed 5 September 2021.

David Thomas and Francis Frizon, 'Resolving Disputes Between Consumers and Financial Businesses: Fundamentals for a Financial Ombudsman – A Practical Guide Based on Experience in Western Europe' (2012) <https://documents1.worldbank.org/curated/en/169791468233091885/pdf/699160v10ESW0P0en0Vol10Fundamentals.pdf> accessed 14 September 2021.

Edwin Saidi, 'Mobile Opportunities, Mobile Problems: Assessing Mobile Commerce Implementation Issues in Malawi' (2009) 14(1) *Journal of Internet Banking and Commerce* 8.

Eleanor Lumsden, 'Securing Mobile Technology and Financial Transactions in the U.S' (2012) 9 *Berkeley Business Law Journal* 139.

Elizabeth Eraker, Colin Hector and Chris J. Hoofnagle, 'Mobile Payments: The Challenge of Protecting Consumers and Innovation' (2011) 10 *Privacy & Security Law Report* 212.

Erik A Hanushek and Ludger Woessmann, 'The Case for Promoting Universal Basic Skills' in OECD (ed), *Universal Basic Skills: What Countries Stand to Gain* (OECD Publishing Paris 2015) <https://www.oecd.org/education/universal-basic-skills-9789264234833-en.htm> accessed 12 September 2021.

European Central Bank, 'Recommendations for the Security of Mobile Payments: Draft Document for Public Consultation' (2013) <http://www.ecb.europa.eu/paym/cons/pdf/131120/recommendationsforthesecurityofmobilepaymentsdraftpc201311en.pdf> accessed 7 August 2021.

Fariba Dehghan and Amirhossein Haghighi, 'E-money Regulation for Consumer Protection' (2015) 57(6) *International Journal of Law and Management* 610.

Federal Trade Commission, 'Paper, Plastic or Mobile? An FTC Workshop on Mobile Payments' (2013) <https://www.ftc.gov/reports/paper-plastic-or-mobile-ftc-workshop-mobile-payments> accessed 14 September 2021.

Financial Conduct Authority, 'Mobile Banking and Payments – Supporting an Innovative and Secure Market' (2013) <http://www.fca.org.uk/static/documents/thematic-reviews/tr13-06.pdf> accessed 13 September 2021.

Financial Conduct Authority, 'Mobile Banking and Payments' (2014) <https://www.fca.org.uk/publication/thematic-reviews/tr14-15.pdf> accessed 5 September 2021.

Financial Services Authority, 'Towards a National Strategy for Financial Capability' (2003) <https://financialliteracygroup.com/wp-content/uploads/2015/10/SM1-UK-National-Strategy.pdf> accessed 13 September 2021.

Franziska Weber, *The Law and Economics of Enforcing European Law: A Comparative Analysis of Package Travel and Misleading Advertising* (Ashgate Publishing 2014).

Friedrich Kessler, 'Contracts of Adhesion: Some thoughts about Freedom of Contract' (1943) 43 *Columbia Law Review* 629.

Fumiko Hayashi, 'M-payments: What's in it for Consumers?' (2012) 1 *Economic Review* 35.

G20, 'High-Level Principles on Consumer Financial Protection' (2011) <https://www.oecd.org/g20/topics/financial-sector-reform/48892010.pdf> accessed 5 September 2021.

Gabrielle Kauffman-Kohler and Thomas Schultz, *Online Dispute Resolution: Challenges for Contemporary Justice* (Kluwer law International 2004).

Gail Hillebrand, 'Before the Grand Rethinking: Five Things to do Today with Payments Law and Ten Principles to guide New Payments Products and New Payments Law' (2008) 83(2) *Chicago-Kent Law Review* 769.

Gail Pearson, 'Reconceiving Regulation: Financial Literacy' (2008) 8 *Macquarie Law Journal* 45, 53.

George Akerlof, 'The Market For 'Lemons': Quality Uncertainty and the Market Mechanism' (1970) 84(3) *Quarterly Journal of Economics* 488.

George Loewenstein, Cass R. Sunstein, Russell Golman, 'Disclosure: Psychology Changes Everything' (2014) 6 *Annual Review of Economics* 391, 412.

Geraint Howells, 'The Potential and Limits of Consumer Empowerment by Information' (2005) 32(3) *Journal of Law & Society* 349.

Geraint Howells and Stephen Weatherill, *Consumer Protection Law* (2nd ed., Ashgate 2005).

Geraint Howells, Hans–Wolfgang Micklitz, Thomas Wilhelmsson, 'Towards a Better Understanding of Unfair Commercial Practices' (2009) 51(2) *International Journal of Law and Management* 69.

Gilberto Martins De Almeida, 'M-Payments in Brazil: Notes on How a Country's Background May Determine the Timing and Design of a Regulatory Model' (2013) 8(3) *Washington Journal of Law Technology & Arts* 347.

Global Partnership for Financial Inclusion (GPFI), "Global Standard-Setting Bodies and Financial Inclusion for the Poor" (2011) <https://www.gpfi.org/sites/gpfi/files/documents/White-Paper-Global-Standard-Setting-Bodies-Oct-2011.pdf > accessed 19 July 2021.

Harry McVea, 'Financial Services Regulation under the Financial Services Authority: A Reassertion of the Market Failure Thesis' (2005) 64(2) *Cambridge Law Journal* 413.

Iain Ramsay, 'Consumer Law, Regulatory Capitalism and the "New Learning" in Regulation' (2006) 28(1) *Sydney Law Review* 9.

Iain Ramsay, *Consumer Law and Policy* (3rd ed., Hart Publishing 2012).

International Finance Corporation, 'M-Money Chanel Distribution Case – Kenya (Safaricom M-pesa)' (2010) <https://www.ifc.org/wps/wcm/connect/e0d2a9bd-16b9-4a36-8498-0b2650b9af8b/Tool%2B6.7.%2BCase%2BStudy%2B-%2BM-PESA%2BKenya%2B.pdf?MOD=AJPERES&CVID=jkCVy-n> accessed 10 September 2021.

Ioannis Lianos, Despoina Mantzari, et al., 'The Global Governance of Online Consumer Protection and E-commerce Building Trust' (World Economic Forum White Paper 2019) <http://www3.weforum.org/docs/WEF_consumer_protection.pdf> accessed 14 September 2021.

Jan M Smits, 'Rethinking the Usefulness of Mandatory Rights of Withdrawal in Consumer Contract Law: The Right to Change Your Mind' (2011) 29 *Pennsylvania State International Law Review* 671.

Jeffery Atik, 'Complex Enterprises and Quasi-Public Goods' (1995) 16 *University of Pennsylvania Journal of International Law* 1.

Jeremy A. Blumenthal, 'Emotional Paternalism' (2007) 35(1) *Florida State University Law Review* 1.

Jette Benn, 'Consumer Education between 'Consumership' and Citizenship: Experiences from Studies of Young People' <http://www.mv.helsinki.fi/home/palojoki/english/nordplus/IJC_364%20Benn.pdf> accessed 10 September 2021.

Julio Cesar Betancourt and Elina Zlatanska, 'Online Dispute Resolution (ODR): What is it, and is it the way forward?' (2013) 79(3) *International Journal of Arbitration, Mediation and Dispute Management* 256.

Katalin Judit Cseres, *Competition Law and Consumer Protection* (Kluwer Law International 2005).

Keith M. Marzilli Ericson and Andreas Fuster, 'The Endowment Effect' (National Bureau of Economic Research Working Paper Series 2013) <https://www.nber.org/system/files/working_papers/w19384/w19384.pdf> accessed 13 September 2021.

Kirsten Thommes, Michael Faure and Klaus Heine, 'The Internal Market and the Consumer: What Consumers Actually Choose' (2014) 21 *Columbia Journal of European Law* 47.

Lauren E. Willis, 'Against Financial-Literacy Education' (2008) 94 *Iowa Law Review* 197.

Loreta Poro, 'Unfair Commercial Practices in Financial Services: Is the EU Legal Framework Sufficient to Protect Consumers?' (2014) 29(7) *Journal of International Banking Law and Regulation* 422.

Magdalena Tulibacka, *Product Liability Law in Transition: A Central European Perspective* (Ashgate Publishing Ltd, 2013).

Marianne Crowe, Susan Pandy, et al, 'US Mobile Payments Landscape: 2 Years Later' (May 2013) <https://abnk.assembly.ca.gov/sites/abnk.assembly.ca.gov/files/mobile-payments-landscape-two-years-later.pdf> accessed 8 September 2021.

Mark Flaming, Alexander Owino, Katharine McKee et al., 'Consumer Protection Diagnostic Study: Kenya' (2011) <http://s3-eu-central-1.amazonaws.com/fsd-circle/wp-content/uploads/2015/08/30095758/11-02-22_Consumer_diagnostic_study.pdf> accessed 13 December 2018.

Martin Ebers, Andre Janssen and Olaf Meyer, (eds), *European Perspectives on Producer's Liability: Direct Producers' Liability for Non-conformity and the Sellers' Right of Redress* (Walter de Gruyter 2009).

Michael J. Trebilcock, Lorne Sossin, Anthony Duggan (eds), *Middle Income Access to Justice* (University of Toronto Press 2012).

Michael Schillig, 'Inequality of Bargaining Power Versus a Market for Lemons: Legal Paradigm Change and the Court of Justice's Jurisprudence on Directive 93/13 on Unfair Contract Terms' (2008) 33(3) *European Law Review* 336.

Nicola Howell, 'Developing a Consumer Policy for the 21st Century' (2008) 33(2) *Alternative Law Journal* 80.

Norton Rose Fulbright, 'Beyond Law: Understanding the Scope of Conduct Regulation' (2014) <https://www.nortonrosefulbright.com/-/media/files/nrf/nrfweb/imported/beyond-law-understanding-the-scope-of-conduct-regulation.pdf> accessed 13 September 2021.

OECD, *China in the World Economy: An OECD Economic and Statistical Survey*, Volume 1 (Kogan Page Publishers, 2003).

OECD, 'Recommendation on Principles and Good Practices for Financial Education and Awareness' (2005) <https://www.oecd.org/finance/financial-education/35108560.pdf> accessed 13 September 2021.

OECD, 'Recommendation on Consumer Dispute Resolution and Redress' (2007) <https://www.oecd.org/sti/consumer/38960101.pdf> accessed 14 September 2021.

OECD, 'Policy Guidance for addressing Consumer Protection and Empowerment Issues in Mobile Commerce' (2008) OECD Digital Economy Papers, No. 149 <http://dx.doi.org/10.1787/230363687074> accessed 10 August 2021.

OECD, 'Consumer Policy Toolkit' (2010) <http://www.oecd-ilibrary.org/governance/consumer-policy-toolkit_9789264079663-en> accessed 6 September 2021.

OECD, 'Consumer Policy Guidance on Mobile and Online Payments' (2014) (OECD Digital Economy Papers, No. 236 <http://dx.doi.org/10.1787/5jz432cl1ns7-en> accessed 12 September 2021.

OECD, 'Report on Consumer Protection in Online and Mobile Payments' (OECD Digital Economy Papers, No. 204, 2012) <http://dx.doi.org/10.1787/5k9490gwp7f3-En> accessed 14 September 2021.

OECD and Russia's G20 Presidency, 'Advancing National Strategies for Financial Education' (2013) <https://www.oecd.org/finance/financial-education/G20_OECD_NSFinancialEducation.pdf > accessed 13 September 2021.

Omri Ben-Shahar and Carl E. Schneider, 'The Failure of Mandated Disclosure' (2011) 159 *University of Pennsylvania Law Review* 647.

Pablo Cortes, 'Online Dispute Resolution Services: A Selected Number of Case Studies' (2014) 20(6) *Computer and Telecommunications Law Review* 172.

Patrick S. Atiyah, *The Rise and Fall of Freedom of Contract* (Clarendon Press 1979).

Paul Latimer and Phillip Maume, *Promoting Information in the Marketplace for Financial Services: Financial Market Regulation and International Standards* (Springer 2014).

Peter Cartwright, 'The Vulnerable Consumer of Financial Services: Law, Policy and Regulation' (Financial Services Research Forum 2011) <https://www.nottingham.ac.uk/business/who-we-are/centres-and-institutes/gcbfi/documents/researchreports/paper78.pdf> Accessed 5 September 2021.

Peter Cartwright, *Banks, Consumers and Regulation* (Hart Publishing 2004).

Rhys Bollen, 'A Discussion of Best Practice in the Regulation of Payment Services: Part 2' (2010) 25(9) *Journal of International Banking Law and Regulation* 429.

Rhys Bollen, 'Recent Developments in Mobile Banking and Payments' (2009) 24(9) *Journal of International Banking Law and Regulation* 454.

Richard A. Posner, 'Rational Choice, Behavioural Economics, and the Law' (1997) 50 *Stanford Law Review* 1551.

Richard A. Posner, *Economic Analysis of the Law* (Little Brown and Company 1973).

Robert D. Cooter and Edward L. Rubin, 'Theory of Loss Allocation for Consumer Payments' (1987) 66 *Texas Law Review* 63.

Roger Miller, Gaylord A. Jentz, *Business Law Today: The Essentials* (Cengage Learning 2007).

Shauhin A. Talesh, 'How Dispute Resolution System Design Matters: An Organizational Analysis of Dispute Resolution Structures and Consumer Lemon Laws' (2012) 46(3) *Law & Society Review* 463.

Shmuel I Becher, 'Unintended Consequences and the Design of Consumer Protection Legislation' (2018) 93 *Tulane Law Review* 105.

Shmuel I. Becher and Tal Z. Zarsky, 'Open Doors, Trap Doors, and the Law' (2011) 74 *Law & Contemporary Problems* 63.

Stefan Wrbka, Steven Van Uytsel et al (eds), *Collective Actions: Enhancing Access to Justice and reconciling Multi-Layer Interests* (Cambridge University Press 2012).

Stephen Lumpkin, 'Consumer Protection and Financial Innovation: A Few Basic Propositions' (2010) 1 *OECD Journal: Financial Market Trends* 117.

Stephen Weatherill, *EU Consumer Law & Policy* (Edward Elgar Publishing 2005).

Stephen Weatherill and Ulf Bernitz, *The Regulation of Unfair Commercial Practices under EC Directive 2005/29: New Rules and New Techniques* (Bloomsbury Publishing 2007).

Steve Trites, Charles Gibney and Bruno Lévesque, Research Division, Financial Consumer Agency of Canada (2013) <https://www.canada.ca/content/dam/canada/financial-consumer-agency/migration/eng/resources/researchsurveys/documents/fcac_mobile_payments_consumer_protection_accessible_en.pdf>

Steven Shavell, 'On Liability and Insurance' (1982) 13(1) *The Bell Journal of Economics* 120.

The Financial Action Task Force (FATF), 'Guidance for a Risk-Based Approach: Prepaid Cards, Mobile Payments and Internet-Based Payment Services' (2013) <http://www.fatf-gafi.org/media/fatf/documents/recommendations/Guidance-RBA-NPPS.pdf> accessed 2 August 2021.

The Office of Communications (Ofcom), 'A Review of Consumer Information Remedies' (2013) <https://www.ofcom.org.uk/__data/assets/pdf_file/0033/91698/information-remedies.pdf> accessed 25 September 2021.

The World Bank Group, 'Complaints Handling within Financial Service Providers Principles, Practices, and Regulatory Approaches' (2019) <https://openknowledge.worldbank.org/handle/10986/32360?locale-attribute=en> accessed 14 September 2021.

The World Bank Group, 'Good Practices for Financial Consumer Protection' (World Bank 2017 ed.) <https://openknowledge.worldbank.org/handle/10986/28996> accessed 12 September 2021.

Toni Williams, 'Empowerment of Whom and for What? Financial Literacy Education and the New Regulation of Consumer Financial Services' (2007) 29(2) *Law & Policy* 226.

United Nations, 'Guidelines for Consumer Protection' (2016) <https://unctad.org/system/files/official-document/ditccplpmisc2016d1_en.pdf> accessed 5 September 2021.

Visa Europe, 'Protected When you Pay' <https://www.visa.co.uk/visa-everywhere/blog/bdp/2019/10/07/protected-when-you-1570458734759.html> accessed 14 September 2021.

Which, 'Unfair Terms in Consumer Contracts: A New Approach' (Which? Consultation Response 2012) <https://www.dropbox.com/s/pwwhdr2sczykdqd/which-response-unfair-terms-in-consumer-contracts-a-new-approach-301590.pdf?dl=0> accessed 9 September 2021.

# Part II

# Mobile Payments and Consumer Protection – Country Studies

# 5 Consumer Protection and Mobile Payments: Canada

## 5.1 Introduction

As is the case in many developed countries, Canadian consumers have access to and use various payment methods. However, there has been a growing shift towards contactless and digital payments in recent years.[1] While card payments continue to account for a significant percentage of contactless payments made, mobile contactless payments continue to grow, with nearly 29 per cent of Canadians using mobile payments (m-payments) to complete transactions in 2020.[2] M-payments are currently offered by a wide range of providers, including traditional banks, technology companies like Apple, Google, and PayPal and retailers like Starbucks.[3] The growing use of m-payments has not escaped the attention of Canadian regulators. As far back as 2013, the Financial Consumer Agency of Canada (FCAC) conducted a thematic review to ascertain whether its consumer protection laws could effectively protect m-payment consumers.[4]

Canada operates a federal system of government which means that federal and provincial authorities have constitutionally defined powers.[5] For example, the federal government has exclusive jurisdiction over telecommunication service providers and federally incorporated financial institutions like banks.[6] However,

1 Payments Canada, 'Payments Accelerated: Global Pandemic Accelerates the Rise of Digital Payments – Canadian Payment Methods and Trends Report 2021' p.8 <https://www.payments.ca/sites/default/files/payments_canada_canadian_payment_methods_and_trends_report_2021.pdf> accessed 20 January 2022.

2 Ibid.

3 Chris Powell, 'Mobile Payments Set to Rise This Year: Catalyst Canada' <http://marketingmag.ca/consumer/mobile-payments-set-to-rise-this-year-catalyst-canada-176794/> accessed 20 January 2021.

4 Steve Trites, Charles Gibney, and Bruno Lévesque, 'Mobile Payments and Consumer Protection in Canada' (2013 Research Division, Financial Consumer Agency of Canada) <https://www.canada.ca/content/dam/canada/financial-consumer-agency/migration/eng/resources/researchsurveys/documents/fcac_mobile_payments_consumer_protection_accessible_en.pdf> accessed 27 January 2022.

5 See the Constitution Act 1867, 30 & 31 Vict, c 3, Part VI.

6 Such as federally incorporated insurance, trust, and loan companies, and federal credit unions. Provincial authorities regulate credit unions, securities dealers and *caisses populaires* incorporated or

DOI: 10.4324/9780429327292-7

other financial institutions may also be registered or incorporated under provincial legislation.[7] The implication is that m-payment service providers will often be subject to a combination of federal and provincial regulations.

This is evident in the area of consumer protection. Although consumer protection is largely considered an area within provincial jurisdiction, federal authorities also regulate the relationship between consumers and federally regulated institutions.[8] Hence, m-payment service providers may be supervised by multiple consumer protection regulators at federal and provincial levels. For example, the FCAC supervises the consumer elements of federal financial services legislation, while provincial regulators oversee provincial consumer protection regulations. Therefore, discussions in this chapter cover both federal and provincial regulatory efforts where appropriate.

## 5.2 Provision of Information

### *5.2.1 Mandatory Disclosures*

The information disclosures required when providing m-payments depends mainly on the service provider's identity and the underlying funding source. Where the service provider is a federally regulated financial institution (FRFI), it is subject to mandatory disclosure obligations under relevant regulatory laws.[9] Previously, while the primary source of disclosure requirements was found in the Bank Act 1991,[10] the specific details were contained in different regulations made pursuant to the Act. Relevant to the funding sources for m-payments were regulations such as the Cost of Borrowing (Banks) Regulations (COBRs) 2001,[11] which governed credit agreements; the Disclosure of Charges (Banks) Regulations 1992,[12] which covered deposit accounts and the Negative Option Billing Regulations (NOBRs) 2012,[13] which dealt with optional products and services offered to existing customers of FRFIs.

---

registered at provincial level. FCAC, 'Who FCAC Regulates' <https://www.canada.ca/en/financial-consumer-agency/corporate/who-we-regulate.html> accessed 5 January 2022.

7 Robert R Kerton and Idris Ademuyiwa, 'Financial Consumer Protection in Canada: Triumphs and Tribulations' in Tsai-Jyh Chen (ed.), *An International Comparison of Financial Consumer Protection* (Springer 2018) pp. 86–87.

8 Catherine Mathieu, 'Do Consumers Really Benefit from the Federal Paramountcy Doctrine? A Critique of *Director of Criminal and Penal Prosecutions v. Telus Communications Inc.*' (2020) 29 *Constitutional Forum* 11, 12.

9 Although FRFIs are subject to federal laws, the recent decision of the Canadian Supreme Court in *Bank of Montreal v. Marcotte* (2014) SCC 55 suggests that provincial laws on disclosure may also apply to them.

10 SC 1991, c 46.

11 SOR/2001–101.

12 SOR/92–324.

13 SOR/2012–23.

In 2018, following legislative intervention, Canada adopted a new Financial Consumer Protection Framework, which sought, amongst other things, to consolidate important consumer protection requirements, including disclosures under a new Part XII.2 of the Bank Act.[14] To support and clarify these amendments, the Financial Consumer Protection Regulations (FCPRs) were also issued in 2021.[15] Most of the new provisions came into effect in June 2022, replacing the aforementioned regulations and consolidating their content into the Bank Act and FCPRs.[16]

Under the Bank Act, banks are subject to general disclosure requirements which apply in the provisions of financial products and services. Specifically, banks must ensure that disclosures are made in language that is clear, simple, and not misleading, and such disclosures must generally be made in writing.[17] Where agreements are made by telephone, disclosures can be made orally, but banks are required to provide the disclosures in writing without delay after the agreement is completed.[18] Banks are also expected to present key information in a prominently displayed information box.[19] Examples of key information will include the description of the product's features and the applicable charges or penalties.[20] Where oral disclosures are used, banks are expected to draw a customer's attention to the information that would usually be included in the information box.[21] Other general disclosure obligations require that banks disclose their complaints procedure and any voluntary codes of conduct and public commitments that they have endorsed.[22] Any changes to existing agreements must also be disclosed to consumers before they take effect.[23]

One important obligation imposed on banks is that before entering into an agreement with a customer by electronic means or mail, they are required to provide the customer with a local or toll-free telephone number of an employee or agent of the institution who is knowledgeable about the terms and conditions of the agreement to which the disclosures relate.[24] This provision appears to provide consumers with additional opportunities to discuss and understand the terms of the agreement disclosed. This is an important obligation in light of the discussions in *Chapter 4* which highlighted that while disclosures can be useful, they

14 Budget Implementation Act 2018, No.2 SC 2018, c 27 (also commonly referred to as 'Bill C–86').

15 SOR/2021–181. These came into force in June 2022.

16 Note that the Cost of Borrowing (Banks) Regulations and the Disclosure of Charges (Banks) Regulations have been repealed in full since they apply to only banks. However, the Negative Option Billing Regulations will continue to apply to other FRFIs like trust and loan companies. See the 'Description' section of the Regulatory Impact Analysis Statement <https://www.gazette.gc.ca/rp-pr/p2/2021/2021-08-18/html/sor-dors181-eng.html> accessed 14 January 2022.

17 s.627.55(1).

18 s.627.55(2)(b).

19 s.627.57(1).

20 s.627.59.

21 s.627.57(2).

22 ss.627.65 & 627.66.

23 s.627.62.

24 s.627.58.

are of little help if consumers do not understand them. By creating an additional opportunity for consumers to consult an expert for free, this obligation can potentially help to alleviate the intellectual limits consumers face in dealing with specialised information.

The general disclosure obligations are supplemented by additional disclosure requirements in the Bank Act and the FCPRs, which apply to specific products and services. For instance, for credit agreements, the Bank Act requires that banks disclose the cost of borrowing, the particulars of the customer's rights and obligations, applicable charges or penalties that may be imposed.[25] Banks must also make ongoing disclosures, including where there have been amendments to the terms or conditions of the credit agreement.[26]

The FCPRs confirm that to implement these obligations, banks must provide the required information in a disclosure statement that is part of the credit agreement or the application for the credit agreement.[27] The disclosure statement may also be set out in a separate document.[28] Where the disclosure statement is part of a credit agreement, then the bank must set out the disclosure statement in a consolidated manner in a single location.[29] Key information must be disclosed in a single prominently displayed information box which must be set out at the beginning of the agreement or separate document.[30] The key information prescribed is dependent on the type of loan agreement but generally includes the term of the loan, the annual interest rate and annual percentage rate, prepayment charges, etc.[31] Where m-payments are funded by a line of credit or a credit card, these disclosure requirements will likely apply.

These disclosure provisions which apply to credit agreements largely mirror the provisions under the COBRs.[32] However, there is one noticeable difference. The COBRs specifically prescribed the manner in which key information contained in the information box should be presented. For example, amongst other things, the COBRs recommended that text be presented in an easily readable font style and size.[33] It also recommended the standard spacing between words and characters and the use of contrasting background and text colours to highlight information.[34] These requirements served to ensure legibility, making it easier for consumers to engage with the information disclosed. As we saw in *Chapter 3*, information overload can trigger consumers to rely on heuristics when making

25 s.627.89(1).
26 s.627.89(4) & (5).
27 s.33(1).
28 Ibid.
29 s.33(2).
30 Bank Act, s.627.57(1); FCPRs, s.33(2).
31 FSPRs, ss. 38, 39, 52 & 59.
32 As earlier stated, the disclosure requirements for credit agreements were formerly contained in the COBRs. See (n 16).
33 s.6(2.4)(a).
34 s.6(2.4)(b) & (d).

decisions which may defeat the aim of disclosures. Thus, the OECD suggests that making disclosures more user friendly may present one option for addressing this problem.[35] The prescribed presentation seemed to reflect the OECD's recommendations.

Nevertheless, these requirements were not replicated in Part XII.2 of the Bank Act or the FCPRs. Some views suggest that the presentation requirements under the COBRs were 'anachronistic in the digital age'[36] and that eliminating them might alleviate challenges associated with disclosing in a digital format.[37] While it is understandable that firms may have struggled to meet the mandated requirements, they served a useful purpose, as highlighted above. Hence, it might have been better to make specific allowances for digital disclosures without eliminating the requirement where paper-based disclosures are used.

Where m-payments services are funded by a personal deposit account or a debit card linked to such an account, the applicable disclosure requirements can also be found in Part XII.2 of the Bank Act and the FCPRs. They were formerly contained in the Disclosure of Charges (Banks) Regulations 1992.[38] Under the Bank Act, banks are mandated to disclose all charges applicable to personal deposit accounts.[39] Where a new charge is introduced, or an existing charge increased, banks must disclose this at least 30 days before the effective date of the proposed change.[40] Thus, where banks charge customers for m-payment services funded by a personal deposit account, such information must be disclosed in a manner compliant with the Bank Act and the FCPRs.

The Canadian Code of Practice for Consumer Debit Card Services ('the Debit Card Code') also contains disclosure requirements that apply where a debit card is the underlying funding source.[41] The Debit Card Code is a voluntary industry initiative that applies to organisations that have endorsed the code.[42] The Debit Card Code has been endorsed by the Canadian Banking Association and the Canadian Credit Union Association. This suggests that m-payment users funding

35 OECD, 'Improving Online Disclosures with Behavioural insights: Towards Better Outcomes for Consumers' (2018) <https://www.oecd.org/sti/consumer/policy-note-improving-online-disclosures-behavioural-insights.pdf> accessed 27 January 2022.

36 Elizabeth Sale and Haley Adams, 'Federal Financial Consumer Protection Framework In-Force Date Announced, New Regulations Published' (2021) <https://www.osler.com/en/resources/regulations/2021/federal-financial-consumer-protection-framework-in-force-date-announced-new-regulations-published> accessed 9 January 2022.

37 Brigitte Goulard, Peter A Aziz, and Marissa A Daniels, 'New Regulations Complete Overhaul of Bank Act Consumer Provisions' (2021) <https://www.torys.com/our-latest-thinking/publications/2021/08/new-regulations-complete-overhaul-of-bank-act-consumer-provisions> accessed 9 January 2022.

38 Trites et al. (n 4) p.36.

39 s.627.68(a).

40 s.627.72(1).

41 The Canadian Code of Practice for Consumer Debit Card Services <https://www.canada.ca/en/financial-consumer-agency/services/industry/laws-regulations/debit-card-code-conduct.html> accessed 9 January 2022.

42 See paragraph 8 for a list of endorsing organisations.

transactions through debit cards issued by FRFIs (like banks and federally incorporated credit unions) and non-FRFIs (like provincially regulated credit unions) are entitled to the same disclosures under the Code of Practice.[43] Where this is the case, the service providers will be expected to inform customers of any fees associated with using the debit cards, how to contact the card issuer if a problem arises, applicable liability rules and dispute resolution procedures.[44] Customers are also entitled to transaction records detailing completed transactions and periodic statements.[45]

Where a bank wishes to offer its existing customers a new optional financial product or service, they were required to obtain the customer's consent before providing the product/service under the Canadian Negative Option Billing Regulations (NOBRs) 2012.[46] These provisions have also been subsumed into the Bank Act and the FCPRs. The new regime confirms that the consent requirement remains.[47] Optional products and services are described as those products or services that are provided as a supplement to another product or service offered by the institution.[48] This definition is technology-neutral and easily applies to FRFIs offering their existing customers new or optional m-payment products/services. To secure a customer's consent to provide an optional service, banks must disclose prescribed information to the customer before such consent is obtained.[49]

The prescribed disclosures should include a description of the product or service, the terms of the agreement, applicable charges, and conditions for cancellation.[50] The disclosure statement must also contain the date from which the product/service is available for use and, if different, the date from which the charges apply and the steps required to use the product.[51] Consumers also have the right to be informed of any changes to terms and conditions at least 30 days before the date the change takes effect.[52] Such disclosures should be in writing using language that is 'clear, simple and not misleading.'[53]

For m-payments funded by direct mobile billing,[54] the relevant disclosure obligations under the Wireless Code apply.[55] The Wireless Code is a mandatory

43 Trites et al. (n 4) p.39.
44 Paragraph 2(3).
45 Paragraph 4.
46 s.3. Provinces also regulate negative option practices; see, for instance, Alberta's Consumer Protection Act RSA 2000, c 26.3, ss. 20–23.
47 s.627.08(1); s.627.42(2).
48 s.627.01.
49 s.627.94 (1) & (2).
50 s.627.94(1).
51 Ibid.
52 s.627.96.
53 s.627.55(1).
54 See *Chapter 2* for an explanation of 'direct mobile billing.'
55 The Code was first issued by the Canadian Radio-Television and Telecommunications Commission (CRTC) in 2013 and revised in 2017 <https://crtc.gc.ca/eng/phone/mobile/codesimpl.htm> accessed 10 January 2022.

code of conduct that only applies to retail mobile wireless voice and data services and therefore applies to mobile network operators (MNOs) providing m-payment services.[56] Under the Wireless Code, service providers must give the customer a permanent copy of the contract and other related documents that set out key contract terms and conditions.[57] In addition, post-paid customers are also entitled to a 'Critical Information Summary' document, which describes the key contract terms, the applicable rates, charges, and fees, information on any limits imposed on services purchases and complaint procedures.[58] The prescribed information must be clear and concise, not exceeding two pages and must be presented using plain language and in an easily readable font.[59]

Where the payment service provider (PSP) is a non-FRFI, they will be governed by provincial laws, which will determine the applicable disclosure requirements. For example, non-FRFIs issuing credit are required to make disclosures similar to those contained under the Bank Act.[60] This is because credit disclosure requirements are harmonised in Canada.[61]

Two points can be made about the existing disclosure regime. First, the Bank Act's general disclosure regime introduces minimum requirements which allow for some consistency amongst banks providing m-payments. For instance, it is clear that disclosure statements and information boxes will be consistently required. Although the content of information boxes may differ,[62] consumers will become accustomed to the fact that they can find a summary of the key information about a product or service in the boxes at the beginning of contractual documents. However, it is unclear if these disclosure requirements are developed with mobile devices in mind. This observation leads Trites et al. to argue that consumers may be disadvantaged if these disclosures are not easy to read on mobile devices. Thus, they suggest that optimising disclosures for use on mobile devices may be helpful.[63] However, they do not elaborate on what 'optimising' connotes. It is clear that mobile devices often have relatively small screens, which may make it challenging to process lengthy disclosure information. Therefore, one may interpret 'optimising' to mean providing a summary of information in a mobile-friendly manner and/or providing mobile links to lengthier disclosures which can be accessed through a more convenient medium by the consumer.[64]

56 CRTC, 'Telecom Regulatory Policy' (CRTC 2017–200), para.1. <https://crtc.gc.ca/eng/archive/2017/2017-200.htm> accessed 10 January 2022.

57 Parts B & C.

58 Part C, paragraph 1(iii).

59 Part C, paragraph 1(iv).

60 See for example, British Columbia's Business Practices and Consumer Protection Act, SBC 2004, c 2, Part 5; Alberta's Consumer Protection Act, RSA 2000, c 26.3, Part 9; Ontario's Consumer Protection Act SO 2002, c 30, Part VII.

61 Trites et al. (n 4) p.39.

62 Depending on whether the disclosures relate to a credit agreement or a personal deposit account.

63 Trites et al. (n 4) p.36.

64 For instance, a consumer may print out a lengthy disclosure document or may decide to open a link on a personal computer with a bigger screen.

Second, while the disclosure regime under the Bank Act is detailed, it only applies to banks. Non-FRFIs will be subject to provincial laws, while specific providers like MNOs will be subject to the Wireless Code. This confirms that disclosure requirements applying to m-payments depend primarily on the existing obligations applicable to the m-payment service provider and the funding source used. This leads to inconsistency in the disclosure mandates. An example of this is with regards to disclosures on consumer liability for loss due to unauthorised transactions. While the Wireless Code does not mandate disclosures on limits to consumers' liability against loss, the FCPRs do.[65] Thus, MNOs are not obliged to make such disclosures while banks offering m-payments are obliged to do so.

### *5.2.2 Consumer Education*

Under Canada's constitution, provinces are responsible for overseeing education.[66] Hence, provinces choose how to promote general (and financial) consumer education, including how these are embedded in their education curriculum.[67] Some provinces maintain online financial literacy resources for consumers, but this approach is not consistent in all provinces.[68] Overall, provincial efforts are fragmented.[69] However, there have been specific efforts at the federal level to champion a coherent approach to financial consumer education. These efforts have been partly influenced by calls from the OECD for member countries to 'promote financial education and awareness.'[70] Hence, discussions in this section focus mainly on federal efforts.

At the federal level, the FCAC manages the implementation of Canada's financial literacy framework. The FCAC is tasked with promoting financial literacy and consumer awareness about all matters connected with protecting their interests in using financial products and services.[71] The FCAC is also charged with coordinating the efforts of stakeholders to foster an understanding of financial services and issues relating to financial services.[72] In line with this mandate, the FCAC commissioned its thematic review of m-payments in 2013. The FCAC primarily sought to understand the extent to which Canadian consumers were

65 See for example, FCPRs, s.64(1)(d).

66 The Constitution Act 1867, 30 & 31 Vict, c 3, s.93.

67 Sue LT McGregor, 'Status of Consumer Education and Financial Education in Canada' (2018) 41(2) *Canadian Journal of Education* 601.

68 For example, Manitoba maintains a financial literacy website which is accessible here: <https://www.gov.mb.ca/finance/literacy/consumer/education_all.html> accessed 8 January 2022.

69 McGregor (n 67).

70 OECD, 'Recommendation on Principles and Good Practices for Financial Education and Awareness' (2005) <https://www.oecd.org/finance/financial-education/35108560.pdf> accessed 8 January 2022.

71 Financial Consumer Agency of Canada Act, SC 2001, c 9, s.3(2)(d).

72 Ibid. s.3(2)(e).

protected when making m-payments. One important conclusion drawn by the FCAC was that –

> For a protection regime to be effective, consumers must be knowledgeable about their rights and responsibilities. Knowledgeable consumers are empowered and better able to make informed decisions ... To implement effective consumer education initiatives, it will be important to determine the best messengers and key target audiences, as well as the most appropriate media for communicating messages.[73]

Since the review, the FCAC has engaged in education initiatives specifically targeting m-payments. These initiatives mainly focus on hosting educative materials on the FCAC website. The information provided covers a range of themes. First, consumers are advised on how to make m-payments with simple explanations on the different supporting technologies.[74] Appropriate examples are also used to show how a particular technology can be used. For instance, consumers are advised that QR codes in a gift card issued by a specific coffee shop can be used to make purchases in that shop and that mobile devices can be used to complete in-app purchases of digital content like extra features in a game.[75]

Second, consumers also receive information on how to get and use a mobile wallet which consolidates their payment credentials in a mobile software application.[76] The FCAC explains how a consumer's payment credentials are stored when a mobile wallet is used and the consumer's rights when using a mobile wallet. For example, the FCAC points out that each payment source must be represented as a separate icon and that consumers have the right to select which payment source they wish to use when completing a transaction. Consumers also have the right to change the default settings that control the payment sources in use.[77]

Importantly the FCAC also highlights the risks involved in using m-payments, emphasising the possibility of fraud due to malicious software that may be installed on smartphones. Following this theme, the FCAC maintains a web page with information on how consumers may keep their mobile devices safe.[78] For example, consumers are advised to lock their devices with a password or a biometric security feature like a fingerprint scan to prevent criminals from accessing

73 Trites et al. (n 4) p57.

74 Financial Consumer Agency of Canada, 'Paying with your Mobile Phone' <https://www.canada.ca/en/financial-consumer-agency/services/payment/mobile-payments/paying-with-mobile.html> accessed 10 January 2022.

75 Ibid.

76 Financial Consumer Agency of Canada, 'Mobile Wallets' <https://www.canada.ca/en/financial-consumer-agency/services/payment/mobile-payments/mobile-wallets.html> accessed 10 January 2022.

77 Ibid.

78 Financial Consumer Agency of Canada, 'Secure the Data on your Mobile Devices' <https://www.getcybersafe.gc.ca/en/secure-your-devices/phones-and-tablets> accessed 10 January 2022.

sensitive financial information stored on the devices. Consumers are also advised to regularly update their devices' operating systems to strengthen security, improve functionality, and remove bugs.[79] They are also advised to be careful when connecting to unsecured Wi-Fi or using Bluetooth technology, as it may leave room for hackers to access their devices. The FCAC also draws consumers' attention to how SMS messages may put their devices at risk and warns against the download of untrustworthy software applications which can compromise their device security.[80] Further guidance is also provided on how consumers can safely download mobile software applications.[81] Finally, where a mobile device is lost or stolen, the FCAC advises consumers on steps to take, such as contacting their mobile wallet provider to disable the wallet and notifying the relevant financial institutions that have issued the payment cards linked to the wallet.[82]

What stands out about the FCAC's efforts in this area is the accessibility of the information provided to consumers. The information is presented in simple, non-technical language. Where technical issues such as the supporting technology are referred to, the FCAC uses appropriate examples to aid consumer understanding. The themes also appear to be informed by the issues highlighted in the FCAC's thematic review, ensuring that the information provided is relevant. For example, the thematic highlighted concerns about the potential for fraud and misuse, which raised privacy concerns and impacted the allocation of liability. The FCAC's efforts address these issues by raising awareness of important security practices that consumers should adopt.

Only one province, i.e., Manitoba, appears to have developed consumer education initiatives that specifically target m-payments. Like the FCAC, Manitoba maintains a web page with user-friendly information on m-payments.[83] Consumers are educated on the risks associated with m-payments and steps that they may take to protect themselves. While less detailed than the information provided by the FCAC, it mirrors the themes covered by the FCAC. An important feature is that the Manitoban authorities also provide web links to the FCAC's resources which consumers can consult to supplement the information provided.

Industry also assists with financial education. For instance, the Canadian Banking Association (CBA) maintains a website with a section dedicated to 'banking basics' which provides information on various financial services that consumers may find helpful.[84] While the CBA's site contains some information on m-payments and mobile wallets, the information is not as detailed or as educative

79 Ibid.

80 Ibid.

81 Financial Consumer Agency of Canada, 'How you can stay cyber secure when downloading and using apps' <https://www.getcybersafe.gc.ca/en/blogs/how-you-can-stay-cyber-secure-when-downloading-and-using-apps> accessed 10 January 2022.

82 FCAC, 'Mobile Wallets' (n 76).

83 Consumer Protection Office (Manitoba), 'Payments on the Go: Mobile Payments' <https://www.gov.mb.ca/cp/cpo/info/payments_to_go.html> accessed 10 January 2022.

84 <https://cba.ca/?cat=Banking-Basics> accessed 10 January 2022.

as that provided by the FCAC.[85] The CBA's publications on m-payments have focused mainly on industry guidelines ensuring the safe and secure delivery of m-payments.[86]

## 5.3 Withdrawal Rights and Cooling-Off Periods

There are provisions for cooling-off periods at both federal and provincial levels which may benefit m-payment consumers. At the federal level, the Bank Act distinguishes two categories of financial services. The first category covers specific products and services such as retail deposit accounts, deposit type instruments, credit cards, and a number of prescribed products and services.[87] The second category covers all products and services not included in the first category.

For the first category of products, the FRFIs contain specific cancellation rules. For example, an agreement in respect of a retail deposit account can be cancelled within 14 business days after the day on which the retail deposit account is opened, while agreements in respect of new deposit type instruments can be cancelled within 10 business days after the day on which the instrument is issued.[88]

For products falling within the second category, the customer has a 14-business day cooling-off period starting after the day the agreement is entered into to cancel the agreement.[89] This applies where the agreement has been entered into by mail or orally by telephone. Where it has been entered into by any other means, then the customer may cancel within a three-business day cooling-off period running from the day after the day on which the agreement is entered into.[90] Where a customer chooses to cancel, they may do so without being charged except for amounts related to the use of the product before cancellation and any expenses that the institution has reasonably incurred in the provision of the service.[91]

If m-payments are broadly interpreted to fall under the second category, then a 14-day or three-day cancellation period applies depending on how the agreement is completed. However, it must be noted that one of the prescribed products falling under the first category includes 'optional products or services that are provided on an ongoing basis.'[92] As explained in Section 5.2.1 of this chapter, the neutral definition of optional products and services can easily capture m-payments

85 For example, see Canadian Banking Association, 'Credit & Debit Cards, Mobile Payments and Cheques' <https://bankingquestions.cba.ca/payments> accessed 10 January 2022.

86 For example, see Canadian Banking Association, 'Canadian NFC Mobile Payments Reference Model' (2012) <https://cba.ca/Assets/CBA/Documents/Files/Article Category/PDF/msc_20120514_mobile_summary_en.pdf> accessed 10 January 2022.

87 Bank Act, s.627.1(1); s.627(11)(1). The prescribed products can be found under the FCPRs, s.4.

88 FCPRs, ss.5(1) & 6(1).

89 Bank Act, s.627.1(1)(a).

90 Or such other period as may be prescribed: Bank Act, s.627.1(1)(b). An example of such a prescribed period can be found in the FRFIs, s.3 which prescribes a period of 14 days for a deposit account other than a retail deposit account.

91 Bank Act, s.627.1(3).

92 FCPRs, s.4(a).

provided by banks. For such optional services, a consumer may cancel the service by notifying the institution of the cancellation.[93] No specific cancellation period is given, but the FCPRs require that the institution cancels the service on the day the billing cycle ends or 30 days after the notification is received, whichever is earlier.[94]

Although consumers can generally cancel optional services, it appears to operate differently from the usual arrangements where a cancellation right is available during a specified cooling-off period. The provisions for optional services can be interpreted as providing a flexible right to withdraw at any time during the contractual period subject to the imposition of any relevant charges.[95] Comparing these provisions to other cancellation provisions highlighted above support this argument. For example, with products falling in the second category, a consumer may notify a bank of their intention to cancel within 14 business days after the day on which the agreement is entered into.[96] Here the 14 days clearly serves as a cooling-off period, but this approach is not replicated with optional products and services. Instead, the cancellation right does not appear to be limited by time.

At the provincial level, cooling-off periods are dealt with under provincial consumer protection statutes. In most provinces, cooling-off periods only apply to specific contracts, most of which cannot be strictly classified as payment services contracts. For instance, under the Ontario Consumer Protection Act (Ontario's CPA),[97] cooling-off provisions only apply to direct agreement contracts,[98] personal development contracts, pay-day loans, timeshares, and contracts to purchase a condominium.[99] In Manitoba, cooling-off periods apply to retail sale and retail hire-purchase transactions.[100]

The provincial cooling-off provisions that may be relevant to m-payments involve optional services provided to consumers who are party to a credit agreement. Provincial statutes allow them to cancel optional services by giving notice to the credit provider. For instance, in Alberta, a borrower may cancel an optional service by giving 30 days' notice or a shorter period of notice provided under the credit agreement.[101] In addition, where the borrower chooses to cancel the

93 FCPRs, s.7(1). See also Bank Act, s.627.94(2).

94 FCPRs, s.7(2). Where the optional service is a credit agreement, prescribed disclosure obligations suggests that a customer may cancel the service by 'notifying the institution that the service is to be cancelled effective as of the day that is the earlier of one month after the day that the disclosure statement was provided to the person and the last day of a notice period provided for in the credit agreement' FCPRs, s.35(1)(a).

95 s.7(3) provides a prescribed formula for determining refunds after cancellation.

96 s.5(1).

97 (n 60).

98 Where a consumer agreement is negotiated or concluded in person at a place other than a supplier's place of business or at an auction, trade fair, etc. s.20(1).

99 See Part IV of Ontario's CPA (n 60).

100 Manitoba Consumer Protection Act 1987 (as amended) CCSM, c 200, s.62(1).

101 Alberta's Consumer Protection Act (n 60), s.67(1). Similar provisions are also contained in British Columbia's Business Practices and Consumer Protection Act (n 60) s.73(1); Manitoba's Consumer Protection Act (n 100) s.23.

optional service, they are not liable for charges relating to a portion of the service that has not been provided at the time of cancellation and is entitled to a refund of any charges period.[102]

It was stated earlier that banking services are federally regulated, which explains why the provincial statutes are mostly silent on cooling-off periods for financial/payment services contracts. This, however, creates an unpredictable situation because m-payments can be provided by non-FRFIs (other than credit providers), which are regulated by the provinces. Therefore, the likely effect is that consumers served by non-FRFIs may be worse off than those dealing with FRFIs or provincially regulated credit issuers. Any cooling-off period applicable to such consumers will entirely depend on their contract with the m-payments provider. However, one possible interpretation of these provincial laws is that although consumers may not enjoy cooling-off periods when subscribing to the m-payment service itself (except where it is an optional service offered by a credit provider), they may enjoy this right where m-payments are used to complete eligible contracts under the provincial laws.

## 5.4 The Regulation of Business Conduct

### *5.4.1 Regulating Unfair Commercial Practices*

Business practices are regulated under the Canadian Competition Act 1985 (CCA)[103] and the various provincial consumer protection statutes. Sector-specific provisions in the Bank Act also contain rules governing responsible business conduct. It is expected that m-payment providers will be subject to these existing regulatory regimes. The CCA focuses on false and misleading representations, which are discussed in Section 5.4.3.

The amendments to the Bank Act dedicate an entire division to provisions promoting responsible business conduct. Responsible business conduct is broadly defined and covers issues pertaining to the prohibition of false and misleading information,[104] a customer's cancellation rights, the need to secure a customer's consent before providing services, accessibility to financial services,[105] and complaints handling processes, amongst others. Certain requirements such as the consent requirements and cancellation rights have already been discussed,[106] while others such as the complaints handling provisions are discussed later in this chapter. Relevant to our discussions in this section is the prohibition of specific behaviours under the Act.

102 Alberta's Consumer Protection Act (n 60) s.67(2). See also British Columbia's Business Practices and Consumer Protection Act (n 60) s.73(2); Manitoba's Consumer Protection Act (n 100), s.24.

103 RSC, 1985 c C–34.

104 This is discussed in Section 5.4.3 of this chapter.

105 These provisions (ss.627.17–627.19) aim to improve financial access and inclusion.

106 For consent requirements, see the discussion on mandatory disclosures in Section 5.2.1 of this chapter and for cancellation rights, see Section 5.3.

First, the Bank Act prohibits banks from imposing undue pressure on a customer or coercing them for any purpose.[107] This includes the use of undue pressure or coercion to force a consumer to obtain one product or service from the institution (and its affiliates) as a condition for obtaining another product or service from the bank.[108] This provision will be useful in discouraging services which, for example, may make the provision of m-payment services to a consumer dependent on purchasing insurance for their mobile device from the bank or its affiliate. The Bank Act further prohibits banks from taking advantage of any consumer.[109] This broadly worded provision presumably provides the regulator with the flexibility to address other forms of unfair conduct.

Second, the Bank Act requires that banks establish and implement policies to ensure that products or services offered or sold to consumers[110] are appropriate having regard to their circumstance, including their financial needs.[111] This prevents situations where consumers are mis-sold inappropriate products, which can negatively impact their financial health, leading to issues such as over-indebtedness or the imposition of liability/financial losses due to a poor understanding of the risks attached to a product. For example, this provision would prevent the provision of m-payment services funded by an underlying credit line that further perpetuates over-indebtedness or the sale of payment insurance products under the guise of securing repayments for m-payment transactions funded by a credit line. Third, to support this obligation, the Bank Act also prohibits practices that provide perverse incentives for bank officers and employees to mis-sell products and services. Hence, banks are required to ensure that the remuneration offered to employees and officers does not interfere with their ability to comply with the obligation to only sell appropriate products to consumers.[112]

Failure to comply with the provisions of the Bank Act is an offence, and guilty parties are subject to criminal sanctions, including imprisonment and the payment of fines.[113] However, while criminal sanctions may serve as a strong deterrent, there are limitations associated with this approach which are briefly highlighted later in this section and in more detail in Section 5.4.3 of this chapter.

Though important, the provisions in the Bank Act are of limited reach because they are sector-specific. At the provincial level, legislative efforts at tackling unfair practices apply irrespective of the sector and, therefore, have a broader reach. The relevant rules can be found in the respective provincial consumer protection statutes. As can be expected, there are similarities and differences in the approach adopted by the provinces.

107 Bank Act, s.627.04(a).

108 Ibid.

109 Bank Act, s.627.04(b).

110 Other than for business purposes.

111 Bank Act, s.627.06.

112 Bank Act, s.627.07.

113 Bank Act, ss.980 & 985.

The provinces generally prohibit the use of unfair business practices.[114] Before proceeding, it is important to note that there is no consistency in the terminology used across the provinces. While the choice of terminology in some provincial statutes is 'unfair,' in others, the term 'unconscionable' is used.[115] Where the latter is the case, the statute appears to categorise unfair practices and unconscionable practices differently but does not explicitly explain the difference between both.[116] In some other provinces, unfair practices consist of subcategories, including unconscionable representations and false and misleading or deceptive representations.[117] Despite these differences, a careful reading of the different provisions confirms that the essence of the provisions is similar.

In giving effect to the prohibition against unfair and unconscionable practices, some provinces include a general explanation of what an unfair or unconscionable practice means. Others simply contain an indicative list of prohibited practices without explicitly defining what unfairness or unconscionability mean in the context of the legislation. Some provinces combine both approaches, i.e., explaining what an unfair business practice means and providing further examples of practices that are deemed to be unfair.

In the first category, where legislation defines the meaning of an unfair practice, the clearest example can be found in Newfoundland's Consumer Protection and Business Practices Act 2010 (Newfoundland's CPBPA). Under the CPBPA, an unfair practice is a 'representation, conduct or failure to disclose material facts that has the effect, or might reasonably have the effect, of deceiving or misleading a consumer.'[118] Taking a less precise approach, Manitoba's Business Practices Act 1990 (Manitoba's BPA) explains that–

> It is an unfair business practice for a supplier–
>
> (a) to do or say anything or to fail to do or say anything if, as a result, a consumer might reasonably be deceived or misled or
>
> (b) to make a false claim or representation.[119]

114 See for example Alberta's Consumer Protection Act (n 60) s.6(1.1); Ontario's Consumer Protection Act (n 60) s.17(1); Manitoba's Business Practices Act 1990 CCSM, c B120, s.5; Newfoundland's Consumer Protection and Business Practices Act SNL 2009 c 31.1, s.9; Prince Edward Island's Business Practices Act RSPEI 1988 c B-7, s.3(1); Saskatchewan's Consumer Protection and Business Practices Act SS 2013 c C-30.2, s.8(1).

115 For example, reference is only made to unfair practices in Alberta's Consumer Protection Act (n 60), Part 2, Manitoba's Business Practices Act (n 114) Part I and Saskatchewan's Consumer Protection and Business Practices Act (n 114) Part II.

116 This is the case in Newfoundland's Consumer Protection and Business Practices Act (n 114) Part III.

117 This is the case in Ontario's Consumer Protection Act (n 60) Part III and Prince Edward Island's Business Practices Act (n 114) s.2(a) & (b).

118 s.7(1).

119 s.2(1). A similar approach is taken under Saskatchewan's Consumer Protection and Business Practices Act (n 114) s.6.

Though both statutes define unfair practices using different wordings, both emphasise the effect of the business practice in question. Where a business practice deceives or misleads a consumer or reasonably has the effect of doing so, then such practice will run foul of the statutes. One possible advantage of adopting broad definitions is that it ensures that acts not expressly identified can still fall within the scope of the statute if they promote the mischief sought to be prohibited.[120]

In the second category, while legislation does not define unfair practices, it either includes a detailed list of practices which are deemed unfair/unconscionable or provides a list of factors which ought to be considered in reaching such a determination. Examples of this approach can be found in Alberta and British Columbia. Alberta's Consumer Protection Act (Alberta's CPA)[121] includes a list of practices that are deemed to be unfair.[122] Under British Columbia's Business Practices and Consumer Protection Act (British Columbia's BPCPA) 2004, unfair practices are divided into broad categories, including the use of deceptive acts and practices and the use of unconscionable acts and practices.[123] Although British Columbia's BPCPA does not define what an unconscionable act connotes, it provides a list of factors that a court may consider in determining if an act or practice is unconscionable.[124] Though couched in different ways, some of the practices singled out in both statutes are similar. For example, under Alberta's CPA, it is an unfair practice for a supplier to exert pressure or influence on the consumer to enter into a consumer transaction.[125] Similarly, under British Columbia's BPCPA, one factor that a court must consider in deciding if a supplier's act or practice is unconscionable is whether the supplier has subjected the consumer to undue pressure to enter into a transaction.[126]

The identification of specific practices which are deemed unfair or particular factors which may aid a court in reaching such a determination may be helpful in the sense that it promotes certainty. Businesses are sure of what types of practices are prohibited, and consumers are also provided with concrete examples of practices to watch out for. However, one problem with this approach is that it may be of limited effect where new unfair practices emerge due to market changes that were not envisaged at the time of drafting. As stated earlier, using a broadly worded definition may solve this problem, but other alternatives exist.

120 A similar approach is found under British Columbia's Business Practices and Consumer Protection Act of (n 60) ss.4 & 8.

121 (n 60). The Consumer Protection Act was formerly known as the Fair Trading Act SA 1998 c F-1.05. A similar approach can be found in the Prince Edward Island's Business Practices Act (n 114) s.2.

122 s.6.

123 See British Columbia's BPCPA (n 60) Part 2. A similar approach is taken under Ontario's CPA (n 60) Part III.

124 s.8(3).

125 s.6(2)(a).

126 s.8(3)(a).

One example can be found in Alberta's CPA which further empowers the relevant minister to make regulations specifying unfair practices.[127] This provision may allow for timely and flexible regulatory responses to changes in market behaviour.

As stated earlier, some provinces combine both approaches, i.e., adopting the flexibility that a broadly worded definition permits while providing some certainty by also including a list of prohibited practices or factors that may guide courts in assessing a business practice. Newfoundland, Manitoba, and Saskatchewan take this approach.[128] Apart from the broad definitions of unfair practices highlighted earlier, they also include a list of practices deemed unfair[129] and factors that help a court determine if a practice is unconscionable.[130]

One important similarity in most provinces is that the evaluation of unfair practices takes the multilingual nature of Canada into consideration. For instance, Section 6(2)(b) of Alberta's CPA provides that it is an unfair practice –

> to take advantage of the consumer as a result of the consumer's inability to understand the character, nature, *language*[131] or effect of the consumer transaction or any matter related to the transaction.[132]

Similar provisions can be found in other provincial statutes.[133] This provision broadly prohibits practices which exploit a consumer's inability to appreciate the nature, language, or effect of a transaction. The particular reference to language can be significant in multilingual societies like Canada. One may argue that one of the aims of fair practices legislation is to support consumers in making rational decisions that are not influenced by biased conduct or information. Like other unfair practices, exploiting linguistic barriers can distort informed decision-making. Hence it is reasonable to prohibit practices which exploit these barriers to the consumer's detriment.

Another significant similarity between provinces is that contravention of the provisions of the relevant statutes (including the use of unfair or unconscionable practices) is criminalised in a fashion similar to the old CCA regime.[134] No

127 s.12.

128 See Manitoba's BPA (n 114) ss.2(1) & 2(3); Newfoundland's CPBPA (n 114) ss.7(1) & 8(1); Saskatchewan's Consumer Protection and Business Practices Act (n 114) ss.6 &7.

129 Newfoundland's CPBPA (n 114) s.7 & Manitoba's BPA (n 114) s.7(1).

130 Newfoundland's CPBPA (n 114) s.8.

131 Emphasis added.

132 See similar provisions in of the British Columbia's BPCPA (n 60) s.8(3)(b), Manitoba's BPA (n 114) s.3(2).

133 See British Columbia's BPCPA (n 60) s.8(3)(b); Manitoba's BPA (n 114) s.3(2)(a); Newfoundland's CPBPA (n 114) s.8(1)(f); Ontario's CPA (n 60) s.15(2)(a); Prince Edward Island's Business Practices Act (n 114) s.2(b)(i).

134 Alberta's CPA (n 60) s.6(1.1); Ontario's CPA (n 60) s.116(1)(b)(ii); Manitoba's BPA (n 114) s.33(1); Newfoundland's CPBPA (n 114) s.109; Prince Edward Island's Business Practices Act (n 114) s.18(2); Saskatchewan's Consumer Protection and Business Practices Act (n 114) s.108. The Old CCA regime is discussed in more detail in Section 5.4.3 of this chapter.

distinction is drawn between situations where default is intentional or otherwise. Regulators are also often empowered with a wide range of administrative powers.[135] Criticisms of criminal sanctions are similar to those applying to the old CCA regime discussed later in Section 5.4.3. Such criticisms emphasise the high cost of prosecution and the possible disproportionate use of criminal sanctions in less serious cases.[136] On the other hand, it may also not be appropriate to over-rely on administrative/civil enforcement tools without any room for criminal sanctions because criminal sanctions may be an appropriate response in more severe cases.[137] Commentators like Ayres and Braithwaite point out that achieving regulatory objectives is more likely when regulators adopt a hierarchy of sanctions and regulatory strategies of varying degrees of interventionism.[138] This is because regulators will be best positioned to encourage cooperation when they can escalate deterrence in a manner that is responsive to the degree of uncooperativeness of a firm.[139] Thus a combination of both approaches (i.e., criminal sanctions alone and administrative sanctions) are useful in responding to different degrees of non-compliance.

Where consumers have been subjected to unfair or unconscionable practices, a range of remedies is available to them. In Alberta, for instance, a consumer may cancel a consumer transaction tainted by unfair practices. This right subsists whether the practice occurred before, during, or after the transaction was entered into.[140] Where cancellation is impossible, the consumer may recover 'the amount by which the consumer's payment under the consumer transaction exceeds the value of the goods or services to the consumer, or to recover damages, or both.'[141] Consumers can also maintain private actions in court against a supplier in most provinces. Where a consumer maintains a court action, courts are empowered to award a wide range of remedies, including damages, rescission, injunction,

135 See for example, British Columbia's BPCPA (n 60) Part 10; Manitoba's BPA (n 114) Part II, Ontario's CPA (n 60) Parts X.1 & XI; Saskatchewan's Consumer Protection and Business Practices Act (n 114) Part VIII.

136 Peter Cartwright, 'Redress Compliance and Choice: Enhanced Consumer Measures and the retreat from punishment in the Consumer Rights Act 2015' (2016) 75(2) *Cambridge Law Journal* 271.

137 Andrew Ashworth, 'Is the Criminal Law a Lost Cause?' (2000) 116 *Law Quarterly Review* 225, 250.

138 Ian Ayres and John Braithwaite, *Responsive Regulation: Transcending the Deregulation Debate* (Oxford University Press 1992) pp.5–6.

139 Ibid. p.36.

140 It is also in addition to any remedy that is available at law, including damages. Alberta's CPA (n 60) s.7(1). In British Columbia, transactions tainted by unfair practices are also not binding on the consumer. BPCPA (n 60) s.10. Rescission is also available under Ontario's CPA (n 60) s.18 and Prince Edward Island's Business Practices Act (n 114) s.4(1).

141 Alberta's CPA (n 60) s.7(3). This is also the case under Ontario's CPA (n 60) s.18(2) and Prince Edward Island's Business Practices Act (n 114) s.4(1).

specific performance, and recovery of monies paid under a contract secured through unfair practices.[142]

Apart from private actions taken by consumers, some statutes empower relevant regulators to bring and maintain actions on behalf of consumers. For example, in Newfoundland, the Director of Consumer Protection and Business Practices[143] may bring an action on behalf of consumers affected by unfair practices.[144] The director may also maintain court action already commenced by consumers or defend court actions brought by suppliers against consumers.[145] Academic literature supports this approach, particularly where individual actions would be costly and where serious issues have been identified in a particular market.[146] However, relying solely on public enforcement is significantly limited. This is because it depends on the actions of public bodies with limited resources, and its intensity may be affected by political considerations.[147]

One response that addresses this limitation is found under Alberta's CPA. While the CPA empowers regulators to sue on behalf of consumers,[148] it goes a step further by empowering consumer organisations to take action against defaulting suppliers.[149] Thus, consumer organisations can step in where public agencies are unable to act.[150] Ayres and Braithwaite also argue that these organisations may provide useful checks against regulatory capture.[151] Actions by consumer organisations will be relevant to m-payments where individual loss may be small, but the provider in aggregate may have caused significant detriment.[152] A large number of small-scale losses caused by one provider may be symptomatic of a bigger problem that requires regulatory attention.[153] However, this issue may go

142 See for example, Alberta's CPA (n 60) s.13; British Columbia's BPCPA (n 60) ss.171 & 172; Manitoba's BPA (n 114) s.23(2); Newfoundland's CPBPA (n 114) s.10; Saskatchewan's Consumer Protection and Business Practices Act (n 114) s.93(1).

143 This is the officer designated to exercise enforcement powers under Newfoundland's CPBPA (n 114) s.4.

144 Newfoundland's CPBPA (n 114) s.104(1)(a). This is also the case under Manitoba's BPA (n 114) s.24(1)(a).

145 Newfoundland's CPBPA (n 114) s.104(1)(b); Manitoba's BPA (n 114) s.24(1)(b). The director may also defend an action brought by the supplier against the consumer: Newfoundland's CPBPA (n 114) s.104(1)(c); Manitoba's BPA (n 114) s.24(1)(c).

146 Geraint Howells and Stephen Weatherill, *Consumer Protection Law* (2nd edn, Ashgate 2005) p.601; OECD, 'OECD Recommendation on Consumer Dispute Resolution and Redress' (2007) p.11 <https://www.oecd.org/sti/consumer/38960101.pdf> accessed 11 January 2022.

147 Iain Ramsay, *Consumer Law and Policy* (3rd edn, Hart Publishing 2012) p.258.

148 s.15.

149 s.17.

150 Inability to act may be for several reasons such as lack of resources (funds, time, and expert personnel), regulatory capture and changing political tide.

151 They refer to this as 'tripartism' – where consumer organisations become 'fully fledged third player(s)' in the regulatory system; Ian Ayres and John Braithwaite, 'Tripartism: Regulatory Capture and Empowerment' (1991) 16 *Law & Social Inquiry* 435, 441, & 449.

152 Howells and Weatherill (n 146) p.17.

153 Ibid. p.48.

unnoticed as it may be unrealistic for all consumers affected to pursue redress.[154] Even where some consumers seek redress, it may not get the desired publicity that will attract regulatory attention. This is where consumer organisations can make a significant difference if they are empowered to act.[155]

### *5.4.2 Regulating Contract Terms*

#### *5.4.2.1 Standard Term Contracts and Fairness*

There is no federal legislation exclusively dedicated to regulating the use of contract terms in Canada. In provinces other than Quebec,[156] protection from unfair contract terms is achieved in multiple ways. These include reliance on the broader statutory regimes prohibiting unfair practices and specific statutes applying to limited transactions.[157] Judicial doctrines like the equitable doctrine of unconscionability and certain principles of contractual interpretation also play a role in regulating contract terms.

Provincial authorities mainly regulate contract terms by relying on the general provisions in relevant statutes which prohibit unfair practices. Thus, the regulation of contract terms is subsumed under the broader regulation of unfair practices. An example of this approach can be found in British Columbia's BPCA. Section 4(1) provides that –

> 'deceptive act or practice' means, in relation to a consumer transaction,
>
> a) an oral, written, visual, descriptive or other representation by a supplier, or
> b) any conduct by a supplier
>
> that has the capability, tendency or effect of deceiving or misleading a consumer or guarantor.

The section further explains that the term 'representation' includes 'any term or form of a contract, notice or other document used or relied on by a supplier in connection with a consumer transaction.'[158] Therefore, based on the above

154 Ibid.

155 This argument does not ignore the fact that in certain cases these groups may become compromised and may not be truly representative of consumer interests. Ramsay (n 147) p.109.

156 Quebec's civil law approach is outside the scope of this book as it belongs to a legal tradition different from the other case studies. For more insight on Quebec, see Section 1437 of the Civil Code of Quebec (1991); ss.8, 316, & 350 of the Quebec Consumer Protection Act 1971 (as amended). See also Union de Consummateurs, 'Ending Abusive Clauses in Consumer Contracts' (Final Report of the Project Presented to Industry Canada's Office of Consumer Affairs 2011) <https://uniondesconsommateurs.ca/endabusiveclauses/> accessed 18 January 2022.

157 For instance, to protect consumers in loan transactions, most provinces have an Unconscionable Transactions Relief Act that allows the court to intervene when there is unconscionability.

158 s.4(1).

provisions, contractual terms which can mislead or deceive a consumer will be declared unfair.

The problem with this provision is that unfair terms can come in several forms. Limiting the scope to situations where they may mislead or deceive suggests that many unfair terms may slip under the regulatory radar. However, some respite is found in other provisions dealing with unconscionable practices in British Columbia's BCPA. In particular, the BCPA lists certain circumstances which courts ought to consider in determining if a practice is unconscionable. One of the listed circumstances is whether –

> the terms or conditions on, or subject to, which the consumer entered into the consumer transaction were so harsh or adverse to the consumer as to be inequitable ....[159]

Similar provisions can be found in Newfoundland's CPBPA[160] and Prince Edward Island's Business Practices Act.[161]

Alberta's CPA offers a more direct approach. Section 6(3)(c) provides that it is an unfair practice for a supplier –

> to include in a consumer transaction terms or conditions that are harsh, oppressive or excessively one-sided ....

The Manitoba BPA adopts similar words to British Columbia's BCPA but adopts the directness found in Alberta's CPA by stating that it is deemed to be an unfair business practice when –

> the terms or conditions on which, or subject to which the consumer entered into the consumer transaction are so adverse or so harsh to the consumer as to be inequitable ....[162]

However, the statutes do not provide any criteria for determining when a term is 'harsh, oppressive or excessively one-sided' or when the term is 'so adverse or so harsh ... as to be inequitable.' As highlighted in the previous section, most do not also explain what 'fairness' or 'unconscionability' signifies in the context of the statutes.

It is possible to argue that these provisions are deliberately set out in imprecise terms so that courts are afforded the flexibility needed to address each case on its merits. However, it is difficult to determine the scope and criteria for determining unfairness from the statutes. More challenging is the fact that terms such as 'good

159 s.8(3)(e). Ontario's CPA (n 60) s.15(2)(f) takes a similar approach.
160 s.8(1)(d).
161 s.2(b)(vi).
162 s.3(2)(b).

faith,' 'fairness,' and 'unconscionable' can mean slightly different things depending on the prevailing legal tradition.[163] However, broader judicial doctrines may shed light on the import of these terms in the Canadian context. As with many Common Law jurisdictions, Canadian courts recognise unconscionability as a factor that may allow an innocent party to avoid certain contractual terms or rescind an entire contract.[164] Important judicial pronouncements show that the review of contract terms for fairness is an important part of the unconscionability doctrine.[165] For example, the Supreme Court of Canada's landmark decision in *Bhasin v. Hrynew*[166] confirms that under Canadian law, there exists a general 'organising principle of good faith' that requires that parties perform their contractual duties 'honestly and reasonably and not capriciously or arbitrarily.'[167] This principle underpins and manifests itself through 'existing doctrines about the types of situations and relationships in which the law requires, in certain respects, honest, candid forthright or reasonable contractual performance.'[168] The judgement recognises the doctrine of unconscionability as one example of such 'existing doctrines.'[169]

*Bhasin* also clarifies that claims of good faith will not succeed if they do not fall within existing doctrines recognised under Canadian law.[170] While acknowledging that the list of such doctrines is not closed, Justice Cromwell emphasised that –

> The application of the organising principle of good faith to particular situations should be developed where the existing law is found to be wanting and where the development may occur incrementally in a way that is consistent with the structure of the common law of contract and gives due weight to the importance of private ordering and certainty in commercial affairs.[171]

Notably, the case confirms that 'the principle of good faith must be applied in a manner that is consistent with the fundamental commitments of the common law of contract which generally places great weight on the freedom of contracting parties to pursue their individual self-interest.'[172]

Although the case emphatically recognises the good faith principle under Canadian contract law, academic commentary suggests that the case did not fully

163 Severine Saintier, 'The Elusive Notion of Good Faith in the Performance of a Contract, Why Still a Bete Noire for the Civil and the Common Law?' (2017) 6 *Journal of Business Law* 441.

164 Theodore Milosevic, 'What Makes a Consumer: Mandatory Arbitration Clauses and Free Digital Services in Canada' (2017) 75 *University of Toronto Faculty Law Review* 9, 33.

165 This doctrine is concerned with fairness in contracts and aims to ensure that one party does not take undue advantage of the other.

166 2014 SCC 71.

167 *per* Justice Cromwell para.64.

168 Ibid. para.66.

169 Ibid. para.43.

170 Ibid. para.66.

171 Ibid. para.66.

172 Ibid. para.70.

'articulate the consequences or limits' of the principle.[173] As a result, there remains some incoherence and uncertainty in the approach taken by Canadian Courts in dealing with the good faith principle.[174] Since the common law did not traditionally understand good faith in the way that civil law did, many common law judges may embrace this principle in varying degrees.[175] Hence, unsurprisingly, *Bhasin* has been interpreted narrowly, with some courts refusing to broaden or extend the applicability of the good faith principle.[176] Even if one concedes that the understanding of these concepts is relatively straightforward, there is still uncertainty on the scope of their application in the context of regulating contract terms. For instance, in some jurisdictions, certain matters are exempt from a test of unfairness.[177] This issue is also not addressed in the provincial statutes discussed.

In regulating contract terms, Canadian courts also place limited reliance on certain principles of contractual interpretation. Although such principles are not directly concerned with ensuring that contractual parties adopt fair terms, Canadian courts employ them where the fairness of a term is an underlying issue.[178] An example is the *contra proferentem* rule which allows ambiguities in a contract to be interpreted strictly against the drafter.[179]

Finally, where unfair terms taint a contract, consumers should be able to enjoy the same remedies available for unfair/unconscionable practices, which are guaranteed under provincial statutes.[180] This is because, as stated earlier, the regulation of contract terms is incorporated under the regulation of unfair practices.

### *5.4.2.2 Transparency*

Owing to the absence of a dedicated regime regulating contract terms, there is also no specific regime dealing with the role of transparency in the assessment of contract terms both at federal and provincial levels. In the absence of provisions

173 Shannon O'Byrne and Ronnie Cohen, 'The Contractual Principle of Good Faith and the Duty of Honesty in Bhasin v. Hrynew' (2015) 53 *Alberta Law Review* 1, 2.

174 Nadia Effendi, Heather Pessione, and Oliver V Nguyen, '*Bhasin v. Hrynew*: Towards Clarity and Coherence with Respect to Good Faith in Contract Performance' (2016) 46 *Advocates' Quarterly* 94, 106.

175 See Bingham LJ's dictum in *Interfoto Picture Library Ltd v. Stiletto Visual Programmes Ltd* [1989] QB 433 at p.439; See Legatt J's dictum in *Yam Seng Pte Ltd v. International Trade Corp* [2013] EWHC 111 (QB) at paras 124–130, 151 and Justice Cromwell in *Bhasin v. Hrynew* (n 166) at paras 32-33.

176 See for example the Ontario Court of Appeal's decision in *Bank of Montreal v. Javed* 2016 ONCA 49.

177 For example, in the United Kingdom, terms which specify the main subject matter of a contract, or the price are exempted from an assessment of fairness if they have been disclosed in a transparent and prominent manner. The UK approach is discussed in more detail in *Chapter 7*.

178 British Columbia Law Institute, 'Unfair Contract Terms: An Interim Report' (February 2005) pp.18–19 <https://www.bcli.org/sites/default/files/Unfair_Contract_Terms_Interim_Rep.pdf> accessed 19 January 2022.

179 See *32262 B.C. Ltd v. Balmoral Investments Ltd* (1999) BCCA 184.

180 See Section 5.4.1 of this chapter for an outline of these remedies.

dealing with transparency and the lack of clarity on the scope and criteria for determining unfairness, it is difficult to ascertain what role transparency plays in the determination of fairness. The statutes leave no clue as to whether transparency on its own would legitimise an otherwise unfair term or whether a lack of transparency will make an otherwise fair term unenforceable.

However, one may turn to judicial decisions to discover what approach may be favoured. Some cases suggest that the Canadian courts require that onerous[181] contract terms must be brought to the attention of a contracting party. In the leading case of *Tilden Rent-A-Car Co v. Clendenning*,[182] the Ontario Court of Appeal stated that –

> In modern commercial practice, many standard form printed documents are signed without being read or understood. In many cases the parties seeking to rely on the terms of the contract know or ought to know that the signature of a party to the contract does not represent the true intention of the signer, and that the party signing is unaware of the stringent and onerous provisions which the standard form contains. Under such circumstances, I am of the opinion that the party seeking to rely on such terms should not be able to do so in the absence of first having taken reasonable measures to draw such terms to the attention of the other party, and, in the absence of such reasonable measures, it is not necessary for the party denying knowledge of such terms to prove either fraud, misrepresentation or non est factum.[183]

To bring onerous terms to the attention of contracting parties, the British Columbia Law Institute considers that 'placing such contract terms in a bold typeface, in capital letters, in a larger font, or a different colour would, in most cases, meet the notice requirement.'[184] However, this only addresses one part of transparency which involves bringing onerous terms to a party's attention. It does not address another arm of transparency which requires that terms are drafted in simple plain language.

Nonetheless, the disclosure mandates discussed in Section 5.2.1 of this chapter may provide some clues about the general regulatory expectation on issues surrounding the transparent use of contract terms. For example, as we saw earlier, under the Bank Act, important terms must be prominently displayed in an information box when disclosures are made.[185] Such disclosures are expected

181 In Canada's Common Law jurisdictions, 'onerous' is often used in the ordinary sense and connotes 'burdensome' or 'troublesome.' In the Civil Law jurisdiction of Quebec, 'onerous' is used in the sense of something that is based upon good consideration. Martin Hogg, *Obligations: Law and Language* (Cambridge University Press 2017) p.213. The meaning of 'onerous' being discussed here is that used in the Common Law jurisdictions.

182 (1978) 83 DLR (3d) 400 at 408–409, per Dubin JA.

183 Ibid.

184 British Columbia Law Institute, 'Unfair Contract Terms: An Interim Report' (n 178) p.9.

185 s.627.57(1).

to be made in language that is clear, simple, and not misleading.[186] Where an important term has not been disclosed prominently in an information box, the supplier would have potentially failed to fulfil their disclosure mandate. In such a situation, one could also argue that it would be unfair for the supplier to rely on such a term since they have not been transparent in adopting it. However, from the perspective of contract terms regulation, this indirect approach leaves some questions unanswered. For example, if the important term is an onerous one but has been prominently disclosed in the information box (thereby meeting the disclosure requirements), will this legitimise the use of the onerous term?

### *5.4.3 Regulating False and Misleading Information*

Rules prohibiting the use of false and misleading information can be found in both federal and provincial statutes. In addition, some rules can be found in sector-specific legislation that is relevant to m-payments. For example, under the Bank Act, banks are prohibited from communicating or providing false and misleading information to customers.[187] This prohibition also extends to the information included in advertisements which must be accurate, clear, and not misleading.[188]

The CCA contains the most important rules and will be considered in more detail in this section. Because the CCA is a federal statute of general application, it applies to all businesses in Canada. Thus, all m-payment providers will be bound by the regulatory regime irrespective of their status[189] and the province they operate in.

The CCA prohibits the use of false and misleading representations that promote the supply/use of a product or a supplier's business interest.[190] The prohibition is divided into two categories. The first category covers the intentional/reckless use of false and misleading misrepresentations.[191] The second category covers the use of false representations, which falls under deceptive marketing practices. These deceptive marketing practices are classified under the category of what is termed 'reviewable practices.'[192] The distinction between the two categories is significant as it informs the sanctions applied. All intentionally or recklessly made false/misleading representations are classified as competition offences[193] attracting

186 s.627.55(1).
187 s.627.03. This prohibition also extends to information provided to the public and FCAC Commissioner.
188 s.627.14.
189 i.e., whether they are financial non-financial institutions.
190 See ss.52(1) & 74.01.
191 s.52(1) & (5).
192 CCA, Part VII.1.
193 CCA, Part VI.

criminal sanctions.[194] Reviewable practices only attract civil sanctions.[195] The civil and criminal sanctions are also mutually exclusive.[196]

This distinction was introduced following amendments to the CCA in 1999.[197] Before this, the use of any deceptive business practice was a strict liability offence attracting criminal sanctions. However, the old regime was criticised on the basis that –

> criminal prosecution as the sole legal instrument of government enforcement for misleading advertising and deceptive marketing practices has a number of shortcomings – a lack of speedy decision-making, specialisation and consistency in decisions … criminal sanctions can be too severe a response for some instances of unintentional misleading advertising, even when the advertiser has failed to meet the due diligence standard. Invoking the criminal process can be unjustifiably expensive, and time and resource-intensive, for both the businesses involved and the Competition Bureau ….[198]

This old regime exemplifies situations in which regulatory offences backed by criminal sanctions are mainly relied on in regulating business conduct. The shortcomings of this approach have been the subject of academic discourse.[199] Cartwright chronicles its notable criticisms, which include the expensive nature of prosecution, the possible disproportionate response it represents in many cases, and the fact that they may be an inadequate deterrence where businesses believe that the likelihood of prosecution and the penalty sums imposed are low.[200] This echoes the criticism of the old CCA regime highlighted above.

Although the new regime retains criminal sanctions for the most serious cases, i.e., intentional or reckless acts, it introduces civil sanctions for less serious cases. This approach is supported by Ashworth, who contends that 'in principle, the fullest enforcement, with the most frequent use of prosecution and the

194 A person found to have made false representations is guilty of an offence and may be liable on conviction to a fine or to imprisonment or to both; s.52(5).

195 s.74.01(1)(a).

196 ss. 52(7) & 74.16.

197 For background information on the amendments, see David Johansen, 'Bill C-20: An Act to Amend the Competition Act and To Make Consequential and Related Amendments to Other Acts' (Law and Government Division, Parliament of Canada, 27 November 1997, Revised 9 March 1999) <https://publications.gc.ca/Collection-R/LoPBdP/LS/361/c20-e.htm> accessed 20 January 2022.

198 Johansen (n 197). This echoes arguments elsewhere on the disadvantages of criminal sanctions for less serious offences, see Philip Hampton, 'Reducing Administrative Burdens: Effective Inspection and Enforcement' (2005) <https://webarchive.nationalarchives.gov.uk/ukgwa/+/http:/www.hm-treasury.gov.uk/prebud_pbr04_hampton.htm> accessed 18 January 2022.

199 Richard B Macrory, 'Regulatory Justice: Making Sanctions Effective' (2006) <https://webarchive.nationalarchives.gov.uk/ukgwa/20070305105024mp_/http://www.cabinetoffice.gov.uk/regulation/documents/pdf/macrory_penalties.pdf> accessed 18 January 2022; Cartwright, 'Redress compliance and Choice' (n 136); Hampton (n 198).

200 Cartwright, 'Redress Compliance and Choice' (n 136) pp.274–276.

highest penalties, should be reserved for the most serious forms of criminality.'[201] Supporting this position, Cartwright adds that 'sanctions may sometimes be seen to be disproportionate, particularly where the trader lacks any moral fault.'[202] Macrory further explains that –

> In instances where there has been no intent or wilfulness relating to regulatory non-compliance, a criminal prosecution may be a disproportionate response, although a formal sanction rather than simply advice or a warning, may still be appropriate and justified.[203]

Thus, the current regime provides more alternatives in the available regulatory toolkit. This allows for more proportionate responses reflecting the different levels of non-compliance.

The CCA targets representations that are false or misleading in a material respect.[204] 'Representations' can cover a wide range of statements, whether they are made through direct mandated disclosures or advertising. The choice of terminology also appears deliberate. Prior to amending the CCA, the conduct targeted was 'misleading advertising.' One may argue that the scope of the old regime was limited as misleading advertising only represents one of the numerous forms in which false/misleading information can be presented. The 1999 amendments change the CCA's focus to 'misleading representations,'[205] which arguably brings more practices under scrutiny.

While the CCA confirms that it is concerned with representations that are false/misleading in a 'material respect,' it does not explain what the term 'material respect' connotes. Although a direct explanation of what this phrase means would have been useful in understanding the scope of the provisions, one may, however, look to other provisions of the CCA to draw necessary inferences. For instance, the relevant provisions indicate that the CCA is concerned with representations which aim at 'promoting, directly or indirectly, the supply or use of a product or for the purpose of promoting, directly or indirectly, any business interest.'[206] Therefore, it is assumed that representations which seek to do either of the aforementioned will be treated as material.

201 Ashworth (n 137) p.8.

202 Peter Cartwright, 'Crime, Punishment and Consumer Protection.' (2007) 30(1) *Journal of Consumer Policy* 1, 9.

203 Macrory (n 199) para.1.14.

204 ss.52(1) & 74.01(1)(a).

205 Calvin S Goldman and John D Bodrug (eds), *Competition Law of Canada: Volume 2* (Juris Publishing, Inc. 2013) s.6.01.

206 ss.52 & 74.01(1) covering both intentional and unintentional acts of non-compliance are similarly worded.

Under the CCA, it is not necessary to prove that any person was actually deceived or misled[207] by the intentional/reckless misleading representations.[208] This approach seems effective as it will ensure that unscrupulous suppliers do not escape sanctions by relying on the technicality that no person has been misled (yet). While regulations prohibiting false representations generally help protect consumers, they also aim to encourage conscientious market practices. It is submitted that imposing sanctions even in the absence of actual consumer detriment ensures that the goal of encouraging conscientious behaviour is also given precedence.

Provincial statutes also augment the CCA's provisions. In particular, the provisions regulating unfair and unconscionable business practices often prohibit the use of misleading and deceptive misrepresentations.[209] M-payment providers will also be bound by the provisions in provincial statutes either because they will have a business presence in the provinces (including being incorporated under provincial laws) or because they will serve consumers resident in them.

## 5.5 Liability Rules

As with disclosures, the liability rules applicable to m-payments depend on the entity offering the service and the underlying funding source of an m-payments transaction.[210] These rules are often determined by the statutes and industry codes applying to the entity or funding instrument. Published advice from the FCAC on unauthorised m-payment transactions appears to support this conclusion.[211] The FCAC confirms that consumers generally do not have to pay for unauthorised m-payments and that the financial institutions which have issued the underlying debit or credit card funding the transactions will have policies that protect consumers from such unauthorised payments.[212] It is, therefore, necessary to consider the liability rules that apply to these payment instruments.

Where credit cards fund m-payment transactions, they will likely be subject to the liability rules for unauthorised transactions under the Bank Act. Under the Bank Act, the maximum liability for the unauthorised use of a credit card is C$50 unless the cardholder has demonstrated gross negligence.[213] The Bank Act clarifies that the unauthorised use of a credit card or the accompanying account infor-

207 s.52(1.1)(a).

208 There is a similar provision with respect to reviewable practices in s.74.03(4).

209 For example, see Ontario's CPA (n 60) s.14; British Columbia's BPCPA (n 60) s.4; Manitoba's BPA (n 114) s.2(3); Newfoundland's CPBPA (n 114) s.7(1); Prince Edward Island's BPA (n 114) s. 2(a); Saskatchewan's CPBPA (n 114) ss.6(a) & (b) and 7.

210 Trites et al. (n 4) p.10.

211 Financial Consumer Agency of Canada, 'Unauthorized Mobile Payments' <https://www.canada.ca/en/financial-consumer-agency/services/payment/mobile-payments/unauthorized-mobile-payments.html> accessed 16 January 2022.

212 Ibid.

213 Or, in Quebec, gross default in safeguarding the credit card, the account information or the personal authentication information: Bank Act, s.627.33(1).

mation or personalised authentication information does not by itself establish that the cardholder has been grossly negligent.[214]

Although the Act does not provide examples of what would qualify as gross negligence, the FCAC provides examples of situations in which a consumer may have to bear liability for unauthorised transactions. These include where a consumer shares the personal identification number (PIN) or password used to make m-payments or where they disable the feature that requires a password for such payments.[215] Consumers would also be liable if they register third party fingerprints on the mobile device, enabling these third parties to approve payments.[216]

Where a cardholder reports to an FRFI that their credit card, account information, or personal authentication details have been lost, stolen, or compromised and is at risk of being used in an unauthorised manner, the cardholder will not be liable for any unauthorised use after the report has been made.[217]

Although the aforementioned provisions do not specifically mention m-payments, they should be able to apply to m-payment transactions without conceptual difficulties. This conclusion can be explained by comparing the Bank Act's provisions to the COBRs. The liability rules for credit cards were initially contained in the COBRs and were couched differently. The COBRs made it clear that 'if a lost or stolen credit card is used in an unauthorised manner, the maximum liability of the borrower is the lesser of C$50 and the maximum set by the credit agreement ....'[218] The COBRs provision centres on the credit card being lost or stolen, and the wording raised queries about whether the liability regime could apply seamlessly to m-payment transactions. For instance, if a mobile device housing an m-payment application is stolen, and the payment application is used to process a payment funded by a credit card, there are two possible ways to interpret if the COBRs regime applies. First, one could argue that the COBRs would apply on the basis that, although the credit card has not been stolen or lost, it is still being subject to unauthorised remote use. In contrast, another argument could be that the COBRs regime cannot apply since it is only triggered if a credit card is actually lost or stolen, which is not the case in the example.

The FCAC's thematic review of m-payments acknowledged that some modifications or further commitments might be required to ensure that existing obligations remain technologically relevant and appropriate given the introduction of new intermediaries.[219] The new provisions in the Bank Act seem to have addressed this problem by adopting broader wording. The liability regime in the Bank Act focuses not only on the credit card itself but also on the account information and personal authentication information. Hence, it is triggered when the card is lost or

214 Or, in Quebec, in gross fault in safeguarding the personal authentication information Bank Act, s.627.33(3).

215 FCAC, 'Unauthorized Mobile Payments' (n 211).

216 Ibid.

217 Bank Act, s.627.33(2).

218 s.12(1)(c).

219 Trites et al (n 4), p.56.

stolen and when the account information or personal authentication information is at risk of being used in an unauthorised manner.

Where debit cards are the underlying funding sourcc for m-payments, it is useful to consider the liability rules in the Debit Card Code, which sets out consumer liability for unauthorised debit card transactions. Paragraph 5(3) of the Debit Card Code provides that –

> Cardholders are not liable for losses resulting from circumstances beyond their control. Such circumstances include, but are not limited to:
>
> 1. technical problems, card issuer errors and other system malfunctions
> 2. unauthorised use of a card and PIN where the issuer is responsible for preventing such use, for example after:
>    - the card has been reported lost or stolen
>    - the card is cancelled or expired
>    - the cardholder has reported that the PIN may be known to someone other than the cardholder
> 3. unauthorised use, where the cardholder has unintentionally contributed to such use, provided the cardholder co-operates in any subsequent investigation.[220]

The Debit Card Code also defines the circumstances in which a cardholder may be deemed to have contributed to the unauthorised use of a card. A cardholder contributes to unauthorised use by –

(1) voluntarily disclosing the PIN, including writing the PIN on the card, or keeping a poorly disguised written record of the PIN in proximity with the card

(2) failing to notify the issuer, within a reasonable time, that the card has been lost, stolen or misused, or that the PIN may have become known to someone other than the cardholder.[221]

The Code indicates that a cardholder deemed to have contributed to an unauthorised use is liable for losses.[222] However, this loss will not exceed the established debit card transaction withdrawal limits.[223]

One issue with the Debit Card Code is that it is very specific to debit cards, which can lead to some difficulty in applying it to m-payments. For example, the criteria for determining whether a customer has contributed to the unauthorised

220 (n 41).

221 Paragraph 5(5).

222 Paragraph 5(4).

223 In some circumstances, the loss may exceed the actual funds in account such as where the account has a line of credit or overdraft protection or is linked with another account or other accounts; or if a debit card transaction is made based on a fraudulent deposit at an automated banking machine (i.e., an ATM), para.5(4).

use of a debit card is not specific to m-payments. The FCAC's thematic review pointed out that it is unclear whether a debit cardholder will be held responsible in situations where a PIN is not necessary to authenticate a debit payment made through a mobile device.[224] The Debit Card Code was last revised in 2004, and unlike the recent amendments to the Bank Act, its provisions may be outdated in light of technological developments.

For m-payments funded by direct mobile billing, the Wireless Code requires that customers notify their service provider when their mobile device has been lost or stolen.[225] A consumer will only be liable for charges incurred before their service provider was notified.[226] There are no conceptual difficulties here since direct mobile billing depends on the direct use of the mobile device with charges placed on the consumer's bill with the telecommunications service provider.

Where m-payments are funded by credit cards issued by provincially regulated institutions, the applicable liability rules will often be found in the provincial consumer protection legislation.[227] These rules are similar to those that were contained under the COBRs. For example, under British Columbia's BPCPA, a cardholder is not liable for unauthorised transactions linked to a lost or stolen credit card after they have reported the situation to the credit card issuer.[228] For unauthorised transactions which occurred before a report was made, the consumer's liability is limited to C$50 or the maximum set by the credit agreement in relation to the credit card, whichever is lower.[229]

Interestingly, unlike the NOBRs, some of the provinces adopt a broad definition of credit card, which may make it easier to directly apply the liability rules to m-payments. For example, in Alberta, British Columbia, Manitoba, and Newfoundland and Labrador, a credit card is defined as a 'card or device that can be used to obtain advances under a credit agreement for open credit.'[230] This definition acknowledges that a device may serve as a credit card. It is arguably

224 e.g., in the use of contactless payment. There may be a precedent to follow under the Canadian Payments Association's Rule E4 which assigns liability for unauthorised PIN-less transactions to the 'payer' financial institution. The rule's scope embraces 'payment applications embedded in a device' (such as a debit card, key fob, or cellular phone). Trites et al. (n 4) p.49.

225 Part F, paragraph (3)(i).

226 Part F, paragraph (3)(i)(b).

227 For example, see British Columbia's BPCPA (n 60) s.99; Alberta's CPA (n 60) s.89. Note that the current liability rules for unauthorised transactions introduced by the amendments to the Bank Act are in harmony with the regime under Quebec's Consumer Protection Act CQLR, c P-40.1, ss.123 & 123.1.

228 s.99(1).

229 Unless the unauthorised transaction is carried out at an automated teller machine using the cardholder's personal identification number, in which case, the maximum liability will be the amount incurred in the transaction. British Columbia's BPCPA (n 60) s.99(2) & (3). See also Alberta's CPA (n 60) s.89(3); Manitoba's CPA (n 100) s.35.8(1); Newfoundland's CPBPA (n 114) s.74.

230 Alberta's CPA (n 60) s.58; British Columbia's BPCPA (n 60) s.57(1); Manitoba's CPA (n 100) s.1(1); Newfoundland's CPBPA (n 114) s.45(1)(n).

broad enough to reduce potential risks of ambiguity if applied to m-payment transactions.[231]

A consumer may install a mobile wallet which houses a debit and credit card to complete m-payment transactions. The same consumer may also purchase digital products like games and ringtones, which may be added to their phone bill. Our discussions above show that the liability rules will be significantly different depending on the underlying funding structure for a m-payment transaction. This is further compounded by the distinction between providers who may be FRFIs or non-FRFIs. The implication of such diverse rules can cause considerable confusion and possible detriment if a consumer erroneously believes that the liability rules applying to m-payment transactions are uniform or that the rules with which they are familiar apply to m-payments.[232] It also introduces higher learning costs as a consumer must consciously navigate and understand the precise liability rules that apply to their transactions.[233]

## 5.6 Dispute Resolution

### *5.6.1 Internal Dispute Resolution Procedures*

The Bank Act sets out the responsibilities of banks with respect to resolving complaints and disputes with customers. These provisions are supplemented by the FCPRs and guidance issued by the FCAC.[234] These existing requirements should benefit consumers using m-payment services offered by banks. Under the Bank Act, banks are mandated to establish internal complaints resolution procedures that are satisfactory to the FCAC Commissioner.[235] Internal procedures will presumably be satisfactory if their design incorporates three core principles – effectiveness, efficiency, and accountability – which the FCAC believes should guide banks in carrying out their responsibility in a manner consistent with the Bank Act.[236]

In particular, banks are required to designate an officer or employee responsible for implementing the internal redress procedures.[237] Officers must also be

231 Trites et al. (n 4) p.39.

232 Clayton P Gillette and Steven D Walt, 'Uniformity and Diversity in Payment Systems' (2008) 83 *Chicago Kent Law Review* 499, 499.

233 Ibid.

234 Financial Consumer Agency of Canada, 'Guideline on Complaint-Handling Procedures for Banks and Authorized Foreign Banks' (2022) <https://www.canada.ca/en/financial-consumer-agency/services/industry/commissioner-guidance/complaint-handling-procedures-banks.html> accessed 20 February 2022; Financial Consumer Agency of Canada, 'Internal Dispute Resolution' (2013) <https://www.canada.ca/en/financial-consumer-agency/services/industry/commissioner-guidance/guidance-12.html> accessed 14 January 2022.

235 Bank Act, s.627.43(1)(a).

236 FCAC, 'Guideline on Complaint-Handling Procedures' (n 234) para II; FCAC, 'Internal Dispute Resolution' (n 234) paras 1–3.

237 Bank Act, s.627.43(1)(b).

appointed to receive and deal with any complaints.[238] In line with the FCAC's guidance, banks must demonstrate that these designated officers are adequately trained and that their skills and authority are appropriate for carrying out the tasks required.[239] Available redress procedures must be also disclosed to customers in written format.[240] In disclosing these procedures, banks must not adopt misleading terms, which suggest that the internal procedures or designated employees/officers are independent of the bank.[241] Accordingly, banks cannot use terms like 'ombudsman' to describe their internal procedures. Presumably, this requirement ensures that consumers can differentiate between internal procedures within the bank's direct control and external procedures that provide a more independent approach.

Where a consumer makes a complaint,[242] the bank must provide them with a written acknowledgement of the date on which the complaint was received.[243] They must also provide the customer with information on the internal procedures for dealing with the complaint, the external complaints body that they can approach if the complaint is unresolved, and any information considered necessary to enable the customer to meet the requirements of the internal redress procedures.[244] These provisions are important as they ensure that consumers have information on the available redress procedures and the requirements for taking advantage of them. This is in line with the OECD's advice that –

> Consumers should be provided with clear, comprehensible, and accurate information on the procedure, including the process for initiating a complaint and selecting a dispute resolution mechanism ....[245]

To further support consumers, the FCAC maintains web pages providing general advice on how consumers may resolve disputes with FRFIs.[246] It also maintains a complaints handling procedures tool that enables consumers to search for

238 Bank Act, s.627.43(1)(c).

239 FCAC, 'Guideline on Complaint-Handling Procedures' (n 234) para III (16); FCAC, 'Internal Dispute Resolution' (n 234) paras.1.2 & 1.3.

240 Bank Act, s.627.65(a); FCPRs, s.17.

241 Bank Act, s.627.43(2).

242 'Complaints' are broadly defined to cover dissatisfaction with the product or service and the manner in which they have been offered, sold or provided. Bank Act, s.627.01(1).

243 Bank Act, s.627.43(4)(a).

244 Bank Act, s.627.43(4)(b) & (c).

245 OECD, 'Recommendation on Consumer Dispute Resolution and Redress' (n 146) para.A(4).

246 For example, see: FCAC, 'Filing a Complaint with a Bank or Federal Credit Union: Rights and Responsibilities' <https://www.canada.ca/en/financial-consumer-agency/services/rights-responsibilities/rights-banking/make-complaint.html> accessed 14 January 2022; FCAC, 'How to file a Complaint with your Financial Institution' < https://www.canada.ca/en/financial-consumer-agency/services/complaints/file-complaint-financial-institution.html> accessed 14 January 2022.

their banks' specific complaints handling procedures.[247] The FCAC recommends a three-stage process that consumers should follow when resolving disputes.[248] Consumers should first seek to resolve a complaint locally by contacting a representative of the bank. Where unsatisfied, the customer can escalate the complaint to the second stage by contacting the bank's official complaints handling department.

Where the complaint cannot be resolved despite using the available internal channels, then the customer can escalate the matter externally (the third stage). The FCPRs require that banks resolve a complaint within 56 days after it is received.[249] Thus, the FCAC recommends that if a complaint has not been resolved internally within 56 days or the consumer is dissatisfied with the outcome, then they can escalate the complaint externally.[250]

Banks are expected to keep a record of complaints for at least seven years, and the retained records should be accessible to the FCAC Commissioner.[251] The Bank Act also imposes reporting requirements. For example, banks must make quarterly reports of complaints received and the complaint records held for the relevant quarter.[252] Annually, banks must also make available on their websites information about the number and nature of complaints dealt with, the average length of time taken to deal with the complaints, including those that were satisfactorily resolved.[253] Apart from ensuring accountability, transparency and compliance, requiring that complaints data is available to the general public is important. First, it provides consumers with important information that assists them in deciding whether to establish a relationship with the bank. Second, it also acts as an incentive. Ideally, banks will strive to maintain a good dispute resolution record if it can affect a consumer's perception of the quality of their service.

### *5.6.2 External ADR Mechanisms*

As stated earlier, where a dispute remains unresolved after internal procedures have been exhausted, a consumer can escalate their complaint externally. Although there is no single federal ombudsman service established by law, consumers can approach external ADR organisations that have been approved to act as an 'External Complaints Body' (ExCB). All banks and federal credit unions are required to be members of an ExCB.[254] Reputable bodies corporate may apply

247 <https://itools-ioutils.fcac-acfc.gc.ca/CHP-PTP/Complain-outilder-eng.aspx> accessed 14 January 2022.

248 FCAC, 'How to file a Complaint with your Financial Institution' (n 246).

249 FCPRs, s.14.

250 FCAC, 'How to file a Complaint with your Financial Institution' (n 246).

251 Bank Act, ss.627.44 & 627.45.

252 Bank Act, s.627.46.

253 Bank Act, s.627.47.

254 Bank Act, s.627.48(4).

for approval to act as ExCBs.[255] Once approved, these ExCBs can accept banks and federal credit unions which apply for membership.[256] Banks must disclose to customers the name and contact information of the ExCB of which they are members.[257]

Consumers who use m-payment services provided by banks will enjoy access to ExCBs. In comparison to litigation, ExCBs provide a less formal atmosphere for dealing with unresolved disputes. As regards cost, the ExCBs also present huge advantages as access is free. Currently, there are two approved ExCBs for banks and federal credit unions, i.e., the Ombudsman Service for Banking Services and Investments (OBSI) and the ADR Chambers Banking Ombuds Office (ADRBO).

To maintain their approval status, ExCBs must ensure amongst other conditions that their services are free of charge to persons who make complaints and also available across Canada in the two official languages.[258] Where a complaint is made, the body is obliged to inform the parties about its terms of reference and procedures for dealing with complaints.[259] ExCBs are also bound on requests to provide any further information and assistance necessary to enable parties to understand the requirements of those terms of reference and procedures.[260] The banks and credit unions who are party to the dispute are also mandated to provide ExCBs with all the information in their possession or control that relates to the complaint without delay.[261] Such information must be provided in a manner using language that is clear, simple, and not misleading.[262]

ExCBs must act independently and impartially.[263] They are also expected to act within defined timelines. For example, if a complaint is received and they find that all or parts of the complaint are not within their terms of reference, they must inform the complaining party within 30 days of receiving the complaint of this determination, including the reasons for reaching it.[264] They must also provide the complaining party with the name of an alternative entity which they may approach to resolve their complaint.[265] Where a complaint falls within its terms of reference, the ExCB must make a final written recommendation within 120 days of receiving all the information required to deal with the complaint.[266] While statutory timelines for dispute resolution are necessary to ensure timely resolution of disputes, they are not always successfully implemented in practice. For instance, a 2020 industry review conducted by the FCAC found that the ExCBs took a longer

255 Bank Act, s.627.49(a).
256 FCPRs, s.16(a).
257 Bank Act, s.627.65(b).
258 Bank Act, s.627.49(b).
259 FCPRs, s.16(d).
260 Ibid.
261 Bank Act, s.627.52.
262 Bank Act, s.627.53.
263 Bank Act, s.627.49(c) & (g).
264 Bank Act, s.627.49(e).
265 Ibid.
266 Bank Act, s.627.49(h).

time to resolve complaints in practice.[267] The review showed that the OBSI took an average of 112 days to propose final recommendations, while ADRBO took 156 days.[268]

ExCBs are also required to publish a summary of their final recommendation within 90 days of making it, on their website free of charge.[269] The summary should describe the nature of the complaint, the name of the institution that received the complaint, the reasons for the final recommendation, and a description of any compensation provided to the complaining party.[270] This requirement aims to encourage transparency, which positively impacts consumer confidence. If consumers are aware that there are independent external procedures to assist in resolving disputes with their financial services providers, they will feel more confident when transacting with providers.[271]

An FRFI is free to leave one ExCB to join another if they wish. However, they must notify the FCAC Commissioner and the ExCB of which they are a member of their intention in advance.[272] If this occurs before an ExCB can make a final recommendation about a complaint received, it must transfer the complaint along with all related information to the other ExCB that the FRFI has joined.[273] Should this occur, the ExCB must write the parties to the complaint to advise them of this transfer.[274]

One interesting requirement is that, at least once a year, ExCBs are required to consult their members and persons who have made complaints to it with respect to the discharge of its functions and the performance of its activities.[275] This opportunity for stakeholder engagement presumably aims to promote accountability. It also provides a feedback loop that allows ExCBs to continuously improve their policies so that they can meet the expectation of the parties that they serve. However, the FCAC found an inconsistent approach to complying with this requirement. For example, the OBSI appeared to consult more widely and consistently and overall was more transparent with these activities than the ADRBO.[276]

ExCBs are supervised by the FCAC and are required to file annual reports detailing, amongst other things, the number of complaints received in respect of each institution, including the number it determined were within its terms of

267 FCAC, 'Industry Review: The Operations of External Complaints Bodies' (2020) paragraph 1.3.1 <https://www.canada.ca/content/dam/fcac-acfc/documents/programs/research-surveys-studies-reports/operations-external-complaints-bodies.pdf> accessed 15 January 2022.

268 Ibid.

269 s.627.49(i).

270 s.627.49(i)(i)–(iv).

271 FCAC, 'Industry Review: The Operations of External Complaints Bodies' (n 267) para.7.

272 This notice must be given at least 90 days before the day on which the bank becomes a member of the other ExCB. s.627.5.

273 FCPRs, s.16(b).

274 FCPRs, s.16(c).

275 FCPRs, s.16(f).

276 FCAC, 'Industry Review: The Operations of External Complaints Bodies' (n 267) para.5.1.

reference.[277] The report must also include the number of final recommendations made and the number of complaints that, in its opinion, were resolved to the satisfaction of the complaining party.[278] In addition, the report must disclose the average length of time taken to deal with complaints, the number of complaints that it determined were not within its terms of reference and the reasons for reaching the determination.[279] It should also cover the number of final recommendations in which compensation was recommended.[280] ExCBs are required to make this report publicly available on its website free of charge.[281]

The recommendations of the ExCBs are non-binding, and adherence to orders made is voluntary. The main tool used to ensure compliance with awards is to publicly name and shame uncooperative firms.[282] Some advantages may be attributed to the non-binding nature of the recommendations. For one, proceedings may be more amicable and less costly if both parties accept findings.[283] It also preserves the right of parties to appeal, unlike most binding arbitral awards, which are often difficult to overturn. However, the non-binding status of awards has been subject to much criticism. For example, in an independent review of the OBSI, it was noted that 'without binding authority to secure fair redress, OBSI, ... has a model that is weighted in favour of firms who are free to ignore its recommendations and negotiate a lower award.'[284] The report pointed out that this operational design prevents the OBSI from securing redress for all consumers who have been wronged, which is the fundamental role of an ombudsman.[285]

Also, in principle, naming and shaming may seem like an effective deterrent because firms will avoid the reputational risks associated with being labelled uncooperative. However, it is not very effective in practice. For instance, the review of the OBSI showed that it did not serve as an effective deterrent, nor did it improve firm behaviour.[286] It has also been counterproductive as publicising refusals reinforces OBSI's limitations and undermines public confidence in the resolution system.[287] There is also the possibility that the non-binding status indirectly increases the cost of dispute resolution, especially if a case ends up in trial. For instance, in the context of m-payments where micro-payments are involved,

277 Bank Act, s.627.49(j)(iii).

278 Ibid.

279 Bank Act, s.627.49(j)(iv) & (v).

280 Bank Act, s.627.49(j)(vi).

281 Bank Act, s.627.49(k).

282 Deborah Battell and Nikki Pender, 'Independent Evaluation of the Canadian Ombudsman for Banking Services and Investments' (OBSI) Investment Mandate' (2016) p.6 <https://www.obsi.ca/en/news-and-publications/resources/PresentationsandSubmissions/2016-Independent-Evaluation-Investment-Mandate.pdf> accessed 7 January 2022.

283 Albert K Fiadjoe, *Alternative Dispute Resolution: A Developing World Perspective* (Routledge 2013) p.27.

284 Battell and Pender (n 282) p.6.

285 Ibid. p.1.

286 Battell and Pender (n 282) p.27.

287 Ibid. p.1.

a binding award may be more appropriate than an extended dispute resolution procedure that may still end up in court. Fiadjoe also notes that where a case ends up in trial, parties may acquire an unfair advantage by using the ADR proceedings to obtain a preview of the opponent's case.[288] Perhaps a better approach may be found in jurisdictions like the United Kingdom, where the recommendations are binding on the business but not on the consumer.[289]

Another issue to consider is the jurisdiction of the ExCBs. Since their mandate covers banks and federal credit unions, disputes arising from m-payment services provided by these institutions will fall under its jurisdiction. However, m-payment providers who are not FRFIs fall outside its jurisdiction. This highlights the concern that applying existing redress procedures tailored to FRFIs, may be insufficient for m-payment users served by non-FRFIs.

The approach of encouraging multiple ombudsman services also raises queries. Although there are only two ExCBs at the moment, nothing bars the registration of more bodies. This multi-institution approach can lead to complexities – an issue acknowledged by the FCAC in its recent industry review of the operations of ExCBs.[290] The FCAC noted that the multiple model is not consistent with international standards and that it introduces 'inefficiencies and increases the complexity of the external dispute resolution system for consumers.'[291]

One shortcoming of this multi-institution approach becomes obvious when considering the important role that ombudsmen play in distilling systemic issues from complaint trends. Although the Bank Act requires that ExCBs notify the FCAC of complaints that raise systemic issues,[292] a single ombudsman service may be better placed to quickly identify complaint patterns that highlight systemic problems. A single ombudsman arguably has the advantage of observing a holistic picture of external complaints and can draw necessary inferences to feed back to regulators. Where several platforms are involved, this may be more difficult as information sharing will need to be carefully coordinated amongst several platforms and the overseeing regulator. This concern is further supported by the FCAC's admission that 'one challenge of having multiple ExCBs is that data about complaints are fragmented and more difficult to use in research.'[293] Moreover, the FCAC's industry review found that the ADRBO and OBSI fell short of this requirement as they deal with too few complaints to be able to identify important trends.[294]

Furthermore, it is arguable that a single statutorily backed service answerable to parliament may be more independent in its operations. Institutions registering as ExCBs are only sustainable if a considerable number of FRFIs decide to join

288 Ibid.

289 See *Chapter 6* for more discussions on this.

290 FCAC, 'Industry Review: The Operations of External Complaints Bodies' (n 267).

291 Ibid. pp.1–2.

292 Bank Act, s.627.49(d).

293 FCAC, 'Industry Review: The Operations of External Complaints Bodies' (n 267) para.7.1.

294 Ibid. para.8.3.

them. FRFIS are also free to exit membership and join any ExCB platform of their choice. Literature suggests that the idea of multiple ombudsmen competing in the same sector may present significant risks to independence and impartiality.[295] This is because a possibility exists that these bodies may adopt a pro-industry approach in order to attract and retain their memberships which will be to the disadvantage of consumers. While the FCAC notes that the OBSI and ADRBO have implemented some policies which ensure independence and impartiality,[296] the possibility of a conflict of interest will always exist due to the multi-institution approach adopted. Moreover, as Thomas and Frizon explain, a multi-institution approach 'overlooks the role of financial ombudsmen as an alternative to the courts and creates one-sided competition – because, unlike the financial businesses, the consumers are not given any choice of ombudsman.'[297]

Although consumers may contact the FCAC for information about the complaints handling process of their financial service providers, the FCAC cannot get involved in individual disputes.[298] Hence it does not provide redress or compensation to individual consumers. Instead, its role focuses on ensuring that FRFIs do not breach their market conduct obligations including the obligation to maintain satisfactory complaint handling procedures.[299]

At the provincial level, publicly funded ombudsman services exist, but these mostly focus on dealing with complaints involving public sector institutions.[300] However, some provinces have ombudsmen created by industry associations which deal with complaints from specific provincially regulated financial institutions. For example, the Credit Union Central of Manitoba deals with complaints involving provincially regulated credit unions in Manitoba.[301] This is also the case with the Credit Union Ombudservice provided by Credit Unions Atlantic Canada, which deals with complaints involving credit unions in New Brunswick, Nova Scotia, and Prince Edward Island.[302] If a provincially regulated credit union offered an m-payment service, its customers would presumably have access to the relevant ombudsman. One issue with these ombudsman services is that their connection with industry associations may undermine consumer confidence since they will be perceived to prioritise industry interests.

295 David Thomas and Francis Frizon, 'Resolving Disputes between Consumers and Financial Businesses: Fundamentals for a Financial Ombudsman – A Practical Guide Based in Experience in Western Europe' (2012) p.38 <http://www.eoi.at/wp-content/uploads/2018/09/Resolving-disputes-between-consumers-and-financial-businesses_Fundamentals-for-a-financial-ombudsman_The-World-Bank_January2012.pdf> accessed 15 January 2022.

296 FCAC, 'Industry Review: The Operations of External Complaints Bodies' para.1.3.4 (n 267).

297 Thomas & Frizon (n 295) p.39.

298 FCAC, 'How to file a Complaint with your Financial Institution' (n 246).

299 Ibid.

300 Note that in Newfoundland, the ombudsman is referred to as the Citizen's Representative. Prince Edward Island's first ombuds office became operational in February 2022.

301 <https://www.cucm.org/ombudsman.html> accessed 15 January 2022.

302 <https://atlanticcreditunions.ca/products-services/credit-union-ombudservice/> accessed 15 January 2022.

Apart from industry-run ombudsmen, consumers using m-payments provided by non-FRFIs may file complaints with provincial financial services regulators who can help to ensure that a customer obtains a clear response from the institutions involved. The general expectation is that the consumers first attempt to resolve the issue with the institution directly.[303] However, it is important to note that some of these regulators cannot mediate on behalf of the consumers,[304] and most cannot deal with purely contractual disputes which are left to the court system.[305] Alternatively, consumers may also contact the relevant provincial consumer protection authority where the nature of the complaint involves conduct that is unfair or deceptive.

## 5.7 Conclusion

This chapter discussed the relevant consumer protection rules that may avail m-payment users in Canada. Canada's federal system of government means that there is a complex maze of federal and provincial rules with important requirements which serve to protect consumer interests. Some m-payment providers will be FRFIs while others will be non-FRFIs, and this can impact the rules that apply to m-payment transactions. For example, the Bank Act contains detailed disclosure rules, but it only applies to FRFIs like banks.

Protections can also sometimes be influenced by the underlying funding source used. This is also, in turn, influenced by the status of the provider issuing the payment instrument that serves as the funding source. For example, where m-payments are facilitated by credit cards issued by FRFIs or provincially regulated credit institutions, disclosure requirements will be uniform as this is harmonised in Canada. Also, m-payment consumers served by FRFIs are assured of detailed complaints handling procedures mandated under the Bank Act. Discrepancies are more noticeable in areas such as the allocation of liability; while the rules applying underlying funding instruments like credit cards are clearer, the same cannot be said for other funding instruments.

In regulating unfair practices generally, provincial statutes play a more prominent role, although the Competition Act contains important rules that specifically target false or misleading representations. Unlike jurisdictions like the United

303 For example, the Financial Services Commission of Ontario advises consumers that the first step and fastest way to resolve a complaint involving a credit union is to contact them in the first instance. Financial Services Commission of Ontario, 'Resolve a complaint about a Credit Union or Caisse Populaire' <https://www.fsco.gov.on.ca/en/creditunions/Pages/complaints.aspx> accessed 15 January 2022.

304 See for example, the British Columbia Financial Services Authority which accepts complaints about credit unions <https://www.bcfsa.ca/public-protection/report-concern/file-credit-union -complaint - :~:text=You can contact the Lawyer,(800) 663-1919> accessed 16 January 2022.

305 For example, this is the case with the Office of the Alberta Superintendent of Financial Institutions Alberta <https://www.alberta.ca/financial-institutions-information-consumers.aspx - credit> accessed 16 January 2022.

Kingdom, which is considered in *Chapter 7*, Canada does not have an independent regime focusing on regulating contract terms.[306] Instead, the regulation of contract terms is subsumed under the broader regulation of unfair practices, supported by the judicial doctrine of unconscionability and the principles of good faith.

In the next chapter, we consider the approach in another jurisdiction. We look at the consumer protection rules that apply to m-payments in Kenya.

## References

Bank Act, SC 1991, c 46.
Budget Implementation Act 2018, No.2 SC 2018, c 27.
Competition Act, RSC 1985 c C–34.
Cost of Borrowing (Banks) Regulations, SOR/2001–101.
Disclosure of Charges (Banks) Regulations, SOR/92–324.
Financial Consumer Agency of Canada Act, SC 2001, c 9.
Financial Consumer Protection Regulations, SOR/2021–181.
Negative Option Billing Regulations, SOR/2012–23.
The Constitution Act 1867, 30 & 31 Vict, c 3.
Business Practices Act (Manitoba)1990 CCSM, c B120.
Business Practices Act (Prince Edward Island) RSPEI 1988 c B-7.
Business Practices and Consumer Protection Act (British Columbia) SBC 2004.
Consumer Protection Act (Alberta) RSA 2000, c 26.3.
Consumer Protection Act (Manitoba) 1987 CCSM, c 200.
Consumer Protection Act (Ontario) SO 2002, c 30.
Consumer Protection and Business Practices Act (Newfoundland and Labrador) SNL 2009 c 31.1.
Consumer Protection and Business Practices Act (Saskatchewan) SS 2013 c C-30.2.
*32262 B.C. Ltd. v. Balmoral Investments Ltd* (1999) BCCA 184.
*Bank of Montreal v Javed* 2016 ONCA 49.
Bank of Montreal v. Marcotte (2014) SCC 55.
*Bhasin v Hrynew* 2014 SCC 71.
*Interfoto Picture Library Ltd. v Stiletto Visual Programmes Ltd* [1989] QB 433.
*Tilden Rent-A-Car Co. v. Clendenning* (1978) 83 DLR (3d) 400.
*Yam Seng Pte Ltd v International Trade Corp* [2013] EWHC 111 (QB).
Albert K. Fiadjoe, *Alternative Dispute Resolution: A Developing World Perspective* (Routledge 2013).
Andrew Ashworth, 'Is the Criminal Law a Lost Cause?' (2000) 116 *Law Quarterly Review* 225.
Brigitte Goulard, Peter A. Aziz and Marissa A Daniels, 'New Regulations Complete Overhaul of Bank Act Consumer Provisions' (2021) <https://www.torys.com/our-latest-thinking/publications/2021/08/new-regulations-complete-overhaul-of-bank-act-consumer-provisions> accessed 9 January 2022.
British Columbia Law Institute, 'Unfair Contract Terms: An Interim Report' (February 2005) <https://www.bcli.org/sites/default/files/Unfair_Contract_Terms_Interim_Rep.pdf> accessed 19 January 2022.

306 Except Quebec.

Calvin S. Goldman and John D. Bodrug (eds), *Competition Law of Canada: Volume 2* (Juris Publishing, Inc. 2013).

Canadian Banking Association, 'Credit & Debit Cards, Mobile Payments and Cheques' <https://bankingquestions.cba.ca/payments> accessed 10 January 2022.

Canadian Radio-Television and Telecommunications Commission, 'Telecom Regulatory Policy' (CRTC 2017–200) <https://crtc.gc.ca/eng/archive/2017/2017-200.htm> accessed 10 January 2022.

Catherine Mathieu, 'Do Consumers Really Benefit from the Federal Paramountcy Doctrine? A Critique of Director of Criminal and Penal Prosecutions v Telus Communications Inc.' (2020) 29 *Constitutional Forum* 11.

Chris Powell, 'Mobile Payments Set to Rise This Year: Catalyst Canada' <http://marketingmag.ca/consumer/mobile-payments-set-to-rise-this-year-catalyst-canada-176794/> accessed 20 January 2021.

Clayton P. Gillette and Steven D. Walt, 'Uniformity and Diversity in Payment Systems' (2008) 83 *Chicago Kent Law Review* 499.

Consumer Protection Office (Manitoba), 'Payments on the Go: Mobile Payments' <https://www.gov.mb.ca/cp/cpo/info/payments_to_go.html> accessed 10 January 2022.

David Johansen, 'Bill C-20: An Act to Amend the Competition Act and To Make Consequential and Related Amendments to Other Acts' (Law and Government Division, Parliament of Canada 27 November 1997, revised 9 March 1999) <https://publications.gc.ca/Collection-R/LoPBdP/LS/361/c20-e.htm> accessed 20 January 2022.

David Thomas and Francis Frizon, 'Resolving Disputes between Consumers and Financial Businesses: Fundamentals for a Financial Ombudsman – A Practical Guide Based in Experience in Western Europe' (2012) <http://www.eoi.at/wp-content/uploads/2018/09/Resolving-disputes-between-consumers-and-financial-businesses_Fundamentals-for-a-financial-ombudsman_The-World-Bank_January2012.pdf> accessed 15 January 2022.

Deborah Battell and Nikki Pender, 'Independent Evaluation of the Canadian Ombudsman for Banking Services and Investments' (OBSI) Investment Mandate' (2016) <https://www.obsi.ca/en/news-and-publications/resources/PresentationsandSubmissions/2016-Independent-Evaluation-Investment-Mandate.pdf> accessed 7 January 2022.

Elizabeth Sale and Haley Adams, 'Federal Financial Consumer Protection Framework In-Force Date Announced, New Regulations Published' (2021) <https://www.osler.com/en/resources/regulations/2021/federal-financial-consumer-protection-framework-in-force-date-announced-new-regulations-published> accessed 9 January 2022.

Financial Consumer Agency of Canada, 'Internal Dispute Resolution' (2013) <https://www.canada.ca/en/financial-consumer-agency/services/industry/commissioner-guidance/guidance-12.html> accessed 14 January 2022.

Financial Consumer Agency of Canada, 'Guideline on Complaint-Handling Procedures for Banks and Authorized Foreign Banks' (2022) <https://www.canada.ca/en/financial-consumer-agency/services/industry/commissioner-guidance/complaint-handling-procedures-banks.html - toc1> accessed 20 February 2022.

Financial Consumer Agency of Canada, 'Filing a Complaint with a Bank or Federal Credit Union: Rights and Responsibilities' <https://www.canada.ca/en/financial-consumer-agency/services/rights-responsibilities/rights-banking/make-complaint.html> accessed 14 January 2022.

Financial Consumer Agency of Canada, 'How to file a Complaint with your Financial Institution' <https://www.canada.ca/en/financial-consumer-agency/services/complaints/file-complaint-financial-institution.html> accessed 14 January 2022.

Financial Consumer Agency of Canada, 'How you can stay Cyber Secure when Downloading and Using Apps' <https://www.getcybersafe.gc.ca/en/blogs/how-you-can-stay-cyber-secure-when-downloading-and-using-apps> accessed 10 January 2022.

Financial Consumer Agency of Canada, 'Industry Review: The Operations of External Complaints Bodies' (2020) <https://www.canada.ca/content/dam/fcac-acfc/documents/programs/research-surveys-studies-reports/operations-external-complaints-bodies.pdf> accessed 15 January 2022.

Financial Consumer Agency of Canada, 'Mobile Wallets' <https://www.canada.ca/en/financial-consumer-agency/services/payment/mobile-payments/mobile-wallets.html> accessed 10 January 2022.

Financial Consumer Agency of Canada, 'Paying with your Mobile Phone' <https://www.canada.ca/en/financial-consumer-agency/services/payment/mobile-payments/paying-with-mobile.html> accessed 10 January 2022.

Financial Consumer Agency of Canada, 'Secure the Data on your Mobile Devices' <https://www.getcybersafe.gc.ca/en/secure-your-devices/phones-and-tablets> accessed 10 January 2022.

Financial Consumer Agency of Canada, 'Unauthorized Mobile Payments' <https://www.canada.ca/en/financial-consumer-agency/services/payment/mobile-payments/unauthorized-mobile-payments.html> accessed 16 January 2022.

Geraint Howells and Stephen Weatherill, *Consumer Protection Law* (2nd ed., Ashgate 2005).

Iain Ramsay, *Consumer Law and Policy* (3rd ed., Hart Publishing 2012).

Ian Ayres and John Braithwaite, 'Tripartism: Regulatory Capture and Empowerment' (1991) 16 *Law & Social Inquiry* 435.

Ian Ayres and John Braithwaite, R*esponsive Regulation: Transcending the Deregulation Debate* (Oxford University Press 1992).

Martin Hogg, *Obligations: Law and Language* (Cambridge University Press 2017).

Nadia Effendi, Heather Pessione and Oliver V. Nguyen, 'Bhasin v. Hrynew: Towards Clarity and Coherence with Respect to Good Faith in Contract Performance' (2016) 46 *Advocates' Quarterly* 94.

OECD, 'Recommendation on Principles and Good Practices for Financial Education and Awareness' (2005) <https://www.oecd.org/finance/financial-education/35108560.pdf> accessed 8 January 2022.

OECD, 'OECD Recommendation on Consumer Dispute Resolution and Redress' (2007) <https://www.oecd.org/sti/consumer/38960101.pdf> accessed 11 January 2022.

OECD, 'Improving Online Disclosures with Behavioural insights: Towards Better Outcomes for Consumers' (2018) <https://www.oecd.org/sti/consumer/policy-note-improving-online-disclosures-behavioural-insights.pdf> accessed 27 January 2022.

Payments Canada, 'Payments Accelerated: Global Pandemic Accelerates the Rise of Digital Payments – Canadian Payment Methods and Trends Report 2021' 8 <https://www.payments.ca/sites/default/files/payments_canada_canadian_payment_methods_and_trends_report_2021.pdf> accessed 20 January 2022.

Peter Cartwright, 'Crime, Punishment and Consumer Protection.' (2007) 30(1) *Journal of Consumer Policy* 1.

Peter Cartwright, 'Redress Compliance and Choice: Enhanced Consumer Measures and the retreat from punishment in the Consumer Rights Act 2015' (2016) 75(2) *Cambridge Law Journal* 271.

Philip Hampton, 'Reducing Administrative Burdens: Effective Inspection and Enforcement' (2005) <https://webarchive.nationalarchives.gov.uk/ukgwa/+/http:/www.hm-treasury.gov.uk/prebud_pbr04_hampton.htm> accessed 18 January 2022.

Richard B. Macrory, `Regulatory Justice: Making Sanctions Effective' (2006) <https://webarchive.nationalarchives.gov.uk/ukgwa/20070305105024mp_/http://www.cabinetoffice.gov.uk/regulation/documents/pdf/macrory_penalties.pdf> accessed 18 January 2022.

Severine Saintier, 'The Elusive Notion of Good Faith in the Performance of a Contract, Why still a Bete Noire for the Civil and the Common Law?' (2017) 6 *Journal of Business Law* 441.

Shannon O'Byrne and Ronnie Cohen, 'The Contractual Principle of Good Faith and the Duty of Honesty in Bhasin v. Hrynew' (2015) 53 *Alberta Law Review* 1.

Steve Trites, Charles Gibney and Bruno Lévesque, 'Mobile Payments and Consumer Protection in Canada' (Research Division, Financial Consumer Agency of Canada 2013) <https://www.canada.ca/content/dam/canada/financial-consumer-agency/migration/eng/resources/researchsurveys/documents/fcac_mobile_payments_consumer_protection_accessible_en.pdf> accessed 27 January 2022.

Sue L.T. McGregor, 'Status of Consumer Education and Financial Education in Canada' (2018) 41(2) *Canadian Journal of Education* 601.

The Canadian Code of Practice for Consumer Debit Card Services <https://www.canada.ca/en/financial-consumer-agency/services/industry/laws-regulations/debit-card-code-conduct.html> accessed 9 January 2022.

Theodore Milosevic, 'What Makes a Consumer: Mandatory Arbitration Clauses and Free Digital Services in Canada' (2017) 75 *University of Toronto Faculty Law Review* 9.

Tsai-Jyh Chen (ed), *An International Comparison of Financial Consumer Protection* (Springer 2018).

Union de Consummateurs, 'Ending Abusive Clauses in Consumer Contracts' (Final Report of the Project Presented to Industry Canada's Office of Consumer Affairs 2011) <https://uniondesconsommateurs.ca/endabusiveclauses/> accessed 18 January 2022.

# 6 Consumer Protection and Mobile Payments: Kenya

## 6.1 Introduction

Kenya's mobile payment (m-payment) platform 'M-pesa'[1] has been described as the poster child for m-payment success in Africa.[2] M-pesa was introduced by a mobile network operator (MNO) (Safaricom) in 2007 with support from the Financial Deepening Challenge Fund of the United Kingdom's Department for International Development (DFID).[3] M-pesa provides a low-cost SMS-based person-to-person money transfer platform which allows users to deposit, send, and withdraw funds using their mobile phones.[4] Users may also purchase prepaid goods and services with the service.

The Central Bank of Kenya (CBK) provided an enabling regulatory environment that allowed Safaricom to leverage its technology, ubiquitous distribution networks, and partnerships with banks to offer m-payment services to the under-served population.[5] There was rapid customer uptake due to a ubiquitous distribution network at the grassroots level, the trusted Safaricom brand and relatively low-cost transactions compared to existing money transfer methods.[6] The success of m-payments in Kenya is evidenced by the fact that as of 2018, more Kenyans had mobile money accounts (72.9 per cent) than accounts with financial institutions (55.7 per cent).[7]

Although M-pesa demonstrated that mobile technology could be successfully deployed to extend financial services to unbanked persons, it also highlighted a

1 'M' stands for mobile while 'pesa' means money in Swahili.

2 'Making Mobile Money Pay in Africa' <https://www.bbc.com/future/article/20120920-making-mobile-money-pay> accessed 14 October 2021.

3 International Finance Corporation, 'M-Money Chanel Distribution Case – Kenya (Safaricom M-pesa)' p.1 <https://www.ifc.org/wps/wcm/connect/e0d2a9bd-16b9-4a36-8498-0b2650b9af8b/Tool%2B6.7.%2BCase%2BStudy%2B-%2BM-PESA%2BKenya%2B.pdf?MOD=AJPERES&CVID=jkCVy-n> accessed 11 October 2021.

4 Ibid. p1.

5 Ibid.

6 Brian Muthiora, 'Enabling Mobile Money Policies in Kenya Fostering a Digital Financial Revolution' (2015) p.6 <https://www.itu.int/en/ITU-T/focusgroups/dfs/Documents/2015_MMU_Enabling-Mobile-Money-Policies-in-Kenya.pdf> accessed 13 October 2021.

7 The World Bank, 'The Little Data Book on Financial Inclusion' (2018) p.84 <https://openknowledge.worldbank.org/handle/10986/29654> accessed 5 October 2021.

DOI: 10.4324/9780429327292-8

gap in the regulation of payment services in Kenya.[8] When Safaricom launched M-pesa in 2007, there were no laws dedicated to m-payments. However, the CBK conducted a review to satisfy itself that M-pesa was not a banking business under the Kenyan Banking Act 1999 (as amended) and did not introduce significant money laundering and operational risks.[9] The CBK also consulted the Communications Authority of Kenya,[10] which was Safaricom's primary regulator as an MNO. The Communications Authority considered M-pesa as a value-added service that Safaricom was licensed to offer but deferred to the CBK for the oversight of the service.[11] When the CBK completed the review, it issued Safaricom a Letter of No Objection, which allowed them to commence business.[12] Hence, in its early years, the service was regulated in an ad hoc fashion which involved open and continuous dialogue between Safaricom and the CBK.[13]

While the CBK adopted a flexible 'test and learn' approach, it became apparent that Kenya required a modern payment services law.[14] Consequently, the National Payments Systems Act (NPSA) and the National Payment Systems Regulations (NPSRs) were passed in 2011 and 2014, respectively. The NPSA provides the general framework for regulating and supervising payment systems and payment service providers (PSPs) in Kenya. To give further effect to the provisions of the NPSA, the NPSRs were introduced to provide additional regulatory rules for the payment sector. The NPSRs set out basic e-money rules and require interested firms to apply for authorisation/registration.[15] In addition, MNOs may be designated as PSPs[16] or e-money

8 Alliance for Financial Inclusion, 'Enabling Mobile Money Transfer: The Central Bank of Kenya's treatment of M-Pesa' (2010) p.6 <https://www.gsma.com/mobilefordevelopment/wp-content/uploads/2013/09/enablingmobilemoneytransfer92.pdf> accessed 2 October 2021.

9 Section 2 of the Banking Act defines what 'banking business' means. In analysing the section, the CBK concluded that M-pesa was not a banking business because the cash exchanged for electronic value was not repaid on terms and effectively remained in the control of the customer. Furthermore, M-pesa agents were required to make an upfront deposit of cash in an M-pesa account held by a local bank, and as such, there was no credit risk for customers or Safaricom. The CBK also established that there was no intermediation as customer funds were not lent in the pursuit of other business, interest, or income. There was also no interest paid on customer deposits. Ibid. pp.4–6.

10 At the time, it was known as the Communications Commission of Kenya.

11 Alliance for Financial Inclusion, 'Enabling Mobile Money Transfer (n 8) p.6.

12 Ibid. pp.4–6.

13 Ibid. p.6

14 Ibid.

15 Regulation 4. A firm issuing e-money on a small scale may apply for registration as a small e-money issuer and will be exempt from complying with some provisions in the NPSRs; Regulation 46(1) & (2).

16 s.2 of the National Payment System Act 2011 defines a 'payment service provider' as –

'i. a person, company or organisation acting as provider in relation to sending, receiving, storing or processing of payments or the provision of other services in relation to payment services through any electronic system;

ii. a person, company or organisation which owns, possesses, operates, manages or controls a public switched network for the provision of payment services; or

issuers.[17] Importantly, the NPSRs identified the CBK as the primary supervisory authority for PSPs.[18]

The NPSRs contain certain provisions which aim to protect customers. These provisions are supported by the CBK's Prudential Guidelines on Consumer Protection (PGCP), which contain enforceable rules issued under the Kenyan Banking Act[19] that apply to institutions licensed under the Banking Act.[20] Sectoral efforts are complemented by constitutional provisions guaranteeing certain consumer rights,[21] provisions in the Kenyan Consumer Protection Act (KCPA) 2012 and the Kenyan Competition Act (KCA) 2010 (as amended), and guidelines issued by relevant regulators e.g., the Competition Authority of Kenya (CAK).[22] Relevant provisions are referenced in subsequent discussions.

## 6.2 Provision of Information

### *6.2.1 Mandatory Disclosures*

Article 46 of the Kenyan Constitution guarantees that Kenyan consumers have a right to 'the information necessary for them to gain full benefit from goods and services.' In line with this constitutional right, the NPSRs and PGCP contain mandatory disclosure requirements that apply to the provision of m-payments. As indicated in the introduction, the NPSRs apply to all PSPs, whether licensed as financial institutions (FIs) or non-FIs. The NPSRs provide minimum requirements for a mandatory disclosure regime. PSPs are mandated to provide –

> a clear and understandable description of the services which it offers and the rates, terms, conditions and charges for such services and shall publish such information and display it prominently at all points of service .... [23]

Disclosure statements are to be issued to consumers free of charge upon their request.[24] Ongoing disclosure requirements are also mandated to ensure that

iii. any other person, company or organisation that processes or stores data on behalf of such payment service providers or users of such payment services.'

17 This is a payment service provider authorised to issue e-money under the NPSRs (Regulation 2).

18 Regulation 30 NPSRs.

19 s.33(4).

20 Central Bank of Kenya, 'Prudential Guidelines for Institutions Licensed Under the Banking Act – Consumer Protection (CBK/PG/22)' <https://www.centralbank.go.ke/wp-content/uploads/2016/08/PRUDENTIAL-GUIDELINES.pdf> accessed 7 October 2021.

21 See Article 46 of the Kenyan Constitution 2010.

22 The Consumer Protection Department is responsible for enforcing the Part VI of the Competition Act which contains the consumer protection provisions: Competition Authority of Kenya, 'Consumer Protection' <https://cak.go.ke/what-we-do/consumer-protection/overview> accessed 4 October 2021.

23 Regulation 35(1)(a).

24 Regulations 35(6) & 35(7).

customers can identify and track individual transactions carried out on their accounts.[25] In addition, PSPs must notify their customers and the CBK of any material changes to information disclosed.[26]

The PGCP, which applies to only FIs licensed under the Banking Act, contains similar provisions. It requires that before choosing a product, an FI should –

> explain clearly in simple and ordinary language which the consumer understands, the key features of the range of products and services that the consumer is interested in so as to enable the consumer to arrive at an informed decision about these products and services.[27]

PSPs should also inform customers of the charges, fees, and other financial liability that they may incur from using the product.[28] Where a consumer has decided to purchase a product/service, an FI must –

> provide the consumer with general information or a summary of the main features of the product or service including the interest rate, charges, fees or other financial obligation relating to the product or service.[29]

Like the NPSRs, the PGCP requires that consumers are given a copy of the applicable terms and conditions.[30] In addition, consumers are entitled to further information on any additional charges, fees, or interest that will be payable if they terminate the contract early.[31] The PGCP also mandates that consumers be notified[32] of any proposed changes to the terms and conditions of services[33] they subscribe to.[34]

The PGCP goes further than the NPSRs by requiring that FIs provide their customers with a 'key facts' document on a product if requested or if the nature of the transaction necessitates.[35] The key facts document essentially contains all the

25 Regulation 35(3) & (4).
26 Regulation 35(1)(c).
27 Paragraph 3.2.3(a)(i).
28 Paragraph 3.2.3(a)(ii).
29 Paragraph 3.2.3(b)(i). The Kenya Information and Communications (Consumer Protection) Regulation 2010 issued by the Communications Authority of Kenya also mandate information disclosures on applicable rates, terms, and conditions of services offered: See Regulation 10(1).
30 Paragraph 3.2.3(b)(ii).
31 Paragraph 3.2.3(b)(iii).
32 The mode of notification shall be agreed at the time of establishing the relationship. Paragraph 3.2.9.
33 The Kenyan Competition Act 2010 (as amended) also prohibits financial institutions from imposing unilateral fees and charges if they are not brought to the attention of the consumer prior to the provision of a service/product: See s.56(3) & (4).
34 Paragraph 3.2.9(a).
35 Paragraph 3.4.3(i).

key information about a product in a summarised form.[36] The PGCP also requires that firms disclose the name and contacts of their regulator. This is to ensure that consumers can contact the regulator where the firm fails to meet its regulatory responsibilities.[37]

Furthermore, the PGCP requires that –

> where a consumer is unable to understand English and Swahili, provide an oral explanation in a language the consumer understands. The institution may also arrange for a written translation of the information into the language the consumer understands should the nature of the transaction require such a translation and as may be mutually agreed upon by the institution and the consumer.[38]

Additionally, it provides that oral explanations should be used where consumers cannot understand written information.[39] These provisions stand out as they encourage alternative routes for passing on information to consumers. They are even more significant when considering that a good proportion of consumers may be uneducated. As we saw in *Chapter 4*, disclosures are meaningless if the consumer cannot make sense of the information.[40] Thus, making necessary allowances by encouraging translated disclosure documents and oral explanations may help support disadvantaged consumers. However, this does not guarantee better decision-making because it is possible to understand the language and words spoken but not the significance of terms used in specialised financial transactions.[41] What this suggests is that although these efforts are important in assisting consumers, they will need to be complemented by financial literacy initiatives that help consumers better appreciate the significance of the disclosed information.

Other enactments support the provisions in the NPSRs and PGCP. For example, the KCA requires that service providers inform consumers of all the charges and fees applying to a product.[42] It further provides that it is unconscionable to impose unilateral fees and charges without bringing them to the consumer's attention.[43] There are also disclosure requirements in the Kenya Information and Communications (Consumer Protection) Regulations (KICRs) 2010, which apply

36 Paragraph 3.4.3(i)(a).

37 Paragraph 3.4.2 (ii).

38 Paragraph 3.4.2(i)(e).

39 Paragraph 3.4.2(1)(f).

40 David Cayne, Michael J Trebilcock, 'Market Considerations in the Formulation of Consumer Protection Policy' (1973) 23 *University of Toronto Law Journal* 396, 406.

41 For this reason, the regulatory approach in countries like the United Kingdom requires that terms are articulated in a way that allows consumers to make informed choices. Hence, the United Kingdom looks beyond the substance and presentation of terms alone and also concerns itself with the significance/effect of terms used. See discussions in *Chapter 7*.

42 s.56(4).

43 s.56(3).

to MNOs.[44] Under the KICRs, consumers are entitled to 'clear and complete information about rates, terms and conditions for available and proposed products and services.'[45]

For m-payments, it appears that the NPSRs provide the minimum disclosure obligations applying uniformly to all PSPs. Additional disclosure requirements in the PGCP and KICRs apply depending on the status of the provider. Thus, banks and other institutions licensed under the Banking Act would also need to satisfy the obligations in the PGCP,[46] while an MNO would need to satisfy the KICRs. This disparity suggests that some consumers will enjoy better disclosures in comparison to others. As shown above, the PGCP contains requirements for oral disclosures to support uneducated consumers. There is no comparable provision in the NPSRs and KICRs. Thus, only m-payment consumers dealing with FIs will benefit from oral disclosures.

The PGCP requires that 'consumer research should be conducted to help determine and improve the effectiveness of disclosure requirements.'[47] This is a good approach because insights from research can assist in evaluating current regulatory policies. Moreover, the literature suggests that there can be disparities between how effective a policy seems on paper and how effective it is when applied to real-life situations.[48] A good illustration of this is evident in the report of a consumer protection diagnostic study conducted in Kenya.[49] The report shows that before the NPSRs were issued, M-pesa was reported to have had transparent pricing schedules with price tariffs being published and made available to users.[50] This pricing schedule adopted a tiered fee model where users were charged according to the monetary value of a transaction. Safaricom adopted this model to ensure that the service would be affordable.[51]

Despite efforts to disclose the pricing schedule, Flaming et al. report that owing to literacy and numeracy concerns, some consumers did not fully understand the tariffs.[52] Consequently, most customers made transactions in the lower tariff tiers and did not transact in other tariff tiers they considered more complex.[53] Thus, although M-pesa focused on transparent tariff disclosures to assist with decision-making, it led to confusion and indirectly limited the choices open to uneducated persons who could only transact on less complex tariffs.

44 For example, see Regulations 3(1)(a), 7(1) & 20(2).
45 Regulation 3(1)(a).
46 See paragraph 1.3.
47 Paragraph 3.4.1(v).
48 See Roscoe Pound, 'Law in the Books and Law in Action' (1910) 44 *American Law Review* 12.
49 Mark Flaming, Alexander Owino, Katharine McKee, et al., 'Consumer Protection Diagnostic Study (Kenya)' (2011) pp.12–13 <http://s3-eu-central-1.amazonaws.com/fsd-circle/wp-content/uploads/2015/08/30095758/11-02-22_Consumer_diagnostic_study.pdf> accessed 7 October 2021.
50 Ibid.
51 International Finance Corporation (n 3) p.5.
52 Flaming et al. (n 49) pp.12–13 .
53 Ibid.

This experience reinforces certain points highlighted in *Chapter 4*.[54] First, it is possible that consumers will not process information correctly for several reasons.[55] In the context of M-pesa, the reason suggested by the consumer study was lack of education. Second, commentators like Cayne and Trebilcock argue that consumers react differently to information. Only those who are psychologically and intellectually equipped to apply the information provided can benefit from disclosures.[56] The consumer report confirms this as it was those consumers who were intellectually handicapped that had a problem understanding the price schedule. Third, the M-pesa experience confirms that information overload and complexity can create undesirable results.[57] Rather than the desired goal of aiding decision-making, some consumers avoided transactions on tariff tiers they could not understand. All these points confirm, as argued in *Chapter 4*, that while disclosures are important in providing the 'raw material upon which rational purchasing decisions depend,'[58] it is not always sufficient on its own. For this reason, efforts in improving disclosures will need to be supported by other consumer policy tools that address its limitations.

### *6.2.2 Consumer Education*

Kenya's financial education regime involves a blend of public-private partnerships and traditional regulatory initiatives. In 2008, a year after M-pesa was launched, Kenya's Ministry of Finance mooted the idea of the government partnering with private stakeholders to drive efforts at improving consumer financial education.[59] Following this, the CBK, in collaboration with the Kenyan Financial Sector Deepening Trust (FSD),[60] sought to develop a National Strategy for Financial Education.[61] To this end, a platform was established known as the Financial Education and Consumer Protection Partnership (FEPP).[62] The FEPP

54 See ss.4.2.1 & 4.2.2.

55 Geraint Howells, 'The Potential and Limits of Consumer Empowerment by Information' (2005) 32(3) *Journal of Law & Society* 349, 355–357.

56 Cayne and Trebilcock (n 40) p.406.

57 Better Regulation Executive and National Consumer Council, 'Warning: Too much Information Can Harm' (2007) <https://www.regulation.org.uk/library/2007-Warning_Too_Much_Information_Can_Harm.pdf> accessed 14 October 2021; Omri Ben-Shahar, Carl Schneider, 'The Failure of Mandated Disclosure' (2011) 159 *University of Pennsylvania Law Review* 647.

58 Cayne and Trebilcock (n 40) p.406.

59 Gerda L Piprek and Ravi Ruparel, 'FSD's Financial Education Programme: Evaluation and Recommendations' (2013) p.1 <https://www.yumpu.com/en/document/read/22036707/fsds-financial-education-programme-evaluation-and-fsd-kenya> accessed 7 October 2021.

60 The FSD programme was established in 2005 to support the development of financial markets in Kenya and expand access to financial services. The programme works in partnership with the financial services industry and operates as an independent trust. <https://www.fsdkenya.org/about-us/> accessed 7 October 2021.

61 Flore-Anne Messy and Chiara Monticone, 'The Status of Financial Education in Africa' (2012) p.33 <https://doi.org/10.1787/5k94cqqx90wl-en> accessed 7 October 2021.

62 It was initially known as the Financial Education Partnership: Piprek & Ruparel (n 59) p.3.

comprised public bodies and private stakeholders[63] and was formed to drive the implementation of financial education and consumer protection initiatives.[64] The CBK's governor served as the 'official champion' of the FEPP while the FSD provided secretariat support.[65]

Under the FEPP initiative, the FSD implemented pilot programmes targeting the mass dissemination of financial concepts. One project stood out in particular. With part funding from the UK DFID Financial Education Fund, the FSD supported a pilot project to convey financial literacy messages through a TV soap opera dubbed 'Makutano Junction.'[66] At the end of episodes conveying financial literacy messages, the audience could send a text message requesting a leaflet containing information discussed in the episode.[67] The leaflets addressed issues of budgeting, saving, investments, and debt management.[68] Where banking services had been referenced in an episode, the leaflets also included an application enabling consumers to sign up with the bank involved.[69]

While this is an innovative way to provide information, one criticism is that the approach may be interpreted as indirect marketing. For example, it is possible that financial institutions may provide sponsorship support or pay for advertising coverage of their services on the show. In such cases, information on their products may be included or given some prominence on the show. This situation will prevent information from being relayed in an unbiased manner. Consumers may, thus, be swayed to deal with the providers receiving more publicity even though others will better serve their needs.

The FEPP initiative lasted from 2008 until 2012.[70] Although it raised awareness about the need for a nationally coordinated effort to improve financial education, it did not lead to the formation of a permanent structure dedicated to the issue. The initiative was primarily donor driven, and when the underlying donor programme came to an end, the project's momentum failed.[71] In addition, the strategic impact of the FEPP was limited because it did not result in key outputs such as a national financial education framework document and no institutionalised entity was created to oversee financial consumer education in the long term.[72]

In the absence of nationally coordinated efforts, the CBK has taken on independent initiatives to encourage financial education. For instance, the PGCP requires FIs to educate their customers using mechanisms such as posting

63 Members include the Central Bank, various Ministries, the FSD, Non-governmental Organisations, financial institutions, and other private sector companies; ibid.

64 Flaming et al. (n 49) p.28.

65 Ibid. p.1.

66 Flaming et al. (n 49) p.28; Messy & Monticone (n 61) p.34.

67 Messy & Monticone (n 61) p.34.

68 Ibid.

69 Ibid.

70 Piprek & Ruparel (n 59 ) p.3.

71 Ibid.

72 Piprek & Ruparel (n 59) p.5.

frequently asked questions on their websites, using brochures, and organising public awareness campaigns.[73] They are also encouraged to maintain call centres with competent staff attending to customer queries.[74] The strategies encouraged under the PGCP have been the most popular methods for disseminating information on m-payments.

M-pesa's history particularly points to the role that targeted education initiatives by private industry stakeholders play in encouraging the uptake of m-payments. Before introducing M-pesa, it was reported that many Kenyans were already familiar with using a mobile phone for basic operations like making voice calls and sending text messages.[75] However, during the pilot phase, it became clear that using a mobile phone for financial transactions was alien to a large percentage of the populace, particularly those in rural areas with low financial literacy rates.[76] Therefore, Safaricom decided to organise training and refresher sessions to familiarise trial participants with the service. Armed with the knowledge that there was a knowledge gap, Safaricom allocated a part of its marketing budget towards educating consumers. It organised awareness promotions, roadshows, and consumer education campaigns in the rural areas.[77] Brochures with clear instructions and illustrations were also distributed to ensure customers could understand how M-pesa worked.[78]

Safaricom's approach meant that within a short time, a large percentage of the population became conversant with the workings of M-pesa. Perhaps this may explain why there have been no specific education initiatives from the CBK targeting m-payments. This issue may have been taken for granted because of M-pesa's success. This is more so because, by the time a full regulatory regime was put in place,[79] M-pesa was already an established service. Although the education initiatives emanated from industry, Safaricom's strategy emphasises that engaging the demand side through targeted consumer education may play an important role in encouraging the adoption of m-payments.

M-pesa's experience raises the question about which stakeholder is best placed to provide targeted financial education for innovative financial products. Safaricom used M-pesa's pilot phase to educate trial participants and gather data informing its consumer education strategy. As indicated in *Chapter 4*, it may not be pragmatic for regulators to make such commitments to a specific product because of the limited information and resources at their disposal. Nonetheless, regulators may be better placed to provide general financial education, which provides the foundation for targeted initiatives. There is an argument that industry

73 Paragraph 3.2.4(d).

74 Ibid.

75 International Finance Corporation (n 3) p.19.

76 Ibid.

77 International Finance Corporation (n 3) p.19.

78 Ibid.

79 The passing of the NPSA and the NPSRs heralded the beginning of full regulatory oversight over the Kenyan payment industry including m-payments.

may be better positioned to educate consumers on specific innovative products. This is because they will likely have more expertise with the product, having developed it.

However, leaving targeted financial education as the sole responsibility of industry can be precarious. This is because industry may not always be motivated to provide financial education since information is a public good.[80] Firms may rely on their competitors who offer similar products to take the lead in educating consumers, thereby causing a free-rider problem. To prevent this, the public-private collaborative approach highlighted in *Chapter 4* should be adopted. This approach will see a national financial literacy framework overseen by a government agency or regulator. This supervising agency should set the national financial literacy baseline and implement initiatives which improve the general knowledge of financial concepts. To support its efforts, the agency can also mandate industry to take the lead with educating consumers on specific innovative products. Industry's efforts will, however, be under the scrutiny of regulators. This collaborative approach will not bar regulators from developing targeted financial literacy initiatives; it will only require that institutions seeking to introduce new products make concerted efforts towards educating intended consumers.

## 6.3 Withdrawal Rights and Cooling-Off Periods

The NPSRs are silent on cooling-off periods and withdrawal rights. The PGCP contains a section marked 'cooling-off periods.'[81] It provides that before contracting, an institution shall –

> inform the consumer of his right to take some time to think over the proposed transaction before signing the contract or committing himself to take the product or use the service.[82]

It further states that the institution shall 'request the consumer to confirm whether he needs some time to reconsider the proposed transaction.'[83] While these provisions seem to ensure that consumers have some time to contemplate before entering a transaction, it does not provide the same opportunities where a transaction has been completed. Thus, these provisions appear to be pre-contractual efforts aimed at preventing pressure sales rather than post-contractual cooling-off periods allowing consumers to cancel contracts without consequences. This point is further buttressed by examining the KCPA.

80 See *Chapter 4* for a discussion on public goods.
81 Paragraph 3.2.6.
82 Paragraph 3.2.6 (a)(ii).
83 Paragraph 3.2.6 (a)(iii).

Part IV of the KCPA also provides for cooling-off periods with attendant cancellation rights. However, these only apply to specific contracts.[84] While contracts for payment services are not expressly recognised as those benefitting from a statutory cooling-off period, the KCPA provides cancellation rights for direct and remote contracts. Direct agreements are consumer agreements negotiated or concluded in person at the supplier's place of business, while remote agreements are consumer agreements entered into between the consumer and supplier who are in different places.[85] Thus, depending on the context, one may interpret a payment services contract as a direct or remote agreement.

Despite a lack of specificity, a comparison may be drawn between the wordings of the KCPA and the PGCP. For instance, for timeshare agreements, the KCPA provides that –

> A consumer may, without any reason, cancel a timeshare agreement at any time from the date of entering into the agreement until ten days after receiving the written copy of the agreement.[86]

It is clear from the wording that the KCPA envisages that for certain transactions, consumers will have the right to withdraw after a transaction is finalised as opposed to the approach in the PGCP, which only recognises a pre-contractual opportunity to contemplate a transaction.

If one were to assume that contracts for payment services can be classified as remote or direct, then it is useful to consider the KCPA's position on cooling-off periods and cancellation rights for such contracts. For remote agreements, the KCPA provides that –

> A consumer may cancel a remote agreement at any time from the date the agreement is entered into until seven days after the consumer receives a copy of the agreement if the supplier fails to comply with section 36.[87]

Section 36 mandates that a supplier must provide a consumer with disclosed information before entering into a remote agreement. The KCPA further provides that –

> A consumer may cancel a remote agreement within one year after the date the agreement is entered into, if the supplier does not comply with a requirement under section 37.[88]

84 e.g., timeshares and personal development contracts.

85 s.2.

86 s.23(1).

87 s.38(1).

88 s.38(2).

Section 37 requires that the supplier delivers a copy of the remote agreement to the consumer. From the above, it is clear that consumers have seven days after receiving the contract to reconsider their commitment. Curiously, this cooling-off period is only available if, in contravention of Section 36, the supplier fails to make initial disclosures before the contract is entered into. As we saw in *Chapter 4*, one of the functions of cooling-off periods is to provide consumers with more time to seek out more information and reconsider the contractual terms. However, the wording of Section 38(1) does not entirely support this function as the cooling-off period will not be available if the supplier complies with Section 36. Hence, consumers do not have any opportunity to rethink a transaction if the supplier has made pre-contractual disclosures.

The KCPA also requires that suppliers send a copy of the agreement to the consumer. To encourage suppliers to meet this obligation, a lengthier cooling-off period is guaranteed to consumers who do not receive a copy of the agreement.[89] This provision can be rationalised on the basis that the usefulness of the cooling-off period depends on the consumer having access to the full contractual terms, which will assist them in deciding whether it is in their interest to continue with the contract. However, this assumption is let down by the fact that if a supplier were to provide pre-contractual disclosures and deliver a copy of the agreement as prescribed, the consumer would not be able to cancel the contract. Hence, the cooling-off period is only triggered by supplier non-compliance and not the need to support consumers' decision-making unconditionally. This conclusion can be supported when one compares the cooling-off provision relating to timeshares which was reproduced earlier. The KCPA expressly states that a consumer who enters a timeshare contract can cancel it '*without any reason*' within ten days after receiving a copy of the timeshare agreement. This cancellation right is not tied to supplier non-compliance and represents a more authentic version of withdrawal rights exercisable during a defined cooling-off period.

The provisions for direct contracts are more ambiguous. Section 35(1) provides that –

> A consumer may, without any reason, cancel a direct agreement at any time from the date of entering into the agreement.

Similar to the cancellation provisions applying to remote contracts, the KCPA also provides that a consumer may cancel a direct agreement within one year after the date of entering into it if they do not receive a copy of the written agreement.[90] While Section 35(1) seems to guarantee an unconditional cancellation right since a consumer can cancel '*without any reason*,' it does not specify a specific cooling-off timeframe. It is unclear why this approach has been taken but failing to specify a timeframe introduces contractual uncertainty, which increases transaction costs.

89 Ibid.
90 s.35(2).

Overall, it will be beneficial for the CBK to clarify whether and how cooling-off periods apply to contracts for payment services and other financial services.

## 6.4 The Regulation of Business Conduct

### *6.4.1 Regulating Unfair Commercial Practices*

Provisions in the KCPA, KCA and, PGCP provide the rules regulating business practices in the financial sector. Therefore, it is expected that these existing rules will apply to m-payments. One of the aims of the KCPA is to promote fair and ethical business practices.[91] It is also dedicated to –

> protecting consumers from all forms and means of unconscionable, unfair, unreasonable, unjust or otherwise improper trade practices including deceptive, misleading, unfair or fraudulent conduct.[92]

To this end, the KCPA states that 'no person shall engage in an unfair practice.'[93] It further provides that 'a person who performs an act referred to in sections 12, 13 and 14 shall be deemed to be engaging in an unfair practice.'[94] The sections mentioned, i.e., Sections 12, 13, and 14 cover three broad categories, namely: the use of false, misleading, and deceptive representations;[95] the use of unconscionable representations;[96] and the adoption of practices which allow a supplier to pressure a consumer into renegotiating the terms of a consumer transaction.[97] Hence, the KCPA provides three broad categories of activity which are considered unfair.

The KCA contains similar provisions but differs in two respects. First, it does not recognise a broader classification of unfair practices with subcategories; instead, it recognises two broad categories of prohibited behaviour, i.e., the use of false and misleading representations and engaging in unconscionable conduct.[98] Second, unlike the KCPA, it expressly criminalises the actions which fall under the prohibited categories. Issues arising from the use of criminal sanctions in consumer protection have been discussed in *Chapter 5*, and those concerns also apply here.

The KCPA does not explain the meaning of the term 'unfair,' and it does not provide a test or criteria to guide the determination of unfairness. Instead, the KCPA lists examples or factors that could be considered when determining if a

91 s.3(4)(c).
92 s.3(4)(d).
93 s.15(1).
94 s.15(2).
95 s.12.
96 s.13.
97 s.14.
98 ss. 55 & 56.

practice falls within the first two categories of unfair practices.[99] The KCA takes a similar approach as it does not define the meaning of the term 'unconscionable' but only lists factors that may be considered in determining if a practice is unconscionable.[100] Although the KCA does not define what 'unconscionable' means in the context of the Act, a further explanation is contained in guidelines issued by the CAK, which elaborate its approach to enforcing the consumer protection provisions in the KCA.[101] The guidelines explain that 'unconscionable conduct is generally understood to mean a statement or an act which is particularly unreasonable, that it goes against good conscience'[102] and that 'transactions or dealings, therefore, may be termed to be unconscionable when they are deliberate, involve serious misconduct or involve conduct which is clearly unfair and unreasonable.'[103] It also further explains that –

> Where a claim is made that certain firm conduct is unconscionable, it must be shown with success that there was inequality in the position of the parties due to ignorance, need or distress of the weaker party which would have him in the power of the stronger party, coupled with proof of substantial unfairness in the bargain. When it has been shown, a presumption of fraud is raised and the stronger party must show the inverse in order to prove his conduct was fair and reasonable.[104]

One may argue that the scope of the KCPA's provisions on unfair practices is limited. This is because unfair practices take a variety of forms which go beyond the categories identified. While one does not expect a statute to list every form of unfair practice, the use of broad definitions and/or standards of fairness allows its reach to extend beyond specific practices listed in the statute. Thus, it is argued that the absence of a broad definition/standard for evaluating unfairness limits the scope of the KCPA's provisions. The same argument can be extended to the provisions of the KCA. Including a broad statutory definition of the term 'unconscionable' would have helped ensure that a wide range of activities is caught under the ambit of the Act. While the CAK's consumer protection guidelines do not define 'unconscionable,' it provides further information on what qualifies as 'unconscionable conduct' which is helpful.

However, the guidelines also raise additional questions. For instance, Paragraph 91 (reproduced above) suggests that where it is alleged that a firm's conduct is

99 i.e., the use of false, misleading. and deceptive representations and the use of unconscionable representations.

100 s.56(2).

101 See Competition Authority of Kenya, 'Consumer Protection Guidelines' (Revised 2017) <https://cak.go.ke/sites/default/files/guidelines/consumer-protection/Consumer Protection Guidelines.pdf> accessed 4 October 2021.

102 Paragraph 84.

103 Paragraph 86.

104 Paragraph 91.

unconscionable and that there exists some power imbalance coupled with proof of substantial unfairness, then a presumption of fraud is raised against the firm. The first issue with the provision is that it is unclear what 'unfairness' means in this context, and it is also unclear what tests will be used to establish 'substantial unfairness.' It also appears that the terms 'unconscionable' and 'unfair' are loosely used interchangeably in the paragraph. The first sentence of the paragraph refers to the firm's conduct being 'unconscionable,' while the last sentence requires proof of 'fair' conduct. The seeming interchangeable use of both terms appears to be at variance with the consistent use of 'unconscionable' in the KCA instead of 'unfair.' More confusing is the introduction of a presumption of fraud against the firm. It is unclear why such a presumption is necessary since the KCA does not mention it, nor does it tie any specific remedies to the failed rebuttal of such a presumption.

Regarding the use of false and misleading representations, the KCA, like the KCPA, only identifies specific examples of targeted representations. The issue of false and misleading representations is discussed in more detail in Section 6.4.3.

Furthermore, the scope of the third category of unfair practices under the KCPA is arguably inadequate. Section 14 of the KCPA provides that –

> It is an unfair practice for a person to use his, her or its custody or control of a consumer's goods to pressure the consumer into renegotiating the terms of a consumer transaction.

The section appears to target the use of duress to secure contract renegotiation. The focus on the supplier using their custody or control of a consumer's goods is narrow. Suppliers may adopt other tactics, including threatening to breach an existing contract to force a supplier to renegotiate contractual terms. However, what is most significant is that the section only targets conduct that pressures a consumer to renegotiate the terms of a completed transaction. It invariably ignores similar unfair conduct, which may be used to pressure the consumer to enter into the agreement in the first place. It also ignores conduct that may affect how contractual terms are enforced to the detriment of a consumer.

The KCA does not directly address the negotiation or renegotiation of contract terms. However, it provides that one factor to be taken into account when determining if a trader has engaged in unconscionable conduct is 'whether any undue influence or pressure was exerted on, or any unfair tactics were used against, the consumer or a person acting on behalf of the consumer.'[105] Although the KCA does not define what 'undue influence' means in the context of the Act, a definition is included in the CAK's consumer protection guidelines.[106] However,

105 s.56(2)(d).

106 The guidelines define 'undue influence' to mean 'exploiting a position of power in relation to the consumer so as to apply pressure, even without using or threatening to use physical force, in a

neither the KCA nor the guidelines clarify what factors will lead to a finding that a consumer has been unduly influenced. Based on Kenya's legal tradition, one may assume that the Common Law requirements for successfully pleading undue influence will apply.

In the financial sector, the PGCP states that the relationship between FIs and their customers shall be guided by certain principles, one of which is fairness.[107] In promoting their services, the PGCP states that an institution shall not –

> engage in unfair, deceptive, oppressive or aggressive practices such as threatening, intimidating, being violent towards, abusing, being non-responsive or humiliating a consumer.[108]

Furthermore, firms must not 'exert undue influence or duress on a consumer to enter into a transaction.'[109] Thus, the PGCP goes a step ahead of the KCPA by identifying the unconscionable practices considered unfair. However, like the KCPA, the PGCP does not provide any definition of fairness. It also does not clarify what criteria will be used to determine if a practice is 'deceptive,' 'oppressive,' or 'aggressive;' neither does it provide guidance for determining if a firm has engaged the use of undue influence or duress.

Where consumers have been subjected to unfair practices, the KCPA provides that –

> Any agreement, whether written, oral or implied, entered into by a consumer after or while a person has engaged in an unfair practice may be rescinded by the consumer and the consumer is entitled to any remedy that is available in law, including damages.[110]

Where rescission is impossible, a consumer may recover any difference by which the amount paid under the contract exceeds the value of the goods or services. The consumer may also recover damages in addition or as an alternative.[111] The PGCP does not provide direct remedies for the consumer. The CBK imposes administrative sanctions on non-compliant FIs on the basis that they are contravening the Bank Act (and not on the basis of providing remedies to consumers).[112]

---

way which significantly limits the consumer's ability to make an informed decision.' See Competition Authority of Kenya, 'Consumer Protection Guidelines' (n 101) p.4.

107 The other principles include reliability, transparency, equity, and responsiveness. Paragraph 3.1(ii).

108 Paragraph 3.2.1(c)(i).

109 Paragraph 3.2.1(c)(vi).

110 s.16(1).

111 s.16(2).

112 Part VI, PGCP.

### *6.4.2 Regulating Contract Terms*

#### *6.4.2.1 Standard Term Contracts and Fairness*

There is no independent regulatory regime for contract terms in Kenya. However, the unfair practices regime can accommodate the regulation of contract terms. For instance, under the KCPA, one factor for determining whether a representation is unconscionable is if the representations are made with the knowledge that the contract terms are so 'adverse to the consumer as to be inequitable.'[113] Similarly, in prohibiting unfair practices, the PGCP directs firms not to include unconscionable or unreasonable terms in their agreements with consumers.[114] The NPSRs are silent on the regulation of contract terms.

While the use of unreasonable and inequitable terms appears to be prohibited by the KCPA and PGCP, both instruments contain no guidance for detecting defaulting terms. As noted in Section 6.4.1, since the KCPA provides no definition/ standards for determining fairness, it is difficult to predict what criteria will be used to determine whether a term is 'so adverse to the consumer as to be inequitable.' The same problem applies to the PGCP, as there are no criteria for establishing that a term is 'unconscionable' or 'unreasonable.' This lack of certainty suggests that clarification may only become available when disputes arise. This is not ideal as regulatory certainty ensures that parties know what standards they are held to and the consequences for falling short. Regulatory subjects should be able to judge the law's reaction to their conduct when choosing between legal and illegal acts.[115] Moreover, uncertainty leads to increased costs as there are higher chances of litigation.[116]

#### *6.4.2.2 Transparency*

Although there is no regime dedicated to regulating contract terms, there are provisions in the PGCP which can be interpreted as encouraging transparency. The PGCP broadly states that the relationship between an institution and its customers shall be based on transparency.[117] Although it does not define transparency, it dedicates some provisions to explaining what is expected of a firm with regards to upholding this principle.

Paragraph 3.4.2(i)(a) of the PGCP states that institutions must –

> ensure that any information given to a consumer on among other things benefits, prices, risks and the terms and conditions; whether in writing, electronically or orally is fair, clear and transparent.

113 s.13(2)(f).

114 Paragraph 3.2.1(c)(v).

115 Iain MacNeil, 'Uncertainty in Commercial Law' (2009) 13(1) *Edinburgh Law Review* 68, 69.

116 Ibid. p.72.

117 Paragraph 3.1(ii).

Firms are to ensure that such information is easily comprehensible so that consumers can make informed choices.[118] Furthermore, firms must not –

> disguise, diminish, obscure or conceal a material fact or warning through, among others, use of small prints which cannot be read easily, describing the material fact or warning in complex language, use of voluminous documents or omitting a material fact or warning.[119]

The information contained in advertising and marketing material is also expected to be written in simple language and in legible fonts that can be easily read.[120] However, these provisions are general and are not specifically framed to apply to contract terms. Hence it is unclear what role transparency will play in the regulation of contract terms used in m-payments.

### *6.4.3 Regulating False and Misleading Information*

The bulk of the provisions controlling false and misleading information are contained in the KCPA and the KCA. Both laws apply generally irrespective of sector and therefore extend to m-payments. In regulating the use of false and misleading information, the KCPA recognises two categories: false representations, which could be misleading or deceptive[121] and unconscionable representations.[122] As noted in Section 6.4.1, the use of representations falling under either category is deemed an unfair practice. The distinction between both categories is a fine one. The false representation category appears to focus on representations which deal with the characteristics and quality of a service as well as the identity of the provider. Unconscionable representations, on the other hand, focus on representations which seek to take advantage of the consumer's personal limitations or bargaining power.

With respect to false representations, the KCPA provides examples of targeted statements. The most relevant to m-payments will include the use of false, misleading, or deceptive representations which suggest that a transaction involves or does not involve rights, remedies, or obligations.[123] Others include representations which suggest that a service has a claimed approval or sponsorship and representations which use exaggeration, innuendo, or ambiguity so as to conceal a material fact or which fail to state a material fact with the intention to deceive.[124] One thing to note is that in introducing the examples of false

118 Paragraph 3.4.2(i)(b).

119 Paragraph 3.2.1(c)(vii).

120 Paragraph 3.4.8(b).

121 s.12; where a person has in good faith published and distributed such representations in the ordinary course of business, they will not be guilty of non-compliance; s.15(3).

122 s.13.

123 s.12(2)(m).

124 s.12(2)(n).

misrepresentations, the KCPA states that the examples are 'without limiting the generality of what constitutes a false, misleading or deceptive representation.'[125] The broad wording suggests that the list is not exhaustive. This introduces the flexibility that will be useful for future enforcement. The only problem lies in the KCPA's failure to provide a clear standard of fairness.

The provisions in the KCA regulating the use of false and misleading representations are less detailed when compared to the KCPA. The KCA provides specific examples of targeted representations like those contained in the KCPA, but the examples are significantly shorter.[126] Also, it does not include any broadly worded caveat, which can support a deduction that the listed examples are not exhaustive. Unlike the KCPA, however, the consumer protection guidelines issued by the CAK further elaborate the meaning of 'representations.' The guidelines explain that representation is 'a statement of account, assertion of facts, declaration, depiction, explanation, illustration, indication, narration, narrative, portraiture, portrayal, presentation, report ….'[127] It further explains that representations may be express or implied.[128] While this broad approach may be beneficial in bringing a variety of practices under the ambit of the CKA, the guidelines do not have the force of law. Also, the use of specific examples in the CKA coupled with the failure to include the broad caveat earlier referred to leads to the conclusion that, in reality, the provisions regulating false and misleading representations in the CKA are limited.

Concerning unconscionable representations, the KCPA states that in determining if a representation falls within the category, certain facts known[129] to the maker of the statement must be taken into account.[130] For instance, a representation may be unconscionable where it is made by a person who knows (or ought to know) that –

> the consumer is not reasonably able to protect his or her interests because of disability, ignorance, illiteracy, inability to understand the language of an agreement or similar factors.[131]

While this provision does not deal with the falsity of a representation, it provides some protection for vulnerable consumers whom suppliers know may be misled due to the factors listed. In addition, this provision indirectly recognises that all consumers have a differing capacity to process information and that a true statement may still be capable of misleading a consumer owing to certain limitations.

125 s.12(2).
126 Compare examples in s.55 of the KCA and s.12(2) of the KCPA.
127 Paragraph 13.
128 Ibid.
129 Or ought to be known.
130 s.13(2). As with false representations, the KCPA also uses broadly worded provisions to introduce the examples of factors that may be considered.
131 s.13(2)(a).

As can be seen in *Chapter 7*, making allowances to protect vulnerable consumers is common practice in other jurisdictions.

Other examples of unconscionable representations listed in the KCPA include statements of opinion that a maker knows are misleading and will be likely relied on by the consumer to his detriment.[132] Unconscionable representations may also be inferred where the price grossly exceeds the price at which similar services are offered[133] or where the consumer is placed under undue pressure to enter into the transaction.[134] The remedies available to the consumer under the KCPA apply to general unfair practices discussed in Section 6.4.1.

The PGCP and NPSRs also contain supporting provisions aimed at preventing the use of false and misleading information. For instance, the PGCP mandates FIs to ensure that advertising and promotional materials are fair, clear, and not misleading.[135] Similarly, the NPSRs require PSPs to ensure that their adverts are precise, easily understood.[136] and not misleading to consumers.[137]

## 6.5 Liability Rules

The NPSRs contain general liability rules for payment services which apply to m-payments. These rules are technologically neutral because they are not drafted to apply to specific payment instruments but instead apply generally to all PSPs. PSPs are defined broadly under the Kenyan National Payment System Act (NPSA) 2011 and easily incorporate traditional FIs like banks and non-FIs like MNOs.[138]

With regards to unauthorised transactions, the NPSRs provide that –

> A payment service provider shall be liable for payment transactions performed without the knowledge of the customer:
>
> Provided that such liability may be contractually excluded in circumstances where the payment service provider—
>
> (a) proves an element of fault on the side of the customer in the use of the service; or
>
> (b) demonstrates at first glance that the payment instruction was carried out by the legitimate customer.[139]

Thus, although PSPs are generally liable for unauthorised transactions, the NPSRs permit the contractual exclusion of liability in two circumstances. While the first

132 s.13(2)(g).
133 s.13(2)(b).
134 s.13(2(h).
135 Paragraph 3.4.8(a).
136 Regulation 37(a).
137 Regulation 37(b).
138 See s.2 NPSA.
139 Regulation 28(5).

circumstance dealing with fault on the customer's side is relatively straightforward, the second circumstance is slightly confusing. PSPs can limit their liability if they can show at 'first glance' that the payment was carried out by a legitimate customer. The NPSRs do not explain how providers may demonstrate legitimacy at 'first glance.' One may argue that in the absence of any report of fraud, most transactions emanating from a customer's account qualify to be treated as legitimate at 'first glance.' The provision offers PSPs a broad basis for avoiding liability. As this significantly impacts consumers' interests, the provision should have been supported by clear guidance identifying the factors that support an assumption of a legitimate transaction at 'first glance.'

Unauthorised transactions occur due to several reasons, such as theft and loss of a payment instrument. However, the NPSRs do not contain provisions acknowledging these possibilities and, thus, do not clarify whether PSPs remain liable if theft or loss of a payment instrument or device occurs though they are not notified at all or within a given timeframe.[140] Hence, if, for example, a mobile phone is stolen and used for unauthorised transactions, it is unclear whether a PSP will remain liable if the consumer does not notify them at all of the theft or if they notify them but do so late. Perhaps in such scenarios, the PSP may seek to avoid any liability for losses occurring before they are notified by arguing that unauthorised transactions carried out after the device was stolen looked legitimate at 'first glance.'

The NPSRs permit PSPs to appoint agents to carry out a wide range of functions on their behalf.[141] For example, an agent may send, receive, or process payments on behalf of the PSP.[142] They can also process or store data on the PSPs' behalf, amongst other things.[143] The NPSRs confirm that 'a payment service provider is liable to its customers for the conduct of its agents, performed within the scope of the agency agreement.'[144] Consequently, it prohibits PSPs from excluding their liability under the agency agreement.[145] This provision was welcome and considered necessary owing to Safaricom's stance on its use of agents to deliver M-pesa. Before the NPSRs were issued, Safaricom asserted in its contracts with customers that it would not be legally responsible for its agents.[146] This was despite the fact that in delivering M-pesa, Safaricom relied on those agents to carry out core aspects of its business.[147] Safaricom's stance worried observers who feared

140 The PGCP requires that firms provide dedicated telephone lines through which consumers may report the loss/theft of payment instruments or suspicious transactions. However, these provisions apply with regards to protecting the account of a consumer and not the allocation of liability; Paragraph 3.3.4(b).

141 Regulation 14(1).

142 Regulation 14(3)(a).

143 Regulation 14(3)(c).

144 Regulation 14(4).

145 Regulation 14(5).

146 Flaming et al. (n 49) p.13.

147 Ibid.

that this would set a troubling precedent and encourage perverse incentives, which would inevitably lead to poor outcomes for consumers.[148] By expressly stating that PSPs would be legally responsible for their agents, the NPSRs put this issue to rest.

With regards to non-executed/improperly executed payment transactions, the NPSRs provide that –

> A payment service provider shall, where it is liable under this Regulation for non-execution or defective execution of an electronic retail transfer, without undue delay, restore the debited payment account to the state in which it would have been had the defective transaction not taken place, including a refund of the charges imposed.[149]

Although it is quite clear that the consumer will be entitled to a refund in such circumstances, the NPSRs do not clarify what falls within the scope of 'defective execution.' Nonetheless, other provisions in the same section of the NPSRs suggest that 'defective execution' will cover situations where the full amount instructed to be transferred is not paid or where improper charges have been deducted.[150] Since a right to refund is involved, it would have been more helpful for the NPSRs to clearly and exhaustively spell out the scope of circumstances considered as 'defective execution.'

## 6.6 Dispute Resolution

Kenya's dispute resolution regime encourages the use of internal redress mechanisms established by firms and other available ADR procedures.

### *6.6.1 Internal Dispute Resolution Procedures*

The NPSRs and PGCP mandate firms to set up internal dispute resolution protocols. The NPSRs require that PSPs shall –

> within a period of six months after commencing the provision of payment services, establish a customer care system within which its customers can make inquiries and complaints concerning its services ….[151]

Before establishing this customer care system, PSPs are mandated to provide adequate means for customers to file complaints.[152] By making this a compulsory

148 Ibid.
149 Regulation 28(4).
150 Regulation 28(2).
151 Regulation 38(a).
152 Regulation 38(b).

requirement for continuing business, PSPs are forced to ensure that complaints handling procedures are given priority.

These internal mechanisms are available free of charge and must be disclosed to the consumer.[153] Thus, the NPSRs require that at the point of service, customers must be informed of the name of the PSP and the contact medium for accessing its customer care.[154] Furthermore, disclosed information must be provided in an easily comprehensible manner.[155]

The NPSRs require that complaints are made within 15 days 'from the date of occurrence.'[156] On receipt of a complaint, a PSP is expected to advise the customer –

(a) of the expected actions and timing for investigation and resolution of the complaint; and
(b) if the payment service provider regards the complaint as frivolous or vexatious.[157]

Although the NPSRs do not specify what event the 'occurrence' refers to, it is reasonable to infer that it refers to the occurrence of the event/transaction that is the cause of the dispute in question. If the customer is dissatisfied with the advice given, the NPSRs indicate that the customer 'shall have further recourse in accordance with these Regulations and the Consumer Protection Act, 2012.'[158]

Regulation 40(1) of the NPSRs indicate a 30-day mandatory timeframe for resolving all disputes received. The use of a mandatory timeframe may ensure that firms give priority to dealing with complaints received. Within the period allocated for resolving complaints, the NPSRs require that mechanisms[159] are put in place to ensure consumers can monitor the progress of the complaint.[160]

One weakness with the NPSRs regime is that there is no mechanism ensuring that PSPs comply with the dispute resolution provisions. For instance, it does not include reporting requirements mandating PSPs to disclose how they are meeting their responsibilities. The NPSRs also do not include mechanisms that assist in detecting systemic problems from the complaints data. If mandatory reports are made to the regulator, they may identify patterns enabling them to draw necessary inferences. As argued in *Chapter 5*, a statutory ombudsman can be particularly useful in this regard because it serves as a central point for complaints, making it easier to identify systemic issues.

153 Regulations 37(d) & 39(7).
154 Regulation 35(2).
155 Regulation 38(d).
156 Regulation 39(1).
157 Regulation 39(3).
158 Regulation 39(4).
159 The regulations suggest the use of complaint reference numbers or other identifiers to facilitate timely and accurate responses to inquiries by consumers. See Regulation 40(3).
160 Regulation 40(2).

Where payment disputes involve MNOs, consumers may, in addition to the NPSRs regime, rely on the redress procedures contained in the KICRs issued by the Communications Authority of Kenya.[161] In the case of payments services offered by banks, their customers may also rely on the dispute resolution processes under the PGCP. The provisions in the PGCP are similar to those in the NPSRs. Firms are expected to establish internal redress procedures[162] which must be communicated to consumers.[163] Unlike the NPSRs, the PGCP includes a mechanism to encourage compliance. It provides that –

> When assessing the track record of an institution in investigating and determining complaints, the Central Bank of Kenya will have regard to the quality and fairness of the institution's investigations and determinations and to the clarity of its written communications to complainants.[164]

The PGCP also includes a mechanism for identifying systemic issues. it requires that –

> Institutions shall put in place arrangements to ensure that, in handling complaints, it identifies and remedies any recurring or systemic problems by:
>
> (a) Analyzing the causes of individual complaints in order to identify any failings in processes, products or services and staff; and
> (b) Correcting any such failings.[165]

The PGCP places the responsibility on FIs to correct identified systemic problems. However, there is no procedure for ensuring that this duty is performed or that the remedial actions adopted are appropriate. It is argued that this duty ought to be closely supervised by the CBK. This is because where systemic issues are caused by an FI's practices, there is no guarantee that these issues will be remedied in the absence of independent supervision and sanctions. For instance, consumer complaints may be linked to unfair advertising practices by banks, which misleads consumers into subscribing to inappropriate m-payment services. While consumers suffer detriment from poor decision-making induced by the misleading information, banks increase their revenue from unfair behaviour. Customers may lodge several complaints about this, which would ordinarily point an unbiased third party to the underlying problem. However, since the banks are the source of the problem and benefit from it, they are unlikely to correct their practices unless closer supervision backed by regulatory sanctions is available.

161 See Regulations 7 & 8.
162 Paragraph 4.1.
163 Paragraph 4.2.
164 Paragraph 4.3(ii).
165 Paragraph 4.6.

### *6.6.2 External ADR Mechanisms*

The Kenyan Constitution 2010 encourages courts to consider the use of 'alternative forms of dispute resolution including reconciliation, mediation, arbitration and traditional dispute resolution mechanisms'[166] The KCPA also aims to promote consumer welfare by 'providing consistent, accessible and efficient system of consensual resolution of disputes arising from consumer transactions.'[167] While encouraging the use of ADR, the KCPA also confirms that a consumer's assent to ADR cannot be used to prevent them from accessing other redress options. The KCPA states that –

> Any term or acknowledgement in a consumer agreement or a related agreement that requires or has the effect of requiring that disputes arising out of the consumer agreement be submitted to arbitration is invalid insofar as it prevents a consumer from exercising a right to commence an action in the High Court given under this Act.[168]

Where parties, however, agree to arbitration and submit to the process, the outcome is binding.[169]

There is currently no financial ombudsman service, although there have been recent unsuccessful attempts to create one. For instance, the Financial Services Authority Bill 2016[170] and the Financial Markets Conduct Bill 2018[171] sought to empower the proposed ombudsman with the authority to 'resolve ... complaints by financial customers about financial service providers in relation to the provision of financial products and financial services ....'[172] Had either bill been successful, m-payments would have been caught under the jurisdiction of the ombudsman because both bills defined financial products to include facilities or arrangements through which a person can make non-cash payments[173] – a definition wide enough to cover m-payments.

In the absence of a statutory ombudsman, other initiatives fill the gap. For example, the NPSRs permit customers to approach the CBK if they are

166 s.159(2)(c).

167 s.3(4)(g).

168 s.88(1).

169 s.88(3).

170 A copy of the Financial Services Authority Bill 2016 (Part XI) is available here: <https://www.treasury.go.ke/wp-content/uploads/2021/03/Financial-Services-Authority-Bill-2016.pdf> accessed 5 October 2021.

171 A copy of the Financial Markets Conduct Bill 2018 (Part XIV) available here: <https://www.treasury.go.ke/wp-content/uploads/2021/03/Draft-Financial-Markets-Conduct-Bill-2018.pdf> accessed 5 October 2021.

172 The Financial Services Authority Bill 2016, s.117(a) and the Financial Markets Conduct Bill 2018, s.122(a).

173 The Financial Services Authority Bill 2016, s.3(1)(c) and the Financial Markets Conduct Bill 2018, s.5(1)(c).

dissatisfied with the internal handling of a complaint.[174] Thus, the CBK indirectly plays the role of an external ombudsman. While this may be useful in the short term, there is some doubt about how the CBK can effectively handle consumer–business disputes in addition to its core responsibilities.[175] In addition, m-payment consumers may also lodge complaints with other relevant regulatory agencies. For instance, where the PSP is an MNO, a consumer may lodge complaints with the Communications Authority of Kenya.[176] The CAK is also empowered to receive and investigate complaints from consumers.[177] Where appropriate, the CAK can also refer received complaints to other specialised government agencies, which must make determinations and inform the CAK and consumer.[178]

The private sector has also come up with initiatives to support dispute resolution. For instance, in 2013, the Kenya Bankers Association consulted the ADR Centre for Development on the possibility of setting up a Banking Industry Mediation Centre.[179] In the same year, the association collaborated with the privately-run Strathmore Dispute Resolution Centre to provide a mediation pilot project that caters to banking-related disputes.[180]

Consumer organisations also assist consumers in externally resolving conflicts. Some of their efforts are statutorily backed; for example, under the KCA, recognised consumer bodies are entitled to notify the CAK of any infringements of the consumer-related provisions in the KCA.[181] They can also represent consumers before the CAK.[182] Where consumer bodies make such notifications, the CAK is obliged to investigate.[183] Other non-statutory initiatives exist. For example, the Consumer Information Network of Kenya (CIN) assists consumers in

174 Regulation 40(5).

175 On the CBK website https://www.centralbank.go.ke/banking-services/ there is a section dedicated to explaining its 'core functions,' consumer protection and dispute resolution are not included on its list.

176 The Kenya Information and Communications (Dispute Resolution) Regulations 2010, Regulation 3,.

177 ss.9(b) & 70(1) KCA.

178 s.68 KCA.

179 ADR Centre for Development, 'Consultancy to Advice the Kenya Bankers Association on the Implementation of an Effective Alternative Dispute Resolution Mechanism' <https://www.adrcenterfordevelopment.com/2018/06/08/kenya-consultancy-to-advice-the-kenya-bankers-association-on-the-implementation-of-an-effective-alternative-dispute-resolution-mechanism/> accessed 6 October 2021.

180 <https://strathmore.edu/news/sls's-centre-to-host-inter-bank-disputes-mediation-center/> accessed 17 October 2021.

181 ss.9(1)(e) & 69(1).

182 Competition Authority of Kenya, 'FAQs on Consumer Protection'<https://cak.go.ke/mandate/Consumer-Complaints/faqs> accessed 4 October 2021.

183 s.69(2). The CAK has also published its Guidelines on Engaging Consumer Bodies <https://cak.go.ke/sites/default/files/guidelines/consumer-protection/Guidelines on Engaging with Consumer Organizations.pdf> accessed 5 October 2021.

seeking recourse from service providers.[184] The CIN's procedure involves first trying to understand the nature of the complaint to determine if any rights have been breached.[185] If a breach is established, the CIN contacts the service provider to obtain its view on the matter. If the matter cannot be settled at this stage, the CIN proceeds to contact the regulator.[186] However, the CIN is not empowered to bring independent actions on behalf of consumers[187] where ADR attempts fail. This is a significant setback because empowering consumer bodies to bring representative actions may force service providers to show more commitment towards the CIN's ADR efforts. Additionally, collective actions by groups such as the CIN will help address issues related to the cost of individual litigation.[188]

## 6.7 Conclusion

In this chapter, we discussed the relevant consumer protection rules that may avail m-payment users in Kenya. In summary, there is no single document containing all the relevant rules; instead, Kenyan consumers must look to provisions contained in several regulatory documents. Also, there is no primary consumer protection agency, and consumer protection mandates are shared between several regulators, including the CBK, which is the primary supervisory authority for PSPs.

The consumer protection rules are more robust in certain thematic areas when compared to others. For example, several documents support the use of mandatory disclosures in the delivery of m-payments. While not entirely perfect, there are also substantial rules regulating commercial conduct and requiring the setting up of internal dispute resolution mechanisms. There is no specific regulatory regime for the regulation of contract terms, and consumers will need to rely on the broader rules tackling unfair commercial practices. There is currently no financial ombudsman which deprives consumers of an important external resolution mechanism.

There are also gaps stemming from a lack of clear guidance on important concepts and terms used in some regulatory documents. For example, key terms like 'fair' and 'unconscionable,' which are central to the regulatory regime for unfair commercial practices, are not given adequate attention. With no clear definition of these terms, the full impact of the regulatory rules remains vague.

184 Another active association is the Consumer Federation of Kenya (COFEK). One of COFEK's subsidiaries, the Monetary Institutions Watch (MIWA) focuses on consumer protection and dispute resolution in the financial sector; Samuel Aywa, 'Consumer Protection in the Financial Services Sector in Kenya' pp.5–6. <https://www.academia.edu/7264338/Consumer_Protection_in_the_Financial_Services_Sector_in_Kenya> accessed 13 October 2021.

185 Flaming et al. (n 49) p.28.

186 Ibid.

187 Ibid.

188 Roger Van den Bergh and Louis T Visscher, 'The Preventive Function of Collective Actions for Damages in Consumer Law' <https://papers.ssrn.com/sol3/papers.cfm?abstract_id=1101377> accessed 13 October 2021.

In the next chapter, we consider the approach in another jurisdiction. We look at the consumer protection rules that apply to m-payments in the United Kingdom.

## References

Banking Act 2012.

Competition Act 2010 (as amended).

National Payment System Act 2011.

The Constitution of Kenya 2010.

The Kenya Information and Communications (Consumer Protection) Regulation 2010.

The Kenya Information and Communications (Dispute Resolution) Regulations 2010.

The National Payment Systems Regulations 2014.

ADR Centre for Development, 'Consultancy to Advice the Kenya Bankers Association on the Implementation of an Effective Alternative Dispute Resolution Mechanism' <https://www.adrcenterfordevelopment.com/2018/06/08/kenya-consultancy-to-advice-the-kenya-bankers-association-on-the-implementation-of-an-effective-alternative-dispute-resolution-mechanism/> accessed 6 October 2021.

Alliance for Financial Inclusion, 'Enabling Mobile Money Transfer: The Central Bank of Kenya's treatment of M-Pesa' (2010) <https://www.gsma.com/mobilefordevelopment/wp-content/uploads/2013/09/enablingmobilemoneytransfer92.pdf> accessed 2 October 2021.

Better Regulation Executive and National Consumer Council, 'Warning: Too much Information Can Harm' (2007) <https://www.regulation.org.uk/library/2007-Warning_Too_Much_Information_Can_Harm.pdf> accessed 14 October 2021.

Brian Muthiora, 'Enabling Mobile Money Policies in Kenya Fostering a Digital Financial Revolution' (2015) <https://www.itu.int/en/ITU-T/focusgroups/dfs/Documents/2015_MMU_Enabling-Mobile-Money-Policies-in-Kenya.pdf> accessed 13October 2021.

Central Bank of Kenya, 'Prudential Guidelines for Institutions Licensed Under the Banking Act – Consumer Protection (CBK/PG/22)' <https://www.centralbank.go.ke/wp-content/uploads/2016/08/PRUDENTIAL-GUIDELINES.pdf > accessed 7 October 2021.

Competition Authority of Kenya, 'Consumer Protection Guidelines' (Revised 2017) <https://cak.go.ke/sites/default/files/guidelines/consumer-protection/Consumer Protection Guidelines.pdf> accessed 4 October 2021.

Competition Authority of Kenya, 'Consumer Protection' <https://cak.go.ke/what-we-do/consumer-protection/overview> accessed 4 October 2021.

Competition Authority of Kenya, 'FAQs on Consumer Protection'<https://cak.go.ke/mandate/Consumer-Complaints/faqs> accessed 4 October 2021.

David Cayne and Michael J Trebilcock, 'Market Considerations in the Formulation of Consumer Protection Policy' (1973) 23 *University of Toronto Law Journal* 396.

Flore-Anne Messy and Chiara Monticone, 'The Status of Financial Education in Africa' (2012) <https://doi.org/10.1787/5k94cqqx90wl-en> accessed 7 October 2021.

Geraint Howells, 'The Potential and Limits of Consumer Empowerment by Information' (2005) 32(3) *Journal of Law & Society* 349.

Gerda L Piprek and Ravi Ruparel, 'FSD's Financial Education Programme: Evaluation and Recommendations' (2013) <https://www.yumpu.com/en/document/read/22036707/fsds-financial-education-programme-evaluation-and-fsd-kenya> accessed 7 October 2021.

Iain MacNeil, 'Uncertainty in Commercial Law' (2009) 13(1) *Edinburgh Law Review* 68.

International Finance Corporation, 'M-Money Chanel Distribution Case – Kenya (Safaricom M-pesa)' <https://www.ifc.org/wps/wcm/connect/e0d2a9bd-16b9-4a36-8498-0b2650b9af8b/Tool%2B6.7.%2BCase%2BStudy%2B-%2BM-PESA%2BKenya%2B.pdf?MOD=AJPERES&CVID=jkCVy-n> accessed 11 October 2021.

'Making Mobile Money Pay in Africa' <https://www.bbc.com/future/article/20120920-making-mobile-money-pay> accessed 14 October 2021.

Mark Flaming, Alexander Owino, Katharine McKee et al, 'Consumer Protection Diagnostic Study (Kenya)' (2011) <http://s3-eu-central-1.amazonaws.com/fsd-circle/wp-content/uploads/2015/08/30095758/11-02-22_Consumer_diagnostic_study.pdf> accessed 7 October 2021.

Omri Ben-Shahar, Carl Schneider, 'The Failure of Mandated Disclosure' (2011) 159 *University of Pennsylvania Law Review* 647.

Roger Van den Bergh and Louis T Visscher, 'The Preventive Function of Collective Actions for Damages in Consumer Law' <https://papers.ssrn.com/sol3/papers.cfm?abstract_id=1101377> accessed 13 October 2021.

The Consumer Authority of Kenya, 'Guidelines on Engaging Consumer Bodies' <https://cak.go.ke/sites/default/files/guidelines/consumer-protection/Guidelines on Engaging with Consumer Organizations.pdf> accessed 5 October 2021.

The Financial Markets Conduct Bill 2018 <https://www.treasury.go.ke/wp-content/uploads/2021/03/Draft-Financial-Markets-Conduct-Bill-2018.pdf> accessed 5 October 2021.

The Financial Services Authority Bill 2016 <https://www.treasury.go.ke/wp-content/uploads/2021/03/Financial-Services-Authority-Bill-2016.pdf> accessed 5 October 2021.

The World Bank, 'The Little Data Book on Financial Inclusion' (2018) <https://openknowledge.worldbank.org/handle/10986/29654> accessed 5 October 2021.

# 7 Consumer Protection and Mobile Payments: The United Kingdom

## 7.1 Introduction

The United Kingdom has a mature payment services market with consumers having access to and frequently using several established non-cash payment instruments like debit and credit cards. Despite this, mobile payments (m-payments) have gained popularity in the last few years. The UK Payments Market Report indicates that as of June 2021, at least a third of the adult population in the United Kingdom, representing about 17.3 million people, have registered for m-payments.[1] This represents an increase of 7.4 million from 2019.[2] Furthermore, 84 per cent of registered m-payment users have recorded an m-payment transaction, while 50 per cent made payments more frequently.[3] The uptake of m-payments can, in part, be attributed to high smartphone penetration, which supports the use of m-payment platforms like Apple Pay and Samsung Pay. Also, established financial institutions have been willing to collaborate in providing m-payment services to consumers, encouraging its uptake. For example, in 2014, an m-payment service called 'PayM' was launched and involved the collaboration of several banks and building societies.[4]

As a former Member State of the European Union (EU), the United Kingdom has transposed several EU Directives which provide important protections for financial services consumers.[5] Consequently, the United Kingdom has an existing consumer protection regime that can be extended to m-payments. Apart from relevant consumer statutes,[6] two other legislative instruments: the Payment

1 UK Finance, 'UK Payment Markets Summary 2021' (2021) p.3 <https://www.ukfinance.org.uk/sites/default/files/uploads/SUMMARY-UK-Payment-Markets-2021-FINAL.pdf> accessed 18 October 2021.

2 Ibid.

3 Ibid.

4 For a list of institutions involved, see <https://paym.co.uk/register-for-free/>.

5 e.g., the Consumer Rights Directive (2011/83/EC), Directive on Unfair Terms in Consumer Contracts (93/13/EC).

6 e.g., the Consumer Credit Act 1974, the Consumer Protection from Unfair Trading Regulations 2008, the Consumer Rights Act 2015.

DOI: 10.4324/9780429327292-9

Services Regulations (PSRs) 2017[7] and the Electronic Money Regulations (EMRs) 2011,[8] are significant in regulating m-payments.[9] This is because they create institutions whose definitions adequately cover m-payment providers.[10] Thus, to fully appreciate the regulatory regime applying to m-payments, it is necessary to take a combined reading of both regulations and the relevant provisions of applicable consumer protection statutes. In addition, regulatory handbooks and guidance documents issued by relevant regulators like the Financial Conduct Authority (FCA) and the Competition and Markets Authority (CMA) also shed light on the regulatory approach to enforcing the relevant legislation.

Before proceeding with our discussions, it is important to note that in the United Kingdom, the issuance of e-money alone does not constitute a payment service.[11] However, where the issuance of e-money is coupled with the issuance of a payment instrument or provision of a platform that facilitates payment transactions, then the e-money issuer is involved in the provision of payment services.[12] E-money institutions (EMIs) that have been registered/authorised under the EMRs may provide payment services without undergoing separate registration/authorisation procedures under the PSRs.[13] EMIs providing payment services are subject to the conduct of business requirements under the PSRs with respect to the payment services part of their business.[14] M-payments fit within the scope of both the PSRs and EMRs. While mobile money falls within the definition of e-money, payment transactions facilitated using mobile platforms fall under the PSRs.

## 7.2 Provision of Information

### *7.2.1 Mandatory Disclosures*

Although several pieces of legislation impose disclosure requirements on financial institutions (FIs), the most relevant obligations for m-payments are

7 Transposing the EU Payment Services Directive II (2015/2366/EU) which replaced Directive 2007/64/EC.

8 Transposing the Second E-Money Directive (2009/110/EC).

9 For a list of other relevant legislation, see Financial Conduct Authority, 'Payment Services and Electronic Money – Our Approach (The FCA's role under the Payment Services Regulations 2017 and the Electronic Money Regulations 2011)' (2021) pp.89–95 <https://www.fca.org.uk/publication/finalised-guidance/fca-approach-payment-services-electronic-money-2017.pdf> accessed 18 January 2022.

10 The EMRs create E-money institutions (s.2 EMRs) while the PSRs create Payment Service Institutions (s.2 PSRs).

11 Financial Conduct Authority, 'FCA Handbook: The Perimeter Guidance Manual (Chapter 3A) – Guidance on the Scope of the Electronic Money Regulations' Question 7 <https://www.handbook.fca.org.uk/handbook/PERG/3A/?view=chapter> accessed 18 October 2021.

12 Ibid.

13 FCA, 'The Perimeter Guidance Manual' (n 11) Question 6.

14 FCA, 'The Perimeter Guidance Manual' (n 11) Question 6; FCA, 'Approach Document' (n 9) para.1.12. In addition, EMIs will remain subject to the conduct of business requirements under the EMRs.

found in the PSRs.[15] The PSRs' conduct of business requirements places detailed disclosure obligations on all payment services providers (PSPs) and will extend to m-payments.[16] This is because m-payment providers assume the role of PSPs under the PSRs. The information obligations depend on the nature of the contract between parties. The PSRs identify two categories of payment contracts, namely framework contracts and single payment transactions. Framework contracts are contracts covering the future execution of individual and successive payment transactions where there is an ongoing relationship between the PSP and the consumer.[17] Single payment transactions represent 'one-off' transactions with no ongoing relationship between the PSP and consumer.[18]

For both categories, PSPs are required to disclose certain information to consumers before and after the execution of payment transactions. For framework contracts, the disclosure requirements are comprehensive. Before entering such contracts, consumers must, amongst other things, receive information about the PSP. This includes the PSP's name, address, and contact details.[19] They must also receive information on the applicable charges, interest, and exchange rates.[20] PSPs must provide further information describing the main characteristics of the service to be provided, including information on the form and procedure for giving and withdrawing consent to the initiation or execution of a payment transaction.[21] Consumers are also expected to receive information on how communication will be maintained throughout the contractual relationship.[22]

Additionally, PSPs are required to inform consumers about the safeguards for keeping their payment instruments safe, the applicable liability rules, the available corrective measures like refunds and the conditions attached.[23] Information disclosed must also cover the rules regarding changes to and termination of the contract.[24] Importantly, PSPs must disclose information on the available redress mechanisms. This includes the laws applicable to the contract, the competent court that can settle disputes, the availability of out-of-court settlement procedures, and how they may be accessed.[25]

15 PSPs are also subject to information requirements under the Financial Services (Distance Marketing) Regulations (FSRs) 2004 discussed in Section 7.3.
16 PSRs, Part 6; Some parties are permitted to exclude certain parts of the information obligations; this is known as the 'corporate opt-out.' This does not apply where the payment service user is a consumer, micro-enterprise, or a charity with an annual income of less than £1 million; Regulation 40(7); FCA, 'Approach Document' (n 9) para.8.6.
17 Regulations 48–54 & Schedule 4.
18 See Regulations 43–47 & Schedule 4.
19 Schedule 4, paragraph 1.
20 Schedule 4, paragraph 3.
21 Schedule 4, paragraph 2.
22 Schedule 4, paragraph 4.
23 Schedule 4, paragraph 5.
24 Schedule 4, paragraph 6.
25 Schedule 4, paragraph 7.

For single payment transactions, consumers must be informed, amongst other things, of the charges and exchange rate (where applicable) before completing payment transactions.[26] Disclosures will also include the maximum time for executing payments and a unique identifier to ensure that the payment order is executed correctly.[27] Furthermore, PSPs must disclose such information applicable to framework contracts that is relevant to the transaction in question.[28] Disclosed information must be contained in a contract made available to the customer.[29] After executing the transaction, PSPs must also provide the consumer with a reference enabling the payee to identify the payment transaction and the payer.[30]

For low-value transactions under which many m-payments transactions will fall, the PSRs also contain specific disclosure requirements.[31] At a minimum, disclosures must include information on how the payment instrument can be used, the charges, and liability rules applicable and where information relating to framework contracts can be accessed.[32]

One easily notices that the breadth of disclosures under the PSRs varies with each category of contract. The explanation for this points to the differing nature and economic impact of payment transactions. Disclosure requirements for single payment transactions are understandably minimal since they are one-off transactions. Hence the disclosures only provide the information needed to perform and identify that specific transaction. This is compared to framework contracts where there is an ongoing relationship between the parties. With framework contracts, several payment transactions will be carried out over a more extended period, and it is reasonable that disclosure obligations are more extensive.

For single payment contracts and low-value transactions with minimal economic impact, it may not be pragmatic to provide very detailed disclosures before a transaction is completed. However, the PSRs balance out this approach by requiring that PSPs indicate where consumers can access more detailed information when engaging in low-value transactions.[33] For single payment transactions, this balance is maintained by requiring broader disclosures where relevant to the transaction. This flexibility ensures that disclosures are appropriate to the transactions involved. This is important because it will not be reasonable to demand that the same amount of resources is dedicated to fulfilling disclosure obligations for transactions with varying economic impact.

26 Regulation 43(2)(c) & (d).
27 Regulation 43(2)(a) & (b).
28 Regulation 43(2)(e).
29 Regulation 43(1).
30 Regulation 45(2)(a).
31 Regulation 42.
32 Regulation 42(2).
33 Regulation 42(2)(v).

The PSRs also require that these disclosures be provided free of charge.[34] Disclosures must be provided or made available[35] in an easily accessible manner and an 'easily understandable language and in a clear and comprehensible form.'[36] Additionally, the PSRs encourage some flexibility in the language of disclosures. Hence, disclosures must be made available in 'English or in the language agreed by the parties.'[37] These provisions support the accessibility of disclosed information to the different members of the consumer class. The PSRs also require that these disclosures be provided on paper or another durable medium in the case of framework contracts and, where requested in the case of single payment contracts.[38] This is to ensure that consumers have a record of transactions should they need to enforce their rights.[39]

From the foregoing, one can conclude that the United Kingdom's mandatory disclosure requirements for payment services are comprehensive. However, as noted in *Chapter 2*, due to cognitive biases and the limits on the human capacity to process information, caution must be exercised in relying on disclosures alone for achieving better consumer protection.

### *7.2.2 Consumer Education*

The United Kingdom's financial consumer education landscape has undergone changes in the last few years. Initially, the Financial Services and Markets Act (FSMA)[40] required that a consumer education body be established with the mandate of educating the public on financial products, dealings, and associated risks. This led to the creation of the Consumer Financial Education Body (CFEB), which was later known as the Money Advice Service (MAS).

Amongst other things, the MAS was charged with enhancing public understanding of financial matters.[41] It promoted awareness of the benefits of financial planning and the benefits and risks associated with financial products.[42]

34 Regulation 56(1). Charges may, however, apply in situations outlined in regulation 56(2).

35 Note that a distinction is drawn between providing information and making information available. Where a PSP is required to *provide* information, they must actively communicate it to the consumer without any prompting by the consumer. In contrast, where a PSP is obliged to *make information available*, then the consumer can be required to take active steps to obtain the information. FCA, 'Approach Document' (n 9) paras 8.70–8.73.

36 Regulation 55(1)(c). Where a question arises as to whether there has been compliance with the information disclosure requirements under the PSRs, the burden of proof rests on the PSP to show that it has complied: Regulation 59.

37 Regulation 55(1)(d).

38 This is subject to other agreements made with the consumer as to the manner in which the information is to be provided or made available. Regulation 55(2)(a) & (b).

39 FCA, 'Approach Document' (n 9) paras 8.75–8.77.

40 2000 (as amended).

41 See s.6A and Schedule 1A FSMA (these provisions no longer have effect).

42 Nathan Willmott, Peter McGowan, Mark Ghusn, et al., 'Equipping the Modern Regulator: Assessing the New Regulatory Powers under the Financial Services Act 2012' (2010) 78 *Compliance Officer Bulletin* 1, 18.

The MAS was also charged with publishing educational materials and providing advice to the public on financial matters.[43] Financial education in specific thematic areas was also carried out by government-sponsored bodies like the Pensions Advisory Service and Pension Wise.

In 2018, the Money and Pensions Service (MaPS) was established as the single financial guidance body.[44] MaPS replaces the MAS, Pensions Advisory Service, and Pension Wise.[45] MaPS aims to provide consumers with financial advice on issues relating to pensions, debt, and money management skills. Importantly, it will work with the FCA to protect consumers.[46]

For specific services like m-payments, it is envisaged that the MaPS's general efforts in educating consumers will be supported by the relevant key regulators such as the FCA, the Payment Systems Regulator and the Phone-paid Services Authority. These regulators will be well placed to alert consumers on the use and risks of using new payment methods. For instance, the FCA maintains a consumer webpage with information on various issues, including firms to avoid, how to report unfair contact terms, scams, or unauthorised firms.[47] Importantly, it compiles warnings to alert consumers of unauthorised firms.[48]

Regarding m-payments specifically, the FCA has carried out thematic reviews of m-payments in the United Kingdom.[49] A key finding highlighted in the reviews was that owing to the novel nature of mobile-based financial services, there was a possibility that consumers may be unclear about their rights and obligations when using such products.[50] The FCA observed that firms have a role in providing consumers with advice on how they may protect themselves against losses, especially those resulting from fraud. The thematic review also concluded that firms were generally providing consumers with advice on keeping their mobile devices safe.[51] In addition to these thematic reviews, the FCA maintains a webpage containing advice on transacting with non-bank payment service providers.[52] The webpage explains the different types of non-bank institutions that may provide

43 Ibid.

44 The body was established pursuant to the Financial Guidance and Claims Act 2018.

45 <https://www.gov.uk/government/organisations/single-financial-guidance-body> accessed 21 December 2021.

46 <https://moneyandpensionsservice.org.uk/who-we-are/> accessed 21 December 2021.

47 <https://www.fca.org.uk/consumers> accessed 15 December 2021.

48 <https://www.fca.org.uk/news/search-results?np_category=warnings&start=1> accessed 15 December 2021

49 See the Financial Conduct Authority, 'Thematic Review: Mobile Banking and Payments' (2014) <https://www.fca.org.uk/publication/thematic-reviews/tr14-15.pdf> accessed 15 October 2021; Financial Conduct Authority, 'Mobile Banking and Payment: Supporting an Innovative and Secure Market' (2013) <https://www.fca.org.uk/publication/thematic-reviews/tr13-06.pdf> accessed 15 October 2021.

50 FCA, 'Thematic Review: Mobile Banking and Payments' (n 49) p.10.

51 Ibid.

52 <https://www.fca.org.uk/consumers/using-payment-service-providers> accessed 19 December 2021.

payment services and clarifies the protection available to funds held with such institutions.[53]

Despite these efforts, there is no specific education initiative dedicated to m-payments. This may be the case for several reasons. First, the thematic review suggested that part of the main concerns for the FCA was whether consumers were losing funds owing to issues like fraud and unauthorised transactions. The review indicated that the FCA was satisfied with the efforts firms were taking in educating consumers on securing their devices to minimise fraud.[54] The FCA also stated that it had found no evidence to suggest that consumers were losing money due to unauthorised transactions. Although they recognised the potential for consumer error due to the smaller screen sizes and keypads of mobile devices, they did not find any significant evidence of problems associated with these issues.[55] They were satisfied that there were sufficient safeguards built into mobile-based financial products to mitigate the risk of such errors.[56]

Moreover, though m-payments continue to grow in acceptability, they do not yet make up the lion's share of consumer payments.[57] Hence coupled with the results of the thematic review, a targeted education initiative may not be a pressing priority.

## 7.3 Withdrawal Rights and Cooling-Off Periods

Although the PSRs are silent on cancellation and cooling-off periods, m-payment users benefit from the provisions in the Consumer Contracts (Information, Cancellation, and Additional Charges) Regulations (CCRs) 2013 and the Financial Services (Distance Marketing) Regulations (FSRs) 2004 depending on the transaction involved.

The FSRs apply to financial services contracts entered at a distance, i.e., a contract for financial services where parties make 'exclusive use of one or more means of distance communication[58] up to and including the time at which the contract is concluded.'[59] This essentially covers contracts where the consumer and supplier are not physically present and rely on distance communication to conclude the contract. It is reasonable to conclude that the FSRs apply to m-payments

53 While the funds are not protected by the Financial Services Compensation Scheme, they are protected through safeguarding arrangements which amongst other things, ensure that the funds are held separately from the firm's operational funds and protected from unrelated claims should insolvency occur. Ibid.

54 FCA, 'Thematic Review: Mobile Banking and Payments' (n 49) p.10.

55 Examples of such errors would include inputting the wrong payment amount or recipient. FCA, 'Mobile Banking and Payment: Supporting an Innovative and Secure Market' (n 49) p.7.

56 FCA, 'Thematic Review: Mobile Banking and Payments' (n 49) p.11.

57 Debit cards accounted for 44 per cent of all the payments in the UK in 2020, followed by cash (17 per cent). 69 per cent of adults also own credit cards. UK Finance, 'UK Payment Markets Summary 2021' (n 1) pp.3–4.

58 Under Regulation 2, this means 'any means which, without the simultaneous physical presence of the supplier and the consumer, may be used for the marketing of a service between those parties.'

59 Regulation 2.

because the term 'financial service' is broadly defined and covers 'any service of a banking, credit, insurance, personal pension, investment or payment nature.'[60] Thus, the FSRs will be relevant to the subscription to m-payment services completed using a means of distance communication.

The FSRs mandate a 14-day cooling-off period that runs from the day the contract is concluded.[61] The statutory cooling-off period is extended where disclosure obligations are not complied with.[62] Disclosure obligations require that PSPs communicate contractual information (including cooling-off periods and withdrawal rights) in good time before the contract is concluded.[63] PSPs will also meet this obligation if disclosures are communicated immediately after concluding a contract that has been facilitated using a means of distance communication requested by the consumer, which does not allow for earlier disclosures.[64] Should a consumer choose to cancel their subscription to an m-payment service during the cooling-off period, the FSRs confirm that the cancellation has the effect of terminating the contract at the time the notice of cancellation is given.[65]

The CCRs apply to consumer contracts which do not qualify as contracts for the provision of financial services. The CCRs also provide cooling-off periods for distance contracts concluded via a means of distance communication but without the simultaneous physical presence of the trader and consumer. It also covers off-premises contracts often concluded in the simultaneous presence of both parties but outside the premises of the trader.[66] The CCRs cover sales and services contracts, notwithstanding the payment instruments used to complete them.[67] Hence, when concluded through a mobile device and facilitated by m-payments, such contracts will likely fall under the scope of the CCRs. The CCRs also apply to contracts for the supply of digital content not provided on a tangible medium. These provisions would apply to digital content such as games, ringtones, and music, popularly purchased via m-payments.

The CCRs provide that –

> a consumer may cancel a distance or off-premises contract at any time during the cancellation period without giving any reason, and without incurring any liability ….[68]

60 Regulation 2.
61 Regulation 10(1) & (2).
62 Regulations 10(3).
63 Regulation 8(1)(a).
64 Regulation 8(1)(b).
65 Regulation 9(2).
66 See Regulation 5 for a more comprehensive definition.
67 The CCRs do not apply to specific contracts which are outlined in Regulation 6: Department for Business, Innovation & Skills, 'Consumer Contracts (Information, Cancellation and Additional Charges) Regulations: Implementing Guidance' (2013) p.18 <https://assets.publishing.service.gov.uk/government/uploads/system/uploads/attachment_data/file/429300/bis-13-1368-consumer-contracts-information-cancellation-and-additional-payments-regulations-guidance.pdf> accessed 21 November 2021.
68 Regulation 29 (1). This is subject to exceptions listed in Regulation 29(1)(a)–(d).

The cancellation period terminates at the end of 14 days after goods come within the physical possession of a consumer in a sales contract or 14 days after a service contract or contract for the supply of digital content is entered into.[69] Owing to the nature of digital content, under contracts for their purchase, traders are not expected to supply the digital content within the cooling-off period.[70] The only exception is where the consumer expressly consents for the digital content to be supplied and acknowledges that the right to cancel will be lost.[71] The consumer must notify the trader of their decision to cancel, and successful cancellation discharges the parties' obligations under the contract.[72]

One notable feature of the CCRs is that a consumer's right to cancel is preserved where they are not informed of the right by the trader.[73] Thus, the CCRs' standard cooling-off period may be extended to 12 months, where the seller fails to inform the consumer of the right to cancel.[74] Therefore, as Loos puts it, if a right of withdrawal is not communicated to the consumer, this implies that the cooling-off period 'never starts to run and therefore does not end.'[75]

This provision is significant for several reasons. First, it provides an incentive that forces traders to comply with the disclosure requirements under the CCRs. One concern traders have is that they are not certain that a transaction is completely finalised until the cooling-off period elapses. It is assumed that traders will seek to avoid situations which would warrant the extension of existing cooling-off periods. Thus, the CCRs incentivise traders to disclose cancellation rights to consumers in order to prevent the extension of the applicable cooling-off period. Additionally, the preservation of cancellation rights where disclosures are not made protects the consumer's interests. As seen earlier in *Chapter 4*, cooling-off periods are meaningless if consumers are unaware of them. By preserving the right to cancel for a significant period, the CCRs indirectly encourage compliance with disclosure obligations.

Like the CCRs, part of the information which must be disclosed under the FSRs includes cancellation rights.[76] However, the effect of non-disclosure differs. Where a supplier does not disclose the right to cancel on or before the conclusion of the contract, the FSRs appear to assume that disclosure obligations will be subsequently complied with, and therefore, only extend the cancellation period to 14 days from the date of compliance.[77] This contrasts with the CCRs, which

69 Regulations 30(1)(a) & (b); 30(3).

70 Regulation 37(1).

71 Regulation 37(1)(a) & (b).

72 Regulation 33.

73 Regulation 31(1).

74 i.e., 12 months from the end of the standard 14 days cooling-off period; Regulation 31(3).

75 Marco Loos, 'Rights of Withdrawal' in Geraint Howells and Reiner Schulze (eds), *Modernising and Harmonising Consumer Contract Law* (Sellier European Law Publishers 2009) p.251; *Heininger v. Bayerische Hypo-und Vereinsbank AG*, Case C-481/99. ECR (2001) I-09945.

76 Regulations 7(1), 8(1) and Schedule 1, paragraph 13.

77 Regulation 10(3). For distance contracts relating to life or personal pensions, the cancellation period ends on the expiry of 30 calendar days after the day on which the consumer receives the required information: Regulation 10(5).

extend the cancellation period to 12 months. The CCRs' approach is preferred as the threat of a significantly longer extension period will likely be more effective. The practical implication of the differences is significant because it suggests that while consumers will enjoy maximum protection with regards to their cancellation rights when completing contracts with m-payments, they will not enjoy comparable protection when subscribing to the service itself.

## 7.4 The Regulation of Business Conduct

### *7.4.1 Regulating Unfair Commercial Practices*

PSPs providing m-payments are subject to the existing regime regulating commercial practices in the United Kingdom. The leading statute regulating commercial practices is the Consumer Protection from Unfair Trading Regulations (CPUTRs) 2008. Regulation 3(1) of the CPUTRs places a general ban on unfair commercial practices. The CPUTRs further explain that –

> A commercial practice is unfair if—
>
> (a) it contravenes the requirements of professional diligence; and
> (b) it materially distorts or is likely to materially distort the economic behaviour of the average consumer with regard to the product.[78]

This broad clause indicates what 'unfair' signifies in the context of the CPUTRs. Abbamonte explains that the broad wording adopted ensures that the statute is 'future proof' because it acts as a 'safety net to catch any current or future practices' not presently categorised under the CPUTRs.[79] Consequently, if it can be shown that a commercial practice violates the requirements of professional diligence and materially alters the economic behaviour of an average consumer with regards to a product, then it would be caught within the CPUTRs' scope.

Apart from the general ban on unfair practices, the CPUTRs also target specific practices. Commercial practices will be considered unfair where they qualify as a misleading action[80] or omission.[81] These practices are further discussed in Section 7.4.3. The CPUTRs also prohibit aggressive commercial practices. Regulation 7 provides that –

> A commercial practice is aggressive if, in its factual context, taking account of all of its features and circumstances—

78 Regulation 3(3).

79 Giuseppe B Abbamonte, 'The Unfair Commercial Practices Directive and its General Prohibition' in Stephen Weatherill and Ulf Bernitz (eds), *The Regulation of Unfair Commercial Practices under EC Directive 2005/29: New Rules and New Techniques* (Bloomsbury Publishing 2007) pp.20–21.

80 Regulations 3(4)(a) & 5.

81 Regulations 3(4)(b) & 6.

(a) it significantly impairs or is likely significantly to impair the average consumer's freedom of choice or conduct in relation to the product concerned through the use of harassment, coercion or undue influence; and

(b) it thereby causes or is likely to cause him to take a transactional decision he would not have taken otherwise.

The CPUTRs single out aggressive practices such as harassment, coercion, and undue influence, which are common vitiating factors impacting contracts under the Common Law. While the CPUTRs indicate that coercion 'includes the use of physical force,'[82] the CPUTRs give a more comprehensive explanation of undue influence, which involves –

> exploiting a position of power in relation to the consumer so as to apply pressure, even without using or threatening to use physical force, in a way which significantly limits the consumer's ability to make an informed decision.[83]

No attempt is made to define harassment or coercion.[84] By failing to define these terms, it is unclear whether they will be given the same interpretation held at Common Law or in statutory instruments such as the Protection from Harassment Act (PHA) 1997. Ryder et al. argue that in the absence of definitions, these words 'must be taken to have their usual meaning.'[85] While this seems reasonable, one difficulty with this position is that the phrase 'usual meaning' can itself be problematic. Take, for instance, the case of harassment; its usual meaning could include a basic Oxford English Dictionary interpretation explaining it to be 'aggressive pressure or intimidation.' It could also imply the interpretation under the PHA, which requires a course of conduct, i.e., at least two incidents must have occurred. Hence, a more explicit definition of these practices may have provided some necessary clarity.

In describing aggressive commercial practices, the CPUTRs emphasise that such practice must be one that significantly impairs (or is likely to impair) the average consumer's freedom of choice. Similarly, in defining undue influence, the CPUTRs require that the exploitation must be one that significantly limits the consumer's ability to make an informed decision. As one may notice, the wordings of the provisions adopt the phrases 'significantly impairs' and 'significantly limits.' This deliberate choice of words suggests that a higher threshold of interference

82 Regulation 7(3)(a).

83 Regulation 7(3)(b).

84 However, under Regulation 7(2), the CPUTRs include a list of factors that a court may take into consideration when determining if a practice involves the use of harassment, coercion, or undue influence.

85 Nicholas Ryder, Margaret Griffiths, and Lachmi Singh, *Commercial Law: Principles and Policy* (Cambridge University Press 2012) p.376.

and impact is required to label a practice aggressive. This view is shared by Ryder et al. who reason that where the impact is slight, it is likely that no breach will be found.[86]

The CPUTRs also blacklist certain commercial practices considered unfair in all circumstances.[87] Hence, for such practices, no case-by-case assessment is needed to prove a lack of professional diligence or a material distortion of decision-making.[88] These blacklisted practices are not expected to be assessed since there is a presumption that they are contrary to the requirements of professional diligence and will materially distort consumer decision-making.[89]

Throughout the CPUTRs, reference is made to the 'average consumer,' and though no definition is provided, the CPUTRs offer some insight into what the reference connotes. It explains that the average consumer is 'reasonably well informed, reasonably observant and circumspect.'[90] The 'average consumer' is a hypothetical person serving as an objective benchmark for determining the effect of a commercial practice under scrutiny. Thus, the CPUTRs provide that –

> In determining the effect of a commercial practice on the average consumer where the practice reaches or is addressed to a consumer or consumers account shall be taken of the material characteristics of such an average consumer including his being reasonably well informed, reasonably observant and circumspect.[91]

It also provides that –

> In determining the effect of a commercial practice on the average consumer where the practice is directed to a particular group of consumers, a reference to the average consumer shall be read as referring to the average member of that group.[92]

Recognising that the circumstances of consumers differ and that the average consumer benchmark would be unfair if applied in all cases, the CPUTRs apply a different standard in certain situations.[93] It explains that –

86 Ibid.

87 Regulation 3(4)(d); Schedule 1.

88 Monika Namyslowska, 'The Blacklist of Unfair Commercial Practices: The Black Sheep, Red Herring or White Elephant of the Unfair Commercial Practices Directive?' in Willem van Boom, Amandine Garde, Orkun Akseli (eds), *The European Unfair Commercial Practices Directive: Impact, Enforcement Strategies and National Legal Systems* (Routledge 2016) p.67.

89 Ibid.

90 Regulation 2(2).

91 Regulation 2(2).

92 Regulation 2(4).

93 Department for Business, Energy and Industrial Strategy, 'Misleading and Aggressive Commercial Practices: New Private Rights for Consumers – Guidance on the Consumer (Amendment) Protection Regulations 2014' (2018) p.9 <https://assets.publishing.service.gov.uk/government/

In determining the effect of a commercial practice on the average consumer—

(a) where a clearly identifiable group of consumers is particularly vulnerable to the practice or the underlying product because of their mental or physical infirmity, age or credulity in a way which the trader could reasonably be expected to foresee, and

(b) where the practice is likely to materially distort the economic behaviour only of that group, a reference to the average consumer shall be read as referring to the average member of that group.[94]

These provisions, particularly the average consumer benchmark, have been the subject of intellectual discourse. Some writers have criticised the benchmark.[95] For instance, Duivenvoorde argues that the benchmark perpetuates the assumption that average consumers are rational and behave similarly, thereby passing this off as 'standard consumer behaviour.'[96] Because consumers differ, Duivenvoorde concludes that it is difficult to work with a benchmark that focuses on how consumers should behave and not how they actually behave.[97] These points raised have some merit, particularly in light of discussions in *Chapter 3*, which highlighted the limitations of consumer rationality. However, one can argue that although the average consumer benchmark is not perfect, it provides a useful normative reference which aids in assessing the effect of commercial practices.

One cannot fault Duivenvoorde's contention that consumers do not all behave the same. However, there is an argument that the CPUTRs take this point into consideration. This view is held for two reasons. First, recognising consumers who are vulnerable due to factors such as physical and mental infirmity, age, or credulity is an acknowledgement that adjustments will need to be made in appropriate circumstances. Second, the reference to the average members of a particular group, as opposed to a static standard, can be interpreted as another attempt to include some flexibility in the use of the average consumer benchmark.

The CPUTRs adopt the use of regulatory offences to deal with non-compliance. Hence, under Regulation 8 –

uploads/system/uploads/attachment_data/file/721872/misleading-aggressive-commercial-practices-guidance.pdf> accessed 11 December 2021.

94 Regulation 2(5). This is without prejudice to legitimate trade puffs; Regulation 2(6).

95 Peter Cartwright, 'The Consumer Image within EU Law' in Christian Twigg-Flesner (ed.) *Research Handbook on EU Consumer and Contract Law* (Edward Elgar 2016) p.199; Bram B Duivenvoorde, 'The Average Consumer Benchmark from a Behavioural Perspective' in Bram B Duivenvoorde, *The Consumer Benchmarks in the Unfair Commercial Practices Directive* (Springer 2015) p.159; Cristina Poncibò and Rossella Incardona, 'The Average Consumer, the Unfair Commercial Practices Directive, and the Cognitive Revolution' (2007) 30(1) *Journal of Consumer Policy* 21; Lisa Waddington, 'Vulnerable and Confused: The Protection of "Vulnerable" Consumers under EU Law' (2013) 38(6) *European Law Review* 757;

96 Duivenvoorde, 'The Average Consumer Benchmark from a Behavioural Perspective' (n 95) p.159.

97 Ibid. p.161.

A trader is guilty of an offence if—

(a) he knowingly or recklessly engages in a commercial practice which contravenes the requirements of professional diligence … and
(b) the practice materially distorts or is likely to materially distort the economic behaviour of the average consumer with regard to the product ….[98]

Similar to the regulatory offences created under the Canadian Competition Act (CCA) discussed in *Chapter 5*, the offence requires proof of knowledge or recklessness on the trader's part. This suggests that criminal sanctions are reserved for cases where the trader has engaged in the practice knowingly or recklessly.[99] Although a trader lacking intent will escape criminal sanctions, they may be subject to an enforcement order sought from the court by the enforcing authority.[100] The order would direct the trader to discontinue the practice. This approach allows for proportionate responses in situations where a trader lacks moral fault.

Another category of regulatory offences sanctions traders indulging in blacklisted practices or any practice that falls within the specified categories of misleading omissions and actions or aggressive commercial practices.[101] These offences apply on a strict liability basis subject to a due diligence defence.[102] This approach is similar to the CCA's old regime. Criticism of this approach was discussed in *Chapter 5*. However, it is important to reiterate that solely relying on criminal prosecution may be too expensive in terms of time and money. Unlike the Regulation 8 offence outlined above, the trader's intention is not put into consideration. As outlined by Cartwright[103] and Macrory,[104] the major problem with

98 Regulation 8.

99 Regulation 8(2) explains that where a trader engages in a commercial practice without regard as to whether that practice contravenes the requirements of professional diligence then the trader will be deemed to be reckless. It would not matter whether the trader had reason to believe that the practice might contravene the requirements. However, Cartwright points out that this provision may prove confusing where a trader considers whether a practice contravenes the requirements of professional diligence but reaches the conclusion that it does not. Although there has been some subjective recklessness in not realising that there is a risk and taking it, Cartwright argues the trader has not been reckless in the context of Regulation 8(2) because he did not fail to have regard for the risk; See Peter Cartwright, 'Unfair Commercial Practices and the Future of Criminal Law' (2010) 7 *Journal of Business Law* 618, pp.624–625.

100 Enforcement orders are brought under the Enterprise Act 2002. A practice which is unfair will amount to a 'community infringement' within the context of the Act; Regulations 26 & 27 CPUTRs, s.218A Enterprise Act. These traders may also be subject to private actions instituted by consumers following the Consumer Protection (Amendment) Regulations 2014.

101 Regulations 9–12.

102 Regulation 17. There is also an innocent publication of advertisement defence under Regulation 18.

103 Peter Cartwright, 'Crime, Punishment and Consumer Protection.' (2007) 30 *Journal of Consumer Policy* 1, 8.

104 Richard B Macrory, 'Regulatory Justice: Making Sanctions Effective' (2006) paragraph 1.14 <https://webarchive.nationalarchives.gov.uk/ukgwa/20070305105024mp_/http:/www.cabinetoffice.gov.uk/regulation/documents/pdf/macrory_penalties.pdf> accessed 18 October 2021.

this is that this may lead to disproportionate responses where fault is lacking.[105] It may also provide inadequate deterrence where businesses believe that the likelihood of prosecution and the sums imposed as penalties are low.[106]

Bodies corporate can also commit the offences highlighted. Hence, m-payment providers will be subject to this regime. The CPUTRs provide that –

> Where an offence under these Regulations committed by a body corporate is proved—
>
> (a) to have been committed with the consent or connivance of an officer of the body, or
>
> (b) to be attributable to any neglect on his part,
>
> the officer as well as the body corporate is guilty of the offence and liable to be proceeded against and punished accordingly.[107]

For the purposes of the CPUTRs, the term 'officer' includes a director, manager, secretary, or other similar officers.[108] Persons purporting to act in the listed roles will also be deemed officers.[109] At first glance, this provision appears uncontroversial. However, the complexities come to the fore when one considers that the Regulation 8 offence requires that *mens rea* is proved (i.e., criminal intent). Since companies cannot think or act as humans do, an unfair practice committed by the company will, in most cases, be committed by an individual connected to the company. Under English law, where *mens rea* is required to prove an offence involving a company, the doctrine of identification is often invoked.[110] This doctrine allows the intent of the company's senior officers to be attributed to the company itself.[111] This is because these offices are presumed to be the 'directing mind and will' of the company. However, this doctrine may make the enforcement of the CPUTRs challenging because, as Cartwright points out, it may be challenging to find a company's senior officer with the required intent.[112]

105 Cartwright, 'Crime, Punishment and Consumer Protection.' (n 103) p.8; Macrory, 'Regulatory Justice' (n 104) para.1.14.

106 Peter Cartwright, 'Redress Compliance and Choice: Enhanced Consumer Measures and the retreat from punishment in the Consumer Rights Act 2015' (2016) 75(2) *Cambridge Law Journal* 271, 274–276; Cartwright, 'Crime, Punishment and Consumer Protection.' (n 104) p.8.

107 Regulation 15(1).

108 Regulation 15(2)(a).

109 Regulation 15(2)(b).

110 *Tesco Supermarkets v. Nattrass* [1972] AC 153.

111 *Tesco* (n 110) suggests that the term 'senior officer' is construed narrowly and will only cover 'superior' officers such as the managing director and the board of directors. The officers mentioned in Regulation 15(2)(a) fit within this category. However, there are cases suggesting that courts may be flexible in construing the term in order to give effect to the purpose of a statute. See *Meridian Global Funds Management Asia Ltd v. Securities Commission* [1995] 2 AC 500.

112 Cartwright, 'Unfair Commercial Practices and the Future of Criminal Law' (n 99) p.628.

The CPUTRs are enforced by public authorities and previously gave consumers no independent civil rights to redress. This position changed following amendments to the CPUTRs.[113] Currently, where consumers have been subject to unfair commercial practices,[114] they have the right to unwind a contract and get a refund,[115] seek a discount in respect of past or future payments due under the contract,[116] or seek damages.[117]

However, these new rights do not apply to credit agreements[118] or other financial services which are classified as regulated activities under the UK Financial Services and Markets Act 2000.[119] This is because these are highly regulated services, and the application of new rights could lead to confusion and inconsistency.[120] The impact of this on m-payments will depend on the underlying activities and business structure facilitating the service. For example, the issuance of e-money[121] and credit is a regulated activity. So, this exception will apply to m-payment platforms built around prepaid accounts storing electronic money[122] or those that provide credit to subscribers to finance a purchase. This will also be the case where the PSP collects deposits and pays out interest from funds received from other customers.[123] However, the receipt of sums solely for the purpose of providing payment services is not regarded as a deposit or electronic money.[124]

113 The Consumer Protection (Amendment) Regulations 2014.

114 i.e., misleading actions and aggressive commercial practices; Regulation 27B (1). Misleading omissions are *not* covered. Thus, although misleading omissions remain an offence under the CPUTRs, consumers have no private remedy against the trader. This is because omissions are more uncertain in scope and English law has never provided redress in these circumstances. However, this limitation is narrow as it only applies where the trader has omitted material information, but the overall presentation of the product/service is not misleading. In most situations, omitting material information would create a misleading overall presentation, and, therefore, count as a misleading action. Department for Business, Energy & Industrial Strategy, 'Misleading and Aggressive Commercial Practices' (n 93) paras 8–10.

115 Regulation 27E.

116 Regulation 27I.

117 Regulation 27J.

118 The only exception is where the consumer has been misled or unfairly pressured to enter a credit agreement to finance a particular transaction ('restricted use credit agreement'): Department for Business, Energy & Industrial Strategy, 'Misleading and Aggressive Commercial Practices' (n 93) para.25.

119 S.22; Department for Business, Energy & Industrial Strategy, 'Misleading and Aggressive Commercial Practices' (n 93) para.23.

120 Department for Business, Energy & Industrial Strategy, 'Misleading and Aggressive Commercial Practices' (n 93) para.23.

121 The Financial Services and Markets Act 2000 (Regulated Activities) Order 2001, Article 9B & 74A.

122 The issuance of e-money by persons certified as small issuers is exempt. The Financial Services and Markets Act 2000 (Regulated Activities) Order 2001, Article 9C.

123 The Financial Services and Markets Act 2000 (Regulated Activities) Order 2001, Article 5; The Financial Conduct Authority, The Perimeter Guidance Manual, Chapter 15.1. <https://www.handbook.fca.org.uk/handbook/PERG/15.pdf> accessed 22 December 2021.

124 The Financial Services and Markets Act 2000 (Regulated Activities) Order 2001, Article 9AB; FCA, The Perimeter Guidance Manual, Chapter 15.2 (Q.5).

Thus, the new rights will apply to some consumers using some m-payment platforms, so it is useful to consider them.

Acccss to the new rights is subject to certain conditions. First, the type of transaction involved must be one covered by the CPUTRs. Transactions covered include those involving a consumer who enters into a contract with a trader for the sale or supply of a product by the trader. It also includes situations where the consumer enters into a contract with a trader to sell goods to the trader or where the consumer makes a payment to a trader for the supply of a product.[125] Second, the trader must engage in a prohibited practice in relation to the product or digital content.[126] The third condition is that the prohibited practice must be a significant factor in the consumer's decision to enter into the contract or make the payment.[127] A consumer with a right to redress under the regulations may bring a civil claim to enforce that right.[128]

For the standard remedies (i.e., a right to unwind a contract and a right to a discount), the consumer need not demonstrate any loss or prove that the trader acted dishonestly, recklessly, or negligently. This is because the standard remedies operate on a strict liability basis. Thus, as long as the trader's actions are misleading or aggressive, the remedies will apply. However, consumers must give evidence of actual losses to be awarded damages. Traders can also plead the due diligence defence. This means that a trader will not be liable for damages if they took reasonable care to avoid committing the prohibited practice.

The impact of the new consumer remedies may be better appreciated in context. As noted earlier, before the amendments, only public authorities could enforce the CPUTRs. This denied consumers direct private remedies under the CPUTRs for losses suffered.[129] There was clearly a need to balance private and public enforcement of the CPUTRs, which is reflected in the amendments. The amendments find favour with academic views which suggest that private enforcement may be the most effective mechanism for ensuring that consumers get adequate compensation.[130] Nevertheless, there are shortcomings associated with private law enforcement of consumer policy. For instance, private enforcement by individuals may

125 Regulation 27A(2).

126 Regulation 27A(4).

127 Regulation 27A(6).

128 Regulation 27K(1).

129 Consumers could, however, sue at Common Law for certain practices like duress, misrepresentation.

130 Andrea Hamilton and David Henry, 'Bricks, Beer and Shoes: Indirect Purchaser Standing in the European Union and the United States' 2012 5(3) *Global Competition Litigation Review* 111; Gordon Downie and Marianne Charrier, 'UK and EU developments in Collective Action Regimes for Competition Law Breaches' 2014, 35(8) *European Competition Law Review* 369. Granting compensation is not only restricted to courts in the United Kingdom but has also become part of the enforcement process under the UK Regulatory Enforcement and Sanctions Act 2008. It has in effect included a compensation function within its public regulatory enforcement system: Christopher Hodges, 'From Class Actions to Collective Redress: A Revolution in Approach to Compensation' (2009) 28(1) *Civil Justice Quarterly* 41, 63.

be less than efficient since it is dependent on the consumer knowing their rights and having the required resources to enforce them.[131]

Private and public enforcement have their respective strengths and weaknesses, and the best outcomes may be achieved by combining both approaches in a complementary way.[132] With the amendments introducing the new consumer rights, it appears that the CPUTRs' approach represents a move towards balancing the use of both enforcement styles.

### *7.4.2 Regulating Contract Terms*

#### *7.4.2.1 Standard Term Contracts and Fairness*

Unlike Canada and Kenya, the United Kingdom has an independent regime regulating contract terms. This regime finds expression in the Consumer Rights Act (CRA) 2015.[133] The CRA generally applies to all consumer transactions and will benefit m-payment users. While the CMA is the primary consumer protection regulator, the CRA recognises that the CMA shares concurrent enforcement powers with other sector-specific regulators such as the FCA.[134] To reduce the duplication of efforts, the FCA enforces the unfair terms regulatory framework in the financial services market. The framework for cooperation between the CMA and FCA is established under a memorandum of understanding.[135] Hence, in addition to the CRA, PSPs (under the FCA's supervision) must also consider the Unfair Contract Terms and Consumer Notices Regulatory Guide (UNFCOG) issued by the FCA.[136] The UNFCOG explains how the FCA will use its powers under the CRA in relation to unfair terms used in the financial services sector.[137] PSPs must

131 Peter Cartwright, 'Consumer Protection in Financial Services: Putting the Law in Context' in Peter Cartwright (ed.), *Consumer Protection in Financial Services* (Kluwer Law International 1999) pp.15–16.

132 Weber describes this as 'optimal mixes' Franziska Weber, *The Law and Economics of Enforcing European Law* (Ashgate Publishing 2014) 8.

133 Note that the regulation of unfair terms in contracts entered into before 1 October 2015, are governed by the Unfair Terms in Consumer Contracts Regulation 1999.

134 Schedule 3, paragraph 8. Note that under the Enterprise Act 2002 (Part 8), a number of regulators are designated as having the power to enforce consumer legislation.

135 Competition and Markets Authority and Financial Conduct Authority, 'Memorandum of Understanding between the Competition and Markets Authority and the Financial Conduct Authority on the use of concurrent powers under consumer protection legislation' (July 2019) <https://www.fca.org.uk/publication/mou/fca-cma-consumer-protection-mou-2019.pdf> accessed 20 December 2021.

136 Financial Conduct Authority, 'FCA Handbook: Unfair Contract terms and Consumer Notices Regulatory Guide' (UNFCOG) <https://www.handbook.fca.org.uk/handbook/UNFCOG/1/?view=chapter> accessed 20 December 2021.

137 UNFCOG 1.1.1.

also consider the FCA's unfair contract terms library, which is a repository of its publications regarding unfair contract terms.[138]

Under the CRA, an unfair contract term is not binding on a consumer.[139] A term is unfair if –

> contrary to the requirement of good faith, it causes a significant imbalance in the parties' rights and obligations arising under the contract, to the detriment of the consumer.[140]

This provision introduces a fairness test which comprises three main elements. For a term to be unfair, the first element requires that the term must not be contrary to good faith. The second emphasises that there must be a significant imbalance in the rights and obligations applicable to both parties. The third element requires that the imbalance should be to the detriment of the consumer. These elements are assessed together and are evaluated in the context of the contract as a whole and all the circumstances in which the contract was entered into.[141]

The UK Supreme Court (UKSC) has explained that the requirement of good faith is one of 'fair and open dealing.'[142] The requirement is given a broad interpretation as it relates to the substance of terms and the way they are expressed.[143] Thus, fair and open dealing suggests that terms should be 'expressed fully, clearly and legibly, containing no concealed pitfalls or traps.'[144] Appropriate prominence should also be given to terms which can operate to the consumer's disadvantage.[145] Thus, in drafting contract terms, a trader 'should not, whether deliberately or unconsciously, take advantage'[146] of the consumers' circumstances to their detriment.[147]

Consumers are often in a weaker bargaining position, especially where standard form contracts are adopted. Hence the fairness test is also concerned

138 UNFCOG 2.1.1; Financial Conduct Authority, 'Unfair Contract Terms Library' <https://www.fca.org.uk/firms/unfair-contract-terms/library> accessed 21 October 2021.

139 s.62(1) CRA; UNFCOG 1.3.6.

140 s.62(4); the CRA covers both negotiated and non-negotiated terms. See also UNFCOG 1.3.2.

141 Competition and Markets Authority, 'Unfair Contract Terms Guidance: Guidance on the Unfair terms provisions in the Consumer Rights Act 2015' (2015) paragraphs 2.10 & 2.18. <https://assets.publishing.service.gov.uk/government/uploads/system/uploads/attachment_data/file/450440/Unfair_Terms_Main_Guidance.pdf> accessed 21 December 2021.

142 *Director General of Fair Trading v. First National Bank Plc*. [2001] UKHL 52, *per* Lord Bingham at para 17.

143 Ibid, *per* Lord Bingham. See also *Aziz v. Caixa d'Estalvis de Catalunya, Tarragona i Manresa (Catalunyacaixa)* (C-415/11) EU:C:2013:164 at paragraphs 44, 45, & 69; Competition and Markets Authority, 'Unfair Contract Terms Explained' (2015) paragraph 28 <https://assets.publishing.service.gov.uk/government/uploads/system/uploads/attachment_data/file/450410/Unfair_Terms_Explained.pdf> accessed 21 December 2021.

144 *First National Bank Plc* (n 142), *per* Lord Bingham at para.17.

145 Ibid.

146 Ibid.

147 Ibid; CMA, Unfair Contract Terms Guidance (n 141) para.2.23.

with the rights and obligations under the contract. Where a term tilts the balance of the contract significantly in the trader's favour, it will suggest that there is a significant imbalance.[148] For instance, if a term in an m-payment contract allocates risks to consumers beyond their control and which the PSP is better-placed to insure against, it may be challenged on the basis that there is a significant imbalance in the obligations.

The Court of Justice of the European Union (CJEU) has noted, with approval from the UKSC, that such imbalance must arise 'contrary to the requirements of good faith,' and this will depend on –

> whether the seller or supplier, dealing fairly and equitably with the consumer, could reasonably assume that the consumer would have agreed to such a term in individual contract negotiations.[149]

In deciding if a term is one that the consumer would have agreed to, certain factors are taken into consideration. These include –

> whether such contractual terms are common, that is to say they are used regularly in legal relations in similar contracts, or are surprising, whether there is an objective reason for the term and whether, despite the shift in the contractual balance in favour of the user of the term in relation to the substance of the term in question, the consumer is not left without protection.[150]

The imbalance must be to the detriment of the consumer; hence Lord Bingham emphasised that 'a significant imbalance to the detriment of the supplier, assumed to be the stronger party, is not a mischief which the regulations seek to address.'[151] In assessing detriment, the CMA notes that although an imbalance must be practically significant, a finding of unfairness does not require proof that a term has already caused actual harm.[152] Hence a term may be open to challenge if it could be used in a way that would cause consumer detriment.[153]

The broad fairness test introduces a degree of flexibility consistent with the general objective of protecting consumers. The elements making up the test are clear[154] and collectively emphasise that a 'supplier should not, whether deliberately or unconsciously, take advantage of the consumer.'[155] By focusing on both

148 *per* Lord Bingham (n 142) para.17; See *West v. Ian Finlay and Associates* [2014] EWCA Civ 316.

149 *Aziz* (n 143) para.69; *ParkingEye Ltd v. Beavis* [2015] UKSC 67 at para 105.

150 *per* Advocate General Kokott in *Aziz* (n 143) quoted with approval in *ParkingEye* (ibid.) at para 106.

151 *First National Bank* (n 142) para.17.

152 CMA, 'Unfair Contract Terms Guidance' (n 141) para.2.19.

153 Ibid.

154 Lord Bingham stated that 'the language used in expressing the test, is, in my opinion, clear and not reasonably capable of differing interpretations' (n 142) para.17.

155 Ibid.

the making and substance of the contract, the scope of the fairness test is also all-encompassing. Importantly, terms are evaluated in the context of the contract as a whole and the circumstances in which it was entered into. This ensures that the regime can adequately address the mischief being tackled.

Furthermore, the CRA blacklists certain terms considered unfair in all circumstances.[156] Thus, if any of the blacklisted terms are used, they will be automatically regarded as unfair without any need to determine if they satisfy the fairness test. The use of blacklists is often considered the 'last resort of a consumer regulator'[157] and is sometimes criticised on the basis that they are 'arbitrary, inflexible and open to abuse.'[158] However, blacklists may be justified where they allow authorities to meet regulatory outcomes with relatively high certainty.[159]

The CRA also contains an indicative non-exhaustive greylist of terms that may be regarded as unfair.[160] Unlike the blacklist, these terms are not automatically unfair but are viewed with suspicion. They are subject to the fairness test. The forerunner to the CRA's parent Directive[161] initially proposed for the terms on the greylist to be incorporated into a blacklist. This proposal was criticised for infringing on the freedom of contract.[162] This criticism brought to fore the tension between balancing competing regulatory interests, which is highlighted below.

It is important to note that the fairness test does not extend to a contract term if it –

(a) it specifies the main subject matter of the contract, or
(b) the assessment is of the appropriateness of the price payable under the contract by comparison with the goods, digital content or services supplied under it.[163]

156 For example, terms which seek to exclude or restrict liability for death or personal injury resulting from negligence. s.65(1); see also ss 31, 47, 57, and 63(6) & (7).

157 Geraint Howells, 'The Potential and Limits of Consumer Empowerment by Information' (2005) 32(3) *Journal of Law & Society* 349, 366.

158 Lara McMurtry, 'Consumer Credit Act Mortgages: Unfair Terms, Time Orders and Judicial Discretion' (2010) 2 *Journal of Business Law* 107, 116.

159 OECD, *Policy Guidance on Resource Efficiency* (OECD Publishing 2016) p.47 <https://www.oecd-ilibrary.org/environment/policy-guidance-on-resource-efficiency_9789264257344-en> accessed 21 December 2021. See also recital 17 of the Unfair Commercial Practices Directive 2005/29/EC.

160 s.63(1) and Schedule 2 (Part 1).

161 Directive 93/13/EEC.

162 See Lord Walker's Judgment in *Office of Fair Trading v. Abbey National Plc* [2009] UKSC 6; Michael Schillig, 'Directive 93/13 and the 'Price Term Exemption: A Comparative Analysis in the light of the "Market for Lemons" Rationale' (2011) 60(4) *International & Comparative Law Quarterly* 933, 934.

163 Section 73 also exempts terms which reflect mandatory statutory/regulatory provisions and the provisions/principles of international conventions. See also UNFCOG 1.3.1.

The legislative history shows that the original proposals for the Unfair Contract Terms Directive did not include this exception.[164] This drew a lot of criticism from academics who believed that the effect of the proposals had far-reaching consequences on the freedom of contract.[165] The exception was subsequently included and represents a –

> compromise between two conflicting regulatory ideologies that obtained at the time in the Commission and the Council, respectively; the consumer rights approach trying to ensure a 'good' bargain for consumers, and the free markets and competition approach relying on the corrective forces of the market.[166]

Hence, this exception, as well as the inclusion of the greylist, represented one of the many compromises aimed at 'balancing the need for consumer protection against the residual freedom of contract.'[167]

While this exception appears straightforward, its application may not always be so. This was evident in *Office of Fair Trading v. Abbey National Plc.*[168] This was a test case seeking to determine if charges for unauthorised overdrafts were exempt from the fairness test since they could be classified as price terms. The Court of Appeal held that the exemption would only apply to price terms that formed part of the essential bargain between the parties. Since the overdraft charges were ancillary payment obligations of a contingent nature, which would not be incurred in the normal performance of the contract, they could not enjoy the exemption.[169] The UKSC, on the other hand, held that the exemption would apply to 'any monetary price or remuneration payable under the contract.'[170] Since the charges were 'monetary consideration for the package of banking services,'[171] they would be exempt from the fairness test.

It must be pointed out that this exemption only applies if the term is transparent and prominent. 'Transparency' suggests that a term must be expressed in 'plain and intelligible language, and it is legible.' This is discussed further below. In a

164 i.e., the Unfair Terms Directive (n 5); this was the forerunner of the Consumer Rights Directive (n 5See Peter Duffy, 'Unfair Contract Terms and the EC Directive' (1993) *Journal of Business Law* 67 for a discussion on the legislative history of Directive 93/13/EEC.

165 See notable criticisms in Hans Erich Brandner and Peter Ulmer, 'The Community Directive on Unfair Terms in Consumer Contracts: Some Critical Remarks on the Proposal Submitted by the EC Commission' (1991) 28(3) *Common Market Law Review* 647; See also Lord Walker's comments in *Abbey National Plc* (n 162) para.6.

166 Anu Arora, 'Unfair Contract Terms and Unauthorised Bank Charges: A Banking Lawyer's Perspective' (2012) 1 *Journal of Business Law* 44, 57.

167 *Abbey National Plc* (n 162) *per* Lord Walker at para 6.

168 Ibid.

169 See paragraphs 93–112 of the Court of Appeal's decision reported at [2009] EWCA Civ 116.

170 *Abbey National Plc* (n 162) para.41, *per* Lord Walker.

171 Ibid. para.47.

similar vein, prominence suggests that a term must be 'brought to the consumer's attention in such a way that an average consumer would be aware.'[172]

The CRA adopts the familiar benchmark of the average consumer used under the CPUTRs. Like the CPUTRs, the average consumer under the CRA is 'reasonably well-informed, observant and circumspect.'[173] However, unlike the CPUTRs, the CRA makes no mention of adjustments to this standard in specific situations. Thus, it is unclear whether the peculiarities of vulnerable consumers will be considered when evaluating a trader's efforts to bring terms to their attention.

Although the CRA specifies that a term must be brought to the consumer's attention, it does not explain how this requirement may be satisfied. The CMA provides some guidance by explaining that a term will be considered prominent if it is –

> brought to the consumer's attention in a way that is practically effective. Steps taken to achieve this should ensure that the average consumer can understand and appreciate all the essential features of the bargain before making a purchase, so as to be able to compare it meaningfully with other available bargains.[174]

The CMA further clarifies that –

> prominence is not merely about highlighting terms visually in the contract document. In determining whether a term is sufficiently prominent, regard will need to be given to several factors – including whether the term itself is onerous, what a reasonable consumer would expect, how other contract terms are presented and what information has been given to the consumer before entering the contract. If a term could come as a surprise to the consumer, it will require more effort to ensure its prominence compared to other terms.[175]

Although the final interpretation lies with the courts, the CMA's guidance is helpful and may influence the courts' assessment. Going by the CMA's statements, m-payment providers must make concerted efforts towards highlighting core terms for the exemptions to apply. In addition, their efforts must be 'practically effective' in ensuring that consumers can appreciate the essential features of the bargain.

In enforcing the regime, the CRA contains some important provisions. First, it imposes a duty on courts to evaluate the fairness of terms used even if none of

172 s.64(4).

173 Regulation 64(5).

174 CMA, 'Unfair Contract Terms Explained' (n 143) para.19.

175 Ibid. para.20.

the parties raises the issue.[176] Courts can carry out this evaluation provided there is sufficient legal and factual material to enable them to do so.[177] This provision aligns the United Kingdom's regime with the broader EU approach to regulating contract terms. The Court of Justice of the European Union argues that 'effective protection of the consumer may be attained only if the national court acknowledges that it has the power to evaluate terms of this kind of its own motion.'[178] Thus, this provision will ensure more vigilance in the regulation of contract terms since an evaluation will be carried out even if the consumer fails to raise an objection. This is significant as consumers may not raise objections because they are unaware that they are subject to unfair terms.[179]

Second, enforcement authorities can pre-emptively challenge the use of unfair terms. Thus, they can act even in the absence of a complaint. The FCA, for example, may, on its own initiative, undertake a review of the contracts used in particular business areas if it is concerned that there may be issues of wider significance to consumers.[180] It is believed that pre-emptive challenges can effectively aid in preventing the use of such terms and will be a useful incentive for changing general contracting practices.[181] Where the regulator finds that contract terms contravene the CRA, it may apply for an injunction against parties which use or recommend such terms or similar ones.[182] Alternatively, the regulator may accept an undertaking from the trader involved.[183] Where a PSP, such as an m-payment provider, has provided an undertaking, the FCA advises that the PSP should promptly notify its clients of the effect of the undertaking on their contracts.[184]

Despite the power granted regulators to pre-emptively challenge the use of unfair terms, the CRA does not accord regulators the power to grant direct redress to consumers who have suffered loss because of an unfair term. However, in the financial services sector, the FCA exercising its broader regulatory powers, can make rules requiring that PSPs establish and operate consumer redress schemes.[185]

Consumers may take independent action where they are subject to an unfair term, but this can be expensive, as highlighted in *Chapter 4*. The CRA contains a helpful response to this issue as it designates a representative consumer organisation (the Consumers' Association) as one of the recognised regulators that can enforce

176 s.71(2).

177 s.71(3).

178 *Pannon GSM Zrt. v. Erzsébet Sustikné Győrfi* (C-243/08) at para 23.

179 *Mostaza Claro v. Centro Movil Milenium SL* (C-168/05) at para 29; *Oceano Grupo Editorial SA v. Quintero* (C-240/98) at para 26.

180 UNFCOG 1.4.3 & 1.4.4.

181 Lord Steyn in *First National Bank* (n 142) para.33.

182 s.70 & Schedule 3, paragraph 3(1).

183 Schedule 3, paragraph 6. The FCA entered one such undertaking with PPRO Financial Limited in 2017: <https://www.fca.org.uk/publication/undertakings/ppro-financial-limited.pdf> accessed 21 December 2021.

184 UNFCOG 1.5.1(1).

185 The Financial Services and Markets Act 2000, s.404: UNFCOG 1.6.1(3); FCA, 'Approach Document' (n 9) para.12.12.

the unfair terms provisions.[186] In effect, the Consumers' Association may apply for an injunction on behalf of consumers to preclude the continued use of unfair contract terms. The designation of a consumer body as a regulator is significant for reasons discussed in *Chapter 4*. As will be recalled, Ayres and Braithwaite argue that involving consumer organisations in the enforcement architecture helps address fears that regulatory capture will leave industry malpractices unchecked.[187] Furthermore, the high cost of individual enforcement suggests that representative actions by consumer organisations may be a more pragmatic alternative.[188]

Apart from the general rules in the CRA, the EMRs, and PSRs contain some provisions addressing specific contract terms used in the provision of payment services. Additionally, the FCA clarifies the effect of some of these provisions in the guidance document clarifying its approach to enforcing both regulations. For example, in the EMRs consumers have the right to redeem the monetary value of their e-money at any time and at par value.[189] The terms of redemption are to be disclosed clearly and prominently to consumers before they are bound by the contract.[190] Any fees charged for redemption must also be proportionate and commensurate to the costs incurred by the e-money issuer.[191] In clarifying these provisions, the FCA states that any term with provisions to the contrary can be challenged, and the onus is placed on the firm to show that the term was clear and prominent and the fees justifiable.[192]

The significance of these provisions is that a term which suggests that a consumer's right to redeem the balance of their e-money ceases to apply after a specified period will be unacceptable.[193] The same goes for a term which charges disproportionate redemption fees. Applying this to m-payments, where consumers are issued e-money stored in electronic m-payment wallets, PSPs are obliged to redeem their unspent funds if they request it. If the PSP's standard form contract charges disproportionate redemption fees or indicates that a request for redemption must be made within less than six years after the termination of a payment services contract, that term could be challenged as an unfair term. Where the terms of redemption have also not been clearly and prominently set out in the contract, they can also be challenged for failing to meet the requirements of fair and open dealing.

186 Schedule 3, paragraph 8(1)(k). Also note that the Consumers' Association is also recognised as a designated enforcer under Part 8 of the Enterprise Act 2002. See The Enterprise Act 2002 (Part 8) (Designation of the Consumers' Association) Order 2005 (SI 2005, No.917).

187 Ian Ayres and John Braithwaite, 'Tripartism: Regulatory Capture and Empowerment' (1991) 16(3) *Law & Social Inquiry* 435, 441 & 449.

188 Geraint Howells and Stephen Weatherill, *Consumer Protection Law* (2nd edn, Ashgate 2005) p.17.

189 Regulation 39(b)(i) & (ii).

190 EMRs, Regulation 40.

191 Ibid. Regulation 41(2).

192 FCA, 'Approach Document' (n 9), paras 8.355 & 8.356.

193 However, note that Regulation 43 permits refusals to redeem where requests are made more than 6 years after the termination of a contract; FCA, 'Approach Document' (n 9) para.8.350.

### *7.4.2.2 Transparency*

The CRA requires that a written term must be transparent.[194] A term is transparent if it is expressed in 'plain and intelligible language, and it is legible.'[195] The CMA has clarified that transparency is both a requirement on its own and a fundamental part of fairness.[196] The transparency requirement reinforces the obligation of fair and open dealing embodied in the requirement of good faith.[197] This implies that terms should be articulated in a way that puts consumers in a position to make informed choices on whether or not to enter into a contract.[198] Of particular relevance to m-payments is the advice from the CMA that terms covering complex and technical issues ought to be presented with care.[199] Providers should not assume that consumers understand how the market operates or the technicalities of a transaction.[200] To satisfy the transparency requirement, firms are expected to provide information in a way that allows a consumer to understand 'both the words used and the practical implications of any unavoidably difficult terms and their relationship with his or her other rights and obligations.'[201]

The CMA stresses that although transparency is important, it is not sufficient on its own to legitimise an otherwise unfair term.[202] This is because good faith relates to the substance of terms and the way they are expressed and used.[203] This confirms that the regime focuses on both the effect/purpose of contract terms and the form in which they are presented.[204]

As stated earlier, a determination of fairness will be carried out in the context of the contract as a whole and all the circumstances in which the contract is entered into.[205] In addition, the CMA has clarified that a term that fails to meet the transparency test alone is not necessarily unenforceable.[206] This suggests that failing the transparency test does not necessarily imply that a term is unenforceable independently of the overall fairness test.[207] The CMA has also stated that if a regulator considers that a term is not transparent, it can take enforcement action

194 s.68(1); UNFCOG 1.3.1(5).

195 ss.64(3) and 68(2); see Chris Willett, 'The Functions of Transparency in regulating Contract Terms: UK and Australian Approaches' (2011) 60(2) *International & Comparative Law Quarterly* 355 for a robust discussion on transparency.

196 CMA, 'Unfair Contract Guidance' (n 141) para.2.4.

197 Ibid.

198 CMA, 'Unfair Contract Guidance' (n 141) para.2.46.

199 Ibid. para.2.47.

200 Ibid.

201 Ibid.

202 CMA, 'Unfair Contract Guidance' (n 141) para.2.42.

203 CMA, 'Unfair Contract Terms Explained' (n 143) para.28.

204 CMA, 'Unfair Contract Guidance' (n 141) para.5.14.5; see Willet, 'The Functions of Transparency in regulating Contract Terms' (n 195) p.384.

205 CMA, 'Unfair Contract Guidance' (n 141) para.2.18.

206 Ibid. para.2.49.

207 CMA, 'Unfair Contract Terms Guidance' (n 141) para.2.6; CMA, 'Unfair Contract Terms Explained' (n 143) para.38.

in the same way as if that term had breached the fairness requirement.[208] Hence, regulators may be able to seek injunctive relief where terms are used in a non-transparent manner.

Finally, where a lack of transparency results in ambiguity, the courts will adopt the interpretation that is most favourable to the consumer.[209] This will also be the position where a term is transparent yet capable of several interpretations.[210] This provision reflects the Common Law approach of interpreting ambiguous terms strictly against the drafter.[211] The CMA has stated that this rule is intended to benefit only consumers in disputes with businesses. It will not be a defence for firms facing regulatory action.[212] This aligns with the CRA's main focus of protecting consumer interests.

### *7.4.3 Regulating False and Misleading Information*

To regulate the use of false and misleading information, the CPUTRs criminalise two categories of practices, namely 'misleading actions' and 'misleading omissions.' While the former deals more with the active use of false information, the latter deals with the omission of material information. As highlighted in Section 7.4.1, both are classified as unfair commercial practices.

A commercial activity may qualify as a misleading action if it fulfils the conditions listed in two circumstances. In the first circumstance, a commercial activity is misleading if –

> (a) if it contains false information and is therefore untruthful ... or if it or its overall presentation in any way deceives or is likely to deceive the average consumer ... even if the information is factually correct; and
>
> (b) it causes or is likely to cause the average consumer to take a transactional decision he would not have taken otherwise.[213]

The information in question must be with regards to specific issues set out in the CPUTRs. The use of 'and' in this provision shows that both conditions must be satisfied. Hence if the information is false but does not affect the transactional decision of an average consumer, then it is not a misleading action. This approach can be justified on the basis that one aim of prohibiting misleading actions is to ensure that consumers can make independent, informed decisions. Therefore, if a consumer's decision-making has not been influenced or is not likely to be influenced by the information called into question, it is only sensible that the trader is not liable for the offence.

208 CMA, 'Unfair Contract Terms Guidance' (n 141) para.2.6.
209 Ibid. para.2.49.
210 s.69(1) CRA.
211 This is known as the *contra proferentem* rule.
212 CMA, 'Unfair Contract Terms Explained' (n 143) para.38.
213 Regulation 5(2).

Moreover, it is important to note that the phrase 'transactional decision' is given a flexible interpretation under Section 2 of the CPUTRs. It means –

> any decision taken by a consumer, whether it is to act or to refrain from acting, concerning—
>
> (a) whether, how, and on what terms to purchase, make payment in whole or in part for, retain or dispose of a product; or
>
> (b) whether, how and on what terms to exercise a contractual right in relation to a product.

Thus, a transactional decision will be interpreted broadly and will go beyond the decision to purchase a product or to refrain from doing so. It will cover a range of pre-purchase and post-purchase decisions made by the consumer with respect to a product.[214] As with most areas of commercial activity, this broad interpretation has implications for m-payment providers. For instance, if an m-payments provider puts out false marketing information about the nature of the m-payment service offered, the provider will contravene the CPUTRs if the information affects a transactional decision made by a consumer. Going by the broad interpretation of 'transactional decision,' the service provider may be liable even where the consumer has not actually subscribed to the service.

Furthermore, the CPUTRs are concerned with the content of the information and its overall presentation. This is significant in light of the findings of behavioural economics discussed in *Chapter 3*. As discussed in *Chapter 3*, due to cognitive biases, consumers can be affected by how information is framed and presented. Hence, it is reasonable that the CPUTRs scrutinises the overall presentation of information.

In the second circumstance, a commercial activity is also misleading action if –

> a) it concerns any marketing of a product (including comparative advertising) which creates confusion with any products, trademarks, trade names or other distinguishing marks of a competitor; or
>
> (b) it concerns any failure by a trader to comply with a commitment contained in a code of conduct which the trader has undertaken to comply with, if—
>
> (i) the trader indicates in a commercial practice that he is bound by that code of conduct, and
>
> (ii) the commitment is firm and capable of being verified and is not aspirational,
>
> and it causes or is likely to cause the average consumer to take a transactional decision he would not have taken otherwise, taking account of its factual context and of all its features and circumstances.[215]

214 EU Commission, 'Guidance on the Implementation/Application of Directive 2005/29/EC on Unfair Commercial Practices' (2016) paragraph 2.3 <https://eur-lex.europa.eu/legal-content/EN/TXT/?uri=CELEX%3A52016SC0163> accessed 22 December 2021.

215 Regulation 5(3).

As with the first category of misleading actions, the emphasis is placed on the effect such practices have on the transactional decisions of consumers. For instance, an m-payment provider will contravene these provisions if they put out false information on the service, which induces consumers to make a transactional decision on the basis that the statement is true. Additionally, where an m-payment provider subscribes to an industry code which is firm and capable of being verified, they must comply with the commitments of that code.[216] This approach reflects marketing realities where consumers may be swayed to transact with particular traders because they are associated with a well-known and respected industry code. It is, thus, reasonable to require that traders comply with the code/standards they have claimed to be affiliated with.

Although non-compliance with a code is potentially a misleading action, it does not attract criminal sanctions. Instead, it is enforced using an injunction.[217] However, it is unclear why this exception was made. While an injunction will force a trader to comply with the code's commitments, it is submitted that this should not stop them from also facing criminal sanctions. Like all other occurrences of misleading actions, the reference to a code can influence a consumer's transactional decision, and as such, it seems more sensible for practices with a similar effect to be sanctioned in the same way. One argument that may justify this exception is that an injunction remedies the situation, negating the need for expensive criminal sanctions. However, this same argument can be used to justify civil sanctions for other misleading actions such as where a product is marketed in a way that causes confusion with another competitor's product.[218]

As already stated, misleading omissions are also prohibited. Unless apparent from the context, a commercial practice is a misleading omission if it omits or hides material information, provides material information in a way that is unclear, unintelligible, ambiguous or untimely, or fails to identify its commercial intent.[219] To qualify, such practices must also result in the average consumer taking a transactional decision they would not otherwise have taken.[220] In deciding if a practice qualifies as a misleading omission, the CPUTRs provide a list of factors that a court will consider. These factors include –

(a) all the features and circumstances of the commercial practice;
(b) the limitations of the medium used to communicate the commercial practice (including limitations of space or time); and

216 Regulation 4 also prohibits a code owner from promoting unfair commercial practices in a code of conduct.

217 Regulation 9; Office of Fair Trading, 'Guidance on the UK Regulations Implementing the Unfair Commercial Practices Directive' (May 2008) Paragraph 11.15. <https://assets.publishing.service.gov.uk/government/uploads/system/uploads/attachment_data/file/284442/oft1008.pdf> accessed 15 October 2021. This guidance has been adopted by the CMA which is the OFT's successor.

218 This breaches regulation 5(3)(a). In such a case, the consumer can maintain an action in misrepresentation while the competitor may rely on the tort of passing off.

219 Regulation 6.

220 Ibid.

(c) where the medium used to communicate the commercial practice imposes limitations of space or time, any measures taken by the trader to make the information available to consumers by other means.[221]

A few points may be made about these provisions. First, the CPUTRs emphasise that the nature of the information in question must be 'material.' The CPUTRs explain that material information covers 'the information which the average consumer needs,[222] according to the context, to take an informed transactional decision.'[223] This is in harmony with other provisions of the CPUTRs, which confirm that the regulations aim to ensure that consumers can make informed decisions without external interference.

Second, it is clear that the main concern here lies with omitting or hiding material information or presenting it ambiguously. In contrast to positive informational responses such as mandatory disclosures, prohibiting the use of false information is classified as a negative informational response.[224] Cartwright explains that while positive informational responses oblige firms to disclose specific information, negative informational responses compel them not to omit information which an average consumer would rely on to make an informed decision.[225] This is significant because mandatory disclosure regimes may unwittingly fail to cover certain matters that can influence a consumer's decision-making. This leaves a loophole which will be exploited by unscrupulous traders who will prefer to keep silent. Although morally questionable, the traders break no law in such situations because they have complied with the mandatory disclosure requirements. Negative informational responses help to address this gap. A combination of both responses will be more effective since both ends of the information spectrum are targeted. Traders will, therefore, be under a positive obligation to disclose vital information under a mandatory disclosure regime. They will also be under a negative obligation not to omit important information under the regime prohibiting misleading omissions.

As seen in Section 7.4.1, engaging in misleading actions or omissions is a strict liability offence with limited defences.[226] But as our discussions show, these offences are only committed if they impair a consumer's decision-making. This implies that an evaluation must be made of the impact of such practices on

221 Regulation 6(2).

222 The courts have emphasised the importance of the word 'needs' and have interpreted it very narrowly. See *Office of Fair Trading v. Purely Creative Ltd* [2011] EWHC 106 (Ch) at paragraph 74.

223 Material information also includes any information required under European Union Law. Regulation 6(3).

224 Peter Cartwright, *The Vulnerable Consumer of Financial Services: Law, Policy and Regulation* (Financial Services Research Forum, 2011) p.29 <https://www.nottingham.ac.uk/business/who-we-are/centres-and-institutes/gcbfi/documents/researchreports/paper78.pdf> accessed 18 October 2021.

225 Ibid. p.29; See also *Office of Fair Trading v. Purely Creative Ltd* (n 222); *Secretary of State for Business Innovation & Skills v. PLT Anti-Marketing Limited* [2015] EWCA Civ 76.

226 Regulations 9 & 10.

consumer decision-making. The OECD suggests that in making such evaluations, authorities will have the task of determining the message actually received by consumers and the importance they attach to it.[227] One way to ensure that this task is carried out consistently is to adopt an objective reference point against which information shared or omitted by traders can be evaluated. This is where the average consumer standard proves to be relatively useful.

English law does not impose liability for trade puffs, and the CPUTRs follow this tradition.[228] Thus, in determining the effect of a commercial practice on the average consumer, cognisance will be given to 'the common and legitimate advertising practice of making exaggerated statements which are not meant to be taken literally.'[229] Ramsay explains that this is justified because trade puffs are often too vague and subjective to represent any factual claim, and it is not expected that a reasonable person would take them seriously.[230] However, there is literature suggesting that the enforcement attitude towards trade puffs may not be optimal because, in many cases, consumers believe the 'false facts that puffing speech implies,' which can significantly alter 'consumption preferences.'[231] There is some truth to the concerns raised because behavioural biases can affect how consumers process information, including those that appear false. Nevertheless, imposing liability for trade puffs may lead to the overregulation of business speech. While it would be desirable to ensure that consumers can make informed decisions, it is also necessary that interventions do not lead to unintended negative consequences.

## 7.5 Liability Rules

The applicable liability rules are partly dependent on the statutes regulating the funding sources of m-payment transactions. For instance, credit and debit cards are subject to different liability regimes under UK law which impact m-payments. Where a credit card funds an m-payment transaction, the consumer may enjoy the rights available under the Consumer Credit Act 1974. Section 75 of the Act permits the credit cardholder to hold the credit card issuer and the merchant jointly and severally liable for any breach of contract or misrepresentation.[232]

227 OECD, 'Consumer Policy Toolkit' (2010) p.38 <http://www.oecd-ilibrary.org/governance/consumer-policy-toolkit_9789264079663-en> accessed 6 September 2021

228 *British Airways Plc v. Ryanair Ltd* [2001] E.T.M.R 24; *Erven Warnink Besloten Vennootschap v. J Townend & Sons (Hull) Ltd* [1979] AC 731

229 Regulation 2(6); *Office of Fair Trading v. Purely Creative Ltd* (n 222).

230 Iain Ramsay, *Consumer Law and Policy* (3rd edn, Hart Publishing 2012) p.137.

231 David A Hoffman, 'The Best Puffery Article Ever' (2006) 91 *Iowa Law Review* 1395, 1438–1439.

232 This only applies to transactions with a value above £100 but below £30,000: s.75(3)(b). It also extends to transactions made with an overseas company using a UK-issued credit card: Which?, 'Section 75 of the Consumer Credit Act' <https://www.which.co.uk/consumer-rights/regulation/section-75-of-the-consumer-credit-act-aZCUb9i8Kwfa> accessed 21 December 2021.

There is no equivalent protection for debit cardholders. Debit cardholders and credit cardholders who do not satisfy the Section 75 conditions will need to rely on chargeback procedures if available. As noted in *Chapter 3*, the liability rules applying to card transactions are often specific to the payment instrument, and the applicable rules may be unclear when m-payment transactions are involved.

However, despite the different regimes applying to various funding sources, the PSRs provide several liability rules which apply uniformly to all payment transactions except those funded by a credit line.[233] For instance, the PSRs provide that –

> where an executed payment transaction was not authorised ... the payment service provider must—
>
> (a) refund the amount of the unauthorised payment transaction to the payer; and
>
> (b) where applicable, restore the debited payment account to the state it would have been in had the unauthorised payment transaction not taken place.[234]

Thus, for unauthorised transactions, this provision may, to an extent, circumvent the problems associated with the varying liability rules applicable to the underlying funding sources. This is more so because the provision is not specific to any payment instrument but targets the payment transaction itself. In effect, the provision creates a minimum set of rules applying to unauthorised payments, thereby providing uniform protection for most m-payment users. However, this does not affect the application of more favourable liability rules associated with the underlying funding source.[235]

There are other notable features of the liability regime under the PSRs. For instance, the PSRs' liability regime for unauthorised transactions is linked to the mandatory disclosure regime. The PSRs provide that, where relevant, PSPs are required to disclose what steps a consumer must take to keep a payment instrument safe.[236] PSPs must also disclose –

> how and within what period of time the payment service user is to notify the payment service provider of any unauthorised or incorrectly executed payment transaction ....[237]

233 Where unauthorised transactions occur where a payment has been funded by a credit line, the liability rules under the Consumer Credit Act 1974 apply. FCA, 'Approach Document' (n 9) para.8.200.

234 Regulation 76(1).

235 FCA, 'Approach Document' (n 9) para.8.217.

236 Schedule 4, paragraph 5(a).

237 Schedule 4, paragraph 5(e).

PSPs are further mandated to –

> ensure that appropriate means are available at all times to enable the payment service user to notify the payment service provider in accordance with regulation 72(1)(b) ....[238]

Regulation 72(1)(b) obliges a consumer to –

> notify the payment service provider in the agreed manner and without undue delay on becoming aware of the loss, theft, misappropriation or unauthorised use of the payment instrument.

This is an important obligation as the consumer is entitled to redress for unauthorised transactions 'only if it notifies the payment service provider without undue delay.'[239] Except where the consumer has acted fraudulently,[240] they will also not be liable for losses arising after the PSP has been notified of the loss, theft, or misappropriation of a device.[241] However, the PSRs include an important caveat. Where the PSP has failed to disclose how it may be notified of an unauthorised transaction, then the consumer is entitled to redress even where they fail to notify the PSP.[242] Thus, the notification requirement, which is tied to the disclosure regime, plays a central role in allocating liability.

The liability regime further connects a PSP's disclosure obligations and the security responsibilities placed on the consumer. On receiving a payment instrument, a consumer must take all reasonable steps to keep all personalised security credentials safe.[243] As noted earlier, PSPs are also mandated to inform consumers of the steps they may take to keep such instruments safe.[244] A consumer will be liable for all losses where an unauthorised transaction occurs because the consumer has acted fraudulently or with 'intent or gross negligence' failed to comply with the security responsibilities placed on him.[245]

This provision seems fair as it targets consumers who have contributed to their losses through serious intentional or negligent failure to secure their payment instruments. However, the severe implication of a consumer's actions being labelled as intentional or grossly negligent requires a careful approach.

238 Regulation 73(1)(c).
239 Regulation 74(1).
240 Or has been grossly negligent in keeping the payment instrument/security credential safe (this is discussed later).
241 Regulation 77(3).
242 Regulation 74(2).
243 Regulation 72(3).
244 Schedule 4, paragraph 5(a).
245 Regulation 77(3)(b). Note that under the Consumer Credit Act 1974, a consumer cannot be held liable for unauthorised transactions on the basis of gross negligence. This suggests that m-payments funded by credit cards will not be subject to this rule. FCA, 'Approach Document' (n 9) para.8.196.

Unsurprisingly, the FCA suggests that the onus is on PSPs to provide evidence to support such claims.[246] This provision also highlights the importance of targeted disclosures and education initiatives which emphasise good security practices. Finally, it supports arguments that disclosures will play a significant role in m-payments because they will help to increase consumer awareness of the risks involved and their responsibilities regarding the safe use of their devices.

The PSRs also require that PSPs apply strong consumer authentication where a consumer seeks to access their payment account online, initiate an electronic payment transaction or carry out actions through a remote channel which may imply a risk of fraud or other abuses.[247] Where the PSP fails to provide strong customer authentication and an unauthorised transaction occurs, the consumer will not be liable for any losses unless they have been fraudulent.[248]

The PSRs further provide that PSPs must maintain adequate security measures to protect the confidentiality and integrity of a consumer's personalised security details.[249] If a payment instrument or any personalised security credentials have to be sent to the consumer, the PSP bears the risks relating to sending it.[250] This provision suggests that if personalised security details are intercepted before they reach the consumer, the PSP will bear any losses arising from their misuse.[251] This provision is reasonable, as a consumer who has not received the security details cannot be expected to bear the losses arising from their misuse. A term suggesting a contrary allocation of risk will contravene the fairness test under the CRA as its effect is to indirectly make the consumer the insurer for losses the business ought to bear. The CMA confirms that –

> A contract may be considered unbalanced if it contains a term imposing on the consumer a risk that the trader is better able to bear. A risk lies more appropriately with the trader if, for instance:
>
> - it is within their control;
> - it is a risk the consumer cannot be expected to know about; or
> - the trader can insure against it more cheaply than the consumer.[252]

However, the CMA notes that if a risk is transferred to a consumer on the basis that they are better positioned to control it or that insurance is available at a reasonable cost, such information needs to be disclosed to them.[253] Consumers must also be informed of what steps they may take to minimise such risks.[254]

246 FCA, 'Approach Document' (n 9) para.8.194.
247 Regulation 100(1).
248 Regulation 77(6); FCA, 'Approach Document' (n 9) para.8.223.
249 Regulation 100 (3).
250 Regulation 73(2).
251 FCA, 'Approach Document' (n 9) para.8.182.
252 CMA, 'Unfair Contract Terms Guidance' (n 141) para.5.31.1.
253 Ibid. para.5.31.5.
254 Ibid.

The PSRs also allocate liability where there has been defective, late, or non-execution of a payment instruction. The payer's PSP is liable to the payer for the correct execution of a payment transaction unless it can prove that the payee's PSP received the amount of the payment transaction.[255] Where a payer's PSP cannot prove this, they must refund the payer the amount of the non-executed or defective payment transaction without undue delay.[256] Where applicable, they must also restore the debited payment account to the state it would have been had the defective payment transaction not occurred.[257] However, where the payer's PSP successfully proves that a transaction has been executed in line with the instructions received, then the payee's PSP is liable to the payee for the correct execution of the payment transaction.[258] Regardless of the liability, a payer's PSP remains under the obligation to make efforts to trace non-executed or defectively executed payment transactions if the payer requests that they do so.[259] The PSP is also obliged to notify the payer of the outcome of their efforts.[260]

As exceptional circumstances can affect the delivery of payment services, the PSRs include provisions to deal with such eventualities. Hence, except where liability arises from a failure to meet the information disclosure mandate under the PSRs, the liability rules will not apply where liability is due to abnormal or unforeseeable and unavoidable circumstances beyond a party's control or due to obligations under EU or national law.[261]

Despite these clear rules, there are some transactions supported by m-payments which fall outside the scope of the PSRs. An example is the purchase of digital content with a value below specified thresholds.[262] In such cases, liability regimes will be dependent on the contracts entered with MNOs. Consumers will rely on the CRA to protect them from contractual terms, which unfairly allocate liability. The CRA nullifies exclusion clauses seeking to limit a trader's liability where the digital content is not as described, is not of satisfactory quality, or is not fit for a particular purpose.[263] The CRA, however, contains no provisions on issues such as unauthorised transactions.

Consumers can also look to the Code of Practice (PRS Code) issued by the Phone-paid Services Authority, the regulator for premium rate services (PRS).[264]

255 Regulation 91(2).
256 Regulation 91(3).
257 Ibid.
258 Regulation 91(5).
259 Regulation 91(8)(a).
260 Regulation 91(8)(b).
261 Regulation 96.
262 The PSRs will apply to the purchase of digital content if the value of a single transaction exceeds £40 and the cumulative value of payment transactions for an individual subscriber in a month exceeds £240. PSRs, Schedule 1, Part 2, paragraph 2(l)(i).
263 s.47(1).
264 The Phone-paid Services Authority was known as PhonepayPlus until 2016. Premium rate services (PRS) are value-added goods or services that consumers can purchase by charging the cost to their phone bill or prepaid phone accounts. Examples include donating to charity by

The Code, amongst other things, requires that PRS consumers be treated fairly and equitably.[265] This can be broadly interpreted to mean that contractual liability regimes will be fair and equitable. The PRS Code also provides that 'PRS must not be of a nature which encourages unauthorised use by non-bill payers,'[266] however, it does not contain any rules on how liability will be apportioned if there is unauthorised use.

In summary, the PSRs contain helpful liability rules that will apply to many m-payment transactions. These rules help to promote certainty and will likely reduce disputes. However, the liability rules will not apply to all m-payment transactions such as those funded by a credit line or low-value purchases of digital content. The practical implication is that this area may prove confusing for consumers. Therefore, it will be helpful for disclosure regimes to explicitly indicate which liability regimes apply so that consumers have clear expectations of their contractual rights and liabilities.

## 7.6 Dispute Resolution

### *7.6.1 Internal Dispute Resolution Procedures*

PSPs providing m-payments will be expected to establish and maintain 'effective and transparent procedures for the prompt handling of complaints' free of charge.[267] The responsibilities of PSPs in this regard are set out in the Dispute Resolution Complaints Sourcebook (DISP) contained in the FCA Handbook.[268]

One key responsibility placed on PSPs is to ensure that consumers are aware of existing channels for resolving complaints.[269] To this end, PSPs are required to publish information regarding their internal complaint procedures and refer eligible complainants to this information.[270] In complying with this requirement, PSPs must summarise how they fulfil their dispute resolution obligations and must indicate that an unresolved complaint may be referred to the Financial Ombudsman Service (FOS) if it falls within the FOS's jurisdiction.[271] In line with disclosure requirements under the PSRs, such information must be disclosed

text, online games, and TV voting: PhonepayPlus, 'Written Evidence Submitted by PhonepayPlus' (2013) paragraph 5 <https://publications.parliament.uk/pa/cm201314/cmselect/cmbis/697/697vw35.htm> accessed 18 October 2021.

265 PhonepayPlus, Code for Premium Rate Services (13th edn), paragraph 2.3.1. <https://www.ofcom.org.uk/__data/assets/pdf_file/0021/36534/code_13.pdf> accessed 19 December 2021.

266 Ibid. para.2.3.5.

267 Financial Conduct Authority, 'Dispute Resolution Complaints Sourcebook (DISP)' DISP 1.3.1 & 1.3.1A <https://www.handbook.fca.org.uk/handbook/DISP.pdf> accessed 19 December 2021.

268 DISP (n 267); FCA, 'Approach Document' (n 9) para.11.4.

269 DISP 1.2.

270 DISP 1.2.1.

271 DISP 1.2.3.

before concluding a payment services contract with a consumer.[272] In addition, the information must be provided in writing and free of charge to complainants who request it and when a complaint is acknowledged.[273]

The DISP also imposes complaints resolution rules to ensure that a complaint is investigated, assessed, and resolved appropriately.[274] For example, PSPs are required to investigate complaints 'competently, diligently, and impartially' and should obtain additional information where necessary.[275] In addition, complaints must be assessed 'fairly, consistently, and promptly.'[276] To ensure prompt resolution, the DISP dictates timelines for resolving disputes. For example, PSPs must send a final response to a complainant by the end of 15 business days after the day on which they received a complaint.[277] Where the PSP cannot comply with this timeline for reasons beyond their control, they are required to send a holding response by the end of 15 business days after the day on which they received a complaint and a final response by the end of 35 business days after the day on which they received a complaint.[278]

A critical feature of the dispute resolution regime is that it recognises the importance of complaints data in identifying systemic problems. Hence firms are required to –

> put in place appropriate management controls and take reasonable steps to ensure that in handling complaints it identifies and remedies any recurring or systemic problems, for example, by:
>
> (1) analysing the causes of individual complaints so as to identify root causes common to types of complaint;
> (2) considering whether such root causes may also affect other processes or products, including those not directly complained of; and
> (3) correcting, where reasonable to do so, such root causes.[279]

This is reminiscent of the obligation under Kenya's Prudential Guidelines on Consumer Protection (PGCP) that required firms to 'put in place arrangements to ensure that, in handling complaints, it identifies and remedies any recurring or systemic problems.'[280] This provision was criticised in *Chapter 6* for the

272 This applies to single payment service contracts (Regulation 43(2)(e) PSRs) and framework contracts (Regulation 48 PSRs); DISP 1.2.1(1)(a).
273 DISP 1.2.1(3).
274 DISP 1.4.
275 DISP 1.4.1(1).
276 DISP 1.4.1(2).
277 DISP 1.6.2A(1).
278 DISP 1.6.2A(2)(a) & (b).
279 DISP 1.3.3R.
280 Central Bank of Kenya, 'Prudential Guidelines for Institutions Licensed Under the Banking Act – Consumer Protection (CBK/PG/22)' para. 4.6 <https://www.centralbank.go.ke/wp-content/uploads/2016/08/PRUDENTIAL-GUIDELINES.pdf> accessed 7 October 2021.

non-inclusion of supervisory mechanisms to ensure that firms act appropriately. Although the duty in the DISP is similar, there are two key differences from the Kenyan regime.

First, unlike the PGCP, the DISP provides guidance on how firms can discharge these functions. The DISP explains that firms can discharge these functions by collecting management information on the causes of complaints, the products/services they relate to, and how they were resolved.[281] The DISP also encourages regular reporting of recurring or systemic problems to senior personnel.[282] Firms must keep records of the analysis and decisions taken by senior personnel in response to management information on the root causes of complaints.[283]

Second, the existence of the FOS (which is discussed in the next section) helps to ensure that if firms do not take reasonable steps to identify and remedy recurring problems, this can be picked up by the FOS.[284] Discussions on the Kenyan approach pointed out that the lack of supervision would allow systemic problems to remain unresolved. The FOS, thus, plays an indirect supervisory function because consumers dissatisfied with internal procedures can approach the FOS. This means that the FOS can spot systemic or recurrent issues that firms have failed to identify. Kenya lacks a statutory ombudsman service; thus, there is no 'safety net' where firms fail to identify recurrent problems.

The DISP also contains provisions on forwarding complaints which may be useful in m-payments. It requires that –

> A respondent[285] that has reasonable grounds to be satisfied that another respondent may be solely or jointly responsible for the matter alleged in a complaint may forward the complaint, or the relevant part of it, in writing to that other respondent, provided it:
>
> (1) does so promptly;
> (2) informs the complainant promptly in a final response of why the complaint has been forwarded by it to the other respondent, and of the other respondent's contact details; and
> (3) where jointly responsible for the fault alleged in the complaint, it complies with its own obligations under this chapter in respect of that part of the complaint it has not forwarded.[286]

This provision may be helpful in m-payments because of the numerous parties involved. Rather than having a situation where all parties avoid responsibility for consumer complaints, this provision obliges firms to consider each complaint and

281 DISP 1.3.3B(1).
282 DISP 1.3.3B(6).
283 DISP 1.3.3B(7).
284 This is also complemented by the complaints reporting requirements imposed on PSPs. PSPs must submit regular reports documenting complaints received to the FCA: DISP 1.10.1R.
285 i.e., the firm receiving the complaint.
286 DISP 1.7.1R.

provides guidance on how to deal with issues falling within their responsibility. For issues outside their responsibility, they are required to forward it to the party they believe is better positioned to handle it.

### 7.6.2 External ADR Mechanisms

Where eligible, m-payment consumers may also enjoy access to the FOS.[287] The FOS is a statutory dispute resolution service established under the Financial Services and Markets Act (FSMA) 2000[288] and operationally independent of the FCA. Currently, the FOS resolves claims between consumers and FIs which do not exceed set monetary limits.[289] The use of the service is free to consumers and is financed by a levy imposed on the financial services industry.[290]

The FOS adopts minimum formality and bases its findings 'by reference to what is, in the opinion of the ombudsman, fair and reasonable in all the circumstances of the case'[291] This allows for flexibility in resolving complaints received. As Afghan explains, this flexibility suggests that the ombudsman can ignore legal technicalities which would have been strictly followed in court.[292] Despite this flexible mandate, the FOS is expected to consider relevant laws and regulations, rules, guidance, and standards issued by regulators, and industry codes of practice in determining what is fair and reasonable.[293] Hence, the ombudsman can conclude that it would be wrong to depart from the strict legal position.[294] Because of this flexibility, the FOS has been criticised for reaching inconsistent determinations. In its defence, Afghan explains that these inconsistencies are unavoidable to a certain extent since the FOS is required to determine each case based on an assessment of what is fair and reasonable.[295]

Where the consumer notifies the FOS that they accept its findings, it becomes binding on both parties and is final.[296] Once binding, the findings also become

287 Complaints may be made to the FCA. While they can influence the FCA's regulatory activities, it is important to note that the FCA does not generally operate a redress mechanism for individual complaints. For individual redress, the FCA will likely advise a consumer to contact the FOS: FCA, 'Approach Document' (n 9) paras 11.51–11.53.

288 See s.225 FSMA.

289 The current monetary limits can be found in DISP 3.7.4. See also Financial Ombudsman Authority, 'Understanding Compensation' <https://www.financial-ombudsman.org.uk/businesses/resolving-complaint/understanding-compensation-maximumlimit> accessed 30 December 2021.

290 s.234 FSMA. Industry funding of the FOS has been challenged and rejected; see *Financial Ombudsman Service Ltd v. Heather Moor & Edgecomb Ltd* [2008] EWCA Civ 643.

291 S.228(2) FSMA; DISP 3.6.1.

292 Shazia K Afghan, 'Commercial Financial Dispute Resolution Platform: A Palliation or Panacea for Consumers of Financial Services?' (2017) 32(5) *Journal of International Banking Law and Regulation* 200, 209.

293 DISP 3.6.4.

294 Khan (n 292) p.209.

295 Ibid. p.210.

296 s.228(5) FSMA; see *Clark v. In Focus Asset Management & Tax Solutions* [2014] EWCA Civ 118.

enforceable in court.[297] However, if the consumer rejects the ombudsman's findings, they are free to pursue that matter further in court.[298] This approach favours the consumers and ensures that their right to redress is not restricted.

The FOS has compulsory jurisdiction over financial service firms, payment service providers and e-money issuers with UK establishments.[299] The jurisdiction of the FOS is acknowledged under the DISP and the FCA's Approach Document.[300] Hence it is clear that disputes between m-payment providers and consumers will fall under FOS jurisdiction. This means that m-payment consumers will enjoy uniform access to the FOS irrespective of the underlying funding source and status of the PSP.

One important feature of the dispute resolution regime is that it communicates an explicit link between the FOS's work and the internal dispute resolution mechanisms maintained by PSPs. It achieves this in several ways. One example is that the compliance requirements mandate that PSPs inform consumers of the availability of the FOS. The DISP requires that such information must be clear, comprehensible, and accessible. The FOS's website address should be included in the PSP's website if one exists and also highlighted in the general conditions of the contract with the consumer.[301]

Another important example is that when setting up these internal procedures, firms are required to –

> ensure that lessons learned as a result of determinations by the Ombudsman are effectively applied in future complaint handling for example by:
>
> (1) relaying a determination by the Ombudsman to the individuals in the respondent who handled the complaint and using it in their training and development;
> (2) analysing any patterns in determinations by the Ombudsman concerning complaints received by the respondent and using this in training and development of the individuals dealing with complaints in the respondent; and
> (3) analysing guidance produced by the FCA, other relevant regulators and the Financial Ombudsman Service and communicating it to the individuals dealing with complaints in the respondent.[302]

This is a significant provision because it obliges firms to keep abreast with the determinations of the FOS and guidance emanating from regulators. This

297 PE Morris, 'The Financial Ombudsman Service and the Hunt Review: Continuing evolution in Dispute Resolution' (2008) 8 *Journal of Business Law* 785, 789.

298 s.228(6) FSMA provides that if by a specified date, the consumer fails to notify the ombudsman of his acceptance or rejection of the determination then it is presumed that he has rejected it.

299 s.226(2)(b) FSMA; DISP 2.1.1(1).

300 FCA, 'Approach Document' (n 9) para.11.31; DISP 2.1.

301 DISP 1.2.1(4).

302 DISP 1.3.2A.

ensures that they can update their internal redress procedures to reflect current best practices. The requirement to incorporate new information into their training and development programmes should also help to ensure that staff charged with resolving consumer complaints are competent and knowledgeable.

Finally, the United Kingdom's dispute resolution regime also provides mechanisms which can assist with the cross-border resolution of payments disputes. For example, the UK International Consumer Centre provides free advice to consumers in cross-border disputes with other traders abroad.[303] This initiative is part of a wider network of European Consumer Centres (ECC-Net).[304] The FOS is also an affiliate of the Financial Dispute Resolution Network (FIN-NET). FIN-NET helps consumers in the European Economic Area resolve cross-border disputes out of court.[305] This will be a viable platform for facilitating cross-border disputes that may arise in the provision of m-payments

## 7.7 Conclusion

In this chapter, we discussed the relevant consumer protection rules that may avail m-payment users in the United Kingdom. In summary, there is a comprehensive network of regulatory requirements which serve to protect consumer interests. For example, key regulations like the PSRs contain mandatory disclosure requirements, which is supported by cooling-off periods guaranteed under the CCRs and FSRs. In addition, commercial practices are generally subject to rules contained in cross-sector consumer protection legislation like the CPUTRs. Importantly, there is an independent regime regulating the use of unfair terms under the CRA.

The enforcement of this regulatory framework also involves several regulators. Two regulators particularly stand out, i.e., the CMA and the FCA. While the CMA has an overarching consumer protection mandate, the FCA authorises and supervises the PSPs providing m-payments, and it also has a consumer protection mandate.

M-payment consumers will enjoy access to internal dispute resolution mechanisms due to PSPs' obligations under the FCA's Dispute Resolution Complaints Sourcebook to maintain such mechanisms. Importantly, m-payment consumers can also access the Financial Ombudsman as PSPs fall under its compulsory jurisdiction.

The next part of the book includes a final chapter which concludes the monograph. The chapter highlights key findings from the case studies and discusses suggestions for countries seeking to develop consumer protection frameworks that can address consumer issues raised in m-payments.

303 <https://www.ukecc.net/> accessed 18 October 2021.

304 <http://ec.europa.eu/consumers/ecc/index_en.htm> accessed 18 October 2021.

305 <https://ec.europa.eu/info/business-economy-euro/banking-and-finance/consumer-finance-and-payments/retail-financial-services/financial-dispute-resolution-network-fin-net/fin-net-network/members-fin-net-country_en> accessed 18 October 2021.

## References


Consumer Credit Act 1974.

Consumer Protection (Amendment) Regulations 2014.

Consumer Rights Act 2015.

Enterprise Act 2002.

Financial Guidance and Claims Act 2018.

Financial Services Markets Act 2000 (as amended).

The Consumer Protection from Unfair Trading Regulations 2008.

The Consumer Rights Directive (2011/83/EU).

The Directive on Unfair Terms in Consumer Contracts (93/13/EC).

The E-Money Directive (2009/110/EC).

The Electronic Money Regulations 2011.

The Enterprise Act 2002 (Part 8) (Designation of the Consumers' Association) Order 2005 (SI 2005, No.917).

The Financial Services (Distance Marketing) Regulations 2004.

The Financial Services and Markets Act 2000 (Regulated Activities) Order 2001.

The Payment Services Directive II (2015/2366/EU).

The Payment Services Regulation 2017.

The Unfair Commercial Practices Directive 2005/29/EC.

The Unfair Terms in Consumer Contracts Regulation 1999.

*Aziz v Caixa d'Estalvis de Catalunya, Tarragona i Manresa (Catalunyacaixa)* (C-415/11).

*British Airways Plc v Ryanair Ltd* [2001] E.T.M.R 24.

*Clark v In Focus Asset Management & Tax Solutions* [2014] EWCA Civ 118.

*Director General of Fair Trading v First National Bank Plc.* [2001] UKHL 52

*Erven Warnink Besloten Vennootschap v J. Townend & Sons (Hull) Ltd* [1979] AC 731.

*Financial Ombudsman Service Ltd v Heather Moor & Edgecomb Ltd* [2008] EWCA Civ 643.

*Heininger v Bayerische Hypo-und Vereinsbank AG* (C-481/99).

*Meridian Global Funds Management Asia Ltd v Securities Commission* [1995] 2 AC 500.

*Mostaza Claro v Centro Movil Milenium SL* (C-168/05).

*Oceano Grupo Editorial SA v Quintero* (C-240/98).

*Office of Fair Trading v Abbey National Plc* [2009] UKSC 6.

*Office of Fair Trading v Purely Creative Ltd* [2011] EWHC 106 (Ch).

*Pannon GSM Zrt. v Erzsébet Sustikné Győrfi* (C-243/08).

*ParkingEye Ltd v Beavis* [2015] UKSC 67.

*Secretary of State for Business Innovation & Skills v. PLT Anti-Marketing Limited* [2015] EWCA Civ 76.

*Tesco Supermarkets v Nattrass* [1972] AC 153.

*West v Ian Finlay and Associates* [2014] EWCA Civ 316.

Andrea Hamilton and David Henry, 'Bricks, beer and Shoes: Indirect Purchaser Standing in the European Union and the United States' 2012 5(3) *Global Competition Litigation Review* 111.

Anu Arora, 'Unfair Contract Terms and Unauthorised Bank Charges: A Banking Lawyer's Perspective' (2012) 1 *Journal of Business Law* 44.

Bram B Duivenvoorde, *The Consumer Benchmarks in the Unfair Commercial Practices Directive* (Springer 2015).

Central Bank of Kenya, 'Prudential Guidelines for Institutions Licensed Under the Banking Act – Consumer Protection (CBK/PG/22)' <https://www.centralbank.go.ke/wp-content/uploads/2016/08/PRUDENTIAL-GUIDELINES.pdf> accessed 7 October 2021.

Chris Willett, 'The Functions of Transparency in regulating Contract Terms: UK and Australian Approaches' (2011) 60(2) *International & Comparative Law Quarterly* 355.

Christian Twigg-Flesner (ed) *Research Handbook on EU Consumer and Contract Law* (Edward Elgar 2016).

Christopher Hodges, 'From Class Actions to Collective Redress: A Revolution in Approach to Compensation' (2009) 28(1) *Civil Justice Quarterly* 41.

Competition and Markets Authority and Financial Conduct Authority, 'Memorandum of Understanding between the Competition and Markets Authority and the Financial Conduct Authority on the use of concurrent powers under consumer protection legislation' (July 2019) <https://www.fca.org.uk/publication/mou/fca-cma-consumer-protection-mou-2019.pdf> accessed 20 December 2021.

Competition and Markets Authority, 'Unfair Contract Terms Guidance: Guidance on the Unfair terms provisions in the Consumer Rights Act 2015' (2015) <https://assets.publishing.service.gov.uk/government/uploads/system/uploads/attachment_data/file/450440/Unfair_Terms_Main_Guidance.pdf> accessed 21 December 2021.

Competition and Markets Authority 'Unfair Contract Terms Explained' (2015) <https://assets.publishing.service.gov.uk/government/uploads/system/uploads/attachment_data/file/450410/Unfair_Terms_Explained.pdf> accessed 21 December 2021.

Cristina Poncibò and Rossella Incardona, 'The Average Consumer, the Unfair Commercial Practices Directive, and the Cognitive Revolution' (2007) 30(1) *Journal of Consumer Policy* 21.

David A. Hoffman, 'The Best Puffery Article Ever' (2006) 91 *Iowa Law Review* 1395.

Department for Business Innovation & Skills, 'Consumer Contracts (Information, Cancellation and Additional Charges) Regulations: Implementing Guidance' (2013) <https://assets.publishing.service.gov.uk/government/uploads/system/uploads/attachment_data/file/429300/bis-13-1368-consumer-contracts-information-cancellation-and-additional-payments-regulations-guidance.pdf> accessed 21 November 2021.

Department for Business, Energy and Industrial Strategy, 'Misleading and Aggressive Commercial Practices: New Private Rights for Consumers – Guidance on the Consumer (Amendment) Protection Regulations 2014' (2018) <https://assets.publishing.service.gov.uk/government/uploads/system/uploads/attachment_data/file/721872/misleading-aggressive-commercial-practices-guidance.pdf> accessed 11 December 2021.

EU Commission, 'Guidance on the Implementation/Application of Directive 2005/29/EC on Unfair Commercial Practices' (2016) <https://eur-lex.europa.eu/legal-content/EN/TXT/?uri=CELEX%3A52016SC0163> accessed 22 December 2021.

EU Payment Services Directive II (2015/2366/EU) which replaced Directive 2007/64/EC.

Financial Conduct Authority, 'Dispute Resolution Complaints Sourcebook (DISP)' <https://www.handbook.fca.org.uk/handbook/DISP.pdf> accessed 19 December 2021.

Financial Conduct Authority, 'FCA Handbook: The Perimeter Guidance Manual (Chapter 3A) – Guidance on the Scope of the Electronic Money Regulations' <https://www.handbook.fca.org.uk/handbook/PERG/3A/?view=chapter> accessed 18 October 2021.

Financial Conduct Authority, 'FCA Handbook: Unfair Contract terms and Consumer Notices Regulatory Guide' (UNFCOG) <https://www.handbook.fca.org.uk/handbook/UNFCOG/1/?view=chapter> accessed 20 December 2021.

Financial Conduct Authority, 'Payment Services and Electronic Money – Our Approach (The FCA's role under the Payment Services Regulations 2017 and the Electronic Money

Regulations 2011)' (2019) <https://www.fca.org.uk/publication/finalised-guidance/fca-approach-payment-services-electronic-money-2017.pdf> accessed 18 January 2022.

Financial Conduct Authority, 'Unfair Contract Terms Library' <https://www.fca.org.uk/firms/unfair-contract-terms/library> accessed 21 October 2021.

Financial Ombudsman Authority, 'Understanding Compensation' <https://www.financial-ombudsman.org.uk/businesses/resolving-complaint/understanding-compensation - maximumlimit> accessed 30 December 2021.

Franziska Weber, *The Law and Economics of Enforcing European Law* (Ashgate Publishing 2014).

Geraint Howells, 'The Potential and Limits of Consumer Empowerment by Information' (2005) 32(3) *Journal of Law & Society* 349.

Geraint Howells and Reiner Schulze (eds), *Modernising and Harmonising Consumer Contract Law* (Sellier European Law Publishers 2009).

Geraint Howells and Stephen Weatherill, *Consumer Protection Law* (2nd ed., Ashgate 2005)

Gordon Downie and Marianne Charrier, 'UK and EU developments in Collective Action Regimes for Competition Law Breaches' 2014, 35(8) *European Competition Law Review* 369.

Hans Erich Brandner and Peter Ulmer, 'The Community Directive on Unfair Terms in Consumer Contracts: Some Critical Remarks on the Proposal Submitted by the EC Commission' (1991) 28(3) *Common Market Law Review* 647.

Iain Ramsay, *Consumer Law and Policy* (3rd ed., Hart Publishing 2012).

Ian Ayres and John Braithwaite, 'Tripartism: Regulatory Capture and Empowerment' (1991) 16(3) *Law & Social Inquiry* 435.

Lara McMurtry, 'Consumer Credit Act Mortgages: Unfair Terms, Time Orders and Judicial Discretion' (2010) 2 *Journal of Business Law* 107.

Lisa Waddington, 'Vulnerable and Confused: The Protection of 'Vulnerable' Consumers under EU Law' (2013) 38(6) *European Law Review* 757.

Michael Schillig, 'Directive 93/13 and the 'Price Term Exemption: A Comparative Analysis in the light of the "Market for Lemons" Rationale' (2011) 60(4) *International & Comparative Law Quarterly* 933.

Nathan Willmott, Peter McGowan, Mark Ghusn et al. 'Equipping the Modern Regulator: Assessing the New Regulatory Powers under the Financial Services Act 2012' (2010) 78 *Compliance Officer Bulletin* 1.

Nicholas Ryder, Margaret Griffiths, and Lachmi Singh, *Commercial Law: Principles and Policy* (Cambridge University Press 2012).

OECD, *Policy Guidance on Resource Efficiency* (OECD Publishing 2016) <https://www.oecd-ilibrary.org/environment/policy-guidance-on-resource-efficiency_9789264257344-en>. accessed 21 December 2021.

Office of Fair Trading, 'Guidance on the UK Regulations Implementing the Unfair Commercial Practices Directive' (May 2008). <https://assets.publishing.service.gov.uk/government/uploads/system/uploads/attachment_data/file/284442/oft1008.pdf> accessed 15 October 2021.

PE Morris, 'The Financial Ombudsman Service and the Hunt Review: Continuing evolution in Dispute Resolution' (2008) 8 *Journal of Business Law* 785.

Peter Cartwright (ed.), *Consumer Protection in Financial Services* (Kluwer Law Int'l 1999).

Peter Cartwright, 'Crime, Punishment and Consumer Protection.' (2007) 30 *Journal of Consumer Policy* 1.

Peter Cartwright, 'Unfair Commercial Practices and the Future of Criminal Law' (2010) 7 *Journal of Business Law* 618.

Peter Cartwright, The Vulnerable Consumer of Financial Services: Law, Policy and Regulation (Financial Services Research Forum, 2011) <https://www.nottingham.ac.uk/business/who-we-are/centres-and-institutes/gcbfi/documents/researchreports/paper78.pdf> accessed 18 October 2021.

Peter Cartwright, 'Redress Compliance and Choice: Enhanced Consumer Measures and the retreat from punishment in the Consumer Rights Act 2015' (2016) 75(2) *Cambridge Law Journal* 271.

Peter Duffy, 'Unfair Contract Terms and the EC Directive' (1993) *Journal of Business Law* 67.

PhonepayPlus, 'Written Evidence Submitted by PhonepayPlus' (2013) <https://publications.parliament.uk/pa/cm201314/cmselect/cmbis/697/697vw35.htm> accessed 18 October 2021.

PhonepayPlus, *Code for Premium Rate Services* (13th ed.) <https://www.ofcom.org.uk/__data/assets/pdf_file/0021/36534/code_13.pdf> accessed 19 December 2021.

Richard B. Macrory, `Regulatory Justice: Making Sanctions Effective' (2006) <https://webarchive.nationalarchives.gov.uk/ukgwa/20070305105024mp_/http:/www.cabinetoffice.gov.uk/regulation/documents/pdf/macrory_penalties.pdf> accessed 18 October 2021.

Shazia K. Afghan, 'Commercial Financial Dispute Resolution Platform: A Palliation or Panacea for Consumers of Financial Services?' (2017) 32(5) *Journal of International Banking Law and Regulation* 200.

Stephen Weatherill and Ulf Bernitz (eds), *The Regulation of Unfair Commercial Practices under EC Directive 2005/29: New Rules and New Techniques* (Bloomsbury Publishing 2007).

The Financial Conduct Authority, 'Mobile Banking and Payment: Supporting an Innovative and Secure Market' (2013) <https://www.fca.org.uk/publication/thematic-reviews/tr13-06.pdf> accessed 15 October 2021.

The Financial Conduct Authority, 'Thematic Review: Mobile Banking and Payments' (2014) <https://www.fca.org.uk/publication/thematic-reviews/tr14-15.pdf> accessed 15 October 2021.

The Financial Conduct Authority, *The Perimeter Guidance Manual*, Chapter 15.1. <https://www.handbook.fca.org.uk/handbook/PERG/15.pdf> accessed 22 December 2021.

UK Finance, 'UK Payment Markets Summary 2021' (2021) <https://www.ukfinance.org.uk/sites/default/files/uploads/SUMMARY-UK-Payment-Markets-2021-FINAL.pdf> accessed 18 October 2021.

Which?, 'Section 75 of the Consumer Credit Act' <https://www.which.co.uk/consumer-rights/regulation/section-75-of-the-consumer-credit-act-aZCUb9i8Kwfa> accessed 21 December 2021.

Willem van Boom, Amandine Garde, Orkun Akseli (eds), *The European Unfair Commercial Practices Directive: Impact, Enforcement Strategies and National Legal Systems* (Routledge 2016).

# Part III

# Mobile Payments and Consumer Protection – Conclusions and Best Practices

# 8 Conclusions

## 8.1 Introduction

Acknowledging that mobile payments (m-payments) can be potentially transformative for financially excluded consumers, the discussion in this book has been centred on the premise that m-payments can only reach their true potential if the innovation functions within a clear regulated framework where parties involved (especially consumers) are protected. Against this background, the book highlighted the concerns associated with adopting m-payments from a consumer protection perspective. Building on recommendations in relevant soft law documents, the book adopted a typology of relevant regulatory tools which can be used to address highlighted consumer issues. This typology guided the book's review of the existing consumer protection frameworks that apply to m-payments in Canada, Kenya, and the United Kingdom.

One general observation from the review is that, in most cases, each country operates some form of regulatory regime covering the themes highlighted. The differences often lie in how comprehensive these regimes are. Nonetheless, the areas of convergence and divergence highlight important trends which provide useful material for policymakers and regulators seeking to tackle consumer issues arising in the adoption of m-payments. Accordingly, this concluding chapter highlights best practices that countries should consider when regulating m-payments from a consumer protection perspective. While these best practices are discussed in the context of m-payments, they remain generally relevant in broader contexts involving the regulation of other innovative financial services.

## 8.2 Provision of Information

### *8.2.1 Mandatory Disclosures*

*Chapter 4* highlighted that mandatory disclosures can make consumer decision-making less difficult since it enables consumers to access key information about the financial services on offer. All the countries examined adopt statutory regimes which require the disclosure of a minimum set of information to consumers. This trend suggests that statutory disclosure frameworks could be a starting point in

DOI: 10.4324/9780429327292-11

protecting consumers using m-payments. In designing a statutory disclosure framework, the following points should be considered:

**As far as possible, all m-payment service providers should be uniformly required to disclose a minimum set of information.** A regime which promotes a uniform approach to disclosing standardised information will make it easier for consumers to compare alternative products. This will assist in reducing search and switching costs for consumers. In the countries reviewed, relevant statutes generally indicate the core information that should be disclosed to consumers. The obligation is often imposed uniformly on all regulated firms that provide payment services, including m-payments. For example, the United Kingdom's Payment Services Regulations (PSRs) 2017 focus primarily on the regulated activity, i.e., the provision of payment services. Therefore, the PSRs apply to all payment services providers (PSPs), including traditional and non-traditional financial institutions. Kenya takes a similar approach. Although the disclosure obligations in Kenya's National Payment Systems Regulations (NPSRs) 2014 are comparatively less comprehensive than the UK PSRs, they apply to all PSPs – a category broadly defined to cover traditional and non-traditional financial institutions.[1]

While Canada's Bank Act[2] contains comprehensive disclosure requirements, there is room for fragmentation since the Bank Act only applies to federally regulated financial institutions (FRFIs) like banks. Non-FRFIs are subject to provincial laws, while specific providers like MNOs are subject to additional obligations under the Wireless Code.[3] As *Chapter 5* highlights, Canada's federal system of government accounts for this approach. Nonetheless, the recent legislative reforms which have seen the consolidation of disclosure requirements in the Canadian Bank Act and Financial Consumer Protection Regulations (FCPRs)[4] suggest a trend towards a more uniform approach to disclosures in financial services.

**The minimum disclosures mandated across the board should include the basic information necessary for consumers to appreciate the nature and costs of the service being offered.** Information covering these core themes can help ensure that consumers are better placed to make informed decisions about adopting m-payments. A close look at the disclosure requirements in the jurisdictions reviewed suggests a convergence on the minimum information which should be disclosed. Based on the practices observed in the jurisdictions, minimum disclosures should include a description of the service offered, the date from which the service is available for use, the price and total cost of the

1 The NPSRs (s.2) adopt the definition of a 'payment service provider' set out in the National Payment System Act 2011, s.2.

2 SC 1991, c 46.

3 The Code was first issued by the Canadian Radio-Television and Telecommunications Commission (CRTC) in 2013 and revised in 2017 <https://crtc.gc.ca/eng/phone/mobile/codesimpl.htm> accessed 10 January 2022.

4 SOR/2021–181. These came into force on 30 June 2022.

service,[5] the charges that may apply, or the method that may be used to determine such charges. It should also cover the potential penalties and risks, available complaints/redress procedures, and termination modalities. Where cooling-off periods apply, this should also be included.

**Disclosure obligations should cover the pre-and post-contractual stages.** Informed decision-making involves the initial decision to sign up for an m-payment service and the subsequent decision to continue using the service. Hence, an ideal comprehensive disclosure regime should cover the pre-and post-contractual stage. The disclosure frameworks in all the countries reviewed contain provisions supporting pre-and post- contractual disclosures. Accordingly, regulators adopting disclosure requirements should explicitly highlight the information that should be disclosed before and after a contract is concluded.

One point to highlight is that it may be helpful for certain disclosures to be accessible to the consumer before they make initial contact with the PSP. Therefore, it is recommended that the minimum disclosures highlighted earlier be available on the PSPs' websites and physical service points. This will allow consumers to compare services before contacting desired providers.

The requirement to provide ongoing disclosures also features in the disclosure frameworks adopted in the three jurisdictions.[6] At a minimum, these will include identifying information for each transaction, such as a payment reference, transaction value, payee identity, account balance and, where possible, updates on the transaction status. These disclosures can help consumers keep track of their transactions which could assist in identifying illegal charges and/or unauthorised transactions.

An important obligation placed on PSPs is to ensure that they disclose any subsequent changes in the terms agreed and the nature of the services provided. This is a necessary obligation to impose on PSPs because it assists consumers in re-evaluating their decision to continue using m-payments. Where a change in the agreed terms substantially conflicts with the commercial expectations of the consumer or jeopardises their financial position, they should be informed of this so they can decide whether to terminate the contractual relationship.

**Disclosures can be lengthy, so key information should be summarised for consumers.** *Chapter 2* emphasised that cognitive limitations impact how consumers process information. This is especially so where there is information overload. To address this, it is pragmatic to require that disclosures covering the key information on an m-payment service are summarised and accessible to consumers. For example, Kenya's Prudential Guidelines on Consumer Protection (PGCP), recommend using a 'key facts' document that summarises key information about

5 This will cover the cost of subscribing (if any), data and/or SMS charges and any additional service charges that may apply.

6 See, Bank Act (Canada), ss.627.62, 627.7, 627.89(4) & (5); NPSRs (Kenya), Regulation 35(1)(c); PSRs (UK), s.50.

a product.[7] Similarly, Canada's Bank Act recommends using prominently displayed information boxes that present key information about a product.[8] This includes information covering the description of the product's features and the applicable charges or penalties.[9] Where oral disclosures are used, banks are expected to draw a customer's attention to the information that would usually be included in the information box.[10]

**Disclosures will only be meaningful if consumers can appreciate the information being provided.** Hence, disclosure frameworks applying to m-payments should be designed to ensure that the information provided is accessible and appropriate. The three jurisdictions reviewed adopt measures supporting this objective. For example, Canada's Bank Act requires that disclosures are made in a language that is clear, simple, and not misleading.[11] To circumvent language barriers, regulators should adopt creative and flexible methods for implementing the disclosure regime. One way to achieve this is by making written disclosures available in alternative languages to support more consumers in accessing the available information. For instance, the UK PSRs, recommend that disclosures can be made in English, or a language agreed by the parties.[12] Oral disclosures may also prove helpful in addressing language and literacy barriers. For example, the Kenya's PGCP recommends that where a consumer is unable to understand English or Swahili, then oral disclosures in a language understood by the consumer may be used.[13] It further recommends using written translations of disclosure documents if it is appropriate and agreed upon by the parties.[14]

**Consumers will benefit from additional opportunities to clarify information disclosed.** Due to cognitive limitations and financial illiteracy, consumers will benefit from further measures designed to support their understanding of the information disclosed. This is particularly important when dealing with a relatively new financial product. Of all the countries reviewed, only Canada includes specific obligations addressing this issue. As highlighted in *Chapter 5*, under the Bank Act, FRFIs are required to provide consumers with a local or toll-free telephone number of an employee or agent of the institution who is knowledgeable about the terms and conditions of the agreement to which the disclosures relate. Such an arrangement is commendable as it provides consumers with an additional

7 Central Bank of Kenya, 'Prudential Guidelines for Institutions Licensed Under the Banking Act – Consumer Protection' (CBK/PG/22), paragraph 3.4.3 <https://www.centralbank.go.ke/wp-content/uploads/2016/08/PRUDENTIAL-GUIDELINES.pdf> accessed 7 October 2021.

8 s.627.57(1).

9 s.627.59.

10 s.627.57(2).

11 s.627.55(1).

12 Regulation 55(1)(d).

13 Paragraph 3.4.2(i)(e).

14 Ibid.

opportunity to consult an expert free of charge and seek further information on the product in question.

**Regulators should design disclosure frameworks with the limitations of mobile devices in mind.** The Financial Consumer Agency of Canada (FCAC)'s thematic review of m-payments highlighted that disclosure frameworks are often not designed to address the inherent limitations of mobile devices, such as small screens and limited storage capacity.[15] With these limitations in mind, regulators should encourage practical measures supporting disclosures on mobile devices. For instance, PSPs should be required to adopt versions of their information boxes or summary boxes which are compatible with display on mobile devices. This would, for example, require that such information boxes adopt large font sizes, easily readable font styles, and a clear layout, making it easy to navigate information on mobile devices. Provision should also be made for consumers to request more detailed information by email or embedded links. Consumers with internet facilities can access the further information requested or linked to the summary document at their convenience on a device with a larger screen, such as a home computer. To cater to a wider range of consumers, the summary provisions should refer to toll-free numbers through which requests could be made for oral explanations and paper copies containing more detailed information.

**Regulators should not overestimate how effective mandatory disclosures are in protecting m-payment consumers.** While disclosures can enable consumers to make better decisions, regulators must recognise its limitations. Discussions in *Chapter 3* highlighted the limits of consumer rationality which suggests that even where mandatory disclosures are in use, they may be inadequate in fully protecting consumers. Kenya's experience with disclosing M-pesa pricing schedules discussed in *Chapter 6* is also particularly instructive.[16] Despite using transparent pricing schedules, the complex information disclosed confused consumers, and uneducated consumers chose to transact on less complex tariffs, effectively limiting their choices.[17] This confirms the concerns documented in academic literature that disclosure regimes can only benefit consumers who are psychologically and intellectually equipped to apply the information provided.[18] Thus, regulators ought to develop other complementary regulatory initiatives

15 Steve Trites, Charles Gibney, and Bruno Lévesque, 'Mobile Payments and Consumer Protection in Canada' (2013 Research Division, Financial Consumer Agency of Canada) p.27 <https://www.canada.ca/content/dam/canada/financial-consumer-agency/migration/eng/resources/researchsurveys/documents/fcac_mobile_payments_consumer_protection_accessible_en.pdf> accessed 27 January 2022.

16 Mark Flaming, Alexander Owino, Katharine McKee, et al., 'Consumer Protection Diagnostic Study (Kenya)' (2011) pp.12–13 <http://s3-eu-central-1.amazonaws.com/fsd-circle/wp-content/uploads/2015/08/30095758/11-02-22_Consumer_diagnostic_study.pdf> accessed 7 October 2021.

17 Ibid.

18 e.g., Omri Ben-Shahar and Carl E Schneider, 'The Failure of Mandated Disclosure' (2011) 159 *University of Pennsylvania Law Review* 647; Geraint Howells, 'The Potential and Limits of Consumer Empowerment by Information' (2005) 32(3) *Journal of Law & Society* 349.

that will assist in presenting a well-rounded response to consumer protection in m-payments.

### *8.2.2 Consumer Education*

Discussions in *Chapter 4* suggested that disclosure regimes may succeed more if consumers are intellectually equipped to appreciate the information disclosed. This can be achieved by adopting well-designed literacy initiatives.

**As a starting point, regulators should recognise that consumers require basic literacy and numeracy skills as a foundation for more specialised consumer financial education.** Thus, general financial literacy objectives and specific initiatives targeting m-payments will need to be complemented by broader initiatives aimed at improving general literacy and numeracy levels.

**In addition to general financial education, consumers will benefit from specific education initiatives targeting m-payments.** Specific initiatives can be advantageous since they complement other regulatory initiatives like disclosures. Disclosures in m-payment services may be better appreciated and acted on by consumers if they have some knowledge of the service. For instance, a consumer aware that third parties can access their mobile payment applications through malicious software may pay more attention to disclosures on how liability for unauthorised transactions will be apportioned. While Canada and Kenya have adopted specific awareness initiatives focused on m-payments, this has not been the case with the United Kingdom. As explained in *Chapter 7* and discussed below, the United Kingdom's failure to adopt any specific initiative may be influenced by the fact that previous thematic reviews did not show any significant evidence of problems associated with the issues of concern to the regulators.

**Regulators should adopt creative ways for furthering financial consumer education goals tailored to meet their populace's needs.** For example, dedicated web pages may be useful in countries with high internet access. Canada adopts this approach as the FCAC's website hosts educative materials focusing on several themes relevant to m-payments. As noted in *Chapter 5*, the FCAC website provides information on how to make m-payments, including information on the supporting technologies.[19] It also highlights the risk associated with m-payments and includes information on how consumers may keep their mobile devices safe.[20] A similar approach is also adopted in provinces like Manitoba.[21]

In countries with limited internet access, other creative options are also available. For example, reference can be made to Kenya's approach in adopting

19 Financial Consumer Agency of Canada, 'Paying with your Mobile Phone' <https://www.canada.ca/en/financial-consumer-agency/services/payment/mobile-payments/paying-with-mobile.html> accessed 10 January 2022.

20 Financial Consumer Agency of Canada, 'Secure the Data on your Mobile Devices' <https://www.getcybersafe.gc.ca/en/secure-your-devices/phones-and-tablets> accessed 10 January 2022.

21 Consumer Protection Office (Manitoba), 'Payments on the Go: Mobile Payments' <https://www.gov.mb.ca/cp/cpo/info/payments_to_go.html> accessed 10 January 2022.

literacy campaigns tailored to the populace's needs. One interesting method adopted by Kenya is the use of TV soap operas to achieve its financial consumer education goals. As seen in *Chapter 6*, at the end of the episodes which convey financial literacy messages, the audience may send a text message requesting a leaflet containing the information discussed.[22] Where banking services have been discussed in the particular episode, the leaflets also include an application allowing the consumers to sign up with the specific bank involved.[23]

Although this approach can help raise consumer awareness about financial products, one must acknowledge that it raises concerns because it could be interpreted as indirect marketing, which would not guarantee that the information discussed is unbiased. Regulators can adopt a modified strategy to address this concern. For example, regulators could sponsor awareness programmes on radio and television which will be perceived as more neutral. They could also include short educational videos circulated on social media. Such programmes or videos should include information on the use, benefits, and current risks associated with adopting m-payments. It should also highlight available service providers and may discuss how they compare against each other. Information on where consumers may access additional information and sign up for a particular service should also be included. Where these programmes are delivered in local languages, it will be easier to reach larger audiences, especially those disadvantaged by literacy and language barriers.

**Empirically backed education initiatives are more likely to be relevant and effective.** Thematic reviews and market studies are important tools that can help inform the direction of proposed education initiatives. They provide empirical data that ensure that regulatory resources are devoted to the most relevant issues. The use of thematic reviews and market studies featured in the three jurisdictions were reviewed. For example, the FCAC's m-payments awareness initiatives have been informed by the results of its 2013 thematic review.[24] The FCAC found that a consumer protection regime focusing on m-payments would only be effective if consumers knew their rights and responsibilities. Thus, the FCAC's focus on explaining the technology supporting m-payments and the options for mitigating security risks directly reflect the findings in its thematic review.

In Kenya, Safaricom's experience with the launch of M-pesa also provides useful pointers. As highlighted in *Chapter 6*, Safaricom included consumer education initiatives in its marketing strategy based on empirical evidence of knowledge gaps observed from its pilot launch.[25] The experience in both

22 Flore-Anne Messy and Chiara Monticone, 'The Status of Financial Education in Africa' (2012) p.34 <https://doi.org/10.1787/5k94cqqx90wl-en> accessed 6 May 2022.

23 Ibid.

24 Trites et al, 'Mobile Payments and Consumer Protection in Canada' (n 15).

25 International Finance Corporation, 'M-Money Chanel Distribution Case – Kenya (Safaricom M-pesa)' p.19 <https://www.ifc.org/wps/wcm/connect/e0d2a9bd-16b9-4a36-8498-0b2650b9af8b/Tool%2B6.7.%2BCase%2BStudy%2B-%2BM-PESA%2BKenya%2B.pdf?MOD=AJPERES&CVID=jkCVy-n> accessed 6 May 2022.

jurisdictions supports the idea that financial education initiatives will be more relevant if they are informed by data highlighting current knowledge gaps and areas of concern.

In the United Kingdom, as noted earlier, the lack of specific education initiatives targeting m-payments can also be explained as reflecting the result of thematic reviews conducted by the Financial Conduct Authority (FCA). The FCA's thematic review suggested that part of the main concerns for the FCA was whether consumers were losing funds owing to fraud and unauthorised transactions.[26] The review indicated that the FCA was satisfied with the efforts taken by firms to educate consumers on securing their devices to minimise fraud.[27] The FCA also stated that it had found no evidence to suggest that consumers were losing money due to unauthorised transactions. Although they recognised the potential for consumer error due to the smaller screen sizes and keypads of mobile devices, they did not find any significant evidence of problems associated with these issues.[28] They were also satisfied that sufficient safeguards were built into mobile-based financial products to mitigate the risk of such errors.[29] Thus, while the FCAC's thematic review in Canada highlighted gaps requiring a targeted response, evidence from the FCA's review in the United Kingdom negated the need for a targeted response.

## 8.3 Withdrawal Rights and Cooling-Off Periods

*Chapter 4* noted that cooling-off periods are important because they give consumers the opportunity to seek out additional information within a specific timeframe. During this period, consumers may withdraw from concluded contracts if they are not optimal. The following key points can be made about cooling-off periods in the context of m-payments.

**A statutory cooling-off period and an accompanying withdrawal right are necessary tools for protecting m-payment consumers.** While cooling-off periods are helpful to all categories of consumers, they are particularly useful to consumers who have been pressured to enter transactions or may be vulnerable due to illiteracy. Cooling-off periods support such consumers by providing them with an opportunity to seek more advice about a product, allowing them to re-evaluate transactions that can have a significant effect on their financial health. PSPs will likely prefer not to include cooling-off periods in their standard term contracts since they introduce uncertainties to otherwise concluded transactions.

26 Financial Conduct Authority, 'Thematic Review: Mobile Banking and Payments' (2014) <https://www.fca.org.uk/publication/thematic-reviews/tr14-15.pdf> accessed 15 June 2022.

27 Ibid. p.10.

28 Examples of such errors would include inputting the wrong payment amount or recipient: Financial Conduct Authority, 'Mobile Banking and Payment: Supporting an Innovative and Secure Market' (2013) p.7 <https://www.fca.org.uk/publication/thematic-reviews/tr13-06.pdf> accessed 15 June 2022.

29 FCA, 'Thematic Review: Mobile Banking and Payments' (n 26) p.11.

Hence, statutory cooling-off periods are desirable in protecting the consumer who has the weaker bargaining power.

**Regulators should explicitly clarify the cooling-off periods and withdrawal rights applying to m-payment services.** Although all the countries reviewed embrace statutory cooling-off periods, it is not always clear if they apply to m-payments. For instance, Kenya's NPSRs are silent on cooling-off periods and withdrawal rights. However, the Kenyan Consumer Protection Act (KCPA) 2012 provides cancellation rights for direct and remote contracts but makes no explicit references to financial/payment services.[30] As discussed in *Chapter 6*, if one interprets a payment services contract as a direct or remote agreement, then cooling-off periods and cancellation rights may be available. However, the conclusion drawn in the chapter was that the Central Bank of Kenya (CBK) needed to expressly clarify whether and how cooling-off periods apply to contracts for payment services.

The situation is not less complex in Canada. At the federal level, the Bank Act distinguishes two categories of financial services and imposes differing cooling-off periods and cancellation rights. The first category covers specific products and services such as retail deposit accounts, deposit type instruments, credit cards, and some prescribed products and services.[31] The second category covers all products and services not included in the first category. As a result, the cooling-off period applying to m-payments will depend on the category under which m-payments fall.

At the provincial level, cooling-off periods are dealt with under provincial consumer protection statutes. As discussed in *Chapter 5*, in most provinces, cooling-off periods only apply to specific contracts, most of which cannot be strictly classified as payment services contracts. The only provincial cooling-off provisions that may be relevant to m-payments involve optional services provided to consumers who are party to a credit agreement. Since banking services are federally regulated, it may explain why provincial statutes are mostly silent on cooling-off periods for financial/payment services contracts. This, however, creates an unpredictable situation because m-payments can be provided by non-FRFIs (other than credit providers), which are regulated by the provinces. Therefore, the likely effect is that consumers served by non-FRFIs may be worse off than those dealing with FRFIs or provincially regulated credit issuers. Any cooling-off period applicable to such consumers will likely depend on their contract with the m-payments provider. However, one possible interpretation of these provincial laws is that although consumers may not enjoy cooling-off periods when subscribing to the m-payment service itself (except where it is an optional service offered by a credit provider), they may enjoy this right where m-payments are used to complete eligible contracts under the provincial laws.

30 See KCPA, Part IV.

31 Bank Act, ss.627.1(1) & (11)(1). The prescribed products can be found under the Financial Consumer Protection Regulations SQR/2021–181 (FCPRs), s.4.

The approach in the United Kingdom is comparatively more straightforward. As shown in *Chapter 7*, there are designated cooling-off periods under the Financial Services (Distance Marketing) Regulations (FSRs) 2004 and the Consumer Contracts (Information, Cancellation and Additional Charges) Regulations (CCRs) 2013 which are relevant to m-payments. Though m-payments are not explicitly mentioned in the FSRs, the definition of 'financial service' adopted under the Regulations covers payment services.[32] The CCRs apply to consumer transactions (not involving the provision of financial services) concluded at a distance or outside a trader's premises.[33] The 14-day cooling-off period under the FSRs will apply directly to m-payment services subscribed to at a distance.[34] On the other hand, the 14-day cooling-off period under the CCRs will cover specific consumer transactions which can be completed with m-payments. The UK approach is preferred as the available cooling-off periods cover the direct subscription to the service and consumer contracts completed using m-payments.

**Consumers should be informed of available cooling-off periods and the accompanying withdrawal rights.** Academic commentary suggests that cooling-off periods will only benefit consumers if they are informed about them.[35] Hence, disclosure frameworks should oblige and incentivise businesses to inform consumers of this right. Of all the countries reviewed, only the UK CCRs link cooling-off periods and cancellation rights to disclosure obligations. Under the CCRs, a consumer's right to cancel is preserved where they are not informed of the right by the trader.[36] Thus, the CCRs' standard cooling-off period may be extended to 12 months, where the seller fails to inform the consumer of the right to cancel.[37] As observed in *Chapter 7*, this approach incentivises traders to comply with the disclosure obligations under the CCRs.

## 8.4 The Regulation of Business Conduct

### *8.4.1 Regulating Unfair Commercial Practices*

Insisting on fair commercial practices ensures that consumer decision-making is not influenced to their detriment and that businesses are incentivised to behave appropriately.[38]

32 Regulation 2.

33 Regulation 5.

34 The FSRs apply to contracts entered at a distance, i.e., a contract for financial services where parties make 'exclusive use of one or more means of distance communication up to and including the time at which the contract is concluded.' Regulation 2.

35 Jeff Sovern, 'Written Notice of Cooling-Off Periods: A Forty-Year Natural Experiment in Illusory Consumer Protection and the Relative Effectiveness of Oral and Written Disclosures' (2014) 75 *University of Pittsburgh Law Review* 333, 356–358.

36 Regulation 31.

37 i.e., 12 months from the end of the standard 14 days cooling-off period; Regulation 31(3).

38 Geraint Howells, Hans-Wolfgang Micklitz, Thomas Wilhelmsson, 'Towards a Better Understanding of Unfair Commercial Practices' (2009) 51(2) *International Journal of Law and Management* 69, 71.

M-payment consumers will benefit from rules regulating the business practices adopted by PSPs. In all the jurisdictions reviewed, there are statutory regimes regulating commercial practices which will apply to PSPs. In Kenya and the United Kingdom, the bulk of the rules are consolidated in a single consumer protection statute, i.e., the Kenyan Consumer Protection Act (KCPA) 2012 and the UK Consumer Protection from Unfair Trading Regulations (CPUTRs) 2008. In Canada, though important rules are contained in the Competition Act 1985 (as amended), which is a federal statute, the bulk of the relevant rules are found in provincial consumer protection statutes.

The main advantage of general rules is that it introduces minimum requirements which apply to businesses in all sectors. In the context of m-payments, this is important as it prevents regulatory arbitrage, which may occur when different rules apply to PSPs who may be traditional or non-traditional financial institutions. For clarity, regulators can emphatically reiterate through published guidance that the general rules apply to all PSPs. For example, the UK's FCA, in published guidance, emphasises that the CPUTRs apply to payment services.[39]

In adopting general rules, the following best practices can be gleaned from the regulatory frameworks in the jurisdictions reviewed.

**Adopting an objective standard for evaluating commercial practices provides clarity in the regulatory framework.** In all three jurisdictions reviewed, unfair or unconscionable commercial practices are prohibited. However, the jurisdictions differ in their approach to evaluating if a commercial practice falls short of the standard expected. In banning unfair commercial practices, the United Kingdom's CPUTRs clearly indicate what 'unfair' connotes in the context of the legislation. A commercial practice is deemed to be unfair if it (1) contravenes the requirements of professional due diligence and (2) materially distorts or is likely to distort an average consumer's economic behaviour.[40] While Kenya's KCPA and KCA prohibit the use of unfair practices and unconscionable practices, respectively, there is no clear test or criteria for determining what is unfair or unconscionable. Both statutes merely provide categories of unfair practices and examples of factors that may be considered in reaching such a finding.

The approach in Canada differs in the provinces. For example, like the United Kingdom, Newfoundland's Consumer Protection and Business Practices Act 2010 (Newfoundland's CPBPA) provides a more precise explanation of what unfairness connotes. Under the Act, a commercial practice is unfair if it has the effect or might reasonably have the effect of deceiving or misleading a consumer.[41] In other provinces, the approach is similar to that taken in Kenya. For example, like the KCPA, British Columbia's Business Practices and Consumer Protection

39 Financial Conduct Authority, 'Payment Services and Electronic Money – Our Approach (The FCA's role under the Payment Services Regulations 2017 and the Electronic Money Regulations 2011)' (2021) paras 8.34–8.40 <https://www.fca.org.uk/publication/finalised-guidance/fca-approach-payment-services-electronic-money-2017.pdf> accessed 18 January 2022.

40 Regulation 3(3).

41 s.7(1).

Act (British Columbia's BPCPA) 2004 provides categories of unfair practices (i.e., deceptive and unconscionable acts or practices) and a list of factors that a court may consider in determining if an act or practice is unconscionable.[42]

The approach taken in the United Kingdom and Newfoundland is preferred as it explicitly provides the criteria for evaluating a commercial practice in issue. In the context of m-payments, this clarifies the standards against which a PSP's activities will be judged.

**A broadly defined standard for evaluating commercial practices will ensure future-proofing.** Where broad standards are used as the basis for evaluating commercial practices, they provide a 'safety net to catch any current or future practices' not categorised or envisaged at the time of developing the rules.[43] The broad definition adopted under the United Kingdom's CPUTRs and Newfoundland's CPBPA focuses on the effect of the practice in question on the consumer's decision-making. This ensures that the rules remain relevant in differing commercial contexts. It also supports future-proofing. This is particularly useful in the face of rapidly changing technology, financial services innovation, and changing consumer behaviour.

A superior approach will combine the approach in the jurisdictions reviewed, i.e., adopting a broad standard and including specific examples of prohibited acts or factors that may be considered in evaluating commercial practices. This is considered a superior approach because it adopts the flexibility provided by broad standards while maintaining a degree of certainty provided by specific examples/ categories of unfair practices.

**Sector-specific rules and regulatory guidance can complement the general framework prohibiting unfair practices.** In all three countries reviewed, general rules are supported by sector-specific requirements. For example, in Kenya, sector-specific rules can be found in the PGCP, which prohibits institutions from engaging in unfair, deceptive and aggressive practices when promoting their products and services.[44] In the United Kingdom, sector-specific rules can be found in the PSRs, FCA Handbook, and accompanying guidance document.[45] For example, the FCA's regulatory guidance confirms that PSPs should avoid giving consumers misleading impressions about the services they offer and should avoid marketing their services in a misleading way.[46]

In Canada, sector-specific rules can also be found in the Bank Act. For example, the Bank Act prohibits banks from using undue pressure or coercion to force a consumer to obtain one product or service from the institution (and its affiliates)

42 s.8(3).

43 Giuseppe B Abbamonte, 'The Unfair Commercial Practices Directive and its General Prohibition' in Stephen Weatherill and Ulf Bernitz (eds), *The Regulation of Unfair Commercial Practices under EC Directive 2005/29: New Rules and New Techniques* (Bloomsbury Publishing 2007) pp.20–21.

44 Paragraph 3.2.1(c)(i).

45 FCA, 'Payment Services and Electronic Money – Our Approach' (n 39) pp.89–95.

46 Ibid. paras 8.35–8.39.

as a condition for obtaining another product or service from the bank.[47] In the context of m-payments, this provision will be useful in discouraging services which, for example, may make the provision of m-payment services to a consumer dependent on purchasing insurance for their mobile device from the bank or its affiliate. In addition, the Bank Act requires that banks establish and implement policies to ensure that products or services offered or sold to consumers[48] are appropriate, having regard to their circumstances, including their financial needs.[49] This provision could discourage the provision of m-payment services funded by an underlying credit line if it would further perpetuate a consumer's over-indebtedness.

**The regulatory framework should support private and public enforcement.** An effective framework should ideally provide consumers with independent statutory rights to redress. However, recognising that private remedies may sometimes be limited, it is also necessary to include arrangements which empower regulators to act on behalf of consumers. In all the jurisdictions reviewed, the regulatory approach, to an extent, adopts a mixture of both forms of enforcement.

Under Kenya's KCPA, consumers are entitled to rescind contracts secured by unfair practices.[50] They may also recover damages.[51] The CBK may also impose administrative sanctions on financial institutions which run foul of their obligations under the PGCP.[52] In the UK, consumers subjected to unfair practices have the right to unwind a contract and get a refund,[53] seek a discount in respect of past or future payments due under the contract,[54] or seek damages.[55] In addition, the Competition and Markets Authority (CMA) and FCA may also carry out enforcement action against PSPs violating CPUTRs.[56]

Consumers in Canadian provinces generally have access to several remedies, including the right to cancel a transaction tainted by unfair practices and a claim for damages.[57] Additionally, in some provinces like Alberta, Newfoundland, and Manitoba, regulators can bring and maintain actions on behalf of consumers

47 Bank Act, s.627.04(a).
48 Other than for business purposes.
49 Bank Act, s.627.06.
50 S.16(1).
51 S.16(2).
52 PGCP, Part VI.
53 Regulation 27E.
54 Regulation 27I.
55 Regulation 27J.
56 Enterprise Act 2002, s.213(5A)(c); See also FCA, 'Payment Services and Electronic Money – Our Approach' (n 39) para.8.40
57 For example, see Alberta's Consumer Protection Act, RSA 2000, c 26.3, s.7(1); British Columbia's Business Practices and Consumer Protection Act, SBC 2004, c 2, s.10; Ontario's Consumer Protection Act SO 2002, c 30, s.18 and Prince Edward Island's Business Practices Act RSPEI 1988 c B-7, s.4(1).

affected by unfair practices.[58] Alberta's Consumer Protection Act 2000 (Alberta's CPA) goes a step further by empowering consumer organisations to take action against defaulting suppliers.[59] Thus, consumer organisations can step in where public agencies are unable (or unwilling) to act.[60] As pointed out in *Chapter 5*, empowering consumer organisations is a laudable approach as they can provide useful checks against regulatory capture.[61] They may also provide collective representation where individual loss may be small, but the provider, in aggregate, may have caused significant detriment.[62]

### *8.4.2 Regulating Contract Terms*

#### *8.4.2.1 Standard Term Contracts and Fairness*

As with most payment services, standard form contracts are used in the m-payments industry. Clear rules are therefore needed to regulate the use of such contracts. All the countries reviewed in *Chapter 3* adopt some form of regulatory rules covering the use of contract terms. However, there are differences in approach. In Canada and Kenya, the regulation of contract terms is subsumed under the general frameworks regulating business practices. On the other hand, the United Kingdom regulates contract terms directly through dedicated provisions in the Consumer Rights Act 2015 (CRA).

While the use of unfair contract terms broadly qualifies as an unfair commercial practice, it is appropriate to design specific rules regulating contract terms. This is because contract terms create binding obligations for the parties involved. In situations where contractual parties are subject to unequal bargaining positions, there is room for exploitation of the weaker party. This is especially so in the provision of financial services where the information available to contractual parties is unequal, and the contract terms are often not individually negotiated. This reality justifies the need for specific rules governing contract terms. Where such rules are designed, regulators and policymakers may consider the following points:

**The evaluation of contract terms should be based on objective guidelines.** To promote clarity in the regulatory framework, it is desirable to clearly identify the benchmarks for evaluating if a contract term is fair. Of the three jurisdictions reviewed, the United Kingdom takes the most direct approach on this. The CRA

58 Alberta's CPA (n 57), s.15; Newfoundland's Consumer Protection and Business Practices Act SNL 2009 c 31.1, s.104(1)(a); Manitoba's Business Practices Act 1990 CCSM, c B120, s.24(1)(a).

59 s.17.

60 The inability to act may be for several reasons such as lack of resources (funds, time, and expert personnel), regulatory capture and changing political tide.

61 Ayres and Braithwaite refer to this as 'tripartism' – where consumer organisations become 'fully fledged third player(s)' in the regulatory system; Ian Ayres and John Braithwaite, 'Tripartism: Regulatory Capture and Empowerment' (1991) 16 *Law & Social Inquiry* 435, 441 & 449.

62 Iain Ramsay, *Consumer Law and Policy* (3rd edn, Hart Publishing 2012) p.153.

adopts a fairness test for assessing contract terms. The test comprises three broad elements. The first element requires that the terms must not be contrary to good faith. The second element emphasises that there must be a significant imbalance in the rights and obligations applicable to both parties. The third element emphasises that the imbalance should be to the detriment of the consumer. These elements are assessed together and are evaluated in the context of the contract as a whole and all the circumstances in which it was entered into.[63]

In Canada, although the regulation of contract terms is subsumed under the broader regulation of unfair terms, certain provisions in provincial consumer protection statutes reflect some of the elements of the United Kingdom's fairness. For example, Alberta's CPA notes that it is an unfair practice for a supplier to include terms or conditions in a consumer transaction that are harsh, oppressive, or excessively one-sided.[64] British Columbia's BCPA emphasises that a commercial practice is unconscionable if the terms or conditions adopted in a consumer transaction are so harsh or adverse to the consumer as to be inequitable.[65] The focus on the contractual terms being excessively one-sided reflects the second element of the United Kingdom's fairness test, which emphasises a significant imbalance in the rights and obligations applicable to both parties. Similarly, references to the contractual terms being oppressive or inequitable replicate the third element of the UK fairness test, which emphasises that the imbalance in the contractual obligations must be to the detriment of the consumer.

Under Kenya's KCPA, one factor for determining whether a representation is unconscionable is if the representation has been made with the knowledge that the contract terms are so 'adverse to the consumer as to be inequitable.'[66] Again, this reflects elements of the UK fairness test, emphasising that the imbalance in the contractual obligations must be to the detriment of the consumer.

The thematic similarities show that similar factors are central to evaluating the fairness of contract terms. However, the explicit approach taken by the United Kingdom is preferred since it provides more clarity.

**The objective guidelines for evaluating contract terms should be broadly drafted to address the mischief targeted.** One advantage of adopting broadly drafted guidelines is that it introduces the flexibility required to respond to varying contractual practices, which are detrimental to the consumer interest. Some firms will seek to employ disingenuous tactics when drafting contract terms to circumvent regulatory rules. Broadly drafted guidelines make it more difficult for such firms to succeed in their efforts. In addition, broadly drafted guidelines are more likely to be responsive to changing contractual practices not contemplated

63 Competition and Markets Authority, 'Unfair Contract Terms Guidance: Guidance on the Unfair terms provisions in the Consumer Rights Act 2015' (2015) paragraphs 2.10 & 2.18. <https://assets.publishing.service.gov.uk/government/uploads/system/uploads/attachment_data/file/450440/Unfair_Terms_Main_Guidance.pdf> accessed 21 December 2021.

64 RSA 2000, c 26.3, s.6(3)(c).

65 SBC 2004, c 2, s.8(3)(e).

66 s.13(2)(f).

at the time of enacting the legal rules. This is particularly relevant in the context of financial services innovation like m-payments which introduce new business models and contractual arrangements.

The UK fairness test comprises broad elements that can serve the abovementioned purposes. Judicial interpretation of the fairness test also confirms this by emphasising that the test aims to ensure that a 'supplier should not, whether deliberately or unconsciously, take advantage of the consumer.'[67] The broad fairness test is also complemented by other provisions which support the general objective of protecting consumers. For example, the CRA provides that contract terms will be evaluated in the context of the contract as a whole and the circumstances in which it was entered into.[68] This emphasises a comprehensive approach which focuses on both the making and substance of the contract. The CRA also clarifies that an unfair term will not be binding on a consumer.[69] Cumulatively, this approach supports the broad objective of protecting consumers in contractual settings irrespective of the specific industry, product, or service involved.

**Blacklists and greylists are useful mechanisms for promoting certainty and providing clear signposts to firms.** In addition to adopting objective criteria for re-evaluating contract terms, it may be useful to adopt the use of blacklists and greylists. A blacklist outrightly invalidates specific unfair contract terms considered unfair in all circumstances. A greylist only raises a presumption of unfairness when certain terms are used. In such situations, the supplier is responsible for rebutting the presumption of unfairness. As pointed out in *Chapter 4*, the advantage of this approach is that it creates certainty and provides clear pointers to firms on the kind of terms that are unacceptable or suspicious. A blacklist also preserves regulatory resources by removing the need to establish that blacklisted contract terms are unfair.

The United Kingdom favours this approach and adopts the use of blacklists and greylists. On their own, blacklists and greylists can be criticised for being relatively inflexible in dealing with unanticipated terms.[70] Also, they can leave room for the continued use of unfair terms since suppliers can exploit the use of disingenuous drafting to avoid falling within the scope of specific blacklisted terms. However, these criticisms are addressed when such lists are used in addition to a broadly drafted standard for assessing fair terms. As indicated earlier, the broad standard can cope with terms that may be drafted disingenuously to avoid contravening specifically listed terms. It can also respond to contractual practices that were not anticipated at the time of drafting the legislation.

67 CMA, Unfair Contract Terms Guidance (n 63) para.2.23.

68 S.62(5).

69 S.62(1).

70 Colin Scott and Julia Black, *Cranston's Consumers and the Law* (3rd edn, Butterworths 2000) p.97.

**Sector-specific rules and regulatory guidance can help contextualise the application of a general framework.** It is recognised that in more specialised transactions such as m-payments, it will be necessary to clarify and contextualise the application of the proposed unfair terms regime. This can be done through specific rules enacted for the financial services sector or guidance issued by the relevant regulators. In Kenya, for example, the PGCP directs firms not to include unconscionable or unreasonable terms in their agreements with consumers.[71] The Canadian Bank Act prohibits FRFIs from taking advantage of consumers.[72] This obligation is broad enough to prohibit the use of unfair terms in the provision of m-payments.

Although the CMA is the primary consumer protection regulator in the United Kingdom, the FCA enforces the unfair terms regulatory framework in the financial services market. In addition to the CRA and regulatory documents issued by the CMA, PSPs (under the FCA's supervision) must also consider the Unfair Contract Terms and Consumer Notices Regulatory Guide (UNFCOG) issued by the FCA.[73] The UNFCOG explains how the FCA will use its powers under the CRA in relation to unfair terms used in the financial services sector.[74] PSPs must also consider the FCA's unfair contract terms library, which is a repository of its publications regarding unfair contract terms.[75] In addition, the FCA's guidance document accompanying the PSRs clarifies the effect of specific provisions in the EMRs and PSRs, which impact the use of specific contract terms in the provision of payment services.[76]

**The framework will benefit from effective monitoring and enforcement mechanisms.** Policy responses targeting unfair terms will only be meaningful if effective monitoring and enforcement mechanisms are in place.[77] One way of ensuring effective enforcement is entrusting a public agency with the authority to monitor consumer contracts and take legal actions challenging offending terms.[78] The United Kingdom adopts this approach. As stated above, while the CMA is the primary consumer protection regulator, the CRA recognises that the CMA shares

71 Paragraph 3.2.1(c)(v).

72 Bank Act, s.627.04(b).

73 Financial Conduct Authority, 'FCA Handbook: Unfair Contract terms and Consumer Notices Regulatory Guide' (UNFCOG) <https://www.handbook.fca.org.uk/handbook/UNFCOG/1/?view=chapter> accessed 20 December 2021.

74 FCA, 'UNFCOG' (n 73) 1.1.1.

75 FCA, UNFCOG (n 73) 2.1.1; Financial Conduct Authority, 'Unfair Contract Terms Library' <https://www.fca.org.uk/firms/unfair-contract-terms/library> accessed 21 October 2021.

76 For example, see the conditions for the redemption of e-money set out in the Electronic Money Regulations 2011, Regulation 40; FCA, Payment Services and Electronic Money – Our Approach (n 39) paras.8.349–8.351.

77 OECD, 'Consumer Policy Toolkit' (2010) p.99 <http://www.oecd-ilibrary.org/governance/consumer-policy-toolkit_9789264079663-en> accessed 6 September 2021.

78 Christian Twigg-Flesner, 'Standard Terms in Consumer Contracts: The Challenges of Law reform in English law' in Larry DiMatteo and Martin Hogg, *Comparative Contract Law: British and American Perspectives* (OUP 2015) p.434.

concurrent enforcement powers with other sector-specific regulators such as the FCA.[79] To reduce the duplication of effort, the FCA enforces the unfair terms regulatory framework in the financial services market.

One important enforcement power given to regulators under the CRA is the authority to pre-emptively challenge unfair terms. As Lord Steyn points out, this approach can prove important in preventing the use of such terms and encouraging a change in business behaviour.[80] Importantly, it also recognises the limitations of private enforcement by consumers. Private enforcement by individuals may be less than efficient as it is dependent on the individual knowing their rights and having the required resources to enforce them, which may not always be the case.[81]

Furthermore, the CRA imposes a statutory duty on courts to evaluate unfair terms even if none of the parties raises the issue. Courts are charged with carrying out this evaluation provided there is sufficient legal and factual material enabling them to do so.[82] This provides an additional layer of vigilance in the use of contract terms. As with the pre-emptive actions by regulators, it also helps address the limitations of private enforcement.

The enforcement of contract terms regulation can be further strengthened if independent third parties like consumer organisations can challenge the use of unfair terms.[83] Under the UK CRA, the Consumers Association is recognised as a regulator.[84] Thus, the Consumers Association may apply for an injunction against a defaulting firm. In addition, as highlighted in Section 8.4.1, in Canadian provinces like Alberta, consumer organisations are empowered to take action against suppliers engaged in unfair practices, including the use of terms in consumer contracts that are harsh, oppressive, or excessively one-sided.[85] Empowering certified consumer associations to take part in the enforcement process can be significant because these associations are often closer to consumers and may be more effective at gathering information about unfair contract terms. They may also ensure that consumer interests are protected when public enforcers are unable or unwilling to act.

79 Schedule 3, paragraph 8. Note also that under Part 8 of the Enterprise Act 2002, a number of regulators are designated as having the power to enforce consumer legislation.

80 *Director General of Fair Trading v. First National Bank Plc.* [2001] UKHL 52 at paragraph 33.

81 Peter Cartwright, 'Putting the Law in Context' in Peter Cartwright (ed.), *Consumer Protection in Financial Services* (1999 Kluwer Law International) pp.15–16.

82 s.71(2) & (3); Alec Samuels, 'The Consumer Rights Act 2015' (2016) 3 *Journal of Business Law* 159, 177; see the 2009 decision of the Court of Justice of the European Union in *Pannon GSM Zrt. v. Erzsébet Sustikné Győrfi* (C-243/08).

83 Michael Schillig, 'Inequality of Bargaining Power Versus a Market for Lemons: Legal Paradigm Change and the Court of Justice's Jurisprudence on Directive 93/13 on Unfair Contract Terms' (2008) 33(3) *European Law Review* 336, 342.

84 See Consumer Rights Act 2015, Schedule 3, paragraph 8(1)(k).

85 Alberta's CPA, s.17.

### *8.4.2.2 Transparency*

**Regulators should encourage the transparent use of contract terms.** A key part of regulating contract terms involves a requirement of enhanced transparency.[86] Transparency in this sense improves fair and open dealing by requiring that contract terms are drafted in simple language and that those terms with significant legal implications are brought to the attention of the consumer. The objective of the transparency requirement is also linked to disclosure regulations. This is because both regulatory responses broadly aim to improve consumer awareness of relevant issues impacting their interests in a proposed transaction. All the jurisdictions reviewed encourage the transparent use of contract terms. However, the United Kingdom is the only one incorporating this requirement as part of the framework for regulating terms regulation.

**Regulators should clarify what role transparency plays in the regulation of contract terms.** Apart from encouraging the transparent use of contract terms, regulators must also clarify what role transparency plays in the overall regulation of contract terms. It should be made clear whether transparency will play a legitimising function on its own or form part of the broader considerations for determining if the use of a contract term is fair. Reference could be made to the approach in the United Kingdom. In the guidance accompanying the CRA, the CMA clarifies that transparency is both a requirement on its own and a fundamental part of fairness.[87] However, although transparency is important, it is not sufficient on its own to legitimise an otherwise unfair term.[88] This is because good faith focuses on both the effect/purpose of contract terms and the form in which they are presented.[89]

The CMA's position is supported by academics like Willett, who argue that transparency should not be capable of legitimising unfair terms because consumers are still unlikely to read terms even when they are transparent.[90] The CMA's approach is pragmatic because the obvious limitations of consumer rationality, illiteracy, and language barriers make it inappropriate for a term to be legitimised solely because it is transparent.

Regulators will also need to clarify how a failure to meet the transparency requirement affects the validity of a term. In resolving this, reference can once again be made to the CMA's position on this. The CMA suggests that failing the transparency test does not necessarily imply that a term is unenforceable independent of the overall fairness test.[91] However, where any ambiguity arises

86 Geraint Howells and Stephen Weatherill, *Consumer Protection Law* (2nd edn, Ashgate 2005) p.25.

87 CMA, 'Unfair Contract Terms Guidance' (n 63) para.2.4.

88 Ibid, para 2.42.

89 Ibid, para.5.14.5; Chris Willett, 'The Functions of Transparency in regulating Contract Terms: UK and Australian Approaches' (2011) 60(2) *International & Comparative Law Quarterly* 355, 384.

90 Willett, 'The Functions of Transparency in regulating Contract Terms' (n 89) p.358.

91 Competition and Markets Authority, 'Unfair Contract Terms Explained' (2015) para.38 <https://assets.publishing.service.gov.uk/government/uploads/system/uploads/attachment_data/file/450410/Unfair_Terms_Explained.pdf> accessed 21 December 2021.

about the meaning of a term, it should be resolved in favour of the consumer. This embodies the *contra proferentem* rule of construction adopted in Common Law jurisdictions and other legal systems with foundations in Roman law.[92] This rule has been codified under the CRA and also forms part of the contract law interpretation principles recognised in Canada and Kenya.

### *8.4.3 Regulating False and Misleading Information*

To prevent the manipulation of consumer decision-making, authorities must prohibit the use of false and misleading information. When innovative services like m-payments are introduced, it is necessary to ensure that PSPs do not mislead consumers about their services. In tackling this issue, regulators can consider some identified best practices identified from the regulatory efforts in the countries reviewed.

**Regulatory frameworks tackling unfair commercial practices should include specific provisions targeting the use of false and misleading information.** Although a broad standard for evaluating commercial practices will cover a wide range of unfair practices, it is helpful also to include specific provisions addressing the use of false and misleading practices. The regulation of false and misleading information is given specific attention in the three jurisdictions reviewed.

In Canada, in addition to the provisions under provincial consumer protection statutes, the Competition Act prohibits using false and misleading representations that promote the supply/use of a product or a supplier's business interest.[93] In Kenya, the KCPA targets false representations, which could be misleading or deceptive[94] and unconscionable.[95] In the United Kingdom, to regulate the use of false and misleading information, the CPUTRs criminalise two categories of practices: 'misleading actions' and 'misleading omissions.' While the former deals more with the active use of false information, the latter deals with the omission of material information.

As is the case with the regulation of unfair practices, the preferred approach is to adopt general rules which apply to all sectors. This introduces minimum requirements which apply to all businesses, including PSPs.

**The regulatory framework should reflect the broader regulatory aim of supporting informed consumer decision-making.** Regulators can support informed decision-making by requiring that PSPs (1) disclose certain information (positive information response) and (2) refrain from providing false and misleading information or omitting material information (negative information response).

92 Joanna McCunn, 'The Contra Proferentem Rule: Contract Law's Great Survivor' (2019) 39(3) *Oxford Journal of Legal Studies* 483, 485

93 See ss.52(1) & 74.01.

94 s.12; where a person has in good faith published and distributed such representations in the ordinary course of business, they will not be guilty of non-compliance; s.15(3).

95 s.13.

In adopting negative information responses, regulators can support informed decision-making by ensuring that regulatory rules focus on the impact of a PSP's practice on consumer decision-making. The United Kingdom takes an explicit approach in this regard by focusing on how the provision of false or misleading information or the omission of material information may impact a consumer's transactional decision.

As earlier stated, the CPUTRs target two categories of practices, i.e., 'misleading actions' and 'misleading omissions.' A commercial activity would be misleading if (1) it contains false information or presents information in a way that is likely to deceive the average consumer and (2) it causes or is likely to cause an average consumer to take a transactional decision that they would otherwise not have taken.[96] Here the second requirement makes it clear that the impact on consumer decision-making is a central focus of the regulatory action.

Regarding misleading omissions, a commercial practice is a misleading omission if it omits or hides material information, provides it in a way that is unclear, unintelligible, ambiguous, or untimely, fails to identify its commercial intent.[97] To qualify, such practices must also cause (or be likely to cause) an average consumer to take a transactional decision they would not have otherwise taken.[98] The CPUTRs also define material information to include information that the average consumer needs according to the context to make informed decisions. This confirms the focus on the broader regulatory goal of supporting consumer decision-making.

**The regulatory framework should target a broad range of activities impacting consumer information.** One way to prevent the use of false and misleading information is to adopt broad terminology covering a wide range of activities impacting the information available to consumers. For example, in Canada, the CCA focuses on false and misleading representations.[99] The choice of terminology appears deliberate. Before legislative amendments were made to the CCA, the conduct targeted was 'misleading advertising.' The current focus on misleading representations brings more practices under scrutiny because 'representations' is an arguably broader term which can cover a wide range of statements, including those made through direct mandated disclosures and advertising. Similar broad terminology, i.e., 'representations,' is used in the KCPA.[100]

The CPUTRs go further than the CCA by including the misleading omissions category. As seen earlier, misleading omissions cover attempts to omit or hide material information. It also covers the provision of such information in a way that is clear, unintelligible, or ambiguous.[101] While not recognising an independent

96 Regulation 5(2).
97 Regulation 6.
98 Ibid.
99 See ss.52(1) & 74.01.
100 KCPA, ss.12 & 13.
101 Regulation 6.

category covering misleading omissions, the KCPA similarly acknowledges that false, misleading, and deceptive representations include the failure to state a material fact if such failure deceives or tends to deceive.[102] By targeting information actively provided and deliberately omitted, the CPUTRs and KCPA ensure broad regulatory coverage of obligations on both ends of the information spectrum (i.e., the positive obligation to provide information and the negative obligation not to omit material information).

**An objective reference point will assist in evaluating the impact of potentially false/misleading information.** In many situations, courts and regulators will have no difficulty determining that a statement is false, deceptive, or misleading. However, there will be more complex situations where a disputed statement is not outrightly false, misleading, or deceptive. In such situations, courts and regulators will have the task of determining the message actually received by consumers and what importance they attach to it.[103] This is not an easy task as consumers are bound to construe things differently. One way of addressing this issue is to include mechanisms which ensure that the disputed information can be assessed objectively.

Of the three jurisdictions reviewed, only the United Kingdom includes a specific mechanism addressing this issue. The CPUTRs adopt the 'average consumer,' a hypothetical person, as the objective benchmark for determining the effect of a commercial practice under scrutiny. The average consumer is understood to be 'reasonably well informed, reasonably observant and circumspect.'[104] Although this is not a perfect standard, it provides a useful normative reference which aids in assessing the effect of commercial practices.

The application of an objective standard should be designed to recognise the differing circumstances of consumers and the particular contexts of a given jurisdiction. For example, the CPUTRs apply a modified standard which recognises that certain groups of consumers may be particularly vulnerable due to their mental or physical infirmity, age, or credulity.[105] In such situations, the reference to the average consumer is interpreted as referring to the average member of that group.[106]

In countries where language and literacy barriers are significant, these factors should be explicitly recognised in the evaluations determining the effect of information communicated to consumers. In such circumstances, even where a modified normative reference point is missing, the regulatory framework could alternatively require that courts and regulators consider whether a firm providing information knew or ought to have known that the intending recipient was disadvantaged due to the inability to understand the language of communication.

102 s.12(2)(n).
103 OECD, 'Consumer Policy Toolkit' (n 77) p.38.
104 Regulation 2(2).
105 Regulation 2(5)(a).
106 Regulation 2(5)(b).

Reference may be made to the KCPA in this regard. The KCPA provides that a representation may be unconscionable where it is made by a person who ought to know that the consumer cannot reasonably protect their interests due to disability, ignorance, illiteracy, or inability to understand the language of an agreement.[107]

## 8.5 Liability Rules

Liability regimes are a contentious issue in m-payments because of the numerous parties involved and the different funding sources that may be used. Based on the policies adopted in the countries reviewed, regulators and policymakers should consider the following points when designing the liability rules applying to m-payments.

**Liability rules in m-payment should focus on promoting certainty, not uniformity.** While it is attractive to have standardised liability rules applying to all m-payment transactions, it is not realistic. This is because the nature of the relationship underlying the payment instruments funding m-payments differs significantly. For instance, credit and debit cards are subject to different contractual arrangements, which is reflected in differing risk allocation rules. While minimum liability rules covering issues such as unauthorised transactions were embraced in the jurisdictions reviewed, there were also allowances for variations owing to the underlying funding source. For example, in Canada, the FCAC acknowledges that consumers will generally not have to pay for unauthorised transactions but concedes that the financial institutions which have issued the underlying debit or credit card funding the transactions will have specific policies protecting consumers. While m-payments funded by credit cards will be subject to liability rules set out in the Bank Act, the liability rules applying to debit card-funded transactions will be determined by the Debit Card Code.[108] Similarly, in the United Kingdom, despite the minimum liability rules contained in the PSRs, liability rules contained in the Consumer Credit Act 1974 will continue to apply to transactions funded by credit cards.[109]

Thus, in developing liability rules covering m-payment transactions, it will be more pragmatic for regulators to concentrate on ensuring certainty rather than uniformity. As discussed in *Chapter 4*, the economic goals for risk allocation will be better served where the rules governing the allocation of risks are clear.

**Disclosure obligations should underpin the liability framework.** It is suggested that disclosures will play a vital role in ensuring that liability rules are clear. Thus, it is reasonable to require that PSPs disclose applicable risk allocation rules to consumers. This is particularly important because consumers

107 s.13(2(a).

108 Bank Act, s.627.33(1); The Canadian Code of Practice for Consumer Debit Card Services, paragraph 5 <https://www.canada.ca/en/financial-consumer-agency/services/industry/laws-regulations/debit-card-code-conduct.html> accessed 9 January 2022.

109 FCA, 'Payment Services and Electronic Money – Our Approach' (n 39) para.8.196.

may wrongly assume that the liability rules applying to other traditional payment services also apply to m-payments. Disclosing the applicable liability rules also supports informed decision-making since consumers are made aware of the risks they are agreeing to bear. For example, under the UK PSRs, PSPs are required to disclose a consumer's liability for unauthorised transactions.

While PSPs are expected to disclose the liabilities of the consumers in all the three jurisdictions reviewed, only the UK PSRs establish a more explicit link between the disclosure obligations imposed on the PSP and the liability framework. Specifically, the PSRs' liability regime for unauthorised transactions is linked to the mandatory disclosure regime. For example, the PSRs provide that, where relevant, PSPs are required to disclose what steps a consumer must take to keep a payment instrument safe.[110] They must also disclose how and within what period the consumer is required to notify them of an unauthorised transaction.[111] Where the PSP has failed to make such disclosures, then the PSP remains liable even where the consumer fails to notify them of an unauthorised transaction.[112] Thus, the notification requirement, which is tied to the disclosure regime, plays a central role in allocating liability.

**The liability framework should include minimum rules applying to unauthorised payments.** The core of the contractual relationship between a PSP and consumers rests on the performance of the authorised instructions given to the former by the latter. Hence, unauthorised transactions are a key area of concern in the provision of payment services. With m-payments, security risks involving the theft of mobile devices and malicious payment software increase the chances of unauthorised payments. Consequently, at a minimum, regulators should clarify how risks and losses will be apportioned in the event of an unauthorised transaction.

Minimum rules should be set in a regulatory or legislative document and not solely determined by contracts. This is because PSPs offering standard form contracts are more likely to include risk allocation rules tilting in their favour. In all the three countries reviewed, liability rules for unauthorised transactions are specifically addressed in legislative and regulatory documents. Generally, PSPs are held to be liable for unauthorised transactions.[113]

Since authorisation is a central issue, one key point that should be explicitly addressed is the scope of what amounts to an unauthorised transaction. This is important because unauthorised transactions could cover straightforward situations where a third party has illegally accessed a consumer's payment account without any fault of the consumer. Unauthorised transactions could also result from more complex situations where a consumer's gross negligence in securing

110 Schedule 4, paragraph 5(a).

111 Schedule 4, paragraph 5(e).

112 Regulation 74(2).

113 Kenya NPSRs, Regulation 28(5); UK PSRs, Regulation 76; Canada Bank Act, s.627.33(1); Canada's Debit Card Code (n 108) para.5(3).

their authentication details has led to illegal access. The Kenyan NPSRs and the UK PSRs address both situations. Under both regulations, a consumer is not liable for unauthorised transactions that have occurred without their fault. However, the presence of fault (e.g., gross negligence and/or fraud) would mean that the consumer is liable for losses.[114]

**Contractual risk allocation rules should be subject to the general frameworks regulating contract terms.** It is unrealistic to expect a regulatory or legislative document to exhaustively contain all the risk allocation rules applying to m-payment transactions. Hence, one can assume that some liability rules will be set out in the contracts entered. One popular method for determining contractual risk allocation includes using exclusion/limitation of liability clauses. Since standard form contracts entrench the unequal bargaining power between the contractual parties, such clauses should be subject to the rules regulating the use of contract terms. Of the three jurisdictions reviewed, only the United Kingdom unequivocally makes it clear that the regulatory framework governing the use of contract terms will also apply to PSPs.[115]

## 8.6 Dispute Resolution

*Chapter 4* highlighted that the ability to file complaints and obtain redress is an important aspect of consumer protection. Academic literature confirms that efficient redress frameworks also increase consumer trust apart from having a deterrent effect on businesses.[116] Since m-payments are a relatively new service in many jurisdictions, the availability of redress frameworks will help boost consumer confidence. This is particularly important for financially excluded consumers who may be accessing formal financial services for the first time. Therefore, regulators should ensure that m-payment consumers can access affordable, fair, and expeditious complaints handling processes. In meeting this objective, the following points should be considered.

### *8.6.1 Internal Dispute Resolution Procedures*

**Regulators should require that m-payment providers implement effective internal dispute resolution procedures.** All the countries reviewed require that PSPs set up internal redress mechanisms. Key areas of convergence suggest certain minimum obligations that should be placed on PSPs. These include: (1) the internal redress system should be available free of charge to m-payment consumers, (2) the internal redress procedures should be disclosed to consumers,

114 NPSRs, Regulation 28(5); PSRs, Regulation 77(3)(b).

115 See FCA, 'Payment Services and Electronic Money – Our Approach (n 39) paras 8.32, 8.33, 8.87.

116 Stefan Wrbka, 'European Consumer Protection Law, Quo Vadis? – Thoughts on the Compensatory Collective Redress Debate' in Stefan Wrbka, Steven Van Uytsel, et al. (eds), *Collective Actions: Enhancing Access to Justice and reconciling Multi-Layer Interests* (Cambridge University Press 2012) p.32.

(3) complaints should be resolved within specific timelines disclosed to the consumer, and (4) where complaints cannot be resolved internally, consumers should be informed of available avenues for pursuing their claim externally.

**Designated officers should be responsible for implementing a PSP's internal dispute resolution mechanisms.** Appointing specific officers to oversee the PSP's dispute resolution policy guarantees that appropriate attention is devoted to meeting the dispute resolution obligation. This is because it ensures that specific persons are responsible and accountable for implementing effective internal dispute resolution procedures. The United Kingdom and Canada explicitly require that specific persons must be appointed to oversee the implantation of the firm's dispute resolution obligations.[117] These officers must be personnel with the requisite authority to meet this responsibility.[118] Guidance from the FCAC also requires that there should be evidence that designated officers are adequately trained and that their skills are appropriate for carrying out the tasks required.[119] The training requirement is notably important in m-payments, as dispute resolution officers ought to know how to resolve the possible complaints they may receive.

**Internal dispute resolution data should feed broader regulatory objectives.** Regulators will need to decide what role individualised internal redress procedures play within the broader consumer protection regime. There is a clear attempt to link internal dispute procedures to wider regulatory objectives in Kenya and the United Kingdom. Hence, both jurisdictions require that these internal procedures be designed to enable PSPs to identify and remedy any recurring and/or systemic problems.[120] The United Kingdom goes a step further than Kenya by providing clear guidelines on how firms may meet this responsibility.[121] For instance, firms are advised to collect and analyse information on disputes received to identify the root causes of problems and remedy them. This approach can assist with gathering information about any systemic issues arising in the adoption of m-payments. This will be particularly relevant in m-payments since the service is facilitated by constantly changing technology which can lead to unexpected problems. Dispute resolution data can also point to key issues which should prompt the internal re-modelling of business practices and in more significant cases, outright regulatory intervention.

117 Bank Act (Canada), s. 627.43(1)(b); Financial Conduct Authority, 'Dispute Resolution Complaints Sourcebook (DISP)' DISP 1.3.7R <https://www.handbook.fca.org.uk/handbook/DISP.pdf> accessed 1 May 2022.

118 DISP 1.3.7(2) & (3)R; Financial Consumer Agency of Canada, 'Guideline on Complaint-Handling Procedures for Banks and Authorized Foreign Banks' (2022) part III(16 https://www.canada.ca/en/financial-consumer-agency/services/industry/commissioner-guidance/complaint-handling-procedures-banks.html> accessed 20 February 2022; Financial Consumer Agency of Canada, 'Internal Dispute Resolution' (2013) paras 1.2 <https://www.canada.ca/en/financial-consumer-agency/services/industry/commissioner-guidance/guidance-12.html> accessed 14 January 2022.

119 FCAC, 'Guideline on Complaint-Handling Procedures' (n 118) part III(18); FCAC, 'Internal Dispute Resolution' (n 118) para.1.3.

120 DISP 1.3.3R; PGCP (Kenya) paragraph 4.6.

121 DISP 1.3.3B.

### *8.6.2 External ADR Mechanisms*

**External dispute resolution procedures should be available and disclosed to m-payment consumers.** Consumers should be able to access external dispute resolution avenues if PSPs cannot resolve their complaints. Consumers must also be aware of the availability of such external procedures. In all the countries reviewed, provisions support consumer access to external dispute resolution mechanisms. For example, in Canada, all banks and federal credit unions must be members of an 'External Complaints Body' (ExCB),[122] which consumers can approach when internal dispute resolution fails. In Kenya, the NPSRs permit customers to approach the CBK when dissatisfied with the internal handling of a complaint.[123] In the United Kingdom, m-payment users can approach the Financial Ombudsman Service (FOS) with any unresolved complaints.

**A financial ombudsman with a broad mandate will benefit m-payment consumers.** Of the three jurisdictions reviewed, only Kenya does not have a financial services ombudsman. As noted in *Chapter 6*, since the CBK receives complaints from consumers, it appears to play an indirect ombudsman role – an arrangement that is less than optimal considering the breadth of its core responsibilities. In the United Kingdom and Canada, ombudsman services are available to m-payment users. There are also certain points of convergence. For example, available ombudsman services are generally funded by a levy on the industry. Consumers are also expected to exhaust internal dispute resolution mechanisms before approaching the ombudsman.

However, the institutional arrangements in both countries differ significantly. In Canada, there is no statutory ombudsman. At the federal level, multiple alternative dispute resolution organisations approved to act as ExCBs and supervised by the FCAC provide ombudsman services. Their decisions are not binding, and their mandate is limited to FRFIs like banks and federal credit unions. M-payment consumers served by provincially regulated PSPs will have to contact ombudsman services often established by industry associations if they are available.

In contrast, the UK FOS is a statutorily backed ombudsman service with a compulsory jurisdiction covering all PSPs operating in the UK. This means that m-payment consumers will enjoy uniform access to the FOS irrespective of the status of the PSP. Furthermore, unlike Canadian ExCBs, the findings of the FOS are binding.[124] The procedural rules are also favourable to the consumer. For instance, although the determinations of the FOS are binding on businesses and enforceable in court, consumers retain the right to reject the ombudsman's determination and further pursue the matter in court.[125]

122 Bank Act, 627.48(4).

123 Regulation 40(5).

124 Financial Services Markets Act 2000 (as amended), s.228(5); see *Clark v. In Focus Asset Management & Tax Solutions* [2014] EWCA Civ 118.

125 PE Morris, 'The Financial Ombudsman Service and the Hunt Review: Continuing Evolution in Dispute Resolution' (2008) 8 *Journal of Business Law* 785, 789.

The United Kingdom's statutory ombudsman is preferred as it will likely face fewer conflicts of interest in its operations. The Canadian approach raises multiple concerns discussed in *Chapter 5*. However, it is necessary to highlight again that private institutions registering as ExCBs are only sustainable if a considerable number of FRFIs decide to join them. As noted in *Chapter 5*, FRFIs are free to exit membership and join any ExCB platform of their choice. Literature suggests that the idea of multiple ombudsmen competing in the same sector may present significant risks to independence and impartiality.[126] This is because a possibility exists that these bodies may adopt a pro-industry approach in order to attract and retain their memberships which will be to the disadvantage of consumers.

**A single financial ombudsman service with a broad sectoral jurisdiction is preferable.** As opposed to multiple ombudsmen platforms as is the practice in Canada, it is argued that a single ombudsman service like the UK FOS will allow for more uniformity and consistency in resolving disputes. Furthermore, a single service may be better positioned to identify systemic problems deduced from complaints. It is predicted that it would be easier to identify patterns and draw necessary inferences where there is a central service evaluating a holistic picture of submitted complaints. Thus, the proposed ombudsman service can play a key role in notifying authorities of any issues that have a regulatory significance in m-payments.

Where the ombudsman's jurisdiction broadly covers the financial services sector, this serves as an advantage to m-payment consumers as they can uniformly access the service irrespective of the status of the PSP. The UK FOS provides a good example of this. Its compulsory jurisdiction covers financial service firms, PSPs, and e-money issuers with UK establishments.[127] Hence, all m-payment users can access the FOS.

## 8.7 Conclusion

The core theme underlying the discussion in this book is that regulators must prioritise consumer protection when encouraging the adoption of financial services innovations such as m-payments. Technology presents multiple opportunities for furthering important policy objectives like financial inclusion. However, these efforts can backfire where poor regulatory frameworks put consumers at a disadvantage. For vulnerable consumers, previously financially excluded for reasons such as poverty and illiteracy, inadequate regulatory protections could be financially devastating with significant consequences on other aspects of their lives.

126 David Thomas and Francis Frizon, 'Resolving Disputes between Consumers and Financial Businesses: Fundamentals for a Financial Ombudsman – A Practical Guide Based in Experience in Western Europe' (2012) p.38 <http://www.eoi.at/wp-content/uploads/2018/09/Resolving-disputes-between-consumers-and-financial-businesses_Fundamentals-for-a-financial-ombudsman_The-World-Bank_January2012.pdf> accessed 15 January 2022.

127 Financial Services Markets Act 2000, s.226(2)(b); DISP 2.1.1(1).

To expand on this central theme, this book sought to explain why regulatory intervention to protect consumers is justified. Having set out the consumer concerns arising in the use of m-payments, the book identified specific consumer policy tools that can be used to address those concerns. Against this background, the book examined the existing consumer protection frameworks that benefit m-payment consumers in Canada, Kenya, and the United Kingdom. Highlighting areas of convergence and divergence, the book identified best practices that should be considered by regulators seeking to design consumer protection responses applying to m-payments. The hope is that by identifying these best practices, policy and regulatory stakeholders can access concrete ideas that may prove useful in reforming and strengthening consumer protection frameworks. This is particularly important for jurisdictions with underdeveloped consumer protection frameworks.

Although the discussions in the book have focused on m-payments, they are of broader relevance to other forms of financial services innovation. This is because certain themes covered in the book are relevant irrespective of the financial product or service involved. For example, the justification for regulatory intervention in financial services markets remains apposite. Moreover, the typology of consumer policy tools adopted in the book also provides a useful reference point for academics, regulators, and policymakers seeking to analyse the suitability and continued relevance of the existing regulatory frameworks applying to any financial product or service in their given jurisdictions.

## References

Bank Act (Canada) SC 1991, c 46.
Business Practices Act (Prince Edward Island) RSPEI 1988 c B-7.
Business Practices Act 1990 CCSM, c B120 (Manitoba).
Business Practices and Consumer Protection Act (British Columbia) SBC 2004, c 2.
Consumer Protection Act (Alberta) RSA 2000, c 26.3.
Consumer Protection Act (Ontario) SO 2002, c 30.
Consumer Protection and Business Practices Act (Newfoundland and Labrador) SNL 2009 c 31.1
Consumer Rights Act (UK) 2015.
Enterprise Act (UK) 2002.
Financial Consumer Protection Regulations (Canada) SOR/2021–181.
Financial Services (Distance Marketing) Regulations (UK) 2004.
Financial Services Markets Act (UK) 2000.
National Payment System Act (Kenya) 2011.
National Payment Systems Regulations (Kenya) 2014.
Payment Services Regulations (UK) 2017.
*Clark v In Focus Asset Management & Tax Solutions* [2014] EWCA Civ 118.
*Director General of Fair Trading v First National Bank Plc.* [2001] UKHL.
*Pannon GSM Zrt. v Erzsébet Sustikné Győrfi* (C-243/08).
Alec Samuels, 'The Consumer Rights Act 2015' (2016) 3 *Journal of Business Law* 159.
Central Bank of Kenya, 'Prudential Guidelines for Institutions Licensed Under the Banking Act – Consumer Protection (CBK/PG/22)' <https://www.centralbank.go.ke/wp-content/uploads/2016/08/PRUDENTIAL-GUIDELINES.pdf> accessed 7 October 2021.

Chris Willett, 'The Functions of Transparency in regulating Contract Terms: UK and Australian Approaches' (2011) 60(2) *International & Comparative Law Quarterly* 355.

Colin Scott and Julia Black, *Cranston's Consumers and the Law* (3rd ed., Butterworths 2000).

Competition and Markets Authority, 'Unfair Contract Terms Explained' (2015) <https://assets.publishing.service.gov.uk/government/uploads/system/uploads/attachment_data/file/450410/Unfair_Terms_Explained.pdf> accessed 21 December 2021.

Competition and Markets Authority, 'Unfair Contract Terms Guidance: Guidance on the Unfair terms provisions in the Consumer Rights Act 2015' (2015) <https://assets.publishing.service.gov.uk/government/uploads/system/uploads/attachment_data/file/450440/Unfair_Terms_Main_Guidance.pdf> accessed 21 December 2021.

Consumer Protection Office (Manitoba), 'Payments on the Go: Mobile Payments' <https://www.gov.mb.ca/cp/cpo/info/payments_to_go.html> accessed 10 January 2022.

David Thomas and Francis Frizon, 'Resolving Disputes between Consumers and Financial Businesses: Fundamentals for a Financial Ombudsman – A Practical Guide Based in Experience in Western Europe' (2012) <http://www.eoi.at/wp-content/uploads/2018/09/Resolving-disputes-between-consumers-and-financial-businesses_Fundamentals-for-a-financial-ombudsman_The-World-Bank_January2012.pdf> accessed 15 January 2022.

Financial Conduct Authority, 'Dispute Resolution Complaints Sourcebook (DISP)' <https://www.handbook.fca.org.uk/handbook/DISP.pdf> accessed 1 May 2022.

Financial Conduct Authority, 'FCA Handbook: Unfair Contract terms and Consumer Notices Regulatory Guide' <https://www.handbook.fca.org.uk/handbook/UNFCOG/1/?view=chapter> accessed 20 December 2021.

Financial Conduct Authority, 'Mobile Banking and Payment: Supporting an Innovative and Secure Market' (2013) <https://www.fca.org.uk/publication/thematic-reviews/tr13-06.pdf> accessed 15 June 2022.

Financial Conduct Authority, 'Payment Services and Electronic Money – Our Approach (The FCA's role under the Payment Services Regulations 2017 and the Electronic Money Regulations 2011)' (2021) <https://www.fca.org.uk/publication/finalised-guidance/fca-approach-payment-services-electronic-money-2017.pdf> accessed 18 January 2022.

Financial Conduct Authority, 'Thematic Review: Mobile Banking and Payments' (2014) <https://www.fca.org.uk/publication/thematic-reviews/tr14-15.pdf> accessed 15 June 2022.

Financial Conduct Authority, 'Unfair Contract Terms Library' <https://www.fca.org.uk/firms/unfair-contract-terms/library> accessed 21 October 2021.

Financial Consumer Agency of Canada, 'Guideline on Complaint-Handling Procedures for Banks and Authorized Foreign Banks' (2022) < https://www.canada.ca/en/financial-consumer-agency/services/industry/commissioner-guidance/complaint-handling-procedures-banks.html - toc1> accessed 20 February 2022.

Financial Consumer Agency of Canada, 'Internal Dispute Resolution' (2013) <https://www.canada.ca/en/financial-consumer-agency/services/industry/commissioner-guidance/guidance-12.html> accessed 14 January 2022.

Financial Consumer Agency of Canada, 'Paying with your Mobile Phone' <https://www.canada.ca/en/financial-consumer-agency/services/payment/mobile-payments/paying-with-mobile.html> accessed 10 January 2022.

Financial Consumer Agency of Canada, 'Secure the Data on your Mobile Devices' <https://www.getcybersafe.gc.ca/en/secure-your-devices/phones-and-tablets> accessed 10 January 2022.

Flore-Anne Messy and Chiara Monticone, 'The Status of Financial Education in Africa' (2012) 34 <https://doi.org/10.1787/5k94cqqx90wl-en > accessed 6 May 2022.

Geraint Howells and Stephen Weatherill, *Consumer Protection Law* (2nd ed., Ashgate 2005).

Geraint Howells, 'The Potential and Limits of Consumer Empowerment by Information' (2005) 32(3) *Journal of Law & Society* 349.

Geraint Howells, Hans–Wolfgang Micklitz, Thomas Wilhelmsson, 'Towards a Better Understanding of Unfair Commercial Practices' (2009) 51(2) *International Journal of Law and Management* 69.

Iain Ramsay, *Consumer Law and Policy* (3rd ed., Hart Publishing 2012).

Ian Ayres and John Braithwaite, 'Tripartism: Regulatory Capture and Empowerment' (1991) 16 *Law & Social Inquiry* 435.

International Finance Corporation, 'M-Money Chanel Distribution Case – Kenya (Safaricom M-pesa)' <https://www.ifc.org/wps/wcm/connect/e0d2a9bd-16b9-4a36-8498-0b2650b9af8b/Tool%2B6.7.%2BCase%2BStudy%2B-%2BM-PESA%2BKenya%2B.pdf?MOD=AJPERES&CVID=jkCVy-n> accessed 6 May 2022.

Jeff Sovern, 'Written Notice of Cooling-Off Periods: A Forty-Year Natural Experiment in Illusory Consumer Protection and the Relative Effectiveness of Oral and Written Disclosures' (2014) 75 *University of Pittsburgh Law Review* 333.

Joanna McCunn, 'The Contra Proferentem Rule: Contract Law's Great Survivor' (2019) 39(3) *Oxford Journal of Legal Studies* 483.

Larry DiMatteo and Martin Hogg, *Comparative Contract Law: British and American Perspectives* (OUP 2015).

Mark Flaming, Alexander Owino, Katharine McKee et al, 'Consumer Protection Diagnostic Study (Kenya)' (2011) <http://s3-eu-central-1.amazonaws.com/fsd-circle/wp-content/uploads/2015/08/30095758/11-02-22_Consumer_diagnostic_study.pdf> accessed 7 October 2021.

Michael Schillig, 'Inequality of Bargaining Power Versus a Market for Lemons: Legal Paradigm Change and the Court of Justice's Jurisprudence on Directive 93/13 on Unfair Contract Terms' (2008) 33(3) *European Law Review* 336.

OECD, 'Consumer Policy Toolkit' (2010) <http://www.oecd-ilibrary.org/governance/consumer-policy-toolkit_9789264079663-en> accessed 6 September 2021.

Omri Ben-Shahar and Carl E. Schneider, 'The Failure of Mandated Disclosure' (2011) 159 *University of Pennsylvania Law Review* 647.

PE Morris, 'The Financial Ombudsman Service and the Hunt Review: Continuing Evolution in Dispute Resolution' (2008) 8 *Journal of Business Law* 785.

Peter Cartwright (ed), *Consumer Protection in Financial Services* (1999 Kluwer Law International).

Stefan Wrbka, Steven Van Uytsel et al (eds), *Collective Actions: Enhancing Access to Justice and reconciling Multi-Layer Interests* (Cambridge University Press 2012).

Stephen Weatherill and Ulf Bernitz (eds), *The Regulation of Unfair Commercial Practices under EC Directive 2005/29: New Rules and New Techniques* (Bloomsbury Publishing 2007).

Steve Trites, Charles Gibney and Bruno Lévesque, 'Mobile Payments and Consumer Protection in Canada' (Research Division, Financial Consumer Agency of Canada 2013) <https://www.canada.ca/content/dam/canada/financial-consumer-agency/migration/eng/resources/researchsurveys/documents/fcac_mobile_payments_consumer_protection_accessible_en.pdf> accessed 27 January 2022.

The Canadian Code of Practice for Consumer Debit Card Services <https://www.canada.ca/en/financial-consumer-agency/services/industry/laws-regulations/debit-card-code-conduct.html> accessed 9 January 2022.

The Wireless Code (2017) <https://crtc.gc.ca/eng/phone/mobile/codesimpl.htm> accessed 10 January 2022.

# Index


Abbamonte, G. 203
access channel 21, 26
ADR Chambers Banking Ombuds Office (ADRBO) 155–158
advertising: regulating false and misleading information 98–99, 145–148, 179; trade puffs 224; transparency 182
agent networks 25; Safaricom 185–186
aggressive commercial practices 204–205
Alberta: cancellation provisions 138–139; Consumer Protection Act 136, 137, 139–140
Alipay 26
Alliance for Financial Inclusion 3
allocative efficiency 53, 60
alternative dispute resolution (ADR) 105; external 108–109, 154–160, 189–191, 232–234; External Complaints Body (ExCB) 154–158; Online Dispute Resolution (ODR) 109
anchoring 56–57
Ashworth, A. 146–147
Au, Y. 23
authentication 34
Automated Teller Machines (ATMs) 2, 19, 29
Ayres, I. 44, 218

back end 21, 22
bailout 48
Bank for International Settlements 6, 24
banks and banking 2, 9, 30, 31, 35; Automated Teller Machines (ATMs) 19; branchless 25, 36; consumer education 130–131; deposit insurance 48; External Complaints Body (ExCB) 154–158; internal dispute resolution 152–154; internet 19; mandatory disclosures 123–124; mobile 25–26; regulation 45; unfair commercial practices 133–134; *see also* financial services
Becher, S. 89–90
behavioural science 62–63
Benn, J. 84
best practices: consumer education 246–248; external alternative dispute resolution (ADR) 267–268; internal dispute resolution 265–266; liability rules 263–265; mandatory disclosure 241–246; regulating false and misleading information 260–263; regulating standard contract terms 254–260; regulating unfair commercial practices 250–254; withdrawal rights and cooling-off periods 248–250
bias 56, 57, 63, 78, 84, 98; indirect marketing 172
Black, J. 79, 97
Braithwaite, J. 44, 218
branchless banking 25, 36
breach of contract: liability rules 102–104
British Columbia, Business Practices and Consumer Protection Act 136, 140–141
bundling 92
business models 49, 86; bank-led 31–32; hybrid 32, 72; MNO-led 31–32

Camerer, C. 87
Canada 72; Bank Act (1991) 122–128, 131, 133, 134, 148–149, 152, 158; Code of Practice for Consumer Debit Card Services 125–126, 150–151; Competition Act (1985) 133, 147, 148; consumer education 128–131; consumer protection 122; contactless payments 121; Cost of Borrowing (Banks) Regulations (COBRs) 122, 124–125, 149; 'Critical Information Summary'

document 127; Disclosure of Charges (Banks) Regulations 122, 125; external alternative dispute resolution (ADR) 154–160; federal system of government 121–122; Financial Consumer Protection Agency 11; Financial Consumer Protection Framework 123; Financial Consumer Protection Regulations (FCPRs) 123, 124, 128, 132; financial services 131–132; internal dispute resolution 152–154; liability rules 148–152; mandatory disclosure requirements 122–128; m-payment/s 121; Negative Option Billing Requirements (NOBRs) 122, 126; standard term contracts and fairness 140–143; transparency of contract terms 143–145; unfair commercial practices, regulation 133–140; Wireless Code 126–127, 129; *see also* Alberta; British Columbia, Business Practices and Consumer Protection Act; Manitoba; Newfoundland
cancellation provisions 201–202; financial service 131–132, 138–139, 175
Cartwright, P. 51, 59, 65, 83, 99, 146–147, 207–208, 223
cases: *Bhasin v. Hrynew* 142–143; *Office of Fair Trading v. Abbey National Plc* 215; *Tilden Rent-A-Car Co v. Clendenning* 144–145
cash payment instruments 21
Cayne, D. 78, 171
Central Bank of Kenya (CBK) 165, 166, 171–172; Prudential Guidelines on Consumer Protection (PGCP) 167–170, 172–173, 175, 180–182, 184
Chatain, P.-L. 30–31
Chicago School of economics 51
classical theory of contract law 54, 94, 94n179
clearing 22
commodities 50–51; public good 73–74
communication protocols 27
Communications Authority of Kenya 166
community values 63–65
comparison tools 75
competition 51, 75
Competition Authority of Kenya (CAK) 167
conditional sales 92
confidence 64; over 56
conflicts of interest 47
consent requirements, financial service 126, 133
consumer education 80; banking 130–131; best practices 246–248; call centres 173; Canada 128–131; decision-making and 84; Financial Consumer Agency of Canada (FCAC) 128–131; financial literacy 83, 169–171; Kenya 171–174; leaflets 172; ‘Makutano Junction’ 172; Manitoba 130; Money Advice Service (MAS) 198–199; M-pesa 173; public-private collaborative approach 174; responsibilisation 85–86; targeted financial literacy initiatives 81–82; training 173; United Kingdom 198–200
Consumer Information Network of Kenya (CIN) 190–191
consumer protection 4, 8, 10, 12, 56, 66; authorisation requirements 47–48; Canada 122–123; *see also* Canada; contract law 55; cooling-off periods 87–90; dispute resolution 104–111; financial 43, 49–50; liability rules 99–104; m-payments 70–73; National Payment Systems Regulations (NPSRs) 166–170; regimes 49–50; regulation of business conduct 90–91; regulation of unfair commercial practices 91–93; responsibilisation 85–86; standard form contracts 95–96; transparency 97–98; withdrawal rights 87–90; *see also* Canada; Kenya; rationale for regulatory; intervention; regulation; United Kingdom
consumers 1, 5; underbanked 36; vulnerability 58–59
contactless payments 121
*contra proferentem* rule 143
contract law 54; cancellation provisions 175, 176, 201–202; classical theory 94; consumer protection 55; contra proferentem rule 143; cooling-off periods 87–90, 131–133, 174–177, 200–203; ‘Critical Information Summary’ document 127; fairness 96–97; fairness test 212–214; financial transactions 78–79; freedom of contract 54–55, 94, 215; good faith principle 142–143, 212–213; limitation clause 101; onerous terms 144–145; *pacta sunt servanda* 87; standard contract terms 95–96, 140–143, 181–182, 211–218; transparency 97–98, 143–145;

unconscionability doctrine 140, 142; withdrawal rights 87–90, 131–133, 174–177, 200–203; *see also* standard contract terms, regulation
cooling-off periods 87–90; best practices 248–250; Canada 131–133; Kenya 174–177; United Kingdom 200–203
Cooter, R. 100
Cost of Borrowing (Banks) Regulations (COBRs) 122, 124–125, 149
Court of Justice of the European Union (CJEU) 212–213, 217
cramming 92–93
credence goods 46–47, 54
credit cards 9, 102, 103; disclosure provisions 124; liability rules 148–149, 151–152
'Critical Information Summary' document 127
Crowe, M. 23

De Almeida, G. 103–104
debit cards 102; Canadian Code of Practice for Consumer Debit Card Services 125–126, 150–151; liability rules 150
deceptive practices 145–148; false and misleading information 98–99, 145–148; m-payment 71; unconscionable conduct 90, 135–138, 141–143, 148, 177–179
decision-making 56–57, 59, 74–79; allocative efficiency 60; consumer education and 84, 171; false and misleading information 98–99; transactional 221, 222
deposit insurance 48
developing countries: financial exclusion 1–2; mobile infrastructure 35
direct mobile billing 28
Disclosure of Charges (Banks) Regulations 122, 125
disclosure regimes 102–103; comprehensive 76; consumer education 80–86; false and misleading information 98–99, 145–148; limits of 77–79; mandatory 74–79, 122–128; micro-payment transactions 79; payment services 75–76; requirements 71; standard contract terms 95–96; standardised 75; timing 76; transparency 97–98, 143–145; vulnerable consumers 78
dispute resolution 55, 71, 104–105, 112; alternative 104, 105; best practices 265–268; external 108–109; external alternative 154–160, 189–191; External Complaints Body (ExCB) 154–158; internal 106–108, 152–154, 229–232; litigation 105; mediation 108, 190; negotiation services 108; ombudsmen 110–111, 158–159; online 109
Dispute Resolution Complaints Sourcebook (DISP) 229–232
distributive justice 57–60
doctrinal research 5–6
doctrine of privity of contract 55
Duivenvoorde, B. 206

efficiency 51n75; allocative 60; market 51–52, 100–101
Electronic Money Regulations (EMRs) 195, 218
e-money: institutions (EMIs) 195; issuers 166–167, 195
endowment effect 90
Eurocheque 9
European Central Bank (ECB) 72
European Union (EU) 108, 109; Product Liability Directive 101
experience goods 46
external alternative dispute resolution (ADR) 108–109; best practices 267–268; Canada 154–160; Kenya 189–191; United Kingdom 232–234
External Complaints Body (ExCB) 154; jurisdiction 158; multi-institution approach 158–159; recommendations 155–158

fairness 102, 177–178, 180; contract law 96–97, 140–143, 181–182; liability rules 102; test 212–214; *see also* unfair commercial practices, regulation
false and misleading information, regulation 98–99, 179; best practices 260–263; Canada 145–148; Kenya 182–184; United Kingdom 220–224
federally regulated financial institution (FRFI) 122, 126; External Complaints Body (ExCB) 156–160
Financial Action Task Force (FATF) 72
Financial Conduct Authority 12
Financial Consumer Agency of Canada (FCAC) 121, 149–151, 153, 154, 158; consumer education 128–131
financial consumer protection 43, 49–50
Financial Consumer Protection Agency 11
Financial Consumer Protection Framework 123

Financial Consumer Protection Regulations (FCPRs) 123
Financial Deepening Challenge Fund 165
financial education 80–81, 173; industry-led 174; public-private collaborative approach 174
financial exclusion 34–35; developing countries 1; rural areas 2
financial inclusion 2–4, 6, 8, 60
financial literacy 81, 83, 85–86, 128, 169–171
financial services 43–44; authorisation requirements 47–48; barriers 35; cancellation provisions 131–132, 175; complaint handling 106–107; conduct rules 90–91; conflicts of interest 47; consent requirements 126, 133; cooling-off periods 87–90; disclosure requirements 71; information asymmetry 45–46; innovation 48–49; mandatory disclosures 74–79; objectives of regulation 8; ombudsmen 110–111; optional 131–132; overproviding 46–47; payment services 7; quality 76; regulation 45; technology 19; underproviding 47; unfair commercial practices, regulation 91–93
Fineman, M. 58
Flaming, M. 82, 170
framework contracts, disclosure obligations 196
fraud 130; m-payment 71
freedom of contract 54–55, 94, 215
Frizon, F. 159
front end 21
funding, m-payment 33, 71, 149–151

G-20, High-Level Principles on Financial Consumer Protection 73
G20/OECD Task Force 50
Gartner 73–74
Ginsburg, D. 63
Glaeser, E. 63
global financial crisis of 2007–2008 49
Global Partnership for Financial Inclusion 2–3, 8
good faith principle 142–143, 212–213
goods 45; credence 46–47, 54; experience 46; search 46
gross negligence 149
Guibert, S. 24
Guru, B. 8–9

hard paternalism 61–62
Herwig, I. 44
Heydon, D. 64
High-Level Principles on Financial Consumer Protection 50, 73
Hirschman, A. 111
Howells, G. 44
hybrid business model 32, 72
Hyde, R. 64
hyperbolic discounting 56

imperfect information 53–54
indirect marketing 172
information: asymmetry 45–46, 70–71, 88, 100; deceptive 99; failure 54; false and misleading 98–99, 145–148, 179, 220–224; imperfect 53–54; mandatory disclosures 74–79; material 223; processing 78; provision 73–74; *see also* provision of information; *see also* disclosure regimes
Information and Communications Technology (ICT) 109
informed consent 81; *see also* consent requirements, financial service; consumer education
innovation 4–7; financial services 19, 48–49; m-payment/s 26; payment services 22; trust and 9–10; *see also* m-payment/s
insolvency 47, 48
internal dispute resolution 106–108; best practices 265–266; Canada 152–154; Kenya 186–188; United Kingdom 229–232
internet 24; banking 19
intervention 43–44; market-based 52–53; paternalistic 60–63, 65; *see also* rationale for regulatory intervention; regulation

Kauffman, R. 23
Kenya 82; Banking Act (1999) 166, 167, 170; Communications Authority 166, 190–191; Competition Act (2010) 167, 177, 180; consumer education 171–174; Consumer Information Network (CIN) 190–191; Consumer Protection Act (2012) 167, 175–178, 182–184, 189; cooling-off periods 174–177; external alternative dispute resolution (ADR) 189–191; false and misleading information, regulation 182–184;

Financial Education and Consumer Protection Partnership (FEPP) 171–172; Financial Sector Deepening Trust (FSD) 171–172; Information and Communications (Consumer Protection) Regulations (KICRs) 169–170; internal dispute resolution 186–188; mandatory disclosure requirements 167–171; M-pesa 7, 11–12, 36–37; National Payment Systems Act (NPSA, 2011) 166–167, 184; National Payment Systems Regulations (NPSRs) 166–170, 184–186; unfair commercial practices, regulation 177–180
Kerschbamer, R. 46–47

learning 84
legal frameworks 9–10
'lemons' problem 47, 54
lender of last resort 48
liability rules 99–104; best practices 263–265; Canada 148–152; disclosure obligations 263–264; Kenya 184–186; m-payment 71; for trade puffs 224; unauthorised payments 225, 264; United Kingdom 224–229
liberty 61
limitation clause 101
literacy 81, 81n80; financial 81–83, 85–86, 128, 169–171
litigation 105; *see also* dispute resolution
Llewellyn, D. 8
loans, disclosure provisions 124
loopholes 49
Loos, M. 202
loss-imposition principle 101
loss-reduction principle 100–101
loss-spreading principle 100

Macrory, R. 147, 207–208
'Makutano Junction' 172
mandatory disclosure/s 74–79, 82; banks 123–124; best practices 241–246; Canada 122–128; Canadian Code of Practice for Consumer Debit Card Services 125–126; consumer education 81; false and misleading information 98–99, 145–148; framework contracts 196; Kenya 167–171; language 198; non-FRFIs 126–128; onerous terms 144–145; oral explanations 169, 170; payment service provider (PSP) 127; Payment Services Regulations (PSRs) 196; PSPs 167–168; for single payment transactions 197; standard contract terms 95–96; transparency 143–145; United Kingdom 195–198; Wireless Code 126–127; *see also* disclosure regimes
Manitoba: Business Practices Act (1990) 135–136, 141; consumer education 130
market 57; -based intervention 52–53; efficiency 51–52; failure analysis 52; information failure 53; 'lemons' problem 47, 54; perfect 50–53, 58, 65, 77
material information 223
McCoy, P. 45
McKay, C. 36
McVea, H. 86
mediation 108, 190
*mens rea* 208
merchants 9, 30
micro-credit, M-Shwari 37
micro-payment transactions 33; information disclosure 79
Miles, D. 45
misleading commercial activity 220–223
Mitchell, G. 63
mobile banking 25–26
mobile devices 6; optimised disclosure statements 77; security 129–130
mobile financial services 25
mobile money 25, 36
mobile network operators (MNOs) 20, 26, 30–32, 72, 103; consumer education 86; Information and Communications (Consumer Protection) Regulations (KICRs) 169–170; internal dispute resolution 188; payment service provider (PSP) 166–167; Safaricom 37, 82; Wireless Code 126–127
moral hazard 48
m-payment/s 4–9, 11, 12, 20; as an additive payment service 32–34; authentication 34; business models 31–32, 72; in Canada 121–122; complexity 78–79; consumer education 86, 128–131; consumer protection 70–73; consumer trust 9–10; cramming 92–93; definitions 23–25; direct mobile billing 28; disputed payments 71, 105; fraud 71; functions 30–31; funding 33, 71, 149–151; information asymmetry 70–71; innovation 26; liability rules 71, 102–103, 148–152,

184–186; mandatory disclosures 76, 79, 122–128, 170; merchants 30; micro-payment transactions 33; near field communication (NFC) 28; novelty of 71–72; ombudsmen 111; overlay system 26; Quick Response (QR) Codes 28–29; security 34, 76–77; Short Message Service (SMS) 27; stakeholders 30; standalone system 26; in Sub-Saharan Africa 7; targeted financial literacy initiatives 81–82; third party providers 32; as transformative payment service 34–38; in the UK 194; unfair commercial practices 92–93; Unstructured Supplementary Service Data (USSD) 27; Wireless Code 126–127; Wireless Identity Module Card (WIM) 30
M-pesa 7, 11, 12, 26, 36–37, 165–166, 166n9, 173, 185; pricing schedule 82, 170–171
M-Shwari 37

National Payment Systems Regulations (NPSRs) 166–170; internal dispute resolution procedures 186–188; liability rules 184–186
near field communication (NFC) 28–29
negative information response 223
Negative Option Billing Requirements (NOBRs) 122, 126
negotiation services 108
neo-classical economic theory 50, 52, 104; unbounded rationality 55–57
Newfoundland 138–139; Consumer Protection and Business Practices Act (2010) 135, 141
non-cash payment instruments 21
non-disclosure, cancellation provisions 202–203
nudge 62–63
numeracy 81

Ogus, A. 55, 61
Ombudsman Service for Banking Services and Investments (OBSI) 155–158
ombudsmen 105, 110–111, 158–159, 267–268
onerous contract terms 144–145
Online Dispute Resolution (ODR) 109
Ontario, Consumer Protection Act 132
optional products and services 131–132
Organisation for Cooperation and Development (OECD) 49, 70, 72, 80, 99, 125, 128, 153, 224
overconfidence 56
overlay system 26

*pacta sunt servanda* 87
paternalism 60, 65; hard 61–62; soft 62–63
PayM 194
payment instruments 21; retail 23
payment service/s 7, 19–20; cancellation provisions 175; information disclosure 75–76; innovation 22; providers 20, 166–168, 184–186, 196, 197
Payment Services Regulations (PSRs) 195; disclosure requirements 196–198; liability regime 225–229
payment transaction 20; access channel 21; back end 21, 22; clearing 22; front end 21; initiation 21–22; person-to-person 27; settlement 22; transfer of funds 20–21
Pearson, G. 85
perfect market 50–53, 58, 65, 77
Pickens, M. 36
policy and policymaking 10, 44, 50, 63; consumer protection 43; market failure analysis 52
positive information response 223
Posner, R. 84
poverty 8, 36; consumer vulnerability and 58–59; financial exclusion 2
premium rate services (PRS), Code of Practice 228–229
private law 54
provision of information 73; consumer education 80–86; decision-making and 77–78; mandatory disclosures 74–79; micro-payments 79; vulnerable consumers 78; *see also* disclosure regimes
proximity payments 29
public good 73–74, 86

Quick Response (QR) Codes 28–29

Rachlinski, J. 61
Ramsay, I. 58, 64, 224; on consumer credit regulation 59–60
rationale for regulatory intervention: community values 63–65; distributive justice 57–60; market realities 53–57; paternalism 60–63; perfect market 50–53

redress mechanisms 104, 105
regulation 4, 5, 8–12, 43, 44; authorisation requirements 47–48; banking 45; of business conduct 90–91; consumer credit 59–60; contract terms 94–98; financial services 45; loopholes 49; mandatory disclosures 74–79; objectives 50; responsibilisation 85–86; unfair commercial practices 91–93, 133–140, 177–180; wholesale payment system 22–23; *see also* rationale for regulatory intervention
Reifner, U. 44
remittances 7
remote payments 29
resources, distributive justice 58–60
responsibilisation 85–86
retail payment services 22–23; market 9; unfair commercial practices 92
risk 4, 79, 85; allocation rules 100–101, 263–265; liability rules 99–104; security 76–77
Rubin, P. 100
rural areas, financial exclusion 2
Ryder, N. 204, 205

Safaricom 37, 82, 165–166; agents 185–186; consumer education 173; *see also* M-pesa
sanctions: providing false and misleading information 145–148; unfair commercial practice 134, 138
Scott, C. 79, 97
search goods 46
security: mobile device 129–130; m-payment 34, 76–77
settlement 22
Short Message Service (SMS) 27, 29, 130; *see also* M-pesa
single payment transactions, disclosure obligations 196–197
soft paternalism 62–63
stakeholders 30
standalone system 26
standard contract terms, regulation 95–96; best practices 254–260; blacklists 214; Canada 140–143; Electronic Money Regulations (EMRs) 218; fairness test 212–214; greylist 214–215; Kenya 181–182; onerous 144–145; transparency 97–98, 143–145, 215–216, 219–220; unfair terms 211–212, 217; United Kingdom 211–218
standardised disclosure 75
sub-Saharan Africa 34; mobile money accounts 36; m-payments 7
Subscriber Identity Model (SIM) 30
supply vulnerability 59
sustainable consumption 64
sustainable development 7
Sustainable Development Goals 3
Sutter, M. 46–47

technology 10; financial services 19; mobile payments 4; m-payments *see* m-payment/s; near field communication (NFC) 28; Quick Response (QR) Codes 28–29; Short Message Service (SMS) 27; Unstructured Supplementary Service Data (USSD) 27
test of good faith 97
third party providers 32
Thomas, D. 159
timeshare agreements, cancellation provisions 175
timing, information disclosure 76
trade puffs 224
traders and trading 51
transactional decision 221, 222
transparency 10, 97–98; contract term 143–145, 181–182, 215–216, 219–220, 259–260; M-pesa pricing 170–171
Trebilcock, M. 78, 171
Trites, S. 77, 127
trust 9–10, 64, 108
two-sided market 9
tying 92

unauthorised payments, liability rules 225, 264
unbounded rationality 55–57
unconscionable conduct 90, 135–138, 140–143, 148, 177–179, 183–184
underbanked consumers 36
unfair commercial practices, regulation 90–93; 'average consumer' 205–206, 224; best practices 250–254; Canadian regulations 133–140; coercion 134, 179–180, 204; consumer remedies 210–211; contract law 96–97; definitions 204; enforcement of regulatory standards 93–94; false and misleading information 98–99, 145–148, 179; freedom of contract and 94–95; Kenyan regulations 177–180; *mens rea* 208; m-payments 92–93; private

enforcement 210–211; prohibited practices 205; public enforcement 139; regulatory offences 206–208; retail 92; sanctions 138, 177–178, 180; standard form contracts 95–96; transparency 97–98; UK regulations 203–211; unconscionable conduct 90, 135–138, 141–143, 148, 177–179, 183–184; undue influence 204–205

United Kingdom 11; Behavioural Insights Team 62; Competition and Markets Authority (CMA) 195, 211, 213, 216, 219–220, 227; Consumer Contracts (Information, Cancellation, and Additional Charges) Regulations (CCRs) 200–203; Consumer Credit Act (1974) 71, 101, 103; consumer education 198–200; Consumer Protection from Unfair Trading Regulations (CPUTRs) 203–211, 220–224; Consumer Rights Act (CRA, 2015) 211–212, 214, 216–218, 227, 228; Consumers' Association 78–79; contract terms, regulation 211–218; Electronic Money Regulations (EMRs) 195; e-money institutions (EMIs) 195; external alternative dispute resolution (ADR) 232–234; false and misleading information, regulation 220–224; Financial Conduct Authority 12, 199–200, 211–212, 227; Financial Ombudsman Service (FOS) 229, 231–234; Financial Services and Markets Act (FSMA) 198–200, 232; Financial Services (Distance Marketing) Regulations (FSRs) 200–202; internal dispute resolution 229–232; liability rules 224–229; mandatory disclosure requirements 195–198; Money Advice Service (MAS) 198–199; Money and Pensions Service (MaPS) 199; Payment Services Regulations (PSRs) 195, 225–229; Payments Market Report 194; unfair commercial practices, regulation 203–211; Unfair Contract Terms and Consumer Notices Regulatory Guide (UNFCOG) 211–212

United Nations (UN) 49; Guidelines for Consumer Protection 64, 73

Unstructured Supplementary Service Data (USSD) 27

Van den Bergh, R. 100, 101

Visscher, L. 100, 101

vulnerability 58–59; consumer 90, 92; supply 59

Weatherill, S. 44

wholesale payment system, regulation 22–23

Wilhelmsson, T. 89

Willett, C. 98

Wireless Code 126–128

Wireless Identity Module Card (WIM) 30

withdrawal rights 87–90; best practices 248–250; Canada 131–133; Kenya 174–177; United Kingdom 200–203

World Bank 1, 36, 50, 106, 109

Wright, J. 63

Zarsky, T. 89–90

Zumbo, F. 95–96

Made in the USA
Las Vegas, NV
19 September 2026

9d1da066-1f4e-4fdf-9bf3-189d2f943fd1R01